Network Nations

D0152461

In *Network Nations*, Michele Hilmes reveals and re-conceptualizes the roots of media globalization through a historical look at the productive transnational cultural relationship between British and American broadcasting. Though frequently painted as opposites—the British public service tradition contrasting with the American commercial system—in fact they represent two sides of the same coin. Neither could have developed without the constant presence of the other, in terms not only of industry and policy, but of aesthetics, culture, and creativity, despite a long history of oppositional rhetoric.

Based on primary research in British and American archives, *Network Nations* argues for a new transnational approach to media history, looking across the traditional national boundaries within which media is studied to encourage an awareness that media globalization has a long and fruitful history. Placing media history in the framework of theories of nationalism and national identity, Hilmes examines critical episodes of transnational interaction between the US and Britain, from radio's amateurs to the relationship between early network heads; from the development of radio features and drama to television spy shows and miniseries; as each other's largest suppliers of programming and as competitors on the world stage; and as a network of creative, business, and personal relationships that has rarely been examined, but that shapes television around the world. As the global circuits of television grow and as global regions, particularly Europe, attempt to define a common culture, the historical role played by the British/US media dialogue takes on new significance.

Michele Hilmes is Professor of Media and Cultural Studies and Chair of the Department of Communication Arts at the University of Wisconsin-Madison. She is the author or editor of several books on media history, including *Hollywood and Broadcasting: From Radio to Cable*; *Radio Voices: American Broadcasting 1922–1952*; *Only Connect: A Cultural History of Broadcasting in the United States* (3rd ed.); *The Radio Reader: Essays in the Cultural History of Radio*; *The Television History Book*; and *NBC: America's Network*.

Network Nations

A Transnational History of British and American Broadcasting

Michele Hilmes

 Routledge
Taylor & Francis Group

NEW YORK AND LONDON

First published 2012
by Routledge
711 Third Avenue, New York, NY 10017

Simultaneously published in the UK
by Routledge
2 Park Square, Milton Park, Abingdon, Oxon OX14 4RN

Routledge is an imprint of the Taylor & Francis Group, an informa business

© 2012 Taylor & Francis

Library of Congress Cataloging-in-Publication Data
Hilmes, Michele, 1953–
   Network nations : a transnational history of British and American broadcasting / Michele Hilmes.
     p. cm.
   Includes bibliographical references.
   1. Television broadcasting—Great Britain—History. 2. Television broadcasting—United States—History. I. Title.
   PN1992.3.G7H57 2011
   384.550941—dc22
   2011004534

ISBN: 978–0–415–88384–9(hbk)
ISBN: 978–0–415–88385–6 (pbk)
ISBN: 978–0–203–84320–8 (ebk)

Typeset in Minion
by Keystroke, Station Road, Codsall, Wolverhampton

Printed and bound in the United States of America on acid-free paper by Edwards Brothers, Inc.

SUSTAINABLE FORESTRY INITIATIVE
Certified Fiber Sourcing
www.sfiprogram.org

Table of Contents

List of Abbreviations

ABC	American Broadcasting Company
ABC, The	The Australian Broadcasting Corporation
ACUBS	Association of College and University Broadcasting Stations (US)
AEFP	Allied Expeditionary Forces Programme (UK/US/CA)
AFRS	Armed Forces Radio Service (US)
ABPC	Associated British Picture Corporation
A-R	Associated Rediffusion (UK)
ASCAP	American Society of Composers, Publishers, and Performers
ATV	Associated TeleVision (UK)
BBC	British Broadcasting Corporation (after 1926); British Broadcasting Company (before 1926)
BEF	British Expeditionary Forces
BFA	Broadcasting Foundation of America
BIS	British Information Service
Blue	NBC Blue Network (US)
BSC	British Security Coordination
CIA	Central Intelligence Agency (US)
CBC	Canadian Broadcasting Corporation
CBS	Columbia Broadcasting System (US)
CED	Committee for Economic Development (US)
COI	Central Office of Information (UK)
CPB	Corporation for Public Broadcasting (US)
ETRC	Educational Television and Radio Center (US)
FAE	Fund for Adult Education, Ford Foundation

FBI	Federal Bureau of Investigation (US)
FCC	Federal Communications Commission (US)
FRC	Federal Radio Commission (US)
FREC	Federal Radio Education Commission (US)
GEB	General Education Board of the Rockefeller Foundation
GPO	General Post Office (UK)
HUAC	House Un-American Activities Committee (US)
IAIC	Inter-Allied Information Committee
IBC	International Broadcasting Company, Ltd. (UK)
ITA	Independent Television Authority (UK)
ITC	Independent Television Company (UK)
ITN	Independent Television News (UK)
ITV	Independent Television (UK)
JCET	Joint Committee on Educational Television (US)
JWT	J. Walter Thompson advertising agency
LSRM	Laura Spellman Rockefeller Memorial fund
MI6	Military Intelligence – Overseas (UK)
MOI	Ministry of Information (UK)
NAB	National Association of Broadcasters (US)
NACRE	National Advisory Council on Radio in Education (US)
NAEB	National Association of Educational Broadcasters (US)
NAS	North American Service of the BBC
NBC	National Broadcasting Company (US)
NCER	National Committee on Education by Radio (US)
NEA	National Endowment for the Arts (US)
NEH	National Endowment for the Humanities (US)
NET	National Educational Television (US)
NETRC	National Educational Television and Radio Center (US)
NPR	National Public Radio (US)
NYT	*New York Times*
OEC	Organization for Economic Cooperation (US)
OFF	Office of Facts and Figures (US)
OWI	Office of War Information (US)
PBS	Public Broadcasting Service (US)
Red	NBC Red Network
RF	Rockefeller Foundation
UNESCO	United Nations Educational, Scientific and Cultural Organization
URI	International Radio University (*Université Radiophonique Internationale*)
USIA	United States Information Agency
WBC	Westinghouse Broadcasting Company (US)

Acknowledgements

This book has been a long time coming. Many people helped and encouraged me along the way, so there are many people to thank.

First of all, I must declare my profound appreciation for the archivists at the Wisconsin Center for Film and Theater Research and the Wisconsin Historical Society, for their work in acquiring and preserving the wonderful media history collections that have enriched not only this book but so many thousands of others over the years. Without their dedication, prescient insight, and constant efforts, so much of this vital part of America's cultural history could never have been known, much less written. I want to include those whose past efforts built up the collections as well as those toiling in the present-day stacks and vaults: Tino Balio, Maxine Fleckner Ducey, Dorinda Hartmann, Peter Gottlieb, Harry Miller, and many others whose names I will never know. Thank you for your care and persistence, and for the advice and help you extended to me.

Other archival collections have been just as important. The wonderful Written Archives Center of the British Broadcasting Corporation in Caversham Park, UK, is one of the most delightful places to conduct research I have ever encountered. Thank you, Jacquie Kavanaugh and your wonderfully competent and helpful staff. What an enormous and well-organized repository of twentieth-century history! I do miss the tea and biscuits.

Thank you Michael Mashon, Alan Gevinson, and Sam Brylawski of the Library of Congress Motion Picture and Recorded Sound Division. Same to Michael Henry and Chuck Howell at the Library of American Broadcasting and Karen King at the National Public Broadcasting Archives, both at the University of Maryland. These are all national treasures.

I am very grateful to the Rockefeller Foundation Archives and to the Lilly Library in Bloomington, Indiana for the research grants that allowed me to consult their fascinating collections in depth. I am also grateful to the Communication Arts Department, the Hamel Family, and the University of Wisconsin-Madison for their funding and support through this long process. And though my fellowship was really intended to further the *next* project, I do wish to thank Susan Friedman and the University of Wisconsin-Madison Institute for Research in the Humanities for the stimulating and yet tranquil environment in which I put the final touches on this book.

Friends and fellow scholars whose work has enormously influenced mine and whose comments and criticisms have enriched not only my scholarship but my life include my colleagues at the University of Wisconsin-Madison (whether they are still there or not), especially Tino Balio, David Bordwell, John Fiske, Vance Kepley, Julie D'Acci, Michael Curtin, Shanti Kumar, Lisa Nakamura, Mary Beltran, and Jonathan Gray, and with them the wonderful graduate students with whom I've had the privilege to work over the past fifteen years.

Further afield, I am grateful for the friendship and scholarship of Brian Winston, Jason Loviglio, David Hendy, Paddy Scannell, Hugh Chignell, Tim Wall, Kate Lacey, Simon Potter, Peter Lewis, Mary Vipond, David Goodman, Jason Jacobs, Andreas Fickers, Jamie Medhurst, Cathy Johnson, Jeannette Steemers, Jonathan Bignell, and Enrico Menduni, all of whom have allowed me to talk about my work at excessive length, and were nice enough not to say so. Their own work, their invitations to speak in various venues, and their advice, have been not only critically important to my development as a scholar, but also to the enormous amount of enjoyment I've taken in getting out of the American box. I look forward to keeping up connections with my distant colleagues as we build up the field of transnational media research.

And, of course, none of this could have happened without the steadfast support of my husband Bruce and daughter Amanda. They are the best listeners and fellow travelers a loquacious academic could have. *Milles mercis et bisous.*

Introduction

Thinking Transnationally: The Anglo-American Axis

Tangled in simplistic relationships with civics education, national historical accounts absorb their surrounding nationalism. Focused on questions of national difference, historical scholarship bends to the task of specifying each nation's distinctive culture, its peculiar history, its *Sonderweg*, its exceptionalism. Since every nation's history is—in fact and by definition—distinct, the move is not without reason. At its worst, however, the result is to produce histories lopped off at precisely those junctures where the nation-state's permeability might be brought into view, where the trans-national forces do their most important work. The narrative field too often shrinks back on the nation; the boundaries of the nation-state become an analytical cage.
　　　　　　　—Daniel T. Rodgers, *Atlantic Crossings* (2)

Transnational studies puts nations back into the dialectical history from which they emerged. Yet to say so is not to dispense with the study of nations.
　　　　　　　—Laura Doyle, "Toward a Philosophy of Transnationalism," (1)

Creative life may be flourishing in widely different ways across Europe, but the most common cultural link across the region now is a devotion to American popular culture in the form of movies, television, and music . . . Even as Europeans visit one another's cities and beaches more than ever, national self-obsessions prevail in the visual arts, new plays, literature, contemporary classical, pop music, and movies.[1]
　　　　　　　—Alan Riding, *New York Times*, 2004

The twentieth century is the century of nationalism. It is also the century of broadcasting. These two facts are deeply and causally related. As empires ripened and disintegrated, as nations warred across the globe, as new nations emerged and defined themselves, they invented and deployed first radio and then television to serve as national circulatory systems, delivering the signs and symbols of the national imaginary across geographical space into individual homes and minds, both reflecting and consolidating key elements of national identity. Yet no previous medium possessed the equally important capacity of radio waves to *transgress* national borders, to defy barriers of both time and space, to travel unseen through the air and enter the ears of private citizens in their homes, undetected by public gatekeepers. For these two linked reasons, no other twentieth century medium of communication was brought more tightly under state control, even in well-established democracies that had long before asserted and defended the freedom of the press. In every nation around the world, radio and then television became state-supported disseminators of the national culture, consolidating linguistic traditions and sending preferred elements of arts and politics into every village. Equally importantly, they held forces from outside the nation at bay, or contained them in a negotiated presence.

This perspective points to the inherent *transnationalism* of broadcasting's cultural economy: constituted both by the demands of the nation and the equally compelling impulse to go beyond, to provide a conduit to speak to other nations and to let other influences stream into the national space. These two capacities operate in considerable tension. Transnational elements in broadcasting's cultural project were (and are) resisted and denied as often as they are acknowledged and encouraged. While the cinema quickly evolved into a transnational medium, dominated by Hollywood, broadcasting took a different trajectory. As British historian John Caughie notes,

> Love it or loath it, the classic Hollywood cinema provides an international standard which allows us to agree or disagree, whether at the academic or the popular level, whether in Sao Paulo or San Francisco . . . Hollywood seems to be the common sense of cinema. Television, on the other hand, is local, defined by quite different systems of national regulation, different historical relations with the state and with capital . . . These different histories add up to different national experiences, and different understandings of what television is. (Caughie 2000, 16)[2]

This core "national-ness" of the broadcasting medium cannot be denied. Yet Caughie, like most historians situated within a national tradition, stops short of drawing the connection between the two elements in his comparison.

Hollywood's troublesome transnationalism played a major role in motivating and shaping broadcasting's national obsession. The threat—and opportunity—of the transnational, symbolized by Hollywood and transnational consumer culture more generally, at every point guided the philosophy and practices of national broadcasting. This tension was equally active in the United States; Hollywood—dominated by immigrants, permeated by *internal* transnational influences, disseminating vulgar mass culture to the unassimilated hordes—displeased the elite protectors of America's national identity as much as it did those of other nations. Often, "Hollywood" (and, abroad, "America") came to stand in for a wide array of culturally denationalizing forces, both within and outside of national boundaries, in the minds and policies of national gatekeepers. Broadcasting promised a powerful agent to contain such forces and to define national cultures around preferred national values.

Thus nation-states imagined broadcasting, and broadcasting imagined the nation-state. Yet theorists of nationalism and twentieth-century historians tend barely to mention this most national of mass media, while media historians frequently adopt a national perspective blindly, without considering why this seems the natural and self-evident framework to employ.[3] The continuing presence of the transnational—cultural influences that could be perceived as "foreign" or that existed in tension with the preferred culture—shaped core values, aesthetics, and practices within each national tradition, whether in opposition, resistance, adaptation, exchange, or emulation, or some combination of all of those. As Daniel Rodgers' astute observation implies, the national framework within which most history is written overlooks precisely those points "where transnational forces do their most important work." One of those points is the transnational relationship of the United States and Great Britain in the field of broadcasting.

I argue here, echoing Rodgers among others, that we cannot understand the cultural history of either the United States or Great Britain without taking into account the continuous flow of mutual influence circulating between them. More uniquely, I argue that this circulation is particularly evident—and resonant—in the field of broadcasting. Though frequently painted as opposites—the British public service tradition contrasting with the American commercial system—in fact they represent two sides of the same coin. Neither could have developed without the constant presence of the other, in terms not only of industry and policy but of aesthetics, culture, and creative hybridity, despite a long history of oppositional rhetoric. Both for Britain and for the United States, this transnational relationship was deeply productive, providing a constant circuit of influence and adaptation that, while often resisted or even reviled, nonetheless worked powerfully to enliven and expand the cultural horizons of both nations. Bound by a common language, British and American broadcasting together constitute a unified system, a powerful symbiotic machine of cultural influence that has spread long tentacles around the globe and affected the ways that culture is practiced and understood far outside the boundaries of these two nations alone: what I call the *transnational cultural economy* of British and American broadcasting.[4]

As Laura Doyle notes in the first issue of the *Journal of Transnational American Studies,* transnational relationships imply the existence of a dialectic, an ongoing process of dialogue between national entities that reveals itself in institutions, in policies, in the trajectory of individuals and populations, in the texts and discourses that circulate between them (Doyle 2009, 1). The dialogue between Great Britain and America holds a unique place in the history of the twentieth century, and particularly in that century's dominant medium. Thus, for historians of the twentieth century, understanding this complex system of trans-Atlantic cultural flow is of particular importance. Yet its full significance extends well outside the media field. The centrality of broadcasting in the twentieth century to all aspects of national life, from arts to politics to the rhythms of everyday domesticity, makes its study vital to our understanding of modern culture.[5] And because broadcasting spread from two of the most powerful twentieth-century axes of empire across the world, their relationship had, and continues to have, a global impact. This book sets out to highlight significant points in the transnational cultural economy established between the United States and Great Britain as they invented the structures, practices, and ethos of broadcasting, in its various forms, from the days of radio's inception in the 1920s to the point at which satellites and other globalizing technologies intervened to break open decisively the national cage in the late 1970s and 1980s. In so doing, it seeks to bring to critical attention the productive dialectic between the national and the transnational to be found in the central cultural project of broadcasting around the world.

It is not a simple tale. Both admiration and abhorrence, marked by vehement opposition on the one hand and blatant appropriation on the other, form the poles of this relationship. British broadcasting pitted itself against the American model, and American broadcasting against the British, as often as each emulated the other. Sometimes the presence of the "other" was real and material, as when imported programs competed with national production economies; more often it was symbolic, as each nation constructed an image of the other in terms that suited the particular circumstances of the day. These two strategies frequently operated together. Open disparagement of American media could almost always be used to justify the existence of the BBC, even as US-inspired broadcast techniques and programs were smuggled in behind the scenes to attract broader audiences. US broadcasters frequently invoked the autocratic horrors of the "state-run" BBC to resist government regulation of their enterprise, even as they raided the British cultural storeroom and adhered slavishly to British definitions of "quality" broadcasting when it suited them. A constant circuit of transnational eaves-dropping and cultural one-upsmanship, as well as cordial transatlantic visits and vital productive relationships, flows through the records of the BBC and ITV as well as NBC, NET, PBS, and other broadcasters; a host of interme-diary organizations actively aided and encouraged this flow for both prag-matic and symbolic reasons, most prominent amongst them the Rockefeller Foundation in the pre-war years and the Ford Foundation postwar.

During World War II both British and American national governments made transnational cooperation in broadcasting a critical imperative, using it to win the war, and developing in the process unique aural documentary and dramatic techniques that would influence radio, film and television when the war ended. Television brought the influence of Hollywood to the fore, as live broadcasting merged with film techniques, and television pro-grams could now be traded not only across the Atlantic but globally. The birth of commercial television in Britain was structured both in rejection and incorporation of the American model; educational and public broad-casting in the United States both embraced and rejected the model of public service broadcasting developed by the BBC. There is a reason why the voice of PBS so often speaks with a British accent, one that has its roots in strong trans-Atlantic relationships that began in the 1920s. And as Alan Riding points out (above), there is a reason why the European Union struggles today with the fact that the one culture truly common across all its member states is American popular culture, delivered into its living rooms by national broadcasters whose own programs are unlikely to be viewed by many of their neighbors.[6]

Yet such a story of transnational cultural economy is rarely told. Sweeping generalities have been brought to bear on the topic of global media influ-ences, but few studies have looked at specific instances of international cross-influence in depth (though see Lacey 1994; Steemers 2004; Tinic 2005). A very few have focused on the US/Great Britain relationship, but only from one side (Camporesi 1994; J. Miller 2000; Rixon 2006). More often, the unthinking national pre-occupation of historians simply overlooks the presence of the transnational, or sweeps it guiltily under the rug. This book attempts to weave the histories of broadcasting in the United States and Britain closely together, foregrounding moments of particular proximity or particular anxiety, setting them out in sufficient detail that the delight-ful specificities of history can be revealed: the personal relationships and intertwined lives, the vexed issues and complaints, the heated debates and behind-the-back sniping, the moments of good faith and bad, the bursts of inspired creativity and bureaucratic dullness, the networks of people's lived experience, both behind the scenes and in public. And since broadcasting, being what it is—a transmitter and participant in all aspects of a nation's life—cannot be isolated from the politics, social conditions, economics, and culture of its period, the story becomes complex indeed. It cannot be told in full—even Lord Asa Briggs' five massive volumes on the BBC have not achieved that—but it is hoped that these pages will give a small indication of the richness, and inter-connectedness, of both these vital cultural traditions.

A secondary goal is to place the study of broadcasting at the heart of the history of the twentieth century, where it belongs, rather than on its margins. Given the prominence of Britain and the US on the world stage, their mutual narrative spreads far beyond the trans-Atlantic sphere. As the world's nations became network nations, the US and Great Britain squared off as the dominant competing models for modern media-centered democratic national cultures, influential across the globe (see S. Potter 2011). From Scandinavia to Japan and across the outposts of empire, nations modeled their broadcasting systems after the BBC, sought its advice and emulated its programming, using strategies of centralization, state ownership, regulation, quotas, tax structures, public funding, and other methods to pull together the national culture and to resist the perceived threat of imperializing American commercial culture, as well as to control "de-nationalizing" elements at home. In the American sphere of influence (notably South and Central America, but felt across the world), private ownership and commercial programming were spread by both government and corporate interests, built on the sale of technology, private investments in national broadcasting infrastructures, advertising agencies marketing American consumer goods, and not least, official international policy initiatives. British and American programs aired on television stations around the globe, and provided the fundamental underpinnings of television forms and genres, aesthetic practices, and production standards for much of the world.

In most nations, the national broadcasting service provides a central outlet and a sturdy pillar of support for a wide range of other arts and cultural activities, from cinema, music, theater and dance to journalism, documentary, education, and civic participation. Those with a publicly funded, state supported system, interlocked with cultural ministries and government agencies of many kinds, owe their basic model to that developed by the BBC in the 1920s—and emulated by the United States, finally, in the late 1960s as one of the central components of President Lyndon Johnson's Great Society programs. Even earlier, and continuing non-stop across the sweep of the twentieth century, American commercial broadcasting moved centrally into place amongst the popular arts and civic culture at home, expanding and supporting Hollywood cinema, popular theater and vaudeville, the music business, sports, journalism, documentary, education, and public events of all kinds. Other nations would later be pushed into extending funding to a similar non-state private sphere in the arts and humanities, as American popular culture's success around the world—driven by the tightly linked engines of cinema, television, and popular music—prompted a widening of the definitions of public culture and a flowering of indigenous popular arts and media, often to the chagrin of traditional national gatekeepers.

Though to trace out these global implications would require another book—probably several books—what follows in this introductory chapter is an attempt to limn them broadly by placing the history of broadcasting within the framework of thinking about nations, national identity, national culture, and flows of influence and resistance. I look at major theories of nationalism, assessing what they have to offer the study of broadcasting history as well as how a consideration of the structures and practices of broadcasting in the twentieth century might inflect theories of nationalism, adding to our understanding of national identity construction and the projection of national interest both internally and externally. Central to this is the concept of "Americanization," the construction of the "American other," so prominent to twentieth century cultural history, and so much a crucial support as well as a product of state-funded media systems. The contested role of popular culture in the formation of national identity closely relates to the problem of "Americanization," especially as the twentieth-century media of film, broadcasting, and recorded music opened up compelling new transnational forms of address to groups considered problematic within the national imaginary—women, the working class, ethnic and religious minorities—while allowing "foreign" products, especially American ones, to circulate widely. Thus, a new kind of transnational cultural history is called for, which I attempt to outline broadly while situating the current project within the Great Britain/United States exchange.

What does a transnational history of broadcasting need to take into account? Here is where the unique concerns and methods of media studies scholarship have something to contribute to both the humanities and the social sciences, because mass media as a field exists at their juncture. Cinema and broadcasting produce texts, both fictional and non-fictional, that involve the kind of narratives, genres, performances, and visual and aural representations well-suited to humanistic analysis and indeed central to any consideration of the development of arts and culture across the twentieth century and into the twenty-first. Yet such texts are produced by institutionalized industries whose structures, economics, sociology, and politics imbricate them inextricably in the realm of the social sciences. These two aspects of culture of course can never truly be separated, despite the tradition in the humanities of treating creativity as the province of the individual author or artist, divorced or at least detached from social and economic institutions, and the propensity of social science to shy away from "texts" or the interpretive aspects of culture. Thus the task of the transnational media historian is to pursue not only traditional humanities concerns—flows of texts and of artists, of influence and innovation—nor only to examine economic and institutional aspects of cultural production such as cross-ownership, national policy, and co-production. Existing as it does at the complex juncture between affairs of state, public culture, and the domain of the arts, the study of broadcasting—particularly understood as a trans-national form—requires attention to the sphere of politics and economics as much as to matters of creative influence, the development of aesthetic practices and forms, and their social and cultural reception. And broad-casting's unique capacity to channel and support other forms of arts and culture means that its history, particularly in the transnational context, must of necessity be a trans-media history as well.

Tom O'Regan, in a rare assessment of the impact of British broadcasting's transnational projections, sums up the task in admirably concise fashion:

> The British television presence is not confined to the international circulation of its programmes. It also involves a history of overseas investment in British television and British investment in television production outside the United Kingdom; the indigenizing of British formats and productions by foreign producers; the adaptation of British policy models; the use of British precedent and program-ming to organize public discussion and debate; and the role played by British television in supplying personnel and training for other television systems. These too are part of the British television story internationally; a story dependent on the cultural resonance its programming, formats, and policy-making have for those who import them. (O'Regan 2000, 304)

These considerations apply as well for British broadcasting's impact on the culture of the United States, and likewise for the impact of United States media culture on Great Britain and elsewhere. Now, try to imagine that statement substituting "literature" for television and "criticism" for policy and see how its sense changes. We are used to thinking about the trans-national circulation of literary texts—as a highly respectable, celebrated, and much-studied phenomenon—but we tend to ignore the economic and institutional structures that underpin it, just as we tend to downplay the distinctly national side of serious literature. This volume attempts to place broadcasting and its texts within the cultural frame usually reserved for more established arts, but also to critique and inform that frame by pointing up both high and low culture's deep imbrication with the national, political, economic, and transnational forces that shape all definitions of culture and cultural production, whether recognized or not.

Here, truly, is an *histoire croisée*, a term developed by Michael Werner and Bénédicte Zimmerman to denote histories in which "social, cultural, and political formations, generally at the national level" (2006, 31) intersect with each other in complex patterns, and in so doing throw into question elements often considered stable in historical accounts, such as historiographical methodology, the accepted categories of analysis, and the object of study itself. They note the particular usefulness of this approach where "nation" makes up the dominant structuring category:

> Within a *histoire croisée* perspective, the transnational cannot simply be considered as a supplementary level of analysis to be added to the local, regional, and national levels according to a logic of a change in focus. On the contrary, it is apprehended as a level that exists in interaction with the others, producing its own logics with feedback effects upon other space-structuring logics. Far from being limited to a macroscopic reduction, the study of the transnational level reveals a network of dynamic interrelations whose components are in part defined through the links they maintain among themselves and the articulations structuring their positions. (2006, 43)

Thus a transnational focus throws the seemingly stable categories of "nation," "national culture," and "national identity" into doubt, showing the forces that permeate them but that constitute them as well. Such a history must take into account "the diversity of transactions, negotiations, and reinterpretations played out in different settings around a great variety of objects" (2006, 43), so that the historian *croisée* finds herself perusing not only Congressional and Parliamentary records, public documents from the Ministry of Information and the Federal Communications Commission, but also the creative texts and records of artists and producers, corporate reports and marketing plans, grant proposals and foundation reports, and critical disputes played out in the press.

A transnational perspective on broadcasting might also contribute to the history of what Akira Iriye calls "cultural internationalism," a specific type of globalizing force that he traces from the mid-eighteenth century up to the present, "not as a story of interactions among sovereign states but in terms of cross-national activities by individuals and groups of people, not always or primarily as representatives of governments but as agents for movements transcending national entities" (1997, 1). Iriye's definition of cultural internationalism implies a more deliberate and disinterested perspective than that possessed by many actors in this history—such as Hollywood television producers or national broadcasting institutions. But others, such as the Rockefeller Foundation, groups of educators and public broadcasters, and occasionally even national governments themselves, did in fact articulate a conscious awareness of both the benefits and pitfalls of such nation-transcending cultural flows. This account positions itself at the intersection of all these forces as it seeks to explore the complex tensions between the national and the transnational, the individual and the institutional, as they crossed and intertwined across one particular field of relations over the tumultuous middle decades of the twentieth century.

Nations, National Identity, and the Transnational

Historians and critics have noted the importance of Anglo-American relations in many other fields, from politics, economics and social policy to art, literature, music, and film. Sharing a common language and a common history, united in the twentieth century through two world wars, and vying for leadership in global influence, Britain and America have a substantial record of both competition and cooperation across multiple spheres of activity that is hard to overlook or deny (Rodgers 1998). Yet their relationship in the field of broadcasting—a medium that stands at the very center of social, cultural and political communication—has been largely overlooked, as though each nation developed radio and television in splendid national isolation. In fact, it requires a real effort of will on the part of the media historian to overlook the constant and constitutive presence of Great Britain in the United States experience, and vice versa, when it comes to broadcasting.[7] Hollywood's influence on the development of the art of film, and the adaptations and resistances to it that various national traditions contribute, has been well established; no such critical transnational historiography has yet been developed for broadcasting.[8]

From the very beginning, as scientists and engineers worked with inspired amateurs to develop the technology of wireless communication, the two nations kept more than a casual eye darting across the Atlantic. At every moment, what went on in the rival empire of the air held immense interest for politicians, producers, artists, critics, and the public alike. I have been fortunate enough to have had access to two of the most extensive archives of broadcasting history in the world, one on each side of the Atlantic: the BBC Written Archives in Britain and the NBC archives in the US (as well as a number of other important collections; see the Bibliography). Their files are full of references to each other, and at certain key points, as this history will show, mutual observation, comparison, and adaptation became all but obsessive. Briggs' invaluable five volumes on the history of the BBC recognizes this intense relationship in a way, referring every few pages to the United States in his detailed account, yet rarely is this thread pulled and taken up as a topic in itself. American historians (and I include my own earlier works) are guilty of ignoring the constant BBC referent in their midst almost entirely, even though it is impossible to understand the evolution of educational broadcasting, the development of serialized drama, or the emergence of today's news form in any other way—to name only a few examples of transnational influence.

Clearly a new kind of transnational media history is called for here, an *histoire croisée* that recognizes that the very strength of the "analytical cage" of nation is a marker of the inherently transnational nature of the medium, and of the transnational cultural economy it creates. A transnational history specifically acknowledges the centrality of nation and the importance of national identity in the events it relates, even as it recognizes that the nation always exists in tension with the transnational and that these forces have enormous constitutive and productive power, particularly in the cultural field. Cinema may well have constituted the first truly transnational medium of the twentieth century, producing works of transcending interest that could be physically distributed to theaters around the world with minimal alteration or translation, reaching audiences at all levels of society who responded to recognizably human narrative dilemmas no matter what the originating nation or language. And though film history is often written from a national perspective—reflecting national imperatives to sustain an indigenous film culture in the teeth of Hollywood's cultural intrusion, a recurring theme in transnational history—film is also recognized as a fundamentally international art form, with influence flowing around the globe as readily as its products. Not so broadcasting: despite the ready evidence of transnational influence and the international flow of programs—particularly, again, from Hollywood—most broadcasting histories read as if only native productions count, as if only nationally produced programs have significance culturally, as if only programs created and circulated by established national institutions exist in the national culture. Here, the national agenda of broadcasting institutions and the discourses they inspire has overwhelmed the evidence before historians' eyes, producing "histories lopped off at precisely those junctures where the nation-state's permeability might be brought into view" (Rodgers 1998, 3).

Even more surprising, viewed from the standpoint of the transnational media historian, is the absence of consideration among theorists of nationalism and national identity of the importance of broadcasting, in particular, as a nationalizing force in the twentieth century. Media historian Richard Maxwell makes the connection between popular broadcast culture and the role of the state as he concludes his study of the development of television in post-Franco Spain:

> As the weight of public opinion became a real force to reckon with in modern democracies, modern state administrations drew more heavily on terms and symbolic assets that had until then only reigned among nationalist intellectuals and protonational affiliations . . . Electronic mass media were fancied as great connectors of peoples to the project of nations. (Maxwell 1995, 150)

However, though nation-builders themselves have certainly appreciated broadcasting's power and the role of the state in shaping it, this is a perception rarely pursued among theorists and historians of nationalism.[9] Eric Hobsbawm simply states, "National identification in [the twentieth century] acquired new means of expressing itself in modern, urbanized, high-technology societies. The first, which requires little comment, was the rise of the modern mass media: press, cinema, and radio" (Hobsbawm 1990, 141)—and turns his attention to sport. Benedict Anderson devotes considerable attention to the role of "print-culture" via the novel and the newspaper, but barely glances at the "new" media of radio and television—this in a book written in 1983!

The neglect of consideration of popular mass media, particularly broadcasting, has created a serious blind spot in our understanding of how nations function and persist, dominate, fracture or reform under the pressures of the modern world. Neglect of the crucial role played by nationalism in the formation of mass media likewise has left a crater in the middle of our understanding of modern media culture. Filling in this blind spot seems especially important for understanding the way both nationalism and culture function in democratic societies, where not only the high culture of the elite counts as vital to national coherence and identity, and where the actions and perceptions of the broad general public (both inside and outside the nation) represent one of the most pressing issues before governments today.

The circulation of national myths and symbols, a sense of shared history, the maintenance of a central language, agreement on national characteristics, all of these work to construct nations by creating the "common public culture" that Anthony Smith designates as the "key attribute of nations" (2001, 14). Modernist theorists such as Eric Hobsbawm, Ernest Gellner, and Benedict Anderson would inflect this with an ideological slant, emphasizing the role of the state and other key institutions in constructing nations and national identities, and in so doing preserving central power hierarchies. In Eric Hobsbawm's words, "Nations do not make states and nationalism but the other way round" (1990, 10), at least in part through the mechanism of "invented traditions": national rituals, ceremonies, myths and symbols that mark the intervention of the state into national culture construction, along with the educational system and other elements of official national culture (Hobsbawm and Ranger 1992). In particular, the creation of what Ernest Gellner calls a "national high culture," produced by the nation's dominant intellectual elite and circulated under the auspices of the state, works to define and celebrate a sense of national identity against all others. Equally important is the consolidation of a national language, seem by many theorists as key to national identity. The work of education and other important media of high culture dissemination, such as literature, theater, and the arts, is to distribute such national cultural symbols, in the official language, from the elite to the masses, a task especially important in modern democracies where national allegiance and consent to state power cannot be imposed but must be consensual.

But what of *popular* culture? Most theories of nationalism have little room for the consideration of popular culture, as distinct from folk culture with its mythologized roots and traditions that discursively underpin national identity (though see Billig 1995). Popular culture is most often seen as a problem, inflected as it is with elements that the state's careful constructions cannot contain or control. Popular culture tends to be marked both by resistance to authorized culture and by living evidence of the "non-national" within the nation's midst: the *sub-national* (local and regional identities in tension with the national), the *pre-national* (those social groups seen as requiring particular assistance in being integrated into the model of national citizenship, such as women, children, and youth, the working class, and ethnic, religious, and racial minorities), and the *trans-national* (influences seen as "foreign" and de-nationalizing). When these three elements coincide to challenge or disrupt the preferred high culture, in their tastes or in their actions—as, for instance, when working class women in rural areas choose American soap operas over domestically produced quality programs—they are seen as a problem that must be addressed, often through state regulation. But such negotiations rarely find their way into histories of nations and nationalism.

In particular, popular culture produced in non-print media such as radio, television, and film has escaped serious attention from historians and theorists of nations. While Karl Deutsch recognized the role played in modern nationalisms by mass media as early as 1966, in his *Nationalism and Social Communications*, mass media are seen primarily as naturally occurring conduits in which pre-existing identity and culture can circulate, not as deliberate state constructions or as a space in which national cultures are constantly challenged and contested. Benedict Anderson focuses on the top-down, centralizing capacities of print media, allowing the (elite) citizen to imagine his membership within the dominant national or imperial culture, yet scarcely aware that at the movie theater or via the radio his wife and daughter might be absorbing very different cultural notions from outside the bounds of dominant print circuits—most likely, in the twentieth century, from Hollywood. Richard Collins, writing about Canada, notes that "Elites have long experienced a transnational 'high' culture . . . However, it is the contemporary pervasiveness of an international *popular* culture in and through which the masses are thought to construct their identities and aspirations *outside* the dominant political institutions of the nation-state that most worries contemporary nationalists" (Collins 1990a, 107–8; emphasis in original). And my use of a gendered distinction above is not arbitrary—typically the national elite citizen is imagined as masculine, leaving women in particular out of the analysis. Popular media, and particularly broadcasting which reached inside the home, reversed this preference. Broadcasters in every nation eventually learned—quickly, in the case of commercial broadcasters; much more slowly in the case of public service broadcasters—that women made up the bulk of their listening audience and had to be addressed as their primary clients. This had some disruptive effects, as we shall see.

Consideration of a transnational popular culture resistant to or inconsistent with the national—a dangerous back door that the sub-national, prenational or transnational other might enter, eroding elite definitions—has been left, first, to theories of cultural imperialism emerging in the 1970s and early 1980s in the work of sociologists and political scientists such as Herbert Schiller, Dallas Smythe, and Armand Mattelart. Though the fears of national cultural erosion propounded by such theorists might at this point seem exaggerated, and certainly have been criticized, they do point the finger squarely at the twentieth century's most pervasive source of transnational popular culture: the United States, especially in the shape of the "transnational corporation" understood to be quintessentially, if not solely, American. In the late 1980s and early 1990s, as changing technologies, economies, and political ideologies in the Thatcher and Reagan era began to erode the standing of public service broadcasters, in Europe in particular, the dangers of "Dallasification" and its "cultural emasculation" (Morley and Robins 1995, 53; Ang 2001) became the rallying cry for those who opposed transnational popular culture in its American guise.

Later theorists of global cultural flows, such as Arjun Appadurai and Homi Bhabha, rejected the one-sidedness of cultural imperialist concepts in favor of notions of cultural hybridity, yet here still it is American popular culture that remains the primary agent of the non- (or even anti-) national. In many cases, the intrusion of non-national (usually American) popular culture acts to spark the oppositional renewal of nationalist cultural production; in others, intra-national regional and local cultures find a space for insertion within the openings provided in formerly heavily centralized and elitist national cultures (see, for instance, Kumar 2008; McCann 2004). Yet when such accounts gloss over the actual sources of transborder cultural influences under the phrase "Westernization," they neglect the specifics of the content and the context of the culture transmitted: for the most part American or British, with their own unique and distinctly differentiated projects of national culture building and dissemination that cannot be dismissed simply as "Western," "imperialist," or "commercial": though they may be all of those things, they are also, importantly, distinctively "American," "British," or deriving from another local center of power, and may contradict and contest each other—particularly in the post-colonial context.

Given the centrality of culture to the formation and maintenance of national identity in the twentieth century, and given the need in modern democratic states to disseminate national culture widely and effectively not only to elite but to middle and lower class populations, the neglect of popular culture in the scholarship on nationalism and national culture histories, and in particular the omission of broadcasting, is somewhat astonishing. From the institution of radio in the 1920s to the growth of television after World War II, and onward to wider dissemination via satellites and the Internet today, broadcasting constitutes the medium most closely linked to nations and nationalism in the twentieth century and most directly established as an institution of national culture by nation-states around the world. Yet literature, journalism, and film have received greater attention in histories and theories of nation-building than broadcasting ever has, despite the fact that most of these activities have remained—often via legal protections—outside the immediate control or financing of democratic states for most of their histories, and in the case of literature, journalism, and the fine arts, outside the grasp of large sectors of the population.

Broadcasting, on the other hand, was taken in hand by governments around the world from the moment of its emergence as a mass medium, and still is used as a primary instrument of national cultural construction and dissemination today. Citizens of every nation spend far more time with the accessible texts disseminated via nationally or transnationally distributed radio and television directly into their homes than with their nation's literature, films, newspapers, arts, or in its classrooms. Yet most theorists of nationalism devote only cursory attention to radio and television as a nation-constructing apparatus—organized sport has received more attention.[10] To a certain extent this is due to the disdain that the academy has shown to broadcasting generally, relegating its texts and audiences to the realm of sociology and low culture (and feminized low culture at that), beneath the radar of humanists and historians. Only very recently has the humanistic study of radio and television entered the academy, producing within the last twenty years a growing body of scholarship that should make the neglect of this central area of national cultural definition and production much more difficult for future social and political historians.

But a certain amount of blame must fall to media scholarship itself, where a concern for the functioning of media in democracy, especially as framed in "public sphere" theory, has deflected attention from the highly nationalistic orientation of broadcasting systems generally, and led to the neglect of the function of nationalism in most of this body of work as well.[11] As several scholars have noted, in some ways democracy and nationalism pull in opposite directions; democracy is concerned with the widest possible spread of political power without disqualifying distinctions, while nationalism is concerned with defining and limiting who is qualified to participate as a citizen in the modern nation-state, rejecting those who do not fall within its restrictive boundaries, whether by gender, ethnicity, class, religion, or migrant status (Ang 2001; Fraser 2010). Democracy is based in principle on inclusion, nationalism in principle on exclusion. As the historical developments described in these chapters will demonstrate, the erroneous conflation of national public service media with the Habermassian public sphere, and the effort to rationalize the exclusion of border-crossing market-based forms from this definition, marks a fundamental misunderstanding of the ways that the ideology of nationalism functioned to set up these basic media structures in the first place, and continues to confound our thought to this day. In particular, the undeniable association between non-state, usually market-based broadcasting forms and the construction of a transnational popular (and the attempt to suppress or control it via national public service systems) brings the clash between democracy and nationalism to the fore, and places the state in the center of the relationship.

Thus we can clearly see the close articulation of broadcasting with the project of the nation-state, despite theories of nation that have ignored this realm of culture and media histories that have taken the national structures of broadcasting for granted. But what is this "nation" that imposes itself so pressingly on the project of broadcasting, and how did radio in its early decades, by providing a technology capable of operating across boundaries and outside of traditional control, mandate a construction of national identity structured in response to fears of de-nationalization?

Since national identity always presupposes difference from another—the nation is unique, it is distinct from its neighbors and from any other existing entity—transnational influences and distinctions assume a crucial constitutive role: the "them" without which the "we" has no meaning. Consideration of the role of the determinant "other" moves us into the arena of discursive construction of the nation. Though some scholars of nationalism maintain the primacy of essential and naturally unique characteristics that arise from within an *ethnie* (see A. Smith 2001, for a discussion), even in such cases the referencing of the "foreign other" usually relies on the construction via discursive devices of certain different and often disdained groups whose claims and essences are repudiated (and all the more strongly repudiated the more proximate and influential they are). Thus to be Serb is to be NOT Croat; to be French is to be NOT German or British, to be Canadian is to be NOT American, to be Japanese is to be NOT Korean (Spencer and Wollman 2005). This universal nation-defining phenomenon has received attention piecemeal and in specific circumstances, notably in the literature on post-colonialism, which deals with the particular relationship between a nation emerging from the dominance of an imperial other and coping with the multiple demands of crafting a nation out of previously suppressed and homogenized identities. Yet it exists at all times and in all states, becoming even more imperative as the traditional, internal and "essential" bases for assertion of national coherence weaken. Kenneth Minogue emphasizes this essentially comparative concept by defining nationalism as "a political movement depending on a feeling of collective grievance against foreigners" (1967, 25). But what is a "foreigner," especially for the modern, democratic, multi-ethnic state? In many cases this can only be answered in the realm of culture, and it is often resistance to threats made by "foreign" culture (again, either internal or external, or more frequently both) that provides the glue to hold a heterogeneous national identity together, defining an "us" against a "them."

Over the twentieth century an important cultural "other" against which the entire world has reacted in one way or another was, and remains, "America." Fears of "Americanization" have driven and continue to drive a significant portion of the discourse of nationalism and other identity movements in nations around the globe.[12] The twentieth century is not just the century of nationalism, nor of broadcasting, but also the century of America's expansion in the world. As David Morley argues, for Europeans, in particular,

> "America" has long provided the negative pole against which "we" have defined ourselves, the image of what "we" are not, or that which "we" do not wish to imagine ourselves to be, or that which it is feared "we" are about to become . . . And "America," as the container of that "experience that cannot be tolerated," assumes a fantasy dimension as that which always threatens to "contaminate" or overwhelm European cultural integrity. (Morley and Robins 1995, 57, 80)

In specific cases, of course, a local "other" remains the more pressing oppositional figure, as Arjun Appadurai notes:

> The central problem of today's global interactions is the tension between cultural homogenization and cultural heterogenization . . . Most often, the homogenization argument subspeciates into either an argument about Americanization or an argument about commodization, and very often the two arguments are closely linked . . . But it is worth noticing that for the people of Irian Jaya, Indonesianization may be more worrisome than Americanization, as Japanization may be for Koreans, Indianization for Sri Lankans, Vietnamization for Cambodians (1996, 32)

In some such cases, American culture may offer a resistant globally available alternative to the local dominant, as for instance South Korea, in part by serving as East Asia's main translator and adaptor of American (and Japanese) popular culture, has not only held off the influence of China and Japan but is threatening a Koreanization of Chinese culture, at least among young people.[13] In the United States itself, the long tradition of "American exceptionalism" constructs the entire world as an "other," (or, in its longterm project of "democratized nationalism," rhetorically rejects the idea of "otherness" altogether, a strongly imperialist construction) while during certain periods a more specific "foreign" presence becomes central, such as the "Communist other" during the period of the Cold War or, in Toni Morrison's construction, the non-white "Africanist other" so persistent in American history and thought (Morrison).[14]

The global role of the American other is driven by its dominant position in the production of popular culture. US popular culture began to spread globally as early as the 1920s, not only in the production of consumer goods but in the "cultural software" often perceived as its advance guard: advertising, movies, popular music. Film, in particular, brought an awareness of American popular culture to world audiences, a phenomenon perceived as particularly threatening by those nations whose own capacity for film production had been decimated by World War I, notably France, Germany, and Great Britain. By the mid-1930s, a British trade paper could ruefully claim, "As far as films go, we are now a colonial people"[15] and British regulators defensively declared, "Trade follows the film"—a reworking of the old empire slogan "trade follows the flag." Film flew the American flag in the "soft" empire of culture.

Broadcasting systems developed just as American domination of the film industry was becoming apparent, and nations around the world adopted structures in the 1920s and 30s designed to combat the incursion of

American popular culture and preserve broadcasting as a uniquely national cultural space. Often, this meant broadcasting systems owned and funded by the state: public service broadcasting, with an explicit mandate to promote and protect national culture from potentially globalizing market influences. Ironically, of course, this confinement of broadcasting within national cultural boundaries freed the field for less-restricted US products to develop a transnational appeal across the global market.

Resistance to Americanization began early in the US/Great Britain relationship, as power shifted from the older empire to the new one in the decades after World War I. Britain had more reasons than most to be concerned about being NOT American (almost as many as Canada): a common language, a common history, shared cultural traditions, strong economic, political, and social ties, and a similar position on the world stage made the relationship indeed "special," and especially fraught. The accommodations and resistances to the American other forged by British broadcasting from the 1920s to the present day profoundly shaped the way that broadcasting was implemented and used in nation-building not only at home and across the nations of the Commonwealth (Canada, Australia, New Zealand, and others) and former Empire (notably India, South Africa, and Egypt) (see S. Potter 2011) but also more broadly in Scandinavia, Africa, and the Middle East. Canada, in particular, assumed a crucial role as "mediator" between American and British broadcasting, frequently providing American-inflected programming and personnel to the BBC and ITV at crucial moments, often when top-down definitions of the "national public" were at stake—all the while fighting its own battle against incursions from both below the border and across the pond.

In the United States, throughout the twentieth century, Britain remained culturally the primary "parent" nation, despite decades of non-Anglo-Saxon-Protestant immigration, and particularly for American elites, lastingly enshrined in the educational establishment. Large portions of the prominent political, professional, and cultural classes in the 1920s and beyond found Britain's solution to the spread of market-based popular culture a compelling model. The BBC, with its non-commercial base and commitment to "quality" culture, remained the standard towards which many believed American broadcasting should strive, a resonant antidote to the culturally threatening influence of Hollywood and other sources of popular culture. It is no coincidence that the nascent Public Broadcasting Service (PBS) in the 1970s found its widest audiences and least troubled reception with programming imported from Britain, and still collaborates heavily with the BBC; indeed, I argue here that it has been difficult for American intellectuals to see beyond the British public service model when it comes to posing alternatives to the commercial system, since the 1930s, and that the idea of British television as "quality television" remains a consistent thread underlying American broadcast innovation. Often, as British policy makers and television producers invoked the horrors of the American system and American programming at crucial moments, they could draw on the criticism of Americans themselves to make their points, especially among intellectuals and academics.

Thus, a picture of a new kind of transnational cultural economy begins to emerge: intellectual classes united across state boundaries in adherence to a carefully managed, state supported, educationally inculcated idea of the "official" national culture (itself significantly transnational) while the working and middle classes (and much of the elite itself) unite in enjoyment of a common, market-driven transnational popular culture, outside the discourses of "official" nationalism (but marked by significant differences in state and economic power). Meanwhile, thousands of local cultures, stimulated by diverse influences, produce their own creative hybrid cultural forms that circulate in a myriad of paths both within and across national boundaries. This is a history that has been lost in the typical nationalist accounts common to the field as well as to their "globalization" oriented counterparts, and it is a perspective on nationalism and national identity that has been lost to historians unwilling to take the social influence of broadcasting and other forms of popular culture into account.

By examining the intertwined histories of the two largest and most dominant broadcasting powers across the twentieth century, I hope to accomplish several objectives, though of course no single volume could explore this complex intersection thoroughly. First, I hope to reveal the central yet neglected role played by broadcasting in twentieth-century nation-building in two key nations, pointing towards similar developments in nations and empires around the world for which, it is hoped, future historians and theorists will find a use. Second, this history points to the ways in which the terms of ongoing competitive relationship between the US and Great Britain affected the conceptual differentiation between public service and commercial broadcasting that has been so central to our thinking—and to national economies and cultures—over the last century. Third, it provides a case study of the ways in which transnational cultural influences were negotiated between two leading producers of broadcast programs and practices, revealing important aspects of cultural hybridity at work and the negotiations between cultural oppositions—high and low, national and "other," quality and popular—that still affect concepts of culture more broadly today, particularly through anxieties over "Americanization." Finally, it provides a transnational perspective on the history of broadcasting as a cultural form in both the United States and Great Britain, correcting the narrow nationalist view that has dominated our understanding up to now and revealing important circuits of influence, adaptation, opposition, and exchange almost always left to the side of traditional nation-based histories. It reveals key transnational figures, texts, and organizations that have been overlooked in both nation-based and globally oriented histories, to the detriment of critical aesthetics and historical understanding.

I argue that we cannot understand either nation's cultural history without considering the "special relationship" outlined here, and further that, given broadcasting's centrality in twentieth century culture more generally, historians of other aspects of the arts and humanities significantly affected by their relationship with radio and television—cinema, theater, music, literature, documentary, history, education, journalism, sociology, and public policy, to name a few—should for the first time perhaps consider how this complex and far-reaching medium has significantly influenced their own fields of study, both within and across national boundaries. What follows is necessarily partial, focusing on key moments rather than providing a comprehensive history, and spans primarily the middle decades of the century, from the 1920s into the 1980s, from broadcasting's inception as a medium up to the point of its increasing dispersal and de-centralization via satellite, cable, and new recording technologies into the digital age of the late 1990s and twenty-first century. Ending just where the many utopian and dystopian analyses of the new "globalization" of culture begin, I hope to show that a constitutive and productive transnationalism runs beneath all those categories of nation, of sovereignty, of cultural purity and social independence that have so engaged us across these decades of nationalism. I hope this work will contribute to a better understanding of the uses to which national discourses have been put as well as of the transnational dialectics that underpin them.

In focusing on this trans-Atlantic dialogue I do not wish to imply that no other transnational relationships are important and indeed crucial in the story of broadcasting and culture in the twentieth century. Many other nations innovated institutions, systems, and programs that vitally affected both the US and Great Britain, as well as their own neighbors and far-flung connections around the world. Both France and Germany developed into leading producers of programs for export after World War II, with the Soviet Union pre-emptively dominant across its sphere of influence, as were both Japan and China in the Asian cultural sphere. In South and Central America, Cuba, Argentina, Mexico, and Brazil operated in a complex dialectic with each other and with culturally proximate nations, including their dominant neighbor, the United States. In Africa, Britain, France, and Germany competed with each other and with the US and the Soviet Union for influence. All of these nations participated in the transnational dialogue—a dialogue that typically ran along the course of larger geo-political alignments. These aspects of transnational cultural economics need to be taken into wider account in histories of global influence and culture. Many theorists have called for the project of tracing such local, regional, and transnational flows of information and culture; few have limned them in detail. That project is overdue. I hope that the story presented here will spur such initiatives and help to pry open our national cages to reveal the many fascinating transnational dialogues contained within.

Chapter Summary

Network Nations is organized into three parts, each comprising three chapters, chronologically organized and defined by distinct stages in the US/British relationship. Though the beginning chapters are broken into sections that consider each nation's historical trajectory separately, as the story progresses the experience of the two nations becomes more interlinked. Part 1 begins during the period of amateur experimentation before and during WWI, and examines the inception of broadcasting as an institution, a social practice, and a cultural forum in both Britain and the United States, looking particularly at the places where their mutual influence is particularly marked. This focus reveals long-standing lacunae in the historiography of both British and American broadcasting: on the American side, matters having to do with the non-profit sector, especially universities, educational groups, foundations, and the federal government; on the British side it reveals the commercial aspects of broadcasting such as the negotiations that founded the early Company, its relationship with adjacent industries like the press, the BBC's magazine publishing operations, and off-shore radio. The BBC's determination to resist "American chaos" spurred the growth of its national network, far ahead of such developments in the United States, and paved the way for the transition from private company to public corporation in 1926. Though the first American network formed in that same year, by the mid-1930s the major chains had all but lost control over the programming sent out over their airwaves, as sponsors and advertising agencies took over the reins of production and formed an alliance with Hollywood.

Many in the United States, including leaders of the educational radio movement, objected strongly to the hyper-commercialization of American radio and looked toward the BBC as a preferable alternative, sparking an outbreak of transnational hard feelings in 1933–34 as the matter came up for national debate. Yet already lines of mutual influence could be clearly discerned. By 1936 the BBC had a permanent American Representative in place, as did both NBC and CBS in London—for CBS, as of 1937, that representative was a young Edward R. Murrow. Murrow's education in broadcasting came at the hands of the BBC, a story taken up in the next chapters, as World War II changed everything.

Part 2 weaves the two nations' histories tightly together as suspicion and self-interest gave way to an urgent need to cooperate. Even before the War, the BBC responded to the need to reach broader audiences, as well as to compete with offshore commercial stations, by selectively adopting previously shunned American practices such as audience research and regular scheduling. In response to German and Soviet radio propaganda, they also broadened the old Empire chain into a new multi-lingual Overseas Service, including, as war broke out, a North American Service (NAS) aimed specifically at the US and Canada. Under its influence the first British serial drama, *Front Line Family*, made its debut, and the NAS became an important conduit for transnational creative innovation, with a heavy influence from Canada that profoundly affected the development of broadcasting on both sides of the Atlantic. The careers of Alistair Cooke, Geoffrey Bridson, Norman Corwin, Alan Lomax, and Edward R. Murrow, among others, were built in the NAS or influenced by it.

The NAS also figures large in the transnational invention of the "radio feature," the highest form of expression of radio art, in programs like *The Columbia Workshop, Transatlantic Call*, and *An American in England*, along with advances in news and documentary in other trans-Atlantically inflected sites, such as the Radio Research Project at the Library of Congress. Meantime US organizations like the Rockefeller Foundation, working with educational radio proponents and leading scholars and critics, began to pull together a plan for public service broadcasting, American style. All pitched in together during the war years, as government organizations like the Office of War Information and the British Ministry of Information turned their focus on the field of radio, leading eventually to the strange story of Boston station WRUL as well as the contested advent of the American Forces Network in Britain. By the end of the war prolonged contact with the national "other" had fundamentally changed both national cultures in ways that would culminate in the new medium of television.

Part 3 begins in the post-war period with television's debut, though radio continued to figure centrally in the media landscape through the mid 1950s in both the US and Britain as television rolled out slowly. In fact the radio sphere expanded considerably in both nations, with hundreds more AM stations and an entire field of FM licenses granted in the US, allowing educational radio a second chance, and setting important precedents for educational television. In Britain the radio service expanded to include the Third Programme, a counterbalance to the popularization of the Home and Light services. Radio's close articulation with national interests during the war led to a spirit of reform and rededication to public service, producing the "Blue Book" in the US and the Beveridge Report in Britain. However, just a few years later commercial television made its contentious debut in Britain as a competitor to the BBC, despite the trans-Atlantic consternation over American networks' handling of the Coronation of Queen Elizabeth II in 1953, one of the first global television events. American television enjoyed an initial period of live anthology programs patterned after the BBC-inspired "single play" tradition, marked too by the Ford Foundation's intervention into "quality" programs with the highbrow variety program *Omnibus*, hosted by Alistair Cooke.

But as US networks quickly converted to filmed series production based in Hollywood, new kinds of transnational production arrangements followed. One was Hannah Weinstein's partnership with J. Arthur Rank and his Independent Television Company (ITC), making British television shows with blacklisted American talent for domestic broadcast as well as export to the US. When British commercial network ABC determined to revitalize its live drama production, it turned to a Canadian, Sydney Newman, so successfully that the BBC made him Head of Drama even as a second channel, BBC Two, emerged. The Ford Foundation also backed the emergence of a new force in educational television, NET, which not only began to provide an alternative "fourth network" to Americans but influenced efforts by ITV in Britain to produce educational and public affairs programming.

Then, in the mid sixties, a period of extensive but often contested relations emerged with the advent of BBC Two in Britain and the passage of the Public Broadcasting Act of 1967 in the US which created a national Public Broadcasting Service backed by new cultural funding organizations like the National Endowments for the Arts and Humanities. British programs enjoyed a period of popularity on American screens, as PBS programs like *Masterpiece Theatre* and *Nova*, underwritten by both public and corporate funds, began to regularize co-production between US and British partners, and commercial television turned to adaptations of British programs rather than direct import. The concluding chapter briefly traces structural changes such as the financial interest and syndication rules and the advent of cable channels in the US and the introduction of Channel 4 in Britain as they breathed life into a new sector of independent production to compete with traditional networks. Co-production with both commercial and non-commercial American producers began to provide considerable revenue to a revitalized British cinema/television industry, led by the powerful BBC Enterprises. By the mid-1980s, with satellite distribution looming on the horizon, there could be no doubt that a transnational cultural sphere existed, spreading around the globe.

Taken together, the necessarily partial and brief histories here attempt to "set the record straight" by placing the development of broadcasting in Great

Britain and the United States in the close conjunction they deserve. In doing so, I risk offending many readers by bursting some of the historical bubbles they are accustomed to, especially in light of the rhetoric of "public service broadcasting = good/commercial broadcasting = bad" so common to both critical and popular analysis in both countries. What I am attempting here is to show how complicated both these categories are, and how they owe their cultural salience as much to the forces and needs of nationalism as to any essential principles or characteristics. More to the point, they are never separate. They grew up together and in relation to each other; public service broadcasting has depended upon and supported a commercial side from the beginning, while for-profit radio and television have frequently incorporated a public service ethos and have leaned heavily upon the non-profit sector for inspiration and validation. I attempt to be even-handed in my history, spreading criticism and praise as it seems due; if it seems at times I am attacking the BBC's pre-eminent achievements and reputation, it is because the dominant rhetoric has left so little room for previous comparative work to develop a more nuanced critical edge. If at times I seem to be defending commercial broadcasting's achievements and social value, I hope it is not within the tradition of industry self-interest but as an objective examination of its strengths and weaknesses, particularly within the American context but with enormous implications for global culture. Above all I hope to dispute the notion that we can organize our histories around a conceptual purity that directly contradicts the experience of everyday people, whose lives have intersected with the compelling products of transnational interaction, in radio and television and film as well as many other spheres of human activity. Culture has never stayed neatly contained in conceptual boxes; it thrives on messy and transgressive border skirmishes. This is a celebration of the productivity of culture across history, outside the box.

The Nations Imagine Radio, 1922–1938

In the beginning we were to some extent guided by the example of America. I do not mean that America indicated the path, but rather that America showed us what pitfalls to avoid; we learnt from her experience. Broadcasting in America was well under way, with a two years' start, when the service was first inaugurated in Great Britain, and it was soon common knowledge that the lack of control in America was resulting in a chaotic confusion . . . Britain, as I say, benefited by America's example, and a centrally controlled system of broadcasting stations was the result.

—John Reith, undated speech @1926[1]

I hold up to you the superior scholarship, the superior good taste, the superior urbanity of the British broadcasting system. It is all that can be said for it in comparison with ours. I hold it up to you and I ask you: Will you for that bribe surrender what America has given to you in your inherent passion for all feasible liberty of utterance? Will you for that bribe surrender all your chances of free expression on the whole American air to the autocratic determination of one selected citizen? If so, vote British. If not, vote American.

—William Hard, NAB spokesman, 1933[2]

Nation and broadcasting are deeply intertwined, as these two quotes demonstrate; they grew up together. "If there was a moment when the nineteenth-century 'principle of nationality' triumphed it was at the end of World War I"—so Eric Hobsbawm begins his chapter entitled "The apogee of nationalism, 1918–1950" (1990, 131). Also triumphant was the technology of radio broadcasting, grown from a hobby of Morse-coded amateur exchanges in the ether to a crucial element of warfare and a hotbed of technological innovation. As military-trained radio enthusiasts streamed back home to pursue the beckoning possibilities of transmitting voice and music over the air, and international corporations squared off over issues of patent control, national governments confronted the pressing issue of how best to handle this new medium that both promised and threatened.

This chapter begins the process of tracing the transnational dialectic between Britain and America with a focus on the politics, economics, and discursive positioning that shaped the founding decisions of broadcasting as a medium and a social institution. During this period of national re-grouping after World War I, when radio remained primarily local and governments and corporations experimented with its potential uses, the United States and Britain, along with Germany, led the world in radio technology. Their constitutive dialogue, and the ways in which they resolved the question of how to handle radio's border-defying and radically demo-cratic properties in an age of nationalism, set up models for all those who would follow.[3] While the US forged ahead blithely into the era of amateur radio experimentation and entrepreneurship, only belatedly attempting to impose controls, Britain pondered its example and devised a broadcasting system specifically intended to hold off the worst of the "American chaos," yet which stifled the democratic potential of radio under a monopoly that protected powerful interests. Later, when pressure built to organize the scattered local business of American radio into national networks and bring it under greater state supervision, the BBC served both as both good and bad example in popular discourse and in regulatory debates. British notions of national "quality" were linked to Progressive social agendas to counter the values of localism and diversity in favor of a higher, more homogenized vision of national culture that strengthened national unity while similarly stifling diversity and protecting powerful interests.

Yet throughout the 1920s and early 1930s, personal and professional relationships, frequent exchanges of observations and ideas, and a growing practice of transnational cultural exchange between the two dominant broadcasting nations stimulated the development of radio as an art and as a cultural force, creating a new space for the kind of cultural internationalism traced by Iriye (1997, 71–2). By the end of the 1930s, as impending war mandated closer collaboration, British and American broadcasters had, in the tension between the two systems, forged the permanent hallmarks of twentieth-century national broadcasting, innovating many of the program forms and genres still prevalent in broadcasting today, extending the reach of music, literature, discussion, and drama into the ordinary domestic sphere, and setting the terms for radio's global development. Out of the productive clash between the values of private profit and public service, commercial enterprise and state support, decentralization and national control, Britain and America built, between them, an "empire of the air" that exists to this day.

This section, broken into three chapters, sets the early development of radio in both countries side by side, and in so doing not only reveals the frequently overlooked history of mutual influence and interaction between these two leading nations, but also their dialectical impact on twentieth-century notions of national culture and national identity. By situating the birth of broadcasting institutions and policy within a larger, transnational context of political, cultural, and economic developments, both similarities and differences in the two systems can be revealed, paying close attention to primary documentation on both sides of the Atlantic as well as the larger rhetorical uses to which broadcasting was put. The essential localism of America's broadcasting system, rooted in the structure and philosophy of the American socio-political system, takes on new significance against the essential centralization of Britain's, and vice versa; the strikingly early formation of national networking in Great Britain, equally relevant to its social and political goals in the early twentieth century, derives greater meaning when counterposed against the slower and more uneven growth of networks in the US. Above all, the fundamental transnationality of radio, despite its national framework, emerges and is shown to be a significant force in the shaping of national identities and relationships as Western nations go from war to peace, and then head for war again.

CHAPTER 1

Chaos and Control

During the years of World War I and the prosperous though brief peace that ensued, radio technology developed from a medium of Morse code transmitted over increasing distances to a medium of analogue sound transmission. The technologies that permitted this new avenue of culture and communication emerged in various places around the globe, growing out of the telephone and telegraph that had preceded them. Yet their institutionalization and transformation into cultural forms was affected by the models set by the two Western nations first to perceive their value in national terms: the United States and Great Britain. This is not to assert that other nations did not initiate broadcasting, either in the public or the private sector, in the years immediately following the war. But nowhere did it develop with more global impact than in the Great Britain and the United States. In the US, radio experimentation was not interrupted by war as it was in Europe, so radio broadcasting proliferated and diversified quickly as a local, popular, relatively uncontrolled medium. Britain, though slower to achieve wide circulation as a popular medium, created in the British Broadcasting Company in 1922 a national structure for radio that accelerated radio's growth above most other European nations. Finally, the global dominance of each of these two nations in the interwar years meant that the institutional structures, policies, technological and creative practices, and decisions as to the social function of radio broadcasting hammered out between 1919 and 1926 would serve as models for much of the rest of the world.

The end of World War I sparked an upsurge of developments in radio. Before the war, transnational corporate expansion had prevailed in the nascent field of communication technology, as the international licensing of patents prompted a boom in cross-investment. The globally dominant Marconi Company, based in Britain, established an affiliate, American Marconi, in the United States, where it assumed a pre-eminent position in telecommunications development. Westinghouse, an American corporation, expanded into Britain with its British Westinghouse subsidiary. American Telephone & Telegraph (AT&T) opened a British branch of its Western Electric division; and the Edison-based General Electric Corporation forged partnerships with companies all over the world, including General Electric in Britain. Wartime alliances encouraged economic and technological co-operation between allies, but with the war over and the spirit of nationalism on the rise, issues of control over key patents in this developing field raised the eyebrows, and hackles, of both corporations and governments.

The Radio Corporation of America

One key piece of technology in particular seemed to mark the major way forward in technological advance: the Alexanderson alternator, an alternating-current generator capable of voice transmission at high power which had been developed by Swiss-born engineer E. F. W. Alexanderson working with Canadian Reginald Fessenden in the General Electric labora-tories in Schenectady, New York. The US Navy had found it very valuable during the war. When, in the spring of 1919, British Marconi approached American GE with a proposal to buy all rights to the innovation, the prospect of foreign control over a key piece of technology prompted a crisis in the United States. Who should oversee radio development? Was it a job for the state—perhaps the Navy—keeping national assets out of the transnational marketplace by bringing radio technology under the direct aegis of govern-ment? Or should radio be left in private hands, insulated from the dangers of government control but with few safeguards against "foreign" influence?[1]

The post-war temperature of the United States ran against government intervention; many felt that the nation had just spent two useless and bloody years in a war that accomplished very little, provoked by a mass-mediated barrage of propaganda engineered by Great Britain and spread by the Committee on Public Information, formed by President Wilson and headed by George Creel (P. Taylor 1999, Cull 1995). Temporarily, at least to many in the US, the idea of linking a new mass medium to government control seemed the worst possible option, detrimental to democracy and contrary to First Amendment freedoms. Yet if radio were left to develop on its own, a foreign corporation, Marconi, threatened to dominate its development worldwide.

In the end, the US government compromised by intervening in the formation of the Radio Corporation of America. This communications giant, pooling the patents of its three parent companies plus the coercively acquired stock of American Marconi, represented the United States' response to the era of technological nationalism beginning to emerge around the globe. RCA's charter stipulated that its stock ownership must be 80% American, that only US citizens were entitled to serve on its board of directors, and that one board member must be a government representative, for most of its early years a Navy man[2] (Finney 2004, 1163). Russian-born David Sarnoff, formerly Director of American Marconi, became General Manager and would later rise to become president. He would exercise considerable influence on the development of American broadcasting. Radio in the US remained in private hands, though with a far greater degree of government oversight than most other segments of the economy—or of the culture. This would create a precedent for later events. RCA became, indeed, *the* radio corporation of America, bringing together the combined expertise of American technological innovation and limiting radio manufacturing in the US to those companies licensed by RCA.

However, by 1919 in the United States radio *broadcasting*, as distinct from radio technology, had already slipped the bounds of both state and corporation and thrived as a field of fiercely defended individual experimentation. Nationalization of patent rights had obvious advantages for America's economic interests—and perhaps political interests as well, given radio's utility during the war—but already organized amateur groups, like the American Radio Relay League, founded in 1914, actively pressed for a vision of "citizen radio" protected by First Amendment rights and outside both government and corporate supervision. As an editorial in the July 1921 edition of *QST*, the ARRL's publication, cogently argued:

> We are trying to . . . establish before the general public the fact that serious communication is being accomplished by private citizens. Do you realize that our radio provides about the only way by which an individual can communicate intelligence to another beyond the sound of his own voice without paying tribute to a government or a commercial interest? It's so, and it's a big thing and becoming increasingly important as new-comers enter the game. When we speak of "Citizen Wireless" we convey a picture . . . of a vast field in which the private citizen of this country may enter and carry on useful communication. And when we stand up before a Congressional committee it's a good term too—just think exactly what it means![3]

The ARRL did speak up before Congressional committees many times before the decade was out, and its vision of the electromagnetic spectrum as a public resource to be used by private citizens undoubtedly went a long way towards keeping US broadcasting in private hands.

Thus RCA's mandate did not include a monopoly of broadcasting itself, as the BBC's would a few years later. RCA and its member companies remained free to operate their own experimental radio stations in the coming years, as did any number of other American businesses, organizations and individuals. For the time being, US broadcasting as a practice and as an emerging mode of cultural expression remained in the hands of the general public, decentralized and largely unsupervised. This fact—taken for granted by most American historians but standing in stark contrast to the status of radio amateurs in most countries in the world—would have a profound effect on the development of broadcasting in the United States, from its financial basis to its emphasis on localism, and on the way it would eventually address the nation. For a brief time, the radically democratic potential of radio broadcasting—communication that paid tribute to neither government nor corporation, in the ARRL's words—prevailed in the US, the way it did in few other places; the powerful strain in American nationalism of individualism linked to populist democracy temporarily triumphed. It helped that no major international challenge from neighboring airspace troubled US sovereignty (as it did in Europe, and for US neighbors such as Canada and Mexico), and that the US, by organizing early and by virtue of size and geography, gained control over more than 80 frequencies to call its own.

Citizens and Entrepreneurs

The roots of this phenomenon lay in America's late entry into World War I. During the crucial years 1914–1917, as Europe dissolved into war and brought all radio experimentation under government control, America's amateurs enjoyed an unrestricted environment. Only between 1918 and 1920 did the US close its airwaves to the public. As soon as wartime restrictions were lifted, thousands of radio amateurs, returning in many cases from training and service in the Signal Corps, perceived radio's developing potential and began to apply for licenses to transmit at low power, at first mostly in code but increasingly switching over to voice. The Department of Commerce, under whose jurisdiction radio licensing fell, had very little authority with which to exert control over who might receive these licenses; in the US, in contrast to Britain and most European nations, communication systems were lightly regulated by the Commerce department but ownership and operation remained in private hands.

Ambitious individuals, civic-minded organizations, and enterprising small businessmen—proprietors of jewelry stores, dry cleaners, chicken farms, and small-town newspapers; schoolteachers, police and fire departments, railroads, theaters, and churches—began to experiment with the promotional and informational capacities of the newly emerging medium. Playing records, bringing in lecturers, sending out live performances, telling jokes, relaying the news and weather, and interspersing it all with self-promotional messages, they competed for attention among the rising crowd of "listeners-in" with the more formal efforts of the radio manufacturing firms, department stores, city and state governments, and universities. Supporting organizations sprang up, such as the American Radio Relay League's numerous local chapters, along with magazines, book series, courses of instruction, retail stores, and listener groups.

By January 1922 over 1 million licenses had been issued (all of them authorizing the holder to both transmit *and* receive), and the untrammeled diversity and populism of the American airwaves provoked the first major move by the Department of Commerce to rein it in. True amateurs, those with the most easily obtainable licenses, most basic equipment and with little institutional backing, were congregated in one isolated band, forbidden from playing records, reading news and weather bulletins, and anything else besides personal communication.[4] More organized broadcasters, who had earlier applied for the standard "station" license, remained classified as "A" stations on the crowded 350 meter band, making their own arrangements to share ether space in localized ad-hoc fashion. But the new "Class B" license on the 400 meter band allowed approved broadcasters to shift their operations to a less congested frequency, in exchange for certain promises of "quality" in performance and in technical standards. Class B stations could be fairly certain of uninterrupted reception wherever they were based (Bensman 1985). Many of the more established broadcasters immediately applied for a "B" license; some of those original stations remain on the air today. "Quality" stipulations included a ban on the playing of recorded music (at least in part a reaction to the social panic over African-American rooted "jazz" that had recently swept the country) and a mandated preference for more expensive "live" performance that would persist into radio's heyday (Hilmes 1997).

A divide began to open between Class A and B broadcasters and the now-segregated amateurs who had pioneered their art, yet these early experimenters remained a considerable force in US broadcasting's early development, and indeed the dividing line between the two groups was anything but clear. By spring of 1923, when *Radio Broadcast* published a survey of radio license holders, 570 stations squawked across the airwaves.[5] Radio and electronics dealers and manufacturers operated the greatest number of stations—231 of the total—with newspapers and other publications second, holding 70 licenses. But the second largest category, with 86 stations, remained "unknown" to the journal, indicating the presence of many individual enthusiasts on the airwaves despite all efforts to constrain them. America's amateurs, numbering over a million by 1922, must be counted as originators of some of the basic characteristics of radio broadcasting itself, from its localized base, to its independent informal spirit, to much of the content that would soon become the standard fare of a professionalized media sphere.

American amateurs took a lively interest in radio's development in other countries, pulling in distant signals not only across the vast reaches of the US but from Canada, Mexico, Cuba, and other nations, and covering radio's development in the pages of their journals and newsletters. Keeping in contact with their counterparts across the Atlantic in Britain remained particularly important, though it was hampered by the restrictions placed on amateurs in the UK (discussed below). A February 1922 article in *QST,* the journal of the ARRL, reported that member Paul F. Godley, "sent overseas with American equipment by the ARRL" and stationed in Androssan, Scotland, succeeded in picking up signals from more than two dozen American and Canadian stations, an achievement that according to the journal was "epoch-making and opens the door to unguessed possibilities in private radio communication."[6] American and British amateurs would cooperate in trans-Atlantic receiving contests frequently in the later 1920s, and their respective publications record overseas visits each way treated with great interest and enthusiasm.[7]

Yet it was precisely the system that American amateurs had created and defended that raised alarms overseas, and at home as well. Pressure was mounting to reign in the amateurs, not least from the commercial corporations who had invested thousands in radio operations only to find their signals interfered with by rambunctious enthusiasts. Secretary of Commerce Herbert Hoover initiated a series of conferences, in 1922, 1923, and 1924, seeking a plan to organize American radio, but with so many players in the field no coherent solution could be reached. Radio still developed apace, with 16% of US households owning a radio receiver by 1926, multiple stations available in most good-sized cities, and a great deal of coordination of signals and frequencies at the local level—such as the institution of "silent nights" during which amateurs could fish for distant signals—on a voluntary basis. Not until 1926, when a case filed by the Zenith Radio Corporation temporarily vacated all licensing authority, did the term "chaos" perhaps become appropriate (though some argue against this interpretation—see Phipps 2001), but to many the course of centralized control pursued by Britain, formulated at least in part to counter the way that radio had developed in the United States, began to exert considerable appeal.

British Caution

The question may well be asked, why was it that wireless telephony, whose possibilities were proved in late 1919 or early 1920, did not come into general use in the autumn of 1920, when things were just beginning to boom in America? The answer lies in a sentence, "We are British."

Let others rush at the new inventions, and do the experimenting, spend the money, get the hard knocks, and buy their experience at a high price. We British sit tight and look before we leap. So it was in this case.

We may often be behind in the early stages of a new science, but once under way, we soon catch up and generally lead the field before long.

How fortunate this national attitude or circumspection was in the case of broadcasting can be seen easily by glancing at the chaotic state of affairs on the other side of the Atlantic.

—Cecil Arthur Lewis, BBC Director of Programmes, 1924 (8)

While American amateurs experimented and organized, their counterparts in war-torn Europe waited impatiently through the post-war period of instability, as nations pulled together their frayed social and economic fabric and wartime restrictions began to ease. The British government had shut down all non-state radio experimentation in 1914, opening the field to non-military uses only in 1920 with extreme caution and careful screening, as authorized by the Defense of the Realm Act, still in effect. Radio fell under the remit of the British Post Office, as did other means of communication such as telegraphs, telephone, and the postal service. Transmitters and receivers were licensed separately; unlike Americans who could both send and receive messages, most British amateurs were barred from transmitting and could qualify only for a license to receive. Transmitting licenses were reserved for those doing approved technical experimentation. About 100 were granted in 1921 at very low power (along with roughly 4,000 receive-only licenses, without which operation of any radio receiving set was forbidden). According to historian Asa Briggs, "All the successful applicants had to be 'men of good character' as well as men of curiosity" and their license applications had to stress not just technical competency but also to include testimonials as to their personal qualities and background (Briggs 1961, 53).

British amateurs and manufacturers chafed at these restrictions and petitioned the Postmaster General in December 1921, who responded by making it clear that wireless was not to be used for mere "purposes of intercommunication" or "personal pleasure" as in America but rather, as Briggs writes, a "definite object of scientific research or of general public utility" (1961, 52–3). But the Post Office did concede to authorize a series of 15-minute concert broadcasts from the Marconi experimental facility at Writtle in early 1922, to which those licensed to receive could sit back and listen.[8] Aside from these and the occasional transmission in English from a Dutch station in Hilversum, British amateurs had literally nothing to tune in to but silence most of the time on domestic airwaves, contrasted to the veritable Babel across the Atlantic. The US publication *Radio Broadcast* reported in September 1922 that "England is still discussing radiophone broadcasting, while numerous English radio amateurs storm and fume as they read our American radio periodicals."[9] It was difficult to develop the art and science of radio under these conditions; it was even more difficult to sell radio apparatus.

British radio amateurs and manufacturers often used the American comparison to push for greater latitude in developing the new medium. By the spring of 1922, British readers not only of specialized wireless publications but of the *Times* of London were being informed on a regular basis of radio's rapid progress in the United States, from its "1,000,000 American Users" who "seem to have caught the 'radio-flu'" to the range of programming available; on April 20, the *Times* reprinted an entire week's broadcast schedule from KDKA-Pittsburgh.[10] Yet even as Marconi director Godfrey Isaacs pushed for radio growth in Britain, envisioning not only a "home service" but possibly "a Continental service as well, from any part of the world which one desires,"[11] more cautious voices warned against the "frantic chaos" prevalent in the US, where radio had "spread like wildfire" resulting in "confusion, congestion, mutual interference, and 'jamming.'"[12] "Clearly," the *Times* editorialized, "if we are to escape the American difficulties, there must be limits to absolute freedom." This characterization of United States radio as a "difficult" situation marked by "chaos" played a key role in the discourse on radio in Britain (and eventually in the US as well), even though by the spring of 1922 the new Class A and B system had begun to separate out the more respectable broadcasting stations from the amateur bands and most urban Americans could receive several stations clearly on their receiving sets.[13]

Yet steps were being taken. Most notably, in the winter of 1921, Mr. F. J. Brown, Assistant Secretary of the British Post Office who had been sent to Washington DC to attend an arms conference, became interested in the "radio craze" that had broken out in the US. He sought out American radio experts and attended the first of the US radio conferences convened by Herbert Hoover in January 1922. On his return, Brown reported back to his superiors at the Post Office his opinion that "broadcasting is the main sphere of wireless in the future."[14] He would become an important influence on the development of British broadcasting.[15] Soon after, the British government referred the question of radio to its Imperial Communications Committee, before which Brown "explained the position which had arisen in America, and the difficulties which were presenting themselves in England."[16] Above all, this meant avoiding what most in Britain viewed as America's major mistake: having allowed radio broadcasting to slip out of government control into the marketplace, and thus into the hands of virtually anyone who cared to venture into the ether, creating both technical and economic "chaos." The ICC formed a Wireless Sub-Committee, headed by Sir Henry Norman, Member of Parliament and a longtime wireless enthusiast, authorized by the Post Office to enter into negotiation with the dominant radio interests in the UK.

These meetings began in May of 1922 on the basis of principles set out in advance by the Post Office. Besides the Marconi Company, twenty-one British electronics firms were represented, amongst them Marconi's two main rivals: Metropolitan-Vickers, formed when British Westinghouse was nationalized under British ownership in 1919, and Western Electric, still with partial ownership by AT&T but under British management and control. The Post Office's restrictions centered on three main concerns: first, the necessity of a cooperative arrangement in Britain along the same lines that RCA had evolved in the US, so as to reap similar national advantages in technological development and keep foreign-manufactured technology out of the British market; second, the avoidance of a commercial monopoly of radio in Britain by the Marconi Company, holder of most key patents and with only a tenuous attachment to British national identity (and a long history of difficult relations with the British government); and third, the restriction of American-style private commercialism "which from the start the Post Office feared," according to Briggs (1961, 55).[17]

Though some of the Post Office's 1922 mandates seem rather comically outdated now—for instance, "Each transmission shall begin 'Hello! Hello! Here message for all stations from (station broadcast)'"[18]—others set the basic parameters by which British broadcasting is organized to this day. Many were clearly crafted with the American comparison in mind. Rather than the "chaos" of hundreds of broadcasters, the six major firms would be encouraged to form one cooperative unit, much like RCA in the US but with an *exclusive monopoly on broadcasting* as well as the manufacture of radio equipment, over eight stations distributed as to cover most of the country. No payment could be solicited for putting on programs; out of deference to the powerful newspaper proprietors and press agencies (from whom the Post Office derived considerable revenue which it did not want to risk), no news could be broadcast nor would advertising be permitted (Briggs 1961, 130); and the operations would be supported by a share of the license fee soon to be charged to all those who would like to operate radio receiving sets.[19] Sir Henry Norman set it out with more *élan* in the Times:

> Of course, every big retail house would like to shout the merits and low prices of its taffetas and tulles, its shirts and shoes. There is no room for this . . . The State has no business to circulate news except news of its own immediate activities. Infinitely less is it the business of commercial [radio] firms to circulate news. Commercial broadcasting will, therefore, necessarily consist of music and songs, spoken entertainment, dance music, lectures, sermons, and suchlike popular non-controversial matter.[20]

His emphasis on innocuous and "non-controversial" content for radio gives a preview of the careful balancing act the BBC would have to perform as a state-sponsored monopoly provider of information, with an uneasy relationship to hard-won press freedoms and to private firms that might find themselves in competition with the publicly funded corporation. However, as the above quote makes clear, the British government would have no direct hand in radio broadcasting either, in contrast to the system being forged in Germany. For the time being, broadcasting remained in private hands, though regulated and licensed by the state, and with some potential uses preemptively foreclosed, especially those that would threaten the lucrative relationship between the press and the Post Office.

Records of these meetings reveal a slowly emerging compromise between Marconi, its competitors, and government representatives to devise a means by which a commercial Marconi monopoly might be avoided, and yet Marconi patents might be made more generally available to build up broadcasting in Britain. It is notable that, though the Post Office's ban on direct advertising was accepted (as distinct from sponsored programs, a possibility kept open) and a pooling of efforts into a single broadcasting company promoted, nowhere in these discussions does the idea of broadcasting as a mission of public uplift and education appear. Somewhat ironically, the strongest spokesman for regarding broadcasting in Britain as a public service undertaking was Godfrey Isaacs of the Marconi Company, who made it clear that Marconi's cooperation, as the sole company controlling sufficient patents to actually begin broadcasting on its own without the need for cross-patenting from the other companies, would only be gained if this generous action resulted in a non-profit cooperative broadcasting venture—not the enrichment of his competitors.

At the meeting of June 2, 1922, Isaacs declaimed, "I will facilitate the Broadcasting Co. for the benefit of the general public, but not for the benefit of individuals," and went on at plaintive length (as transcribed in summary, not verbatim):

> I came here with quite a fair proposition. I offered everything in the interests of broadcasting for the benefit of the public, I waived any question of payment for licences, I offered to make no profit on the building of the stations, I agreed my Company would in no way figure as the company. I cannot go further, I do not think anyone at the outset could have expected the Marconi Company would have gone further than that. Where we break down is that the Marconi Company has absolutely no fish to fry for its own advantage, it could, had it wanted to, have gained advantage from this business because of its past history; it does not want to do so, but what it says is, I am not going to give to individual firms a selfish or individual advantage, that is what they are aiming at obtaining, their object is the benefit of the individual firms for purposes other than broadcasting. If they genuinely believed they had something of advantage to the stations it would be perfectly easy for them to submit it and have it adopted; but that is not the question for them, the question is the individual advantage for the individual firms. And that the Marconi company is not going to give."[21]

Briefly, a plan for two separate companies evolved, one dominated by Marconi, the other by Metropolitan-Vickers and Western Electric.[22] Not until Isaacs and Archibald McKinstry of Metropolitan Vickers went off on their own and hammered out an agreement between them in a series of meetings held between July 19 and August 8 did the formation of a single British Broadcasting Company move forward, to the relief of the Post Office and smaller players. On August 8, 1922, Isaacs and McKinstry brought their decision back to the Sub-Committee, and subsequent meetings devoted themselves to working out the details.[23]

At no point in these proceedings was the notion of broadcasting itself as a public service discussed, except for a brief mention in press release circulated on October 18: "The BBC will, in the words of the Memorandum, be a public utility service for the broadcasting of news, information, concerts, lectures, educational matter, speeches, weather reports, and theatrical entertainments."[24] It would be left to the BBC's young manager John Charles Walsham Reith, hired in December of that year, to develop the concept of public service broadcasting into a philosophy of national high culture-building. The manufacturers merely wanted a broadcasting service that would sell receiving sets—British receiving sets.

Clearly, elements of British broadcasting later attributed to its public service function—centralized monopoly, license-fee funding, exclusion of advertising—actually *precede* the definition of a public service mission for this barely emergent medium, and stem instead from concerns of nationalism and the state, at this point focused on the economic and political: to prevent transnational companies and the troublesome Marconi from dominating radio development in Britain, to keep the practice of broadcasting from escaping into the general population as it had in the United States, and to placate powerful press interests and protect government revenues. Invocations of "American chaos" became increasingly crucial in achieving these objectives. Between 1922, when the Company was formed, and 1926, when the BBC as a public corporation was established, the emphasis rested primarily on technological and economic definitions of "chaos"; after 1926, it was American *cultural* chaos that primarily concerned critics, a shift in definition stemming primarily from the efforts of John C. W. (soon to be Sir John) Reith.

The Uses of Chaos

On November 15, 1922, broadcasting officially began in Britain from a Marconi station based in London; stations in Manchester and Birmingham would quickly follow. Receiving licenses began to be authorized in November of that year. All British listeners were required to pay a license fee as well as a tax on receivers (this would later be dropped). Only British-manufactured receivers, stamped "B.B.C.", were allowed to be sold in Britain, to hold off intrusive American and German manufacturers looking for overseas markets (this would be relaxed by the end of 1924). The new British Broadcasting Company received its official license in December 1922. However, by the spring of 1923 the system that the Post Office and the radio manufacturers had crafted was being contested from a variety of directions: enforcement of license fees, the BBC monopoly over broadcasting, the ban on advertising, the provision of news. A committee was convened to address them, headed by Major General Sir Frederick Sykes, M. P.

This time one of Britain's leading populist newspapers, the *Daily Express* (owned by a Canadian, Max Aitken, later Lord Beaverbrook), took up the campaign against the BBC joined by a consortium of some of the smaller manufacturers, bringing a measure of public attention to the arrangements that had taken place behind closed doors the previous year. In the Parliamentary debate leading up to Sykes, the fundamental nationalist rationale for the creation of the BBC and the suppression of private broadcasting was articulated more clearly. Again, F. J. Brown's testimony proved crucial for the Sykes Committee, as it had for the Post Office a year earlier.

Brown stressed at first in his testimony that the BBC had been formed because "The Post Office held that it was essential that there should be no monopoly" in British broadcasting, referring to the danger of Marconi's dominant position.[25] He was questioned on this point by a member of Parliament, Mr. Trevelyan:

> There is no monopoly there [in America], and there are a large number of Broadcasting companies. That is how I come to question . . . why the Post Office here has set itself, apparently, to adopt an entirely different system from the American, whether it was because of the failure, in their view, of the American?

Brown answered:

> Yes, it was. The American system was leading to chaos, it was doing so already while I was there, and because of that chaos Mr. Hoover called a Committee of Officials and Manufacturers . . . with the view of arriving at some agreed scheme for preventing that chaos.[26]

Here he has managed to use the term "chaos" linked to the US three times in a single sentence; obviously this is a crucial point. This construction becomes a central one. It is echoed in the statement by Lord Gainsford later in the proceedings: "Within six months we have achieved more than America did in two years, and have avoided the chaos which exists in the USA."[27] Or, as a BBC official statement summarized at the beginning of the Sykes Committee deliberations: "The initiative which led to the formation of the Company came from the Post Office. They knew that, if the American chaos were to be avoided, one broadcasting authority was essential."[28]

However, even Mr. Brown had to admit that this characterization might not necessarily be accurate as regards US radio, at least technically. Questioned in Parliament, he was asked,

Q: (Mr. Eccles) Did you listen in at all?
A: (Brown) Yes, what I head was fairly good and was not interrupted.
Q: (Mr. Eccles) What I heard was fairly good; I was wondering whether the chaos might not have been exaggerated?
A: (Brown) It may have been exaggerated.[29]

This exchange points to the fact that the power of the "American chaos" construction cannot be attributed to careful study of technical and economic problems actually existing in that country, any more than later US invocations of "government controlled" British broadcasting could be supported by an examination of the facts. Instead, "American chaos" is used as a powerful discursive device, standing in for a number of things that influenced the shape and form of British broadcasting but were sensitive enough that they could not be discussed openly. These had to do with the set of specifically national factors discussed above that the American example might tend to point up if not cut off by charges of "chaos": restrictions on the general public's access to broadcasting, misgivings about Marconi's position in the British economy, fear of commercial competition that might undercut national control of a powerful new technology, and unwillingness to offend powerful business interests and jeopardize government income. It also reflects the increasingly contentious role that America and its interests—political, economic, and cultural—would play in British life in the decades to come.

The BBC weathered the challenge of the Sykes investigation with the help of a new articulation of its public service mission constructed primarily by John Reith, shifting the association of American chaos away from its technological and economic meanings and linking it more clearly to the *cultural* chaos of United States commercial competitive broadcasting, and indeed of American culture more generally. As Briggs puts it, by the mid-1920s, "the argument had shifted. Concern for technical control was giving way to concern for standards and taste" (1961, 67). He gives the example of advertising, later to become the key component of the BBC's rejection of the American system:

> Radio advertising had been strongly opposed by the newspapers on the grounds that it would interfere with their own interests, but in reaching its conclusions the committee was swayed by a different argument – that advertising 'would lower the standard' (Briggs 1961, 165).

Broadcasting "standards," now in the cultural, not the technical sense, became the new focus of BBC justification, and Reith argued strongly for the principle of "having a uniform policy of what can or cannot be done in broadcasting," in sharp contrast to "the trouble which arose in America" (Reith 1924, 182, 5). This spoke directly to the need for, as Reith would later term it, "the brute force of monopoly" (Reith 1949, 99) to implement those uniform standards of quality, but as Briggs argues, for Reith it was the rejection of the profit motive more than anything else that marked out and made possible public service in broadcasting.

Though he faithfully served the combined commercial manufacturing interests that made up the BBC, Reith began to articulate as early as 1924, in his book *Broadcast Over Britain*, his desire to see the company take on an expanded cultural function, above and beyond the simple coordinating task of its original mandate, to build up a center for British culture at its best that would contrast to the vulgarities of American culture and hold off its influence:

> In America broadcasting had been developed wholesale, largely on a commercial basis, and without any method of control whatsoever. There is no co-ordination, no standard, no guiding policy; advertising, direct or indirect, is usually the sole means of revenue. (81)

As with previous—and many subsequent—British observers of the American scene, he did not hesitate to exaggerate the chaotic, out of control qualities of US broadcasting and link it to lack of standards and guidance (as did many American critics as well). Reith was hardly alone either in his distrust of mass culture or in his articulation of cultural "uplift," on either side of the Atlantic. Andrew Higson points to this same formulation around British national cinema developing in 1923 and 1924 and leading to the protectionist Cinematographic Act of 1927, and in the Leavisite movement to promote "minority culture" against "mass civilization" in a defense of the English language and literature between the wars (Higson 1995). Bruce Lenthall traces the trajectory of similar rhetoric in the US (Lenthall 2002, 2007; see also LeMahieu 1988). Throughout this movement there is a strong current of anxiety over the role of American mass culture in general and the influence of "mongrelized" Hollywood in particular, lending a nationalist element to notions of public service and cultural uplift that is frequently perceptible though rarely noted: what Higson calls "the threat of denationalization" (Higson 1995, 20).

In contrast stands Reith's articulation of a newly conceived public service mission for the BBC, an Arnoldian vision of national high culture that would certainly have come as a surprise to those gathered in the Post Office meetings two years before.

> As we conceive it, our responsibility is to carry into the greatest possible number of homes everything that is best in every department of human knowledge, endeavour, and achievement, and to avoid the things which are, or may be, hurtful. It is occasionally indicated to us that we are apparently setting out to give the public what we think they need – and not what they want, but few know what they want, and very few what they need . . . In any case it is better to over-estimate the mentality of the public, than to under-estimate it (Reith 1924, 34).

Many powerful politicians and intellectuals in the United States as well as Britain agreed strongly with Reith's point of view. Within a few years American broadcasters would have to debate these contentions head-on, in the context of the passage of the Communications Act of 1934. But few by this time would have disagreed with Reith's conclusion: "Broadcasting is a national service the full importance of which will in due course come to be recognized, even if it not be adequately appreciated already" (1924, 219).

CHAPTER 2

National Broadcasting in Britain

The great significance of the demonstration which radio broadcasting is making tonight is in the vista which is opened of national
as well as world service by radio . . . It brings into view a national
broadcasting service that will transmit to every home in the land the
cultural and educational advantages developed by the best thought
of the nation.

—David Sarnoff, January 1, 1926[1]

1926 marks the emergence of broadcasting as an organized national and
international force. Most nations lagged behind the US and Great Britain; in
contrast to the hundreds of stations in the US, and Britain's unified national
service which by this time reached most of the country via 9 main stations
and 10 repeaters, in Europe only Germany with thirteen stations and France
with eight came anywhere near.[2] The *New York Times* reported in 1925 that,
in Hungary, "possession of a broadcasting set was a criminal offense . . . until
six or eight months ago" and other nations could boast of only one or two
stations, most of them under some kind of government control.[3] Yet clearly
radio had now become a world phenomenon, and celebration of radio's
international potential was planned for New Year's Eve, 1926: a "world-wide
New Year's celebration by radio" beamed primarily from New York and
London via the emerging technology of "transoceanic superbroadcasting"
on special high-power transmitters.[4]

RCA station WJZ and the BBC's 2LO in London cooperated in sending
out their own broadcasts, then relaying messages sent back to them from
radio stations who had heard the programs around the world. The *New York
Times* breathlessly reported "Parts of the American program were heard in

London, Paris, Buenos Aires, Havana and Bermuda, as well as everywhere in the United States . . . Thus virtually the entire Western world was linked together for a few minutes by invisible strands." The London program suffered some atmospheric difficulties, but could be heard across the US as well as throughout Europe. This was indeed a demonstration of radio's capacity to transcend national borders. RCA's David Sarnoff, however, indicated where the major interest of most broadcasters lay in his trans-nationally distributed address, which in the quote above reveals the funda-mentally national concerns underlying the occasion. If his words sound virtually Reithian, it should be remembered that RCA was just about to launch America's first network, the National Broadcasting Company (NBC), for which the BBC would serve as both an exemplar and a contrast.

Making the Nation as One Man

It is agreed that the United States system of free and uncontrolled transmission and reception is unsuited to this country, and that Broadcasting must accordingly remain a monopoly – in other words that the whole organisation must be controlled by a single authority.
—Great Britain, Report of the Crawford Committee, 1926 (6)

By 1926 Britain had gone much further in pulling the nation together under a unified broadcasting service than had America's competing local broad-casters. The Crawford Committee, convened in 1926 to review the BBC's charter, strongly endorsed John Reith's eloquent re-articulation of the national function of the BBC, resulting in the transformation of an awk-wardly coordinated private enterprise into a ground-breaking public cor-poration. By this time the organization had grown from 10 to over 700 employees, established a regular broadcasting service of 1,200 hours per week (averaging 8 hours per day per station) to more than 2 million license holders throughout Britain.[5] It had also weathered the General Strike of May 1926 by springing into action on behalf of the British government, against the strikers.[6] This brought it more fully into the fold of national institu-tions, and persuaded many in the upper echelons of British society of the important role that radio must play in the maintenance of national order, and of the dangers that might result should less unified control be permitted. It also won Reith his knighthood.

The Crawford Committee's report validated Reith's vision and defended the BBC's monopoly position by again employing the American comparison (above). This new endorsement stands in strong contrast to the *avoidance* of monopoly so strongly desired by the Post Office in its original charge. The essential difference is that the British Broadcasting *Corporation* was formed as a public rather than a private monopoly, supported and guided by the state rather than by the commercial marketplace. Now, with monopoly a solution rather than a problem, the definition of broadcasting in the public service begins to focus on *centralized control* and *a unified national culture* as the twin pillars of its mission, as Reith argued strongly in his statement before the Committee.[7]

In terms of centralized control, the BBC had begun immediately in 1923 to assert coordinated management over the operations of the distinct and disconnected stations built by the various members of the initial partner companies: Marconi with 2LO, the London station, as well as 5NO in Newcastle and 5WA in Cardiff (Marconi's famed experimental station, 2MT at Writtle, closed down in 1923); Metropolitan-Vickers' 2ZY in Manchester; and Western Electric's 5IT in Birmingham. In 1923 the BBC added 6BD Bournemouth, 5SC Glasgow and 2BD Aberdeen, with 2BE Belfast joining the group in 1924. To ensure greater national signal coverage, relay stations—transmitters that merely relayed a signal from the nearest originating station—were set up in Nottingham, Leeds/Bradford, Sheffield, Hull, Liverpool, Stoke on Trent, Plymouth, Swansea in Wales, and Edinburgh and Dundee in Scotland. Later, another would be added in the far south of England at Plymouth. This system of using low-power repeaters to bring radio reception into easy reach of even the most rudimentary crystal set has been blamed by some for slowing the growth of more sophisticated valve sets in Britain—necessary for pulling in more distant signals—and thus also for using up much more bandwidth to transmit BBC signals than might have been necessary (due to crystal sets' inability to tune in sharply). But it did ensure that coverage would be almost universal (reaching 70% of the public by 1926), that low-cost sets could be afforded by all (especially important in view of the license fee, a considerable expense for working class listeners), and that reception of stations from outside Britain would not be possible, for the time being at least.

All the main stations had their own station directors and program organizers, now employees of the BBC rather than of their original operators, and commenced program provision to their coverage areas for several hours a day. The BBC concentrated its forces at 2LO in London, setting up headquarters in 1923 at Savoy Hill where it would remain until 1931. This would become the BBC's flagship station from which the National Service would go out to all points; stations like Swansea in Wales, Sheffield in the north, and Dundee in Scotland became (at their own insistence) "London's babies" rather than transmit the geographically closer Cardiff, Manchester, or Glasgow signals, respectively (Briggs 1961, 219). Unlike the United States, where the establishment of as many local and regional broadcasters as possible remained at the heart of public policy (see below), it was the BBC's intent from the beginning to *reduce* the number of stations, sacrificing any benefits there might have been in local diversity to the advantages of a cohesive, unified national service. Regional stations would continue to produce a certain amount of programming from their local areas (later forming a separate Regional Service) but one that would always remain secondary to the London based national program. A single unified national service was the goal, to be made available to all. In Reith's words, "conclusive proof has been given that under no other system than unity of control can Broadcasting be conducted . . . it is essential ethically, in order that one general policy may be maintained throughout the country and definite standards promulgated."[8] Later he would describe this mission as "making the nation as one man."[9]

By 1924 the BBC under Reith had taken management of all stations into centralized hands and had begun to experiment with linking them together via telephone wires to be able to provide simultaneous programs. At this point a central Control Committee was established, and Reith's second in command, Admiral Charles Carpendale, was named Controller. A Programme Committee was created to make policy for the entire system, reporting to the Control Committee. By 1926, the Assistant Controller of Programmes (Roger Eckersley) oversaw five separate divisions, each with its own director: Talks, Music, Productions (including Variety and Drama), Executive (overseeing program finance and publicity), and London Station operations. Education would be added in 1927, an important acknowledgement of the new Corporation's expanded public role. Each department acted as a self-contained unit reporting to the central committee, acquiring properties, writing scripts and adaptations, employing performers, and working with engineers on productions, with an ever-increasing in-house staff of producers, directors, writers, and assistants. In the late 1920s and early 1930s, as US networks lost their control over program production by dispersing it amongst advertisers, agencies, and independent companies, the BBC consolidated and centralized in a manner reminiscent of Hollywood during the heyday of the studio system. This meant that many program forms pioneered by the local stations, responding to local interests, had no room in the expanding national service. Scannell and Cardiff argue that "the values and attitudes that began to emerge in the local stations between 1923 and 1927 were quite deliberately eradicated by the policy of centralization" (1991, 304).

However, coverage by the regional/relay system remained insufficient as the twenties progressed, and plans were made for building a new, high power station on long waves that could reach the entire nation with one strong signal. The first, built at Daventry in 1925 (call letters 5XX) represented, according to Briggs, "not only the biggest broadcasting station in the world but the first long-wave station" (1961, 224). It required adaptations to the receiving set, but could reach 85% of the population of Britain and brought a second service into many households. In 1927 a new high power station, 5GB, opened at Daventry as well, but with the aim of replacing many of the regional and relay stations with a high power Regional service, an alternative to the National. The Birmingham station became the main studio from which regional programs originated (sent to Daventry and distributed via 5GB) (Briggs 1965, 25).

By 1930 two full daily national services were in place; eventually, more powerful transmitters replaced Daventry's at Huddlesford and Droitwich. Former local stations either closed down or cut back drastically in programming and in staff. The major stations retained some production facilities, now serving a public conceptualized regionally: Midlands, North, West (including Wales), Scotland, and Northern Ireland. This centralization of service was not merely technical; Briggs points out its cultural basis as well: "No provincial station, it was decided, was to do anything which could be better done from London, and in normal circumstances it was in London that 'the best talent and the greatest facility' were available."[10] Reith's vision of a cohesive national service directed firmly from London had been realized. This arrangement would later be challenged by Charles Siepmann, named Director of Regional Relations in 1936. He would go on to become an important, though now largely forgotten, figure in American broadcasting history.

A Unified National Culture

> There were . . . at the head of the British Broadcasting Company men not merely of great organising and technical ability but men with vision, men with high purpose, men with wide outlook, men who looked at the problem not from the trade angle but from the national angle. It is to that happy circumstance we owe the great development which has attended broadcasting here. They set broadcasting upon a plane of high ideals, and they based it on a broad conception of their duty to the public and to public morality.[11]
> —Sir William Mitchell-Thompson, Post Master General, 1926

In terms of Reith's other main tenet, the establishment of a unified national culture, the avoidance of market-based competition for audiences along American lines formed the first line of defense, with the promotion of specifically British culture the closely related second. The BBC was never entirely detached from the market. Not only Marconi but a wide variety of British manufacturing firms would make considerable profits through their exclusive sale of transmitters and other operating equipment to the

Corporation, and the Company's original mission, of course, was to stimulate receiver sales in the British market, which it certainly did. And the BBC itself would eventually establish a thriving ancillary business in advertising-supported publications—the *Radio Times,* the *Listener,* and *World Radio*—which by 1932 would provide nearly a third of BBC revenues (since the British government continued to siphon off more than half the license fee proceeds into its own coffers) (Briggs 1965, 483–4). But in Reith's vision, and increasingly in the vision of Britain's national elite, there was something about broadcasting itself, something unique and powerful, that mandated its detachment from commercial concerns and set it up in resistance to the vulgarizing powers of the marketplace, to be pursued "not from the trade angle but from the national angle." It helped to point to America to make this distinction clear—and particularly to the threatening example set by American film.

Precisely as broadcasting rose to new heights, British domestic film production sank below the onslaught of American movie imports. Before World War I, 25% of films shown in Britain were produced in British studios, and circulated successfully around the world. By 1926 that figure had fallen to 5%, with films from the United States making up more than 80% of box office revenues (Glancy 2006; Higson 1995; Sarah Street 2009). This stark differential would worsen with the introduction of sound. As the Crawford committee in 1926 debated the future of British broadcasting, much anxiety had begun to surface in the press about the threat of American films, not only to the British box office but to British national culture and identity. *The Daily Express* fumed in 1926 that far too many British film viewers "talk America, think America, and dream America. We have several million people, mostly women, who, to all intent and purpose, are temporary American citizens" (quoted in Maltby and Vasey 1999, 34). Parliament began the debates that would eventually lead to the Cinematographic Act of 1927, which would place quotas on American imports by requiring that theater owners show a certain percentage of British films. Many supporters of the BBC and defenders of British cinema pointed to the commercial nature of the film industry as the fundamental problem: not only did US studios dominate economically, distributing films at costs far below that which home producers could afford, but they catered to the mass "lowest common denominator" audience culturally, driving down cultural quality and promoting American products and lifestyles as well.

That these two phenomena—national broadcasting and de-nationalized cinema—were not regarded as separate issues can be seen in a speech given in 1926 by Prime Minister Baldwin at a dinner in celebration of the BBC's first years of service. It is clear as well that more than just national industry is at stake:

In the same way, it is too early yet to say what the influence on civilisation of the moving picture may be, but I confess that there is one aspect of it upon which I look with the gravest apprehension, and that is the effect of the commoner type of film, as representing the white races, when represented to the coloured races of this world (Hear, hear). I need say no more on that subject except this, that in my view the whole progress of civilisation in this world is bound up with the capacity that the white races have, and will have, to help the rest of the world to advance, and if their power to do that be impeded by false ideas of what the white races stand for, it may well be that their efforts will not only fail, but that the conception of the white races generated in the hearts of the coloured races throughout the world may be an initial step in the downfall of those white races themselves. *I have ventured to say these things to you because we all felt here how different have been these past four wonderful years in the development of this great gift of science to mankind; how different from what they might have been had those in charge of them been actuated merely by mercenary and "get rich quick" motives* (Cheers).[12] (emphasis added)

Here Baldwin explicitly congratulates the BBC for adopting a system designed to keep threatening "foreign" influences, of more than one kind, under control. Implicit is the argument that a commercial broadcasting system ruled by "get rich quick" motives, as in America, would have thrown open the airwaves to the disruption of the dominant cultural order, linking it not only to national interests but to racial identity and empire as well. National cultural elites had lost control of the medium of film; they did not intend to let that happen with broadcasting.

Sir William Mitchell-Thompson, Post Master General, echoed these sentiments in the debates over the Crawford Report before Parliament in November 1926, in the quote at the beginning of this section. Trade led to de-nationalizing market exchanges and culturally debasing competition; a publicly funded monopoly service could stay above the fray on a higher moral plane (though of course investors in British radio manufacturing firms were profiting nicely). Opening up the British airwaves to competition could mean allowing American business directly into the British broadcasting market. In 1929, Gerald Cock of the BBC wrote a report on "American control of the Entertainment Industry" in which he worried not only that "the national outlook and with it character is gradually becoming Americanized" but that US interests might try to dominate television in the UK:

With a practically non-existent film producing industry in Great Britain, unsubstantially financed theatres, inefficient managements and dependence on American films and technical apparatus, the position is ripe for U.S.A. control, and with it propaganda more undesirable even than the present tributes levied by U.S.A. on the British public and managements for entertainments, in rentals, installations, and royalties . . . Against all this, there is left but one strong point (strongly organized and with satisfactory finance) namely the B.B.C.

Such influences, he warned, if not checked could lead to "the end of the B.B.C. as an independent organization and the advent of competitive American-influenced broadcasting."[13] Through the late 1920s and 1930s periodic warnings arose that American interests were just about to establish broadcasting stations just outside British jurisdiction: in Athlone, Ireland or in Hilversum in the Netherlands, for instance. Later, American commercial interests in fact made Radio Luxembourg and Radio Normandy their European bases (discussed in Chapter 3). The "American octopus" always threatened, and the BBC remained the first line of defense against the de-nationalization of British national culture.

Yet the public monopoly status of British broadcasting itself brought some difficulties in its wake when it came to forging a broadcast schedule to serve the public. National broadcasting culture in Britain faced some severe limiting factors in the 1920s and 1930s. First of all, the relationship of the early BBC with the state meant close supervision of anything deemed controversial or political, particularly in the area of news and public affairs. A careful neutrality had to be maintained in any matters having to do with politics, since taking sides would have undermined the fledgling service's relationship with its governors. As Scannell and Cardiff put it, during its early years "the BBC was on trial and must not do anything without the consent of the Postmaster General." (1991, 24)

The Post Office's cooperative relationship with the press would continue to limit BBC news coverage into the mid 1930s. The leading newspapers' position from the very beginning had been that to expect them to compete with a government-funded monopoly—for advertising revenue, had advertising been allowed, as well as in news coverage—would have been fundamentally unfair. The BBC's national monopoly position gave it an advantage over competing regional and national newspapers that threatened revenues and readership, and put the state itself in competition with private enterprise.[14] In the US, a similar conflict between the press and radio had also occurred, but it was resolved by the fact that many newspapers themselves owned radio stations and that radio broadcasters were free to simply set up their own wire service, which they did. No such options were possible for British newspapers, nor for the BBC. Reith fought hard for the easing of restrictions on news coverage and on presentation of controversial subjects, finally succeeding in winning relative independence from both in the late 1930s.

But state supervision of political topics, particularly foreign affairs, would continue well into and past the years of WWII. As Scannell and Cardiff conclude:

> For over thirty years, throughout the era of the BBC's monopoly, political broadcasting was structured in deference to the state. The struggle to make politicians answerable and accountable to the electorate through broadcasting was not joined until the establishment of commercial television and the new forms of broadcasting journalism inaugurated by Independent Television News in the late fifties. (1991, 101–2)

Monopoly itself led to some of these problems, enforcing a neutrality of opinion that cut off exploration of important issues and any meaningful debate; lack of competition stifled the development of alternative sources of news and opinion. Monopoly joined to state ownership and financing reinforced a narrow and fundamentally undemocratic definition of the national interest in which the vast majority of the British public had little power to intervene.

On the other hand, by the time war broke out in the late 1930s, the British public had a nationally distributed source of news and information, produced by an organized and well-structured news and talks division, that was capable of moving decisively into wartime news coverage not only for Britain but, through the developing Empire Service (later named the Overseas Service), around the world. By 1938, a staff of more than 30 newsmen, most of them trained journalists, provided more than 90 minutes of news each evening between 6 and 9 pm in reports balanced between news, discussion, and sports (Scannell with Cardiff 1991, 120–21). This stood in stark contrast to the situation in the US, where networks had barely begun to see news coverage as something that they should provide. Emerging newsmen such as Edward R. Murrow, thrust into covering breaking news in Europe by CBS even though he had no journalistic training or background, would learn from the BBC how a news department might be structured and run (see Chapter 3). American public affairs programs might have been freer from political interference and more prolific than was possible in Britain, but on the downside demagogues like Father Coughlin gained a national audience. Sponsored network commentators combined with local station coverage did not provide the news service that Americans would soon find they needed. National monopoly broadcasting produced both problems and advantages.

In music, which took up most of the broadcast day, the BBC's national position quickly placed it at the very center of musical production in Britain. By the time the American networks organized later in the decade, they had to work with a highly developed and powerful music industry. By contrast, the BBC in effect called a British music industry into being, as Scannell and Cardiff argue, pulling not only musicians and music publishers but the very definition of national music culture itself into a centrally organized system that had not before existed. Music in Britain, previously the product of scattered sites of production and divergent regional tastes, was brought together by the BBC in a "strange new abstract unity . . . universaliz[ing] music as a socio-cultural category in a quite unprecedented manner" (1991, 182). Music rights and performers organizations quickly emerged to counterpose the BBC's power, but had to work within the aegis of the emergent state monopoly. By the end of the 1930s fully 54% of the revenues of the Performing Rights Society—the British equivalent of ASCAP—derived from a single organization, the BBC. Channeling musical development through such a large and powerful bureaucracy resulted in a rapid canonization of musical forms and a hierarchy of taste, producing standards of preference for both classical and popular music that not only clashed internally but also failed to suit many members of the listening public. While a carefully calculated transnationalism prevailed in the realm of classical music—and the BBC became one of the standard-bearers of advanced musical culture in Europe—nationalism at the popular level ruled musical selections. This was particularly problematic in the arena of jazz and swing music; the BBC came to see itself as the incubator of British talent and musical traditions in the face of Americanized incursions (Baade 2011; Camporesi 1994, 2000).

Yet, as many have argued, the BBC did more to advance British music culture—an area where Britain had traditionally lagged behind the other nations of Europe—than any alternative force could possibly have done. Radio became a major supporter of music and arts organizations throughout the nation, not only creating its own orchestras and musical companies but subsidizing others. The BBC Symphony Orchestra was formed in 1930 under the leadership of Sir Adrian Boult, who also directed the Music Department, employing 119 musicians full-time. Eventually it was joined by a Theatre Orchestra, a Variety Orchestra, the Empire Orchestra, the BBC Military Band, and five regional orchestras based in each of the major stations, employing more than 266 musicians by the late 1930s (Scannell with Cardiff 1991, 235). The BBC also heavily supported the Promenade Concerts, Covent Garden (home of the Royal Opera), Sadlers Wells (specializing in opera performed in English by British performers), and a touring company, the Carla Rosa Opera Company (Scannell with Cardiff 1991, 236).

The amount invested in serious music by the BBC became controversial later in the 1930s, as nascent listener research showed that it attracted a fraction of the audience of more popular entertainments like drama and variety, yet took up not only a significant percentage of BBC expenditures but also large chunks of the broadcast schedule. The BBC took music seriously, with worldwide cultural impact that only a centrally organized monopoly could have engendered.

While music and talk took precedence in BBC schedules, it was what would later be called "light entertainment" that listeners most desired (as would be conclusively demonstrated once audience research was developed after 1938). But Britain's music hall and theater owners resisted state monopoly competition the same way that newspaper proprietors had, refusing to cooperate in a field in which they were asked to cede control to this powerful organization without adequate financial return. Performers balked at using up comedy and musical routines in a single night on air that would have sustained them in national tours for months, at a rate of return far above that which the BBC was willing to pay. As Briggs writes, "These difficulties would have been avoided only if broadcasting had been directly sponsored and promoted by the entertainment industry," (1961, 252) as it was in America; instead the BBC and the entertainment industry were established as competitors. Not until the late 1930s would popular program forms along the lines developed in the US in the mid 1920s find their way onto British airwaves. They would come in on a wave of changes, discussed in the next chapter, brought about by shifts in institutional structure at the BBC as well as a need to reach audiences on their own terms as war threatened.

Cultural Chaos and Change

Throughout the late 1920s and 1930s, the concept of American chaos assumed increasing importance as a motivating factor in BBC program-ming, representing the "commercial low other" against which British public service quality could shine. In 1924, A.R. Burrows could write half-admiringly about American radio, "It mattered not whether one station overlapped another in wave-length or in hours of transmission, or whether the performance of a classical masterpiece was followed by an appeal on behalf of somebody's soap or pickles. It was all part of a new game" (Burrows 1924, 55). By 1927, however, a more critical tone had begun to emerge in the reaction of another British visitor, Peter Eckersley, to the US: "Some of the concerts were good, but the majority suffered through commercialism, and to our ears would sound extremely crude. For example, I heard an announcement that a particular hour was to be the "Brightness Hour", brightness means smiles, smiles means white teeth, teeth will be whiter if you use X tooth paste, the manufacturers of which are responsible for the program. In other cases the advertisement is less crude."[15] A 1929 editorial in *Radio Times* put it even more strongly:

> In America, the ether is racked and torn with competing broadcasting stations filling the air with advertising matter . . . In America, even the wireless reception of a Beethoven Symphony cannot be free from association with someone's chewing gum or pills. In England, the tired worker who has been all day shouted at and advertised to in his newspaper, on the hoardings, in train or omnibus, may settle down to his evening's wireless entertainment with the feeling that at last he is free from the necessity to listen to someone who has something to sell.[16]

"Chaos" became associated with the rampant spread of advertising-based mass culture, with its "crude" and "vulgar" and above all "American" manifestations. Another *Radio Times* opinion piece concluded:

> The thoughtful listener will come away with the double impression that, while American radio has startling vitality in its method of presentation, its material, which largely consist of songs of the jazz order sung by artists of the genus "crooner", is, to British ears at least, confined within a rut of lowering and monotonous sentimentality . . . much that this vitality contributes to radio on that side of the Atlantic would be termed "vulgar" on this.[17]

The BBC sent various visitors to the United States during the early 1930s who returned to report back on what they had found. Sir John Reith himself made a well-publicized tour of the US and Canada in 1933. Spending time first in Ottawa and Montreal, he traveled by train to New York, where Merlin Aylesworth of NBC and William Paley of CBS with much ceremony put their organizations at his disposal, splitting his time carefully between them. At one point Paley and Aylesworth jointly entertained Reith at a private luncheon, "and I was informed that it was the first occasion on which the Presidents of these two competitive organizations had ever joined in hospitality to any individual."[18] Reith's report, written on his return, shows an attempt to judge the American situation fairly, but he remains fundamentally critical.

> Good programmes are put over; there is no question about that; and in many parts of the country there is an astonishing range . . .

But with few exceptions the best programme items are sponsored, which means the insertion of advertising ballyhoo.

And he goes on to note, "The more educated and intelligent the American, the more I found him or her critical of the radio service, and the more commendatory of the English programmes, either from direct listening or from hearsay." However, on his return, it was reported by *Popular Wireless* (and discussed in NBC interdepartmental memos) that Reith planned to encourage more visits to the US by senior BBC personnel, particularly so that "his organization learns the technique of that crisp presentation at which the Americans are so adept."[19]

The following year Sir Noel Ashbridge, the BBC's Chief Engineer, visited New York primarily to study the reception of the newly established Empire Service station in North America, but his observations on what he heard there sounded a familiar note:

[T]he extent to which the advertised products were mentioned was greater than I expected, and their mention interfered much more with the programme than one would have thought necessary . . . This even extends to Children's Hours, where, during an adventure story, children are suddenly exhorted to persuade their parents to let them consume a certain breakfast food, the exhortation frequently being made a propos the exploits of a cowboy, or something of that kind.[20]

He accuses even religious programs of being "syrupy" and "sickly" and concludes, "In general, so far as programmes are concerned, I feel almost sure that they would not be acceptable in any country in Europe which I have visited." Americans became so accustomed to hearing this kind of criticism that when Peter Eckersley made a second visit in 1932—fresh from being fired by Reith from his former position as the BBC's chief engineer, it should be noted—his sarcastic summary of a day of British broadcasting combined with favorable remarks about American radio led to a surprised headline in the *New York Times*: "Praise from an Englishman."[21]

Criticism of American broadcasting, and of American culture more generally, found increasing resonance during the 1930s in what LeMahieu calls "the reassertion of cultural hierarchy" (1988, 103) not only in Britain but among educated elites across Europe and North America. On both the left and the right, cultural critics such as F. R. and Q. D. Leavis, T. S. Eliot, George Orwell, and Aldous Huxley excoriated the rise of "mass civilization" and its erosion of all that was excellent in literature, music, and the arts.

"America" and "Americanization" played a particular role in such theories as the source and primary perpetrator of mass culture, with its popular appeal that not only substituted mass produced cultural products for the legitimately authored works of the past, but implied a criticism of the idea of cultural hierarchy itself, on which such theories were based. America's increasingly dominant role in the international marketplace tapped into fears of market-based culture forms more generally and a rising "disgust with the vulgarities and sensationalism of commercial culture" among embattled elites (LeMahieu 1988, 139). American "cultural chaos" threatened not only the culture-producing industries of other nations, but the very definition of culture itself. And not only for European critics: as LeMahieu points out, "some of the most searing observations about American life in the early twentieth century came from American intellectuals, whose ideas British writers appropriated freely and occasionally without acknowledgement," such as Robert Lynd, Upton Sinclair, Sinclair Lewis, and H. L. Mencken (LeMahieu 1988, 118; see also Lenthall 2002, 2007). During the mid 1930s, as the Communications Act of 1934 was being debated, and again during World War II as government came closer to broadcasting than ever before (or since) in the US, these arguments would be aired vociferously, with the BBC representing all that American culture must either accept or reject.

But, as Camporesi and LeMahieu point out, this discourse increasingly had to contend in Britain with disturbing tendencies in the other direction as the 1930s drew to a troubled close. Centralization and nationalization of broadcast culture had begun to produce a reaction that disparagement of American radio and invocation of American chaos could no longer conceal. Forces from within the BBC itself, as well as from the actions of the British public, began to introduce competition to the unified national service, dominated by London and the South of England, that Reith had made his hallmark. They also allowed British audiences to experience American radio directly, for the first time, and find it to their taste.

First of all, there was new competition at home. The regional stations, reduced in number and significance in the centralizing years of the twenties and early thirties, began to assert themselves as sites of legitimate cultural production, ironically aided by the nationalistic discourse that had originally worked to repress them. Where better to look for sources of authentic British culture, as far removed as possible from the de-nationalizing influence of Americanization, than local culture growing out of the regions? This was especially true of the working-class regions of the North, and both Briggs and Scannell and Cardiff focus on Manchester in particular as the base of a growing grass-roots definition of national culture.

As centralization took hold, many within the BBC realized that the pendulum had swung too far in a national direction. In 1935, Reith removed Charles Siepmann from his post as Director of Talks and placed him (somewhat against his will) in a newly created position as Director of Regional Relations. Though Siepmann had earlier been one of the strongest proponents of London control, his observations of regional broadcasting made over a three month period traveling from one to another persuaded him that the regions had much to offer British national culture. His "Report on the Regions," submitted in January 1936, was widely regarded as a "Charter of Regional Rights."[22] Regional broadcasting, after a decade of suffering diminishment at the hands of an imperious London-oriented program board, gained new-found respect that would have a profound effect on BBC programming in the late 1930s and 1940s, as the regions became centers of popular program production.

Second, competition threatened from outside the national borders. Unlike regional broadcasting, these stations lay entirely outside the BBC's control, violating not only the call for centralization and unity of standards so close to the BBC's central mission, but its resistance to market forces as well. Taking advantage of France's more liberal pre-war stance towards privately owned stations, as well as that of independent states like Luxembourg, private commercial stations based on the continent could be heard by the mid 1930s across most of Britain. Radio Normandy and Radio Luxembourg (along with several lesser stations, such as Radio Lyons, Radio Toulouse, and Poste Parisien), though serving local audiences with programming in French during the day, took advantage of the weaknesses of the BBC schedule, particularly the "Reithian Sundays" which eschewed all popular programs, as well as early mornings (the BBC began broadcasting at 10:30), late afternoons and early evenings (during schools and children's hours), and late evenings (when the BBC turned to more serious fare). Their signals, particularly those of Luxembourg, could reach most of Britain over short wave.

British advertisers, long baulked by the BBC's non-commercial stance, quickly began to sponsor programs along American lines. Primary producers in London were the British branch of J. Walter Thompson (JWT) and the International Broadcasting Co. Ltd. (IBC) headed by Captain Leonard F. Plugge. Sometimes simply airing transcriptions of American programs— including a block of US soap operas in the afternoon that exposed British female audiences to such programming for the first time—and at other times airing original variety and musical programs employing British, American, and European talent, by the late 1930s these stations had an audience that was sometimes estimated at one third of British license holders

(Sean Street 2006). Suddenly, the "American other" threatened from just offshore. The way that the BBC, in the end, responded to these threats would usher in a whole new approach both to public and to programming—and a new relationship to American radio—even as war rumbled in the distance.

CHAPTER 3

The "American System"

I can promise you finer programs, better music and no long
speeches. We have only sixteen hours at our disposal and we cannot
afford to crowd the air with programs which will not interest
people . . . We shall not cram education down the throats of people
who do not want it. What we shall strive for is to make people
everywhere happier.[1]
—Merlin H. Aylesworth, President of NBC, 1926

As early as 1922, some American journals praised the system that was
emerging in Britain and relayed with sympathy British criticism of American
radio; the *Literary Digest* reprinted part of an article from the *Newark Call*:
"English analysis of the radio situation in this country is that we have gone
'wireless crazy' and have lost all perspective of the basic economic principle
of broadcasting." However, others favorably compared American radio to
British, noting "striking similarity in the material chosen to entertain and
instruct listeners here and abroad." Some even claimed superiority for US
radio, in distinction to criticisms that would be made later, as in this 1924
article from the *New York Times*:

American program directors have laid more stress on educational
subjects than have the foreign studio managers. In England education lectures comprise a fair percentage of the program, but in
the United States there is scarcely a station of any size, power, or
importance that does not broadcast educational subjects. Nearly a

hundred American colleges and universities maintain and operate broadcasting stations.[2]

Others noted the progress that Britain had made in the practice of networking, which both AT&T and RCA were experimenting with in the US. However, before 1926 most decried British radio's slow and cautious roll-out, and made boosterish numerical comparisons, as in this headline: "London Has Only One Station; New York District Has 14".[3]

Local versus National

Until 1926, and RCA's formation of America's first national broadcasting network, radio remained primarily the province of individual local stations, large and small. Though some areas of the country, notably the South and the far Western states, lagged behind in radio reception, most American cities and less isolated rural areas could receive signals from at least one or two stations by 1926; larger urban areas boasted multiple stations. Both AT&T and RCA had experimented with linking stations together with telephone wires in the mid 1920s, but it remained unclear that this would prove the path of the future—especially since AT&T retained a monopoly over use of high quality landlines and showed little willingness to let any radio competitor use them. At one point RCA announced plans for a series of high-power stations, along the lines of the BBC's Daventry, by which it could provide nearly national coverage, though this never materialized.

By 1926, however, as a lawsuit filed by the Zenith Radio Corporation challenged all the attempts at licensing and allocation that the Department of Commerce had devised since 1922, a consensus finally arrived that something must be done to create order in the airwaves. The establishment in Britain of the Crawford Committee to consider a "commission to control broadcasting," as the *New York Times* put it, gained attention in the spring.[4] RCA's plans, too, gained strength from the British example of networked national broadcasting. In July 1926, after a series of complex negotiations, AT&T sold its flagship station WEAF to RCA and retreated to its primary business, the manufacture of telephone equipment and the provision of land lines and service, with the prospect of AT&T-connected national networks in the offing.

David Sarnoff paid a visit to London in August, where he spent several days in the offices of the BBC (for the second time; his first visit in July 1925 had prompted Reith to predict, "I believe that the States are shaping to our system.") (Briggs 1961, 316). Just two months later, on September 9, 1926, RCA launched its new business in momentous terms:

ANNOUNCING THE NATIONAL BROADCASTING COMPANY, INC. *National radio broadcasting with better programs permanently assured by this important action of the Radio Corporation of America in the interests of the listening public* . . . The purpose of that company will be to provide the best programs available for broadcasting in the United States . . . The Radio Corporation of America is not in any sense seeking a monopoly of the air . . . It is seeking, however, to provide machinery which will insure a national distribution of national programs, and a wider distribution of programs of the highest quality. [emphasis in original][5]

RCA's articulation of "national" with "quality," along with its disclaimer of intention towards monopoly, would provide the nascent network's keynotes throughout its early years, always with the example of the BBC in the background. A public advisory council, along the lines of the BBC's Board of Governors, was announced and took shape quickly (Benjamin 1988). Merlin H. Aylesworth, a Colorado-based lawyer with a background in public utilities management, was named president of the new network, and though his version of his task differed considerably from that of John Reith (his reference above to "cram[ming] education down the throats of people who do not want it" was an obvious slap at the BBC), the two would form a relationship over the next ten years that would prove influential in both countries.

Network broadcasting in the United States had little choice but to develop in tension between the local and the national, thanks to the hundreds of stations that had sprung up in its early years and the strong political advocacy of American amateurs. But localism's central position in the US system of radio—as indeterminate and contradictory a concept as it has proven to be in application—did not merely reflect the facts of US radio's early history. It also functioned as the guarantor of *decentralization*, both cultural and political, a concept as deeply rooted in American political thought as centralization was in Britain's. In a country divided into forty-eight states, each with their own legislatures that often exhibited a contentious relationship with the federal government and, in a nation consciously constructed from a multiplicity of national origins and cultures, centralized institutions remained few and far between in the 1920s. Market-based private enterprise, rather than threatening national unity as it seemed to do in Britain, was conceptualized as a force that kept America free from centralized government control and allowed individual citizens, based in local communities, to create their own locally based culture which resonated with the whole. Localism became a central tenet of US broadcasting policy. To further this policy, US regulators regarded allocation of "the maximum technically feasible number of stations around the country" as a vital part of their task (Newton 2004, 870). One of the first actions of the Radio Act of 1927 was to divide the nation into five zones for frequency allocation purposes; the Davis Amendment in 1928 required equality of allocation across the zones (when this proved nearly impossible the requirements were loosened).

Yet by the mid 1920s new forces advocating a more uniform, centralized American national identity and government had emerged onto the scene. Progressive reformers in the teens and twenties not only advocated for increased federal oversight of business, labor conditions, agriculture and the food processing industry, and education, but also advocated for restrictions on the immigration to America that had changed the face of US society so profoundly in the decades since 1880. Reform of electoral processes to restrict the power of the party machines (organized along ethnic lines) of the previous century began to take hold, and conscious attempts made to define what it meant to be an American and how new Americans could be formed (Schudson 2000). A new discipline of sociology, combined with applied social work, grew out of the effort to understand the process of national assimilation and to put those concepts into effect in America's crowded immigrant ghettos. Social theorists agreed that the expanding arena of popular media and entertainment held the key to drawing diverse populations into the social order—or, unsupervised, allowing cultural chaos to spin out of control (Czitrom 1982). Radio's potential to address the entire nation, and thus to shape a truly national culture as exemplified by the BBC, seemed to offer a solution to the Progressive's dilemma (Goodman and Gring 2000; Kirkpatrick 2006). Yet the forces of national unity and centralization in the United States would always have to work within a framework of cultural diversity, political decentralization, and the persistence of the local in broadcasting.

On February 19, 1927, the US Senate passed a radio bill and sent it to President Coolidge for his signature. The Radio Act of 1927 set up the Federal Radio Commission with the assigned task of bringing order to the American airwaves, both technical and social.[6] Effectively, this move to order ushered in the era of network dominance, despite public ambivalence about NBC's emergent "chain" and its parent RCA's monopoly position in the radio market. Though cautions against monopoly were sounded throughout the Act, with so many voices in the airwaves, dispersed unevenly about the country, chaos seemed to be a more pressing problem than monopoly. The FRC's first task was to restructure the system for assigning station licenses, under a basic operating principle that held "the success of radio broadcasting lay in doing away with small and unimportant stations" while still preserving radio's local base (quoted in McChesney 1993, 19). But heavy opposition from smaller station owners made outright revoking of licenses too risky politically.

Instead, the FRC developed a practice based on its earlier Class B decision. First, it created a number of national "clear channel" stations—superior quality broadcasting stations with enough power to be heard over an entire region, assigned to a frequency where they would have no competition. Such stations were intended to provide radio service across the vast remote rural areas with few centers of population and few existing radio stations. Most of these clear channel assignments went to stations either owned by or affiliated with one of the major broadcasting manufacturers or with a major newspaper. For the other, lower power stations, the FRC designed a complicated system of frequency sharing, with one station assigned, say, to the morning hours on a particular wavelength, another the afternoons and a third the right to broadcast in the evenings. After coming up with a plan for dividing radio stations into three categories based on service requirements and signal strength—clear channel, regional, and local—across the five regions, the FRC next required some criteria on the basis of which such assignments would be made.

1928's General Order 40 developed a framework that created a preferred category of "general public interest" stations—commercial stations selling time to any and all—and gave such stations higher power and more favorable frequency allocations. Those owned and operated by nonprofit groups, schools, religious and social organizations, and political groups were classified as "propaganda" stations: stations committed to representing only one point of view or set of interests and thus not open to the general public. These stations were to be discouraged, and many of them soon found themselves assigned to shared frequencies operating on the lowest power (Federal Radio Commission 1929, 32–36; McChesney 1993, 23–29). "General public interest" stations—a category that included all the powerful clear-channel and most of the regional licensees—were constrained only to operate in the "public interest, convenience, and necessity," a phrase borrowed from public utility law and never clearly defined.[7]

This distinctly American conception of the public interest, privileging commercial business operations over nonprofit public service, exactly reversed the BBC's Reithian definition, which had come to consider commercial broadcasters inherently private and thus not able to operate in the service of the public. Rather than making licensing decisions that might violate First Amendment freedoms by giving preference to one group's point of view over another, the FRC deflected control over broadcasting speech onto the marketplace. Commercial stations would sell time freely to all on the basis of their ability to pay, not the content of their speech, and with many small, local stations available in every market, every speech could find an audience. This was the concept. National broadcasting, however, would be dominated from the beginning by large commercial corporations, and decisions made on the basis of their corporate interests would limit the scope of radio's free speech.

Networks and Affiliates

Within three years of the Act's passage and the extensive reassignment of frequencies that followed, hundreds of small, nonprofit stations had lost their licenses or gone out of business due to unfavorable time and frequency assignments as well as more stringent technical requirements, while the more powerful stations owned by larger commercial interests thrived. Many of them received the "clear channel" assignments that enabled them to be heard across large sections of the country and in rural areas far from city stations. Though networks owned and operated some of their stations, all affiliates were local stations, licensed to serve a specific geographical area, most of them owned by local businesses or other organizations in the community.[8] They elected to air NBC or CBS programs for part of their broadcast day, or in many cases during the first decade switched from NBC to CBS depending on the program and local audience tastes. The rest of the time they provided either locally produced or, increasingly, syndicated recorded programs (Russo 2009).

Starting out with 28 affiliates by the end of 1927, NBC claimed 71 by 1930, 88 by 1934, and 182 affiliates (by now on two networks: the Red and the Blue) by the end of 1940. The growth of NBC's main rival, the Columbia Broadcasting System (CBS) is equally impressive; debuting a year after NBC in 1927 and purchased by William Paley in 1928, it went from 17 affiliates that year to 112 in 1940 (Sterling and Kittross 2002, 830–31). In 1929, the three networks combined put out approximately 351 hours of national programs per week; by 1935 that had risen to 809, and by 1941 the figure was 1,078—distributed over four networks by then, since the Mutual Network had joined the competition in 1934 (Sterling and Kittross 2002, 848).

This meant that most affiliate stations broadcast local, or at least locally selected, programming for a portion of their day, usually early morning, late night, and weekends, with network programs aired largely in the evenings and at certain key parts of the daytime. The amount of network time slowly grew; by 1939, NBC provided "approximately sixteen hours" of programs to its affiliates each day, stating as its philosophy, "To help create a true democracy of the air, NBC has sought to preserve the individuality which characterizes every station's approach to its own audience" (NBC 1939, 14–15). Of course, affiliates had to agree to "clear" the best parts of their schedules for network transmissions, leaving an increasingly limited number of hours for expressing such individuality.

However, this tells only half the story. American network radio underwent an enormous transformation between 1926 and 1936. From 1926 until roughly 1932, the two major networks briefly enjoyed more creative control over broadcast production than they would again until the 1960s. Part of NBC's promise to the nation was to step up its own production of programs; rather than relying solely on other self-promoting businesses to fill up the broadcast hours, NBC itself would, BBC-like, take responsibility for the production of network programs in the name of quality. In November 1926, Bertha Brainard, newly named Director of Commercial Programming, wrote to a potential client:

> This department secures suitable talent of known reputation and popularity, creates your program and surrounds it with announcements and atmosphere closely allied with your selling thought.[9]

By 1932, however, the shoe began to shift to the other foot. Sponsors came to perceive that they—or more likely, their advertising agencies—might more successfully produce programs "allied with their selling thought" than could a network whose loyalties were divided.

By the mid-1930s, in contrast to the BBC's centralization of production and increasingly in-house control over its programming, in the US almost all evening and a large proportion of daytime programs were originated and produced by sponsors and advertising agencies, with the networks on the sidelines. During the daytime, in fact, networks frequently sold time in hour-length blocks to big advertisers like Procter & Gamble, who might produce four 15-minute serials, each promoting a different P&G product, during that time. Sponsors effectively took out long-term leases on a particular day and time slot, filling it with the program of their choice, and since networks had very little stake in programs, sponsors frequently moved them to a rival network if a better deal, or a better time, were offered.[10] And as national advertisers devised plans to attract the largest possible audiences to their programs, they began to reach out to established stars and modes of entertainment. By 1936, Hollywood had become the center of broadcast program production, drawing on a roster of stars and celebrities established in film and vaudeville, and adapting stage, screen, and print-based forms to a new medium (Hilmes 1990). As the BBC centralized and unified, American broadcasting, though now national in reach, grew increasingly dispersed and decentralized in its task of program production, but with Hollywood its increasingly powerful common denominator.

Thus, though US national networks can take credit for originating early forms of many popular radio broadcast genres that soon became standard around the world—the variety show, the serial drama, the quiz program, the news commentary, homemakers talks, the public affairs roundtable, and many more—it was in the creative meetings and planning sessions of advertising agencies and their sponsors that these genres developed and grew into staples of modern popular culture. NBC had promised "quality" national programs; sponsors took that promise and ran with it, all the way to the bank. On the way they innovated cultural forms known today around the world. Yet the programs they created also marked a closer relationship of commerce to culture, within the very fabric of the medium, than had previously been experienced. Radio programs often integrated their sponsor's message right into the narrative of the drama, or into the program announcer's commentary, placing advertising slogans into the mouths of fictional characters and glamorous stars alike. This was certainly not the system that Progressives had envisioned, with the local station owner almost entirely displaced and powerless, and networks themselves handing over program control to invisible, unregulated advertisers. This was what most caused shudders in the observations of British listeners, and also for an increasing number of American critics. Even in a nation that linked the free operation of the marketplace with liberty of expression in its founding documents, commercial radio began to be perceived as a threat to the development of a strong and vital American national culture.

Meantime, awareness of alternatives to the American system grew. The early 1930s witnessed a closer relationship between British and American networks than had ever existed before. A certain amount of program exchange between the BBC and US networks had occurred since the 1920s. Though direct transmission by shortwave proved problematic (for both technical and time difference reasons), the occasional broadcast of a recorded program from across the Atlantic provided novelty. A special broadcast of *Amos 'n' Andy* lightened BBC New Year's schedules on January 1, 1930, much to British listeners' bemusement (and generally negative reviews from the critics).

But as shortwave technology improved, transatlantic broadcasts increased. Most of the exchange was from East to West, as American networks aired a constant stream of talks, concerts, and special events from Europe, with the BBC the main originator. A few programs went the other way: CBS began a series of specially prepared broadcasts in February 1932, called "Stars of American Radio," which the *Radio Times* greeted ambiguously: "We ourselves felt slightly faint before the hour was over, but could not deny the perfection of the thing within its own limits; it was *so American*."[11] More complex relationships began to emerge. In 1933 the BBC began an occasional program that both satirized and showcased American radio, produced by Eddie Pola for Eric Maschwitz in the newly formed Variety department. *America Calling* featured British radio performers creating parodies of American stars and radio genres, such as "chatty talks on the most embarrassing details of health, travelogues, serial dramas that run for months, gossip columns of the air, propaganda speeches by every sect and faction"—in short, all that was forbidden on the BBC.[12] They were popular, and received an occasional airing in the US as well, under the title *Is America Calling?* Policies against the broadcast of recorded programs would keep most BBC regular programs (as opposed to stand-alone broadcasts) off American airwaves until Mutual began to explore this area in the late 1930s, though British personalities and performers turned up with regularity on US schedules. Program exchange would develop rapidly after 1935, as discussed in the next chapter.

Partly this was due to institutional changes, notably the acknowledgement by both organizations that each needed to have personnel permanently stationed in the other country. CBS had established Caesar Saerchinger as its European representative in 1932, where he made arrangements for relays of live events and lined up suitable personalities and stories for rebroadcast in the States. A green and impressionable Edward R. Murrow would replace him in 1937. In 1933 NBC appointed its own man in Europe, Fred Bate, who would go on to become a well-regarded fixture at the BBC and would take on the role of NBC's primary British correspondent in the early years of WWII. The BBC responded in 1935 by hiring Felix Greene as their man in New York, mostly concerned with expanding Empire Service operations. He would play a much more vital role in advising the Canadian system than in the US, where his criticisms of American broadcasting were not always appreciated.[13]

Meantime, the head of NBC, Merlin Aylesworth, and John Reith of the BBC had developed a cordial and even personal friendship based on frequent, polite correspondence and of course a visit or two. Their letters, housed in the Wisconsin NBC papers, show an increasing if somewhat affectedly intimate tone, especially on Aylesworth's part. They addressed each other as "My dear Merlin" and "Dear Sir John" and Aylesworth signed off "Affectionately yours." Reith visited Aylesworth at his home in the autumn of 1933, following up a 1931 visit made by Aylesworth to Britain. Aylesworth informed Reith in a letter written in December of 1933 that, "we all consider you as a part of our family" (which he copied to David Sarnoff).[14] Yet all too soon the family would begin to look somewhat dysfunctional.

Debates and Change

By the early 1930s, criticism of the way that American radio had developed began to circulate widely through intellectual circles and the popular press, making increasing use of a comparison with British and European broadcasting. A visit by Sir John Reith to the US and Canada in May 1931 for the purposes of "studying the American broadcasting system" sparked an initial round of articles both pro and con the British system. Reith visited the Federal Radio Commission on May 27, where he asked the commissioners if they "thought anything of the British system might be possible in America, beginning with the commissioners taking more power and building up on the public interest clause rather than the no-censorship one." His Diary entry, quoted by Briggs, concluded that "they were immensely tickled with the idea that they should exert their powers" and in general he portrayed them as unimpressive bumpkins.[15] In a speech before the National Advisory Council on Education by Radio (NACRE) Reith predicted that it would only be a matter of time before the US would come around to adopting British structure, since its commercial base had occurred only "more or less by accident" and emphasized what he called "the risks of ballyhoo" on American radio.[16]

On his return, Reith published an essay on "Broadcasting in America" in *The Nineteenth Century*, a journal published in both London and New York, elaborating on his observations made in the States. Here he returned to the idea of "American chaos," claiming that "It may be inaccurate to speak of an American 'system' at all. There is actually no system in the ordinary sense of the term . . . In the United States competition is practically unlimited and practically unbridled . . . there is little if any control of the quality of the matter offered for public consumption" (Reith 1931, 205–8). He had praise for some of the programs put on by the major networks, but concluded that "the absence of the institution . . . is preventing the best men from doing their best work" (206) and painted a picture of American radio as a wild and wooly outcast, stubbornly refusing to learn from the wise council and experience of Britain and Europe.

Many American intellectuals could not have agreed with him more. Leading pundit H. L. Mencken wrote in the *Baltimore Evening Sun* in June 1931, inspired by Reith's reported remarks: "The B.B.C. is a Government agency, and is supported by a small annual tax on radio outfits. It sends nothing shabby, cheap or vulgar onto the air. There is no bad music by bad performers; there is no pestilence of oratory by ignoramuses; there is no sordid touting of tooth-pastes, automobile oils, soaps, breakfast foods, soft drinks and patent medicines. In America, of course, the radio program costs nothing. But it is worth precisely the same."[17] Upton Sinclair declaimed in 1931:

The conditions of our radio at the present time constitute a national scandal and disgrace . . . If they are allowed to continue for another ten years we shall have the most debased and vulgarized people in the world, and the fault will not rest with the people, who are helpless, and have to take what is handed out to them by exploiters and commercialists of the basest type.[18]

Part of this new wave of criticism stemmed from the efforts of educational broadcasters who had suffered in the FRC's station license reassignments, buttressed by other groups who believed that radio's potential for national cultural and political development had been undercut by the demands of the marketplace. Both Susan Smulyan and Robert McChesney have traced this movement in detail, as it led up to the debates surrounding the Communications Act of 1934. Suddenly, the example of the BBC became central to American reformist arguments. And they tapped into larger criticisms of mass culture in the 1930s as well, directed by American critics not at the "foreign other" designated by British intellectuals but at forces much closer to home.

Bruce Lenthall identifies two divergent strands of thought within the political critique directed against American radio, in particular, in the 1930s (Lenthall 2002). One group, represented in Lenthall's analysis by British-born Smith College professor and social commentator William Orton, objected to American radio's promulgation of a standardized "mass culture," oriented towards the common man and detrimental to the maintenance of high cultural standards. Orton was loosely affiliated with one of the educational reform groups, the National Advisory Council on Radio in Education (NACRE), headed by Levering Tyson, before which Reith had spoken in 1931. NACRE generally followed a policy of providing educational programming for the networks with funding by the Rockefeller Foundation and the Carnegie Corporation.

The other, more radical group consisted of the National Committee on Education by Radio (NCER), chaired by Joy Elmer Morgan with strong backing by Armstrong Perry and Tracy Tyler. NCER was funded in 1930 by the Payne Fund, a private Cleveland-based foundation dedicated to social and educational reform. Its president, H. M. Clymer, was a leader in the thirties' "ferment among the educators," to use McChesney's phrase (McChesney 1993, 38). Clymer made a decisive trip to visit the BBC in 1926 and came back convinced of the value of BBC-style, non-commercial and centrally organized educational radio (Leach 1983). It was the danger of monopoly corporate control over broadcasting that most concerned Clymer and the NCER, especially that of RCA, and they lobbied for a plan by which 15% of all station assignments would be set aside for educational broadcasters, with federal funding to support the efforts of educational stations.

Though the bitter disagreements between these two groups—one seeking to "improve" the commercial system, the other insisting on a separate educational structure—would fracture the reform movement fatally, as McChesney concludes, the one thing that united them was admiration for the BBC. Levering Tyson, Joy Elmer Morgan, and Tracy Tyler all visited the BBC in the early 1930s and kept up a lively, though somewhat one-sided, correspondence with various BBC executives. Both groups rallied behind a series of bills introduced in Congress to reform the radio situation between 1931 and 1933, proposing changes as sweeping as the complete overhaul of the American system along BBC lines, to more specific suggestions like requiring RCA to divest itself of some of its holdings, to the incremental, such as setting aside certain frequencies for educational broadcasters or demanding more time on commercial schedules. Both groups approached the BBC for endorsement during this period, which the BBC scrupulously avoided providing.[19]

American educators and other reform-oriented groups were energized, as well, by developments taking place in Canada. Spurred by the findings of the Aird Commission in 1929, which recommended reconfiguring Canadian broadcasting along national public service lines, activists Alan Plaunt and Graham Spry founded the Canadian Radio League in October 1930. According to historian Mary Vipond,

> The league was the culmination of a decade of organization and networking among English-Canadian cultural nationalists striving to foster unity among the different provinces and peoples of Canada and to strengthen the sense of national identity, particularly vis-à-vis the United States. (1992, 227)

The domination of Canadian radio by American broadcasters had long troubled Canadians concerned with resisting the behemoth to the south. As Spry himself put it, in a 1931 letter to an American broadcasting executive, "The strength of the Canadian Radio League is really based on [a] two-fold foundation, distaste for commercialism, and apprehension of Americanization . . . Indeed, if the fear of the United States did not exist, it would be necessary, like Voltaire's God, to invent it" (quoted in Vipond 1992, 228). Elsewhere, Spry memorably claimed that, for Canadian broadcasting, "It is either the State or the United States" (Spry 1931, 247). This nationalist vision dictated a more centralized approach, along the lines of the BBC, than even the Aird report had recommended. As Canadian plans moved forward, American reformers as well as British broadcasters took note, and several testified before the Canadian commission deliberating the proposal in the spring of 1932.[20]

The developments in Canada and the unrest at home did not go unnoticed by those who saw advantages in the US system, such as William Hard, news commentator for the NBC network. In an October 1932 article titled "Europe's Air and Ours," noting frequent British and domestic criticism of the US system, Hard takes a hard line, not on the field of high culture and taste, but in the arena of political and public affairs broadcasting and on the field of democratic citizenship, as opposed to national culture.

> My thesis, then, is simple. I concede that European governmental broadcasting generally exceeds American private broadcasting in the potential cultivation of good taste—by a graceful margin. I will contend that American private broadcasting exceeds European governmental broadcasting in any European country, in the potential cultivation of free citizens—by a vital margin.[21]

He cites freer access to the airwaves by politicians of all stripes, programs produced by citizens' groups, a broader international perspective, a greater diversity of views allowed on the air, and a comparative lack of censorship. This political argument, in turn, held considerable appeal in Britain amongst those who wished to reform the BBC, especially as German broadcasting became the mouthpiece of National Socialist propaganda.

The US reform movement achieved its biggest publicity coup in 1933, once again with the BBC at the heart of it. NACRE persuaded the National Forensic League and the National Extension University Association to choose for their annual debate topic *Resolved: That the United States Should Adopt the Essential Features of the British System of Radio Control and Operation.* An outpouring of articles, speeches, editorials, pamphlets, and press coverage ensued, bringing the British versus American question firmly across the Atlantic to American shores and spotlighting it deliberately in an effort to influence legislation pending before Congress. In January 1932 the Senate had passed a bill requiring the FRC to investigate the commercial basis of American radio and "the feasibility of Government ownership and operation of broadcasting facilities." The resulting report itself did not make any radical proposals, but in the spring of 1933 alone, six bills to amend the regulation of radio were introduced into Congress, recommending changes as radical as a complete overhaul of the system and as simple as licensing radio in vehicles.

The *Congressional Digest* devoted its August 1933 issue to the topic of radio reform in the context of the US vs. Britain debate, laying out the history, scope and pros and cons for each side. Reith's 1931 article was reproduced, as was William Hard's. In addition to these two, the pro-British side was represented by the BBC itself, in an excerpt from the 1933 Year Book.

A wide range of opinions was aired, and throughout the example of Canada played a key role. But by far the most controversial publication published during all the tumult was a 191-page pamphlet assembled by the National Association of Broadcasters entitled, "Broadcasting in the United States." It consisted of a 32-page, highly complimentary description of "American Radio," with charts and graphs enumerating the many hours of high quality sustaining and commercial broadcasting purportedly put out by American networks and stations, followed by a 26 page denunciation of the British system called "The American vs. the British System of Radio Control." Similar to the British use of "American chaos," the NAB-authored pieces made heavy use of the tactic of praising the US system by denigrating the British, in such constructions as:

> American radio is the most competitive in the whole world. Hundreds of local stations are forever looking for local entertainment talent. The two competing "chains" are forever trying to develop new competitive entertainment stars. Additionally the advertisers, in multitudes, are forever competitively flinging new entertainment stars into the radio firmament. You have to take the volcanic dust of their advertising convulsions along with the stars; but you get the stars. You get them because each of these competitors has to stay awake . . . The British Broadcasting Corporation does not have to stay awake. It doesn't even begin broadcasting— for instance—till after ten o'clock in the morning, on week days; and on Sundays, till recently, it didn't begin broadcasting till three o'clock in the afternoon. And then, on Sundays, it always laid off and did no broadcasting from six-thirty to eight in the evening. It can afford to rest. It knows that no rival will broadcast while it's sleeping. And it takes a sort of social revolution to wake it up. (Hard 1933, 95)

Here American initiative and "wide awakeness", all based on commercial competition, is contrasted with British complacency and sleepiness, with underlying attributions of elitism that only a "social revolution" could shake free. This native American vitality was then linked to innate characteristics of the US as a nation in contrast to England:

> It must be remembered that not only is Great Britain a small country, but that on the whole, its population possesses similar traits of mind and character—similar viewpoints and interests. There is not the marked diversity in racial, cultural, social and economic backgrounds which one finds in the United States. Each part of the

country has priceless cultural heritages of its own, which color its viewpoint, and affect many of the radio programs it desires. Likewise the many races which have gone to make up our nation have a right to programs ministering to their racial consciousness, for each of them have brought something of great value to the evolution of the American character. (NAB 1933, 48)

Or, to put it another way:

The nervously-active American is never in a mood to take educational punishment. You *must* interest him—or he quickly tunes you out. This characteristic is in only slightly lesser degree fundamental to any discussion of listener reaction in any country. It is the rule and the law and the testament upon which every successful broadcast structure is based. It is the risk, for instance, that Sir John Reith runs in Britain when he avowedly gives his public what he believes it is good for it to have. (18)

Here a liberal-pluralist concept of America's racial background is contrasted to Britain's putative homogeneity—this in a country which effectively barred African Americans from the airwaves and had made *Amos 'n' Andy* its most popular show. Education is termed "punishment" and commercial competition becomes practically a Biblical mandate.

After this diatribe, the pamphlet offered a compilation of various articles and talks about the competing paradigms by US broadcasting spokesmen. This section included a collection of mostly critical responses to the BBC from the British press compiled by Major Joseph Travis of London, in the preface to which it is asserted, "the great mass of radio listeners, realizing that the BBC is a monopoly and can do as it pleases (which impression is given in most of the addresses and articles by BBC officials), have decided that it is a waste of time and money to send their criticisms to either the BBC or the press" (NAB 1933, 114). It concluded its most vehemently argued section, the reprint of a speech by news commentator William Hard, with the rhetorical flourish quoted at the beginning of this chapter.

The pamphlet appeared in early January 1934 and caused considerable stress in BBC/US relations. On January 10 an urgent telegram from NBC's Fred Bate in London to Merlyn Aylesworth breathlessly wailed:

DEEPEST RESENTMENT HERE NAB PUBLICATION EVEN REACHING CONSIDERATION SEVERING RELATIONS STOP FEEL ADVISABLE YOU CBS DEFINE ATTITUDE TOWARD STATEMENT SURE TO BE CHALLENGED STOP FAILURE

ADVISE ME PUBLICATION IN TIME OR PROVIDE COPY
RESULTED MOST EMBARASSING SITUATION TODAY STOP
... SUGGEST LINE OF ACTION STOP SITUATION TENSE.[22]

A frantic, and rather humorous, exchange of telegrams and letters ensued. Aylesworth attempted to reassure Bate and Reith, by downplaying the NAB as a fractious bunch of small time station owners, as opposed to the big network guardians of more enlightened culture. Reith in turn expressed his dismay in a telegram back to Aylesworth, pointing out that many members of the reform opposition (notably, Armstrong Perry and Levering Tyson) had lobbied for a BBC endorsement of their views, which the BBC had honorably stayed away from, only to be insulted in this way.[23] Aylesworth reassured Reith, at great length and with considerable disingenuousness, considering the strength of the reform movement in the US: "We consider the whole matter of little importance in this country and just a lot of fun between school children who have a good time debating the subject."[24]

The major networks, NBC and CBS—in contrast with the more outright self-interest of members of the NAB—attempted to distance themselves from the debate but also tried to reap its benefits, at once rigorously defending commercial broadcasting against any thought of a public service system in the US, while simultaneously attempting to get credit for supporting and exemplifying the "high culture" goals of just such a system. This sort of rhetoric prompted in defense of American radio displaced onto "Britishness" the whole concept of broadcast reform, projecting undesirable "foreign" influences onto those who object to commercial radio's narrow limits. It limited the reformist agenda to a definition of "public service" that was eminently criticizable in American terms: elitist, focusing on high culture and formal education—and above all British. This American articulation of the de-nationalization argument effectively excluded and marginalized the rationale underlying the reform movement at home, such as the concentration of station ownership in mainstream commercial hands, US radio's exclusion of people of color and representatives of labor from the airwaves, and censorious network practices. It was a tactic for which American broadcasters and their lobbyists would find ample use in the future.

For the most part, however, the BBC and the major American networks sat on the sidelines of the battle, refusing to endorse any one point of view. The BBC's conclusion in the whole affair seems to have been that better information was needed in the US on how British broadcasting actually worked. A spate of articles, in BBC publications like *The Listener* but also published more broadly in journals like *Harper's Monthly* and *The Saturday Evening Post*, laid out the BBC's version of itself, with the explicit negative comparison with US radio so prevalent in earlier articles now much toned down. Felix Greene's appointment in 1935 as BBC representative in the US also reflected the perceived necessity of having a spokesman available to provide more accurate information on the BBC to the press and other interested groups; indeed, Greene reported himself inundated with requests to speak on the topic and besieged by all manner of interested parties.[25] And in the US, passage of the Communications Act of 1934 in June of that year ushered in a new era in network programming in which the BBC was more frequently taken as model than as foe.

However, in the context of regulatory reform, the educators' efforts and the publicity they gained did contribute to the inclusion of the Hatfield-Wagner Amendment on the communications bill finally submitted to Congress in May of 1934. This would have given the reformers what they desired: a portion of frequencies set aside for non-profit educational broadcasting. Though the amendment was defeated, a clear mandate for commercial broadcasters to improve their public service by working with educational groups was included in the Act, leading to the formation of the Federal Radio Education Commission (FREC) in 1935. Their efforts, though not living up to the vision of the educational reformers, would still work to transform American broadcasting. American and British broadcasting would draw closer together over the next ten years than ever before.

Part 1 Conclusion
Towards Transnationalism

These chapters have attempted to set the early history of broadcasting in a transnational framework, revealing forces and aspects that previous nationally oriented histories have tended to obscure or misrepresent. The first decade and a half of radio broadcasting not only set a new conduit of national culture in place, it established the terms of a highly productive set of discursive frameworks employed in both Great Britain and the United States (and eventually around the world) to support and justify decisions made in the course of radio's roll-out. Broadcasters and policy-makers on both sides of the Atlantic worked hard to establish a contrasting position to their chief global rival. "American" radio became, in the British context, symbolic of all that the BBC resisted, not because US broadcasting itself presented a serious threat (as did Hollywood film) but as a stand-in for a set of domestic de-nationalizing forces. These included not only radio-specific factors such as the desire to control amateurs, appease press interests, and curb the power of the Marconi Company, but other more broadly diffused social pressures that broadcasting threw into high relief, such as the changing status of the working class, the tension between local, regional, and national identities, and the increasing globalization of consumer culture. Close attention to the Post Office debates surrounding the formation of the British Broadcasting Company show that it was these national factors that led to the initiation of broadcasting as a license fee-funded monopoly under the direction of the central government, preceding the later formulation of public service mission and goals that the BBC's young director, Sir John Reith, would articulate.

In the US, due in large part to the campaign for reform of American broadcasting mounted by educational radio supporters and social critics,

"British" broadcasting became a rallying point for the construction of a much-needed public broadcasting sector, even though many aspects of the British system—such as its lack of localism and exclusion of educational and civic institutions as broadcasters—would not have suited American conditions at all. It would take the intervention of highly transnational private forces in the late 1930s and 40s—notably the Rockefeller Foundation—to bring British and American broadcasters together in a way that would prove productive to both, with the urgent incentives of WWII further driving the process.

Yet the construction of "British quality" versus "American chaos" helped to set and hold in place vital national communications systems in both countries, both marked by public service as well as commercial considerations, that in fact accomplished many of the same goals: the promotion of a unified national culture, the support of central national hierarchies (of class, race, gender, language, religion, and other facets of identity), the formation of a new kind of public sphere and public address, and the creation of a vital new platform of national cultural production that would both ally itself with and resist certain elements of a growing transnational mass consumer culture, whether nominated as "America" or "Hollywood." Its contrasting association in Britain with a sphere of education and uplift, dominated by graduates of Oxford and Cambridge, and in the United States with a Hollywoodized commercial culture based in all the vulgar diversity of America itself, both helped to support the system across the Atlantic by providing its symbolic opposite and to contribute vital elements to be drawn upon by its early creative innovators.

Throughout this period, the other model of national broadcasting strongly contending for the world's attention was that of Germany. Radio in Germany had started off partly privatized and based in the separate Länder, or provinces, but by 1932 had been centralized under government control, financed by a license fee on set purchases. As the Nazi party came into power in 1933, Joseph Goebbels, Minister for Public Enlightenment and Propaganda, took charge of broadcasting along with all other media in the Third Reich. By 1936, a single government channel not only dominated all of Germany but reached out beyond its borders to other nations as well. Here, clearly, was state power linked directly to the medium of radio in a form of nationalism dominated by political ideology and military aggression. Italy's state-owned and -run RAI provided another example of how nation building and broadcasting might work together all too efficiently. Even those most critical of the hyper-commercialism of American broadcasting had to admit that the state/radio alliance developed in some parts of Europe did not bode well for world peace. Yet could the dispersed, market-driven nationalism of the United States system adequately serve the nation—and the world—in times of war? And could the BBC retain its arms-length relationship with the state under pressure from outside attack? These were the questions that faced broadcasting as it matured into prominence on a troubled world stage.

PART 2

Trans-Atlantic Convergence, 1938–1946

Wartime brought Britain and America into closer relationship than ever before, not always in ways that were comfortable and pleasant for either side. Central to the wartime relationship was communication; first, as Nicholas Cull has argued, Britain had to convince the United States to take up its cause through both overt and covert means as Europe fractured and fell. The propaganda efforts mounted by the British government through its Ministry of Information and Overseas Service were extensive, beginning in 1939 and continuing until the US set up its own agencies of persuasion in 1942 (Cull 1995). British advisors and undercover agents played a large role in this process, as will be detailed below in the case of radio, mostly on a covert basis since a strong strain of resistance to Britain and its influence remained from the World War I years, kicked up by groups like the America First Committee and isolationist individuals such as Charles Lindbergh (D. Goodman 2007a). After Pearl Harbor, radio continued to act as a means of keeping up troop morale, building up transatlantic goodwill, and keeping citizens around the world informed about the progress of the war, as the provision of what we now know simply as broadcast news evolved. Radio also provided an opportunity to deceive and mislead, a route for enemy propaganda to enter national space, and even between allies the airwaves became a place where national values could conflict and diverge.

Yet during this era, as television debuted in both Britain and (less extensively) in the US, broadcasters in these two nations largely set aside their differences, acknowledged the strengths they could perceive on both sides of the Atlantic, and worked together to defeat the threat of totalitarian forces both as part of the military effort and as crucial supports of democracy at home. To subvert freedom of communication in a war to defend freedom would have been to undermine the allied nations' case for war, yet many dangers surrounded the uncontrolled use of radio that governments and broadcasters struggled to negotiate. War brought to the surface enduring inequities of class, race, and gender; to the credit of both nations radio became a means of acknowledging and addressing those problems while uniting the citizenry not only within national boundaries but across them.

This meant closer cooperation with the State on both sides than ever before, with all the threats of censorship and government intervention that it implied; it also meant an increased critical attention to radio's national role, to its central function as the purveyor and exemplar of democracy and open exchange, and to the crucial part it would play in addressing not only world politics but the politics of discrimination and exclusion at home. However, international conflict brought a new awareness of the power of propaganda, at home and abroad; as radio became a primary site for the deployment of national ideologies and politics in the air it also became a contested ground for the emerging field of communication research in order to understand and manage these contradictions. In both of these activities US and British interests sometimes struggled, sometimes coincided. Out of this disputatious exchange came some of the governing ideas about media and culture that would shape the remainder of the century.

British broadcasting became more "American": instituting audience research, using the results to make programs more accessible and enter-taining to broader audiences, creating a second national channel—the Forces Network—to compete with the Home Service for those audiences, introducing American programs and adaptations of American forms and styles onto British airwaves, and eventually allowing a foreign power to invade British airspace itself in the form of the American Forces Network. American broadcasting became more "British": introducing more public service programs, encouraging original dramatic and documentary work that addressed issues of American national identity, working more closely with government agencies, toning down its commercialism (even elimi-nating advertising in military programs), and recognizing the role that American network radio must play as a cohesive national force, against all decentralizing and localizing influences. American educational radio recovered from the setbacks of the 1930s to build new bridges with the BBC via private encouragement from such powerful forces as the Rockefeller Foundation, which also served as a key support for a heightened level of scholarly inquiry into the promise and perils of radio communication in the era of propaganda.

Important transatlantic careers were built during the war, as Alistair Cooke's broadcasts established him in his long-running role of explaining

America both to England and to itself, Norman Corwin and D. G. Bridson established reputations as creative radio dramatists on both sides of the Atlantic, Charles Siepmann left the BBC to become American broadcasting's most prominent critic and reformer, and Edward R. Murrow and his associates pulled together a new kind of news operation combining British and American practices that would contribute to the transformation of news broadcasting around the world. The BBC would find itself reluctantly producing its first domestic serial drama, a form long disdained within the hallowed halls of BBC Drama and Features, leading eventually to the dominance of that form on British airwaves today, while in the US writers would draw on British precedents to forge a new type of dramatized documentary form. Cooperatively produced programs such as *Transatlantic Call*, *Transatlantic Spotlight*, *Britain to America*, and *An American in England* literally bridged the ether between the two nations, promoting the convergence of program forms and performers across national boundaries, a tradition on which the new Light Programme would build after the war. Indeed, from this period forward, though differentiation by national values and characteristics might assert themselves, the US and Great Britain would increasingly form the nucleus of a single cultural system in broadcasting, a circuit of continuous influence that would shape the development of radio and television around the world.

CHAPTER 4

Enormous Changes at the Last Minute

From 1932 to 1939, when the war saved the BBC from itself, was the great Stuffed Shirt era, marked internally by paternalism run riot, bureaucracy of the most hierarchical type, an administration system that made productive work harder instead of easier, and a tendency to promote the most negative characters to be found amongst the staff. Externally it was similarly marked by aloofness, resentment of criticism, and a positive contempt for the listener, which was only finally to be broken down by the joint influence of Listener Research and the war.
—Maurice Gorham, Head of the BBC Light Programme, 1948 (5)

The BBC underwent enormous transformations in the four brief years between 1936 and 1940, changes that started out slowly, rose to a decisive crescendo just as war broke out, then continued with permanent impact on the future. But even before war loomed on the horizon, as Gorham indicates, pressures for change had been building up within the deceptively tranquil hallways of Broadcasting House. Though most of these pressures responded to developments within British broadcasting itself or to situations unique to Britain, as always there was an American motif that ran beneath, constantly threatening to break out if not contained. Each door that the BBC opened to relieve the pressures building up, or to let new practices in, freed a new route for American influence (or, at least, influence characterized as American) to slip past the gatekeepers. No wonder Sir John Reith felt increasing besieged in his own fortress. Not only audience research, but also threats from commercial stations broadcasting from the continent, the creeping encroachment of more popular program forms, and the increasing influence of the Overseas Service throughout the organization produced the combination of factors that would lead to the formation of the Light Programme after the war, and eventually to the advent of commercial television.

Listener Research

The first crack in the BBC's façade of "peculiarly British" self-sufficiency stemmed from dissatisfaction within its own ranks. Some of the staunchest defenders of the London-centric definition of national culture forged over the first decade of operations, such as Val Gielgud, appointed Head of Drama in 1929, and Charles A. Siepmann, succeeding Hilda Matheson as Director of Talks in 1932, recognized that it was hard to know in which direction to extend their efforts to serve the public if they possessed no reliable way to assess the reactions of that public as a whole. Existing channels of feedback, primarily letters from listeners and the reviews by radio critics in newspapers and journals, provided a constant barrage of criticism and praise (annoyingly, almost always more criticism than praise) but could not be said to represent the average listener. It was well known that in the United States frequent audience surveys were made by stations, networks, and sponsors, and their reports often found their way into the hands of BBC executives and producers.

As early as May 1930, a feeling that some form of audience survey might aid in the process of program planning arose at a meeting of the Programme Board, at which a copy of one of NBC's audience research surveys was passed around and examined. Gielgud summarized his reaction in a memo written a few days later to the senior programming staff:

> I cannot help feeling more and more strongly that we are fundamentally ignorant as to how our various programmes are received, and what is their relative popularity. It must be a source of considerable disquiet to many people besides myself to think that it is quite possible that a very great deal of our money and time and effort may be expended on broadcasting into a void. I believe it is now generally agreed that the information to be gained from our correspondents is both inaccurate and misleading. The plain listener is not a person who ever writes a letter, except under very startling circumstances, and we obviously do not wish to broadcast for the benefit of cranks and people with a great deal of spare time on their hands.[1]

Though a flurry of memos evoked some support, most reactions came out firmly against such a plan, such as this reaction from J. C. Stobart of the Talks division:

As I hold very strongly that the ordinary listener does not know what he likes, and is tolerably well satisfied as shown by correspondence and license figures with the mixed fare now offered, I cannot escape feeling that any money, time or trouble spend upon elaborate enquiries into his tastes and preferences would be wasted.[2]

The issue was tabled, though it would continue to arise, often through pressure from outside groups such as the Radio Manufacturers Association who were less concerned with cultural standards than with selling more radio receivers.

In 1934 a Programme Revision Committee was formed under the direction of the new Controller of Programmes, Col. Alan Dawnay, in response to growing criticism and in anticipation of the upcoming charter renewal process to take place in 1936. The need for audience research formed one of the committee's recommendations, though with reservations as expressed by Dawnay:

In considering programme revision as a whole both I and the committees concerned were faced at every turn with an absence of reliable evidence on which to base our judgments and recommendations. Assertions that this or that item is popular can only be based on individual belief, and the analysis of listeners' habits and of their opportunities of hearing a particular programme at a given time are based on almost equally flimsy grounds. A primary recommendation, therefore, is that the Corporation should actively pursue listener research . . . Research should be directed to discovering listening habits rather than tastes, since the Corporation should rely mainly on its own professional judgment to produce the widest possible range of programmes, each good of its own kind, and should use the knowledge of listening habits which it acquires to place these varied programmes in such a way as to meet the reasonable demands of a considerable audience.[3]

It is clear that the BBC desired information as much to combat the critical assertions made by critics, policy makers, and the general public as to use it to actively shape their own practices and opinions, and that the expectation on the whole was that listener research was apt to reflect their own experienced judgments far better than those of others. The appointment of Sir Stephen Tallents in 1935 as Controller of Public Relations moved the idea forward decisively. Tallents had previously served as Secretary of the Empire Marketing Board where he had sponsored the pioneering documentary work of John Grierson and had become Britain's leading proponent of promoting the image of Britain in the world. His background made him well versed in the developing science of market research, and in the summer of 1936 a Listener Research Group was appointed.[4]

Bringing in Robert J. Silvey from the London Press Exchange, Britain's largest advertising agency, as an advisor (he would later become Director of Listener Research) opened up a new era in BBC radio practice. Though both Tallents and Silvey were committed to a vision of research that would avoid the "purely" quantitative and audience-pandering techniques of US broadcasters in favor of a more nuanced and sociological approach, the use of the "audience barometer" survey as it developed over the next several years opened BBC executive eyes to many differences between their own perceptions of what properly constituted British culture and the perceptions of their wider public. As Silvey notes, the BBC was the first public service broadcaster in Europe to initiate an organized program of audience research; most public service broadcasters saw little point in tracking audience reaction since, unlike commercial operations, their income did not derive from audience size but from license fees or from direct government funding (Silvey 1974, 18). It was more important to hold up a distinguished national image and to satisfy those whose decisions mattered, as a rule the elite concerned with national culture. Many in the BBC were beginning to chafe at this vision.

Offshore Commercial Competitors

It is no coincidence that one of Silvey's first areas of inquiry concerned an insidious attack on the BBC's national monopoly status: stations broadcasting commercial programs from the continent across much of England. Part of Silvey's suitability for the job rested on his expertise in this area. In his former post at the London Press Exchange he had prepared a survey on the extent of listening to European commercial stations for clients interested in their advertising potential (Sean Street 2006, 168). As early as 1932, stations broadcasting off the coast of Britain, most notably in France and Ireland, began to draw the attention of British firms interested in using radio to advertise to the British public. Noting the success of radio as an advertising medium in the US, a growing dissatisfaction with the BBC's non-commercial monopoly began to inspire experimentation with the sponsorship of entertainment programs, usually 15 to 30 minute programs of popular gramophone records interspersed with short commercial messages. These were found to be particularly effective on Sundays, when Reith's strict sabbatarianism allowed only the most serious and dignified of programming on the BBC, causing many listeners, in *Variety*'s flippant words, to "tune to continental stations the moment they wake up with a hangover and realize it's Sunday."[5]

The reach of such broadcasts was constrained, however, by the fact that only a small proportion of British radio homes could bring in their signals, and the refusal of virtually all British newspapers to carry such station's program listings or allow advertising of the programs, in protest against advertising revenue competition.[6] Then, in May 1933, a new threat appeared on the scene: Radio Luxembourg, "the MOST POWERFUL IN EUROPE" declared itself "available for British sponsored programmes." Readers of this ad were instructed to apply to International Broadcasting Co, Ltd. of Portland Place, London.[7] This was a feisty start-up founded by Captain Leonard F. Plugge in 1930 as an ad brokerage firm placing British advertising primarily on Radio Normandy but also working with Radio Athlone, Poste Parisien, Radio Lyons, Radio Toulouse, and several others. Because of the ban on publicizing English commercial programs in British magazines and newspapers, IBC started its own journal, *Radio Pictorial*, in January 1934, as a privately owned competitor to the BBC's *Radio Times*, providing not only commercial radio schedules but those of the BBC as well. Reith, in a sporting gesture, graciously contributed his congratulations in the first issue.[8]

Aiding the growing audience and revenues of the commercial stations was the unique phenomenon of what were called "wireless exchanges" or "relays" in Britain. Both for reasons of poor reception and because of the cost associated with owning and operating a radio set in the UK, an inexpensive alternative had sprung up, serving particularly those working-class enclaves of the Midlands and North nestled in industrial river valleys where BBC's signals did not reach very clearly. For a small monthly sum, households could subscribe to a relay service, which supplied them with a receiver box hooked up to a line that brought in up to four channels of radio from a central transmitter located distantly: essentially, wired subscription radio. Owners of relay sets had neither to buy a radio nor pay the license fee, and tuning in was as simple as flipping a switch. By the mid-1930s over 300 separate relay exchanges served more than 230,000 mostly working-class households (Sean Street 2006, 153). Most exchanges provided not only the BBC national and the nearest BBC regional channel, but also one or two continental commercial stations, with far greater clarity than possible over the air. In Briggs' words, "It was no longer possible for the BBC to watch quietly what was happening. Relay stations putting across commercial programmes could break the BBC's monopoly with the ordinary British listener" (Briggs 1965, 359). The BBC responded by persuading the International Broadcasters Union in 1933 to ban the existence of "the systematic diffusion of programmes or messages, which are specifically intended for listeners in another country and which have been the object of a protest by the broadcasting organization of that country" (Briggs 1965, 360). Though the nation's newspaper proprietors strongly supported the

BBC's cause (even tempering their usual criticism of BBC programs for a time), such measures proved ineffective.

With the stations themselves outside of regulatory reach, another defense was needed. By early 1934 rumors of American plots to take over British radio were flying. The *Daily Sketch* ran a sensational headline, "Plot to Capture British Radio Fails – But Danger From US Not Yet Past," next to a picture of one of America's most popular radio stars, "Roxy" (Samuel F. Rothafel), who had just returned from a trip to London. It's unclear what relationship Roxy might have had to "one of the big American corporations with £1,000,000 of capital waiting for investment in what it foresees to be a rich new field for exploitation"—except for his role as former host of a program on the NBC network.[9] But the *Sketch* would not have been reassured by a memo written in June of that same year by NBC executive Alfred Morton to the network's London representative, Fred Bate, advising Bate that "The National Broadcasting Company is planning to supplement its present services to American advertisers by including the placement of advertising on foreign radio stations."[10]

However, it did not require a plot by Americans to bolster the cause of commercial radio. IBC published the results of a 1935 survey showing that 61% of British radio homes listened regularly to English programs on foreign stations, most of them to Luxembourg.[11] By October 1935, the practice had become so commonplace that the British trade journal *Shelf Appeal* could lead off an article with:

> Nine-tenths of the money outlayed on Broadcast Advertising by English advertisers is spent on Sunday. In other words, the whole of the radio advertising business of this country depends primarily on the attitude of the British Broadcasting Corporation towards its Sunday programmes. That these programmes are highly unpopular, and not what the mass of people really want and care to listen to, not even the staunchest supporters of Broadcasting House will deny.[12]

By December of that year, the American trade journal *Broadcasting* smugly claimed "British Advertisers Clamoring for Commercial Radio Outlets," reporting on an appeal made to the British government by the Incorporated Society of British Advertisers.[13] Many harbored hopes that the report of the Ullswater Committee, due out in early 1936, would provide at least for some sponsored programs on home airwaves.

When these hopes were dashed, and the BBC's noncommercial monopoly reaffirmed, commercial broadcasting from offshore stations became a permanent part of British national broadcasting; as Sean Street points out, from 1934 on it is essentially incorrect to speak of British radio as only consisting of the BBC, not only in terms of what Britons actually listened to but what Britain produced. An entire alternative production sector set itself up in London, with studios to rival those of the BBC's; a *Radio Pictorial* article in 1939 about Plugge's company IBC was titled, "Britain's Other Broadcasting House."[14] Besides IBC and LPE, one of the biggest production companies was the London branch of the US-based J. Walter Thompson advertising agency.[15] All led in the adaptation of US commercial programs for British audiences, produced in London, recorded on discs or film, and carried across the channel for broadcast. Sunday afternoons at 1:00, Radio Luxembourg featured the *Lux Radio Theater*, based on the same scripts as the popular American show but performed by British actors. Drama based on US originals dominated during the day, including what Luxembourg's ads called "the Wonder Hour": back to back 15-minute serials, comprising *Mr. Keene, Tracer of Lost Persons*; *Mary Noble, Backstage Wife*; *Young Widow Jones*; and *Stella Dallas*.[16] Several of these also aired on Radio Normandie. Shows created along American lines predominated, but most of them had very little actual American content: they simply used popular techniques to put across popular music announced by popular figures in a manner generally scorned by the BBC.

At the same time, the BBC began to respond to the offshore migration of its audience, especially as the Listener Research office brought in convincing statistics about audience preferences. John Reith's departure from his long-held office in 1938 to a new post at Imperial Airways accelerated the trend, and the increasing independence of the regional stations lent fresh ideas.[17] Audience participation programs in the form of spelling bees made their debut, a format widespread on American radio that could be defended as deriving from venerable British schoolhouse traditions. Comedy/variety expanded on the evening schedule, some of it scheduled on a recurring weekly basis as had been the practice in American radio from the beginning (called "fixed point" scheduling and ardently resisted by the Reithian BBC); *Monday Night at Seven*, the first to debut, made this new practice plain in its title. *Band Waggon* followed in January 1938, scheduled for Wednesday evenings[18] and starring Arthur Askey, whose comic character—as "himself," the host of a radio show, who lived in a flat at the top of Broadcasting House, with a recurring crew of comic types such as Mrs. Bagwash and her daughter Nausea and Richard Murdoch as his sidekick Dicky—seemed to be patterned very much after Jack Benny. The Sunday schedule "brightened" considerably.[19]

But the biggest change was the rise of serial comedy/drama, a form hitherto disdained in favor of the more "serious" single play, whether in the form of literary adaptations or based on comic character sketches spun off from variety shows. The Listener Research bureau discovered that these constituted some of the most popular programs on radio, particularly among working-class listeners who formed the vast bulk of the listening audience, and more with women than men.[20] Early examples, from 1937 and 1938, included *The Plums, Mr. Muddlecombe JP, Inspector Hornley, Cad's College,* and *The English Family Robinson,* a skit by Mabel Constanduros and Howard Agg that built on their famous Buggins Family sketches, a regular feature on the BBC *Children's Hour* since 1925.[21] In accordance with usual BBC practices, these were not the continuous, virtually endless serials as practiced on US radio, but discrete serialized fictions that ran for a limited number of weeks, scheduled intermittently at various times, with an end always clearly in sight. British and American radio practices and programs were drawing closer together, but retained their distinctive identities.

Competition at Home: The Forces Programme

Sir — How can we expect to make a nation of soldiers from a nation of boys nourished on a diet of jazz, blues, syncopation, tickety-boos and other inanities!

Colonel, Golders Green, NW

Sir — Is it not time that we old fogeys who dislike crooning stopped trying to dictate on matters of taste to the fighting men? That the sort of entertainment provided is, on the whole, what they like can be proved by anyone who takes the trouble to listen to the "Forces' Choice" programmes. And, after all, people living in retirement in delectable spots of the country can always choose their own "virile entertainments" and turn off the "flabby amusements" selected by ableseamen and sergeant pilots.

Yours truly, D. M. E—, Queen's Court, W2[22]

Luxembourg and Normandy closed down abruptly in September 1939 with the outbreak of war, though before this happened historian Philip Taylor describes a fascinating episode of the British government using Luxembourg for "black propaganda" aimed at the German people.[23] With the continental stations off the air, British military commanders realized that keeping up morale among the British Expeditionary Forces (BEF) stationed in France, feeling considerable stress but with little to do, presented a potentially serious problem. Plenty of stations across Europe were broadcasting light popular music interspersed with announcements and news in English—the only drawback was, most of these were based in Germany and Italy and were aimed explicitly at getting an Axis point of view across. An easy turn of the dial by a soldier bored with BBC uplift could bring the enemy directly into the British camp. Many within both the BBC and the British government resolved to provide the troops with a radio service designed to suit their tastes, not a paternal vision of their educational welfare. For a short time, an independent group calling itself Radio Internationale, based in France but with some British direction (including the indomitable Leonard Plugge), forged ahead and in November 1939 began the Fecamp BEF Programme, using the old Radio Normandy transmitter and providing mostly American recordings—even distributing a program guide to the troops called "Happy Listening." [24]

But in December this too ceased. Colonel A. P. Ryan, one of Tallents' deputies, wrote a humorous poem addressed to Sir Frederick Ogilvie, Director General of the BBC, on 30 November 1939, concisely stating what many felt was needed:

Lo, the poor private in the black of night
Prepared for war, not yet required to fight . . .
With two large armies largely unemployed
It's up to radio to fill the void. . . .
Enough, dear Mr. O., of titled hacks
And talks on bees and non-stop Sandy Macs,
And orchestras that drool the time away
Among the drearier tunes of yesterday.
No more announcers in whose accent lies
Unmanly comment on their old school ties . . .
If not, be sure our Lady of the Lamp
Which shines (for Nazi pilots) at Fecamp
Sweet Leonard Plugge, Belisha's Beacon Bright
Will cheer the troops by day, the Czechs by night.
So pull your socks up, do, dear Mr. O.
And make your programmes glamorous and low.[25]

The time was right to get such a point across, and on 7 January 1940, the BBC began its own Forces Programme, using frequencies and transmitters formerly employed for the Regional Programme, which had shut down upon declaration of war. A lighter touch, more popular music, more participation from the audience, a new informal style, and the appearance of new and old stars (many of them American) from stage, sound, and screen quickly became hallmarks: glamorous indeed, and low only to those who clung to the Reithian ideal.

The Forces Programme quickly filled a void on the domestic front as well. One BBC higher-up, Sir Basil Nicholls, would go so far as to claim that the whole concept "ultimately sprung from the BBC's desire, after a month or two of war, to give an alternative programme to its Home listeners"—never mind the troops.[26] And in fact, the new service soon obtained such popularity among domestic audiences, particularly women, that one observer claimed the Forces Programme "might have been renamed 'the Housewives Programme."[27] Or, as Cardiff and Scannell state, "Suddenly there was a spate of programmes about and for the working class . . . In the Forces Programme the tastes of the audience came first, and public service a long way second" (Cardiff and Scannell 1986, 98). American programs, especially variety shows, began to find their way into the schedule. Bob Hope and Jack Benny debuted in June of 1941; later, as the AFRS swung into action, programs like *Command Performance* and the *American Sports Bulletin* would also waft across the airwaves. Programs especially for war workers on the home front became popular, such as *Music While You Work* and *Workers' Playtime.* Program concepts borrowed from US broadcasting found a new British form, such as *The Brains Trust* (based on CBS's *Information, Please,* a humorous quiz show in which listeners won prizes for writing in with questions for a panel of experts) as well as home-grown favorites, such as *Sincerely Yours,* with Vera Lynn. The Listener Research department confirmed that this kind of popularization of program policy brought in greater numbers of listeners and therefore could serve more effectively to rally the national sense of purpose. Soon even more radical programming departures would ensue. In 1944, in order to ensure that British troops stationed around the world could still hear their favorite programs, the English-language General Overseas Service (the old Empire Service) was merged with the Forces Programme to form the General Forces Programme.

Reaching Out: The North American Service

The BBC Empire entertainment programs are wasted as far as the USA is concerned. They do not seem to be selected with a view to short-wave transmission, or for the American public . . . Americans tend to act on their emotions. It is necessary, therefore, to discover and build up microphone personalities for USA listening; and to acquire a reputation for frankness and authenticity in the material broadcast.

— "Report on USA Attitude to European War,"
Gerald Cock, 1940[28]

Throughout the mid-1930s, growing levels of external shortwave broadcasting from Germany, Italy, Russia, and other politically ambitious nations, including US commercial networks in Latin America, created pressure in Britain to better fund the struggling Empire Service. The BBC's Empire Service had begun transmitting in 1932 in the English language on shortwave, introducing its trademark phrase "This is London calling" to British citizens and colonial subjects in Empire and Commonwealth countries throughout the world. By 1938 it was beginning to seem more and more imperative to counter German propaganda by reaching out with a British point of view to other areas of the world, in their languages as well as in English. Broadcasts in Arabic to the Middle East were instituted that year, followed by Spanish language broadcasts to Latin America. Over the next two years hosts of others debuted, and the division was renamed the Overseas Service. But by September 1939 it was the English language service that had begun to worry officials most; now, drawing the still-neutral United States into the war effort on the side of the Allies became a primary objective. When German troops finally invaded Belgium, the Netherlands, and Luxembourg in May 1940, the waiting was over—and the formation of a new North American Service aimed directly at the hearts and minds of North Americans took center stage, with an enormous impact on home broadcasting. A staff of talented Canadians would guide the relationship.[29]

The North American Service built on the considerable aerial exchange between the US and Great Britain that had already developed by the late 1930s. An early period of experimentation with direct shortwave transmissions back and forth had given way, under pressure of nationalization, to fewer but more regular exchanges. As noted in Chapter 3, far more material flowed east to west, from Britain to the US, than the other way across, such as CBS's regular 1932 sustaining series called "Sunday Overseas Pickups," featuring a variety of figures and personalities from around the world brought to the microphone by CBS European Representative, Caesar Saerchinger, in London. NBC's Fred Bate was appointed in 1933 to handle similar tasks, but with a mandate to encourage west-to-east traffic across the ether as well. One result was the program *Five Hours Back,* originally designed "to rely solely on reception from a short-wave broadcasting station for regular transatlantic relaying" on an experimental basis, simply transmitting a half hour of NBC morning programming across to the BBC for its afternoon schedule, beginning on February 16, 1935.[30] However, NBC quickly realized that since "our regular morning programs are not as strong as our late afternoon and evening programs," they might be playing right into the hands of those in England who would like to retain a low opinion of American radio.[31]

So a special program was produced, employing prime-time-quality performers and transmitted over short wave frequencies, unheard by American audiences. It was well received in Britain, particularly by critics of the BBC like Collie Knox of the *Daily Express*, who wrote:

> The *Five Hours Back* relay from America emphasized once more just how dull and ponderous is the BBC method of presenting pro-grammes. Did you notice how each item and announcement came on with hardly a break? Did you notice how the whole show was smooth and slick and polished? I'll bet you did . . . No hesitation. No rustling of papers. No shuffling and coughing. No announce-ments like 'There will now be an interval of three minutes.' Those irritations were reserved for the BBC programmes that followed.[32]

He had to admit, though, that the shortwave reception proved so problem-atic that the show sounded "like a relay from a pier in a storm." It was a highly favored project at NBC, where John Royal urged the BBC to extend the experiment perhaps by broadcasting an American serial program. Fred Bate suggested that a "woman's program" would be worth considering. These suggestions were not taken up.[33] *Five Hours Back* was, however, renewed for the 1936 season.

Also in 1935 the BBC appointed its own representative to the US, Felix Greene (cousin both to novelist Graham Greene and to Hugh Carleton Greene, later BBC Director General), with an aim towards increasing the US to Britain flow of programs, as well as the other way around. Greene had already spent two years in the U.S., then several more in the BBC Talks Department. In one of his first reports back to the BBC, written in 1935, he recounts a meeting that would have future consequences:

> Ed Murrow, Talks Director, I particularly like; I have seen him on several occasions since my first meeting and we have spent some evenings together. He has only recently joined the staff. Broad-casting is a new medium to him of which he knows nothing. There are many ways in which I can help him from our longer experience with broadcast talks and adult education. Ed Murrow . . . has a wide knowledge of international affairs and is a cultural and intellectual person. He has never before faced the hurly burly of a commercial organization. I sometimes wonder how long his academic mind will stand it. He is one of the few people who have a vision of the place broadcasting should fill in the community or its potentialities in the education of the people.[34]

It is from such BBC contacts as Greene that Murrow would in fact learn the broadcasting business—though Greene's own career with the BBC would end abruptly in 1939 when he quit over conscientious objections to the war and the BBC's wartime role.[35]

Transatlantic cooperation resulted in a few more experiments with live shortwave broadcast. In February 1938, an "Anglo-American Spelling Bee" connected a team from Oxford on the BBC London Regional frequency with their counterparts from Harvard in the NBC studios in Boston. It was aired live on both sides of the Atlantic. *Variety* proclaimed "Spelling Bee Wows England" and forecast that "a new craze [was] likely to sweep the length and breadth of England."[36] The show brightened up the BBC Sunday schedule at 4:55 pm, putting it at 11 am in Boston. Such contests were continued irregularly over the next couple of years. The vagaries of shortwave transmission itself presented another series of problems with which such programs had to contend, though a positive benefit could be found even there; as one reviewer commented, "The reception is sometimes shaky, fading in and out, like the sound of the sea across which they travel. In a domestic show that would merely be annoying. To these reports it adds a certain sense of wonder, a suggestion of places at once so far and so near" (Hutchens 1942).

In another form of exchange, Raymond Gram Swing, a veteran American news reporter, began in 1935 a series of talks for the BBC on political conditions in America titled *American Commentary,* shortwaved three times a week from New York to London for British consumption only. This innovation occurred at the request of President Roosevelt, who felt his New Deal was misunderstood in Britain (Culbert 1976, 102; Swing 1964). Swing became an early supporter of American intervention, winning him a considerable fan base in Britain and much influence in the upper echelons of British thought. By 1941 over 6 million Britons tuned in weekly. In 1936 he began, in addition to his BBC program, a long-running stint as a news commentator on the Mutual Network, which brought him comparable fame in the US.

Also during this period a more familiar figure makes his debut: Alistair Cooke, known to Americans today as the long-running host of PBS's *Masterpiece Theatre.*[37] Cooke's first experience with the United States came in the form of a two-year fellowship at Yale and Harvard from 1932–34, financed by the American Commonwealth Fund. The young man's ambitions as a critic led him to contribute occasional reports on American culture to the British newspaper *The Observer,* but it was radio that truly interested him. Writing to offer his services to the BBC in January 1934, he presciently proposed:

> I don't know if English people are still as tiredly indifferent as they were to the force, policies, humour, literature of America. If they are

I imagine nobody proposes to do anything about it until America makes it even clearer she is moving towards a contemporary civilisation, while we perpetuate—prolong rather—a less apt, a less contemporary one. And that would be all. But if anybody is interested, I am mooting the proposal of some series of talks about these things.[38]

No one was interested, at least not yet. However, returning to England, the ambitious Cooke succeeded in wangling a position from Charles Siepmann, BBC Director of Talks, to "undertake a series of broadcast talks for us on The Cinema." He parlayed this into an appointment as BBC film critic from 1934 to 1936.

In spring of 1935, perhaps as a reciprocation for "Five Hours Back," Cooke was commissioned to put on a special series of feature programs titled "The American Half-Hour," "a weekly review of American news, ideas, music, literature and entertainment"[39] in which two characters, "the Englishman" and "the American," encounter various characters and have interesting experiences as they explore various parts of the United States, starting in Manhattan. Cooke produced the series from England in cooperation with the NBC network, via its London representative Fred Bate. Each program was to feature the voice of one or two American creative or public figures, and NBC found itself scrambling to make recording dates with those nominated by Cooke. They included, for the first broadcast, Eugene Rostow, Washington Lee, Robert Maynard Hutchins, Irvin Cobb, Will Rogers, and George Nathan—an ambitious plan, especially for a program that the American network itself would not be able to carry since it was based on recordings. Cobb, Rogers, and Hutchins declined. The American ambassador to England inaugurated the first broadcast, on April 6, which met with general approval. The second program, though, ruffled NBC feathers. It featured a trip to Harlem and frank discussion of American racism with lines like, "With all our boasted equality in New York, it's an unwritten law that certain streets are for negroes, others are not. If a Negro family does appear in a new street, the white families move out; so a landlord will move heaven and earth to keep his tenants white." This, and a comment made by an American character about the "bad teeth" to be found generally around England, made John Royal, in particular, begin to regret all the time and trouble NBC was putting into the program, despite the fact that the BBC was paying the costs. When the series ended two weeks later, no one proposed continuing it.[40]

By 1937, Cooke found himself back in the US. Fred Bate, whom Cooke had gotten to know in London, set up an appointment with NBC's program director John Royal. Royal hired him on the spot to do a weekly Wednesday evening cultural commentary on New York events (Clarke 1999, 134–35) as well as the intermission talk during the Sunday Metropolitan Opera broadcasts. He pitched to the BBC a series called *I Hear America Singing*, in cooperation with Alan Lomax, succeeding in getting permission from the Library of Congress to borrow and re-record rare folk music from its Archive of Folk Culture (Winick 2005). He produced it in London in the summer of 1938 to good reviews, and may have opened up the BBC to the kind of folk song program that Alan Lomax would eventually produce for the Third Programme after the war. In the fall of 1938, returning to New York, Cooke finally persuaded Felix Greene and Lindsay Wellington of the BBC New York office to give him a six month contract for a program called "Mainly About Manhattan," very much along the lines he had proposed years before, but confined to the cultural activities of New York City. Not until January 1940, in the midst of the phony war but with pressure building all around, did Cooke propose the program that would figure so centrally in his career:

> A regular talk, a sort of diary of a country at peace . . . taking in two or three topics each time, touching on life away from the East coast; on democratic festivals or celebrations it might be good for Britons to know about; on a new invention; a great man dead; on a new writer; on American experiments in democracy – the country teems with projects that are gallantly run . . . To be called, say, *A Letter From America*. (Clarke 1999, 160)

However, Raymond Gram Swing was already filling this role in the eyes of the BBC, and Cooke's proposal met with a cold response back in London:

> Whilst I think there is need for the USA to understand the British, and indeed the European, situation, I do not feel that at this stage there is an equivalent need for us to understand the American point of view. It is put well enough for us by Swing . . . I think AC has become a good deal more Americanised than in the 'Mainly About Manhattan' days.[41]

Soon, this would be perceived as an advantage rather than a disqualifier. As luck would have it, Swing gave up his BBC program to focus on his Mutual broadcasts that summer, and with the debut of the North American Service in May 1940, a new man, Gerald Cock, was making the decisions. Cooke went on to take over the role as host of *Letter From America* that he would fill for an astonishing fifty years, an icon of Anglo-American culture in the United States and a primary interpreter of America to Britons.

In 1938 the old Empire Service changed its name to the Overseas Service, with Sir Stephen Tallents, formerly head of Public Relations, as Controller. Under him was Tony Rendall as director of all English and Empire language broadcasts; he was also appointed head of the American Liaison Unit that would work closely with US reporters and representatives as war accelerated. The North American Service was officially constituted in May 1940. The motto of the NAS was "British in content, American in appeal" and to achieve this Tallents looked first to the pool of accomplished Canadian broadcasters already in their midst, involved in arranging programs for the Canadian troops stationed in Britain. In July 1940 he appointed Ernest Bushnell, former program director of the CBC and already seconded to the BBC, to the post of Organizer of Programmes. Another Canadian, Stanley Maxted, produced the dramatized news program, *Radio Newsreel* (modeled after *The March of Time*), which soon figured as the most popular program on the regular Overseas schedule and would later be re-broadcast on both the CBC and on the Mutual network in the States (Gray 2010). H. Rooney Pelletier, also from Canada, would take over from Bushnell as program organizer in 1942[42]; the whole Service came under the direction of Maurice Gorham, a feisty Irishman and longtime editor of *The Radio Times*, in 1941. They would build the NAS into a sort of popularizing and Americanizing spearhead within the BBC over the course of the war, despite efforts by others to contain its influence. It is no coincidence that both Gorham and Pelletier took leading roles in the Light Programme after the war.[43] A staff of "American advisors" also lent their expertise to NAS operations as the war went on, among them Wells "Ted" Church, Morris Gilbert, John Hooley, and Arthur Feldman.

At first Empire programs consisted mainly of items taken from Home programs and re-broadcast (often from recordings); a growing number of programs produced especially for the service would later be developed. One big concession was won in the news arena. Though Reith continued to battle restrictive newspaper interests at home, with news coverage still limited on the national network to brief post-press-time news reports, the Empire Press Union put up no such objections to Empire Service news broadcasts (Briggs 1965, 393). J. C. S. MacGregor was appointed Empire News Editor, with a staff of three, in 1934. News broadcasts quickly become the most highly valued part of the service, and the Empire news service would aid the BBC greatly when it came to establishing its first true national news programs in the early 1940s.

The British government's increasing need to convince not just the American elite—who tended to be pro-intervention—but the vast American middle and working class public that the US should enter the war effort on Britain's side (and to keep up Canadian morale) meant a deliberately different approach to programming. This could be seen in the NAS's debut program, beamed across the Atlantic on the afternoon of May 28, 1940. Vernon Bartlett addressed his audience frankly, "I am going to talk to you three times a week from a country that is fighting for its life. Inevitably I'm going to be called by that terrifying word 'propagandist.' But of course I'm a propagandist. Passionately I want my ideas—our ideas—or freedom and justice to survive" (Rolo 1942, 184). *Britain Speaks* was a very different kind of program from those the BBC had previously produced; as Gladstone Murray, former BBC controller now Director of the CBC, explained in the 1941 *BBC Handbook*:

> [F]urther efforts were employed to please North American listeners. Thus, a Canadian announcer was employed; the news bulletins were shortened; news commentaries on the American model were introduced; the custom of announcing the names of news readers and others was adopted; and the general style of announcing and presentation was radically changed. (56)

Besides Bartlett, commentators included Leslie Howard, J. B. Priestley, George Slocombe, and A. G. Macdonnell. Reaction in the US was favorable. *Time* magazine reported, "*Britain Speaks,* now a fortnight old, is a vast improvement over the stodgy stuff that BBC used to short-wave to North America."[44] It was received particularly enthusiastically in Canada, as the CBC began to put together its BBC-inflected national service, but could be heard over much of the United States as well. As Nicholas Cull observes, "Broadcasting House soon noted that it received more correspondence from American listeners than Canadian, and assumed audience figures to match" (Cull 1993, 404).

But extending the listening audience beyond the short waves meant encouraging re-broadcasting by regular US stations. By 1941 over 80 American stations provided some NAS programs, though this would always be hindered both by the American networks' prohibitions against recorded programs and the BBC's refusal to allow any of its shows to be sponsored, even after the fact in the US. The Mutual network proved the most receptive to BBC broadcasting, but CBS and NBC participation picked up as programming developed, the prohibition against use of recorded programs weakened, and the US edged towards war; some experimentation with joint production of live shortwave programs over American networks and other creative cooperative transatlantic productions would follow in 1942 and 1943, and the BBC would develop at least a partially blind eye when it came to sponsorship.[45] The North American Service proved a fertile ground for transnational influence, familiarizing North American audiences not only with Britain's plight as Nazis advanced, France fell, and bombs dropped on London, but with British culture itself in the form of commentators, performers, political figures, and the man on the street. It also opened an avenue of information about the United States for audiences in Britain, though to a lesser degree since most NAS programs were not broadcast on BBC home networks. It would take the American Forces Network to fully expose Britain to American radio—and with US troops stationed there starting in 1942, with an even more direct, though less controllable and positive, exposure to Americans and their culture.

As the urgency to persuade the US to enter the war increased, and then as America and Britain engaged in full scale war as allies, the North American Service would expand enormously both in size and in impact. That story will resume below. In the end, however, it can be argued that the North American Service had a greater impact on the BBC itself than on North America.[46] It became an "Americanizing" beachhead within the heart of British national culture, with an advance guard made up of Canadians, whose broadcasting culture seemed to bridge the two. Between the forces of listener research, competitive popular broadcasting, and a new influx of influence from across the Atlantic, the stage was set for a new era. British broadcasting would never return to its old ways—though it would find a way to preserve the best of them. American broadcasting would find itself altered as well; encouraged by a variety of forces it would experiment with new forms, build up its news and public service programming, and develop wartime broadcasting structures in close complicity with British goals and models. That story is taken up in the next chapter.

CHAPTER 5

The Politics and Poetics of Neutrality

A few weeks ago a tall, bushy-haired young man landed in England. Since then he has been traveling about the country, absorbing its atmosphere. Midst the rubble of Coventry he has talked with men and women who have survived attacks from the skies. He has dropped in on workers at their homes. In the halls of Parliament he has spoken with statesmen and in Whitehall gathered ideas about the workings of government . . . He has felt the pulse of a hard-pressed nation and set down in verse and prose the story of Britain's war . . . These playlets are written to epitomize the feelings of millions in the words of a few . . . With talk, music, and sound effects he tells the story in poetic form.
      —S. J. Woolf, "Corwin Presents – Britain at War"[1]

[Such programs are] not, in the usual sense, "written." The creator of such a program . . . uses as his material not merely the voices but the minds and emotions and impulses of the people themselves . . . *not* to put words into their mouths, but to draw the people out, to get "on the record" their currents of thought, the feelings they had about their environment.
      —Erik Barnouw, *Radio Drama in Action* (49)

In the United States network radio hit the apex of its social influence, creativity, prosperity and popularity in the late 1930s and early 1940s, yet in many ways still fell short of fulfilling the role of central national institution that the BBC had occupied from the beginning. Forces were at work, however, to amend the fragmented, decentralized, primarily commercial system of American radio. Some came from within the industry itself, some worked from the outside, and others simply swept the radio industry along in the tide of social upheaval brought about by impending war. By 1946, as wartime efforts disbanded, American radio had transformed itself into a national cultural institution with obligations and responsibilities it had never recognized before, even as a greater transformation loomed: television.

Though critics of the American system of broadcasting had been dealt a setback in the Communications Act of 1934, by the late 1930s two significant developments rose out of the ashes to shape American broadcasting in definitive ways, both influenced by the relationship forged with British broadcasting as part of the earlier campaign, both with indelible effects on the future of broadcasting in the US. First, educational radio regrouped and found serious new backers in the emergent sphere of America's private foundations, during these years rapidly becoming a force to rival governments in influence as they would continue to do over the course of the century. The involvement of the Rockefeller Foundation, in particular, with the cause of educational radio would create a host of new initiatives, in both broadcasting and in communication research, that would decisively guide US radio in a more explicitly national and public service direction as it entered the war years.

Second, educators' organized efforts worked to change commercial network broadcasting substantially in the late 1930s. CBS and NBC both recognized that they would have to pay far more attention to providing the sort of public service program that responded to the need to protect and support a national high culture, the kind built into the very foundations of the BBC but vacated early on by American networks in favor of a dispersed system of both sponsored and sustaining programs. In the years before the war finally drew the US fully in, networks returned to the role of program innovator and producer that they had given up a decade before. They did this with the support and direct involvement of many public-service-minded groups, from private foundations to universities, civic organizations, and government agencies. As before, when such groups and the network themselves looked for program ideas to support their objectives, they first thought of the BBC. Many careers were built on criss-crossing the Atlantic, and the shape of radio—and television—after the war would owe much to the exchange of ideas and influence that wartime radio inspired.

Radio, Rockefeller, and Reform

Both private foundations and educational institutions had played a role in shaping American radio from the beginning. As noted in Chapter 2, many of the earliest stations on the air in the US were university-based, totaling an impressive 202 in number between 1921 and 1936. However, as Powell points out, these numbers are somewhat misleading since a high proportion of them "were assigned to the electrical engineering departments of the institutions concerned, for the purpose of experimentation . . . Not many of these licensees were concerned with, or even aware of, the educational potential of the new medium."[2] These stations were training engineers but not reaching out with educational fare to the general population.

Though their numbers dropped dramatically after the regulatory and economic difficulties of the late 1920s and early 1930s (only 38 remained in 1937) many key educational and community stations had begun to develop outreach broadcasting along a number of lines, supported by a combination of university, state, federal, and industry funds. And by the mid-1920s a few prescient private foundations began to move into the educational radio field, often prompted by more general interests in child welfare and the social effects of education. The Carnegie Corporation's American Association for the Education of Adults in 1926 provided backing for the formation of the National Advisory Council on Radio in Education (NACRE), directed by Levering Tyson, for the purpose of guiding educators, universities, and commercial broadcasters towards cooperative efforts. The Payne Fund in 1931 gave a five-year, $200,000 grant (over $2.5 million in today's dollars) to establish the National Committee on Education by Radio (NCER), a more radical group bent on reform of radio policy and the set-aside of dedicated frequencies, headed by Joy Elmer Morgan. The NCER used these funds to found the Institute for Education by Radio at Ohio State University, initiating a series of annual conferences that brought together educational and commercial broadcasters in a productive exchange through the 1930s, one that would influence key policy makers over the next two decades. In 1935, the Rockefeller Foundation's General Education Board (GEB) provided substantial funding for the Federal Radio Education Committee, formed under the aegis of the US Department of Education to address radio educators' concerns in the wake of the Communication Act of 1934 debates.

The connection between education and communication can be associated with Rockefeller funding in many ways, starting with the very existence of the University of Chicago, founded by John D. Rockefeller in 1892. The University of Chicago took the lead in the development of "new" disciplines such as sociology and political science, and its faculty and alumni "played a disproportionate role in the historical development of American thought about communication" from the 1920s onward, according to Peters and Simonson.[3] Associated with John Dewey (who earned his doctorate there), long linked to Progressive forces in education and social thought, the University of Chicago also pioneered in educational radio (in its *University of Chicago Round Table* program, most prominently) and trained or employed a long line of influential scholars and practitioners active in the communications field, from Harold Lasswell and James Rowland Angell to Herbert Blumler, Douglas Waples, Robert M. Hutchins, Paul Hoffman, and William Benton.

The Rockefeller family had initiated direct intervention into American educational thought and practice as early as 1903 with its General Education Board (GEB), which funded rural schools as part of a campaign "to uplift isolated populations without access to either modern medicine or public education" (Richardson and Johanningmeier 2006, 6). The Rockefeller Foundation (RF) was established in 1913 to further work in education and public health, along with its sister organization, The Laura Spelman Rockefeller Memorial (LSRM) fund, dedicated to the welfare of women and children (later folded into the RF). The GEB and LSRM became early supporters of educational radio, sponsoring radio broadcasts by the Child Study Association in 1924 at the University of Iowa, and funding scholars to study this new medium.[4]

Other key foundation-supported organizations include the Association of College and University Broadcasting Stations (ACUBS), formed in 1925 at the third national radio conference and later to become the National Association of Educational Broadcasters (NAEB). This group provided cohesion and guidance for educational stations and coordinated lobbying efforts as radio regulation took shape in the late 20s and early 30s; many of its members benefited from Rockefeller Fellowships and would later take leading roles in the development of public television and radio in the 1960s. Most prominent among the NAEB's station members were universities belonging to the "Big Ten" and the "Big Seven"[5] with Wisconsin (WHA), Illinois (WILL), Iowa State (WOI), Ohio State (WOSU), and Oklahoma (WNAD) the most significant among the early players. Almost all received some form of foundation funding as they sought to define their role in providing educational and informational programming, defend their licensees and frequencies, and reach out to US audiences with a service that contrasted sharply with the prospering commercial networks and their affiliates.

The story of private foundations in American life is an interesting one, and has been traced by a number of historians (Fisher 1993; Gary 1996; Lagemann 1989). Now a familiar type of organization around the globe, they are by most accounts largely an American invention, emerging in the decades before World War I as the founders and heirs of some of America's largest fortunes such as Andrew Carnegie, John D. Rockefeller, and Henry B. Payne turned to philanthropy and set up trusts to carry such activities on for many subsequent generations. The Ford family would join their ranks in the 1950s with the eponymous foundation whose impact on US broadcasting cannot be overstated (see Chapter 8).[6] In many ways such foundations stepped into the gap created by US broadcasting's dispersed structure and hands-off relationship with the federal government.[7] It is doubtful that public broadcasting as a national institution could have emerged in the US were it not for the positive intervention and active policy-setting of major foundations. Educational broadcasters themselves certainly played a dynamic role, but at certain key junctures foundations took the initiative and set the broadcasters on a course they might not have taken otherwise.[8]

Furthermore, as Richardson and Fisher point out, for the decentralized, scattered United States as the twentieth century began, "the Rockefeller family was larger than the state in terms of economic resources" (1999, 4). Private foundations thus came to constitute a kind of "shadow government" active in all aspects of American social and cultural life; often, their international operations served as a counterbalance to the more nationalistic focus of governmental policy and took the lead in establishing transnational initiatives. At other times—during World War II, for example (Gary 1996), and also during the Cold War (Saunders 1999)—they have collaborated closely with government on national and international political agendas. This is certainly the case with the Rockefeller Foundation, whose crucial intervention in broadcasting research and policy in the late 1930s brought with it a strongly favorable attitude towards British broadcasting and culture, served both British and US government interests during the War, and remained an important conduit of British influence on American public radio and television.[9]

Of all the players in this shadow history, John Marshall of the Rockefeller Foundation must be credited with an extraordinary, if little recognized, role at the heart of the machine. His impact has been understood in bits and pieces. Many educational broadcasting histories make grateful, if brief, mention of his name, but historian Brett Gary is one of the first to provide an assessment of Marshall's initiative not only in setting up an infrastructure for communications research in the US but in guiding leading thinkers into cooperation with the Roosevelt administration's (and Great Britain's) interventionist strategies and propaganda before and during the war (Gary 1996, 1999). William Buxton also draws attention to Marshall's impact as "a modernizing force in communications" who "encouraged innovation in educational radio, documentary film, library microphotography, the study of communications and public opinion, the study of culture, and museology" (Buxton 1999, 2003). Some of the leading intellectuals in the field including Paul Lazarsfeld, Theodor Adorno, Siegfried Kracauer, Charles Siepmann, and John Grierson owe their prominence to his support; his name or the Foundation's frequently crop up in footnotes or indexes to histories. But his full impact comes into focus when we link Marshall's contributions to the fields of educational broadcasting and communication research with his key role in fostering transnational connections, particularly with Britain and the BBC.

Marshall, scion of an old New England family with a Harvard M.A. in Medieval studies, joined the Rockefeller Foundation in 1933 as assistant director of the Humanities Division. The Division's director, David Harrison Stevens, also acted as vice-president of the Foundation's General Education Board (GEB), headed from 1922 to 1929 by Beardsley Ruml, who had studied at the University of Chicago under James Rowland Angell, a disciple of John Dewey. Ruml served under Angell as his executive assistant during the brief year Angell spent as Director of the Carnegie Corporation, another key foundation, in 1920. Angell went on from there to become President of Yale University (and later, educational director for NBC); Ruml became, at age 26, director of the Laura Spelman Rockefeller Memorial fund, mentioned above for its pioneering work in educational radio.[10] Though Ruml would leave the Rockefeller Foundation in 1929 (returning to Chicago to become Dean of Social Science[11]), his associate David H. Stevens—also trained at Chicago—and Stevens' assistant John Marshall would take Ruml's concerns in a productive direction in the dynamic years ahead. As a harbinger of things to come, in early 1934 the Foundation moved into new offices on the 55th floor of the recently completed Rockefeller Center in central Manhattan, just below NBC's offices and next door to what would become the home of the BBC's North American Service (as well as some other more covert operations, as we shall see).

The Humanities Division of the Rockefeller Foundation had long maintained an interest in scholarship and libraries, and in the early 1930s funded several European projects, including construction of the New Bodleian Library at Oxford. John Marshall was sent over to tour these sites in the spring of 1934, visiting Dublin, Oxford, Paris, Brussels, Geneva, and Rome and coming away impressed with what he saw and eager to foster connections with European institutions, especially those, like the BBC, that reached out to a broad public with humanities-based culture (Buxton 2003). Towards the end of that year, he participated in the decision to make a strategic shift in the Foundation's perspectives and policies away from a sole focus on academic scholarship at elite institutions and towards the wider sphere of popular culture. As a Foundation Report in 1936 put it:

> [T]he Foundation, in 1934, decided to put greater emphasis upon the attempt to bring the results of humanistic study from books, seminars, and museums more directly into the current of modern life. If instrumental in determining esthetic values, surely one of the first answers would be the radio and the moving picture. (42–43)

As a result of this, as Buxton explains, "Marshall began to move away from the traditional humanities and towards the educational and commercial media," particularly radio and film (Buxton 2003, 142). He also began to develop the links with British broadcasting that would prove crucial in the Foundation's work, for himself and for others in the educational radio field; in 1935 the RF sponsored a three month internship at the BBC for two men who would become leaders in American educational broadcasting: Harold McCarty and Lester Ward Parker. McCarty, program director at the University of Wisconsin station WHA, would draw strongly on his BBC experience as president of the NAEB (Blakely 1979, 238) and as director of Wisconsin's pioneering state-wide public service broadcasting network. Parker returned from England to write a book on *School Broadcasting in Great Britain* (1937). Many more educational broadcasters would benefit from Rockefeller Fellowships enabling travel to England and training at the BBC over the next several decades.

Throughout the 1930s the Rockefeller Foundation, via Marshall, funded a number of efforts directly involved in producing programs for educational radio. The University Broadcasting Council in Chicago (a consortium of the University of Chicago, Northwestern University, and DePaul University), with Rockefeller funding had created the prestigious public affairs discussion program the *University of Chicago Round Table*, aired on the NBC network since 1933.[12] In 1935 the World Wide Broadcasting Foundation in Boston received RF funds "to develop, produce, and broadcast programs of a cultural, educational, artistic, or spiritual character, and to arrange for an interchange throughout the world of constructive radio programs" via shortwave station W1XAL (Rockefeller 1935, 279); this station's interesting history will be discussed below. In 1938 the Foundation began its long-running support for the Rocky Mountain Radio Council, a cooperative pro-duction venture eventually involving 37 Western educational broadcasters under Robert B. Hudson, later Director of Education for CBS and, after that, program director of the National Educational Television and Radio Center (NETRC). Though it is certainly true, as Hugh Slotten argues, that "the organizers of radio stations at institutions of higher education in the USA drew on local traditions of adult education, agricultural extension and university-based community service" to direct their operations, they also benefited from foundation-inspired visions of European-style public service broadcasting with the BBC as preeminent example, particularly through the efforts of John Marshall and the Rockefeller Foundation (Slotten 2006, 224). These are the two competing poles between which US public broadcasting philosophy would swing for the rest of the century.

Marshall's second trip to Europe in 1936 solidified British connections. His primary purpose was to see "what was being done in England in film and radio" (Buxton 2003, 143) and included several meetings with John Grierson[13] and his associates at the Film Centre in London and to the headquarters of the BBC, where he met with John Reith and Charles Siepmann, among others. Marshall was so impressed by Siepmann's ideas on regional broadcasting that he suggested that Siepmann might make a visit to the US to survey the radio situation there (Buxton 2003, 143). Though the notion was originally dismissed by Sir Cecil Graves, then joint Director General of the BBC—"much as we appreciate the suggestion, no useful purpose could really be served by a grant of money enabling someone from the BBC to go to America to study American broadcasting and exchange ideas with American broadcasters and educationalists"[14]—it eventually met with Reith's approval, and in 1937 the Rockefeller Foundation funded a three-month tour of educational and other stations that would set Siepmann's life on a new course as well as consolidate a lively exchange between British and American radio broadcasters that continued at least into the 1970s.[15] Marshall became a frequent correspondent with Reith and other BBC high officials as these exchanges were arranged, with the only hitch resulting from the Foundation's eagerness to fund employees of NBC and CBS for BBC internships as well—something the BBC found potentially awkward, given recent events.

In a memo written by the BBC's North American Representative Felix Greene to the Director of Programmes, Siepmann's trip was put in terms not especially flattering to US educational radio:

> Marshall's idea is that Siepmann should spend most of his time in visiting the small regional stations run, not by commercial firms, but by Universities, States, and schools. Many of these are struggling in a not very effective way to make some contribution to educational broadcasting in this country. What they need (and here Marshall is dead right) is intellectual stimulus. He wants Siepmann to travel and spend a week or so at each centre, talk to those responsible for the station and programmes, and attempt to give them some imaginative grasp of what, on a regional basis, they could accomplish . . . I know these people: intellectually they are not very alive; in radio they are hindered by the general acceptance of the standards of the commercial companies, and they themselves are tied to these standards because they have had experience of no other. I personally do not know of anyone in the BBC who could help this awakening process more than Siepmann. He, on the other hand, will get experience of American broadcasting (particularly when he returns to spend the last of the three months in New York) which might be very valuable to the BBC.[16]

The disdainful tone of this message says more about Greene and his attitudes, however, than it does about Siepmann or educational radio in the US, and indeed productive and mutually respectful relationships were established, along the lines that Marshall wished to cultivate.

Siepmann would become an important resource for educational radio organizations, and would return to England not particularly impressed with US radio's current state but highly enthusiastic about its possibilities. He even put himself forward for a job in NBC's Educational Programming department under Angell, who had become its director after retirement from the Presidency of Yale, though this effort failed.[17] Siepmann returned to Britain and the BBC, where he was appointed Director of Programme Planning as wartime changes loomed. Soon, however, through another intervention by John Marshall, a further transatlantic opportunity would bring Siepmann to the US for good, where he would play an influential role in the development of educational and public broadcasting, as well as broadcasting policy, for decades to come (see Chapter 7).

John Marshall continued his efforts to further US-European connections in the radio and film fields, returning to Europe in 1938 for a three-month stay.[18] In London he spent time with Siepmann and with Siepmann's close friend and protégée, Edward R. Murrow, whom Marshall had known from Murrow's New York days. As Buxton notes, "It was evident that the BBC and the Rockefeller Foundation were forging a special relationship, and as Marshall was to note, 'everyone in the Foundation . . . thought of the BBC in a way quite different from what they thought of American broadcasting.'"[19] Marshall also actively pursued other non-profit European cultural groups in the film and radio fields, seeking "to generate a new publicly-oriented network in mass communications, as a counterweight to the dominance of commercial media" (Buxton 2003, 149).

He returned to New York with important cultural connections that shaped the Foundation's strategies. By 1939, Marshall's European networking had resulted in a long list of Rockefeller-funded projects, including the Film Library of the Museum of Modern Art under John Abbott, Iris Barry, and Siegfried Kracauer, modeled after the London Film Society[20]; the American Film Center headed by Donald Slesinger, a sister to Grierson's London Film Centre (which also received RF support); the International Film Exchange with the Paris Institute of Cinematography; and the National Film Society of Canada, linked both to New York and to London. It also included a number of more research-oriented organizations: the Princeton Radio Research Project under Hadley Cantril and Frank Stanton, the Office of Radio Research at Columbia University directed by Paul Lazarsfeld, the Ohio University Institute for Education by Radio, and the Radiobroadcasting (sic) Research Project of the Littauer Center at Harvard University, among many others.

Also in 1938, upon his return from an increasingly politically volatile Europe, Marshall embarked on a project that would set the Foundation on a new course and take important steps towards preparing American radio for the challenge of war.[21] As productive as Rockefeller educational radio projects had been, a new urgency now prompted a deeper consideration of the theoretical underpinnings and strategic direction of American radio and communications research. What were the responsibilities of researchers, broadcasters, foundations, and the state in a world at war? With radio used ever more widely for political propaganda, and facing the challenges of mobilizing national democracies against a common enemy, how should radio theorists and practitioners respond? Britain's declaration of war against the Axis powers and the Nazi/Soviet pact of August 1939 brought these questions to a head. Marshall sought to turn the attention of US scholars to an intensive study of the role of persuasive communication in a democratic society. To this end he convened a consortium of scholars to meet for what would prove to be fifteen sessions over the next ten months from September 1939 through June 1940; these would become known as the "Communication Seminars." Among those in regular attendance were Harold Lasswell (Princeton), Robert Lynd (Columbia), Paul Lazarsfeld (University of Vienna/Columbia), Hadley Cantril (Princeton), Lyman Bryson (Columbia), Donald Slesinger (Chicago), I. A. Richards (Harvard), Lloyd Free (Princeton), and Douglas Waples (Chicago), all of them well known scholars affiliated with prestigious universities, most of them heading a major Rockefeller-funded project.

Also present were two British participants, both recipients of Rockefeller funding to promote US/British exchange: Geoffrey Gorer, an Oxford-trained anthropologist, funded by Marshall to make a study of the impact of film and radio on American culture; and Charles Siepmann of the BBC, now back in the US for the long term. Earlier that year Marshall had persuaded the Rockefeller Foundation to fund a special three-year lectureship in broadcasting at Harvard University "to encourage and give direction to studies of broadcasting as a means of mass communication" (Rockefeller 1939, 324–25). Siepmann was selected for this honor, at Marshall's prompting and with Angell's assistance. He arrived in the States in the fall of 1939,[22] fresh from putting the BBC's wartime programming plans into place, and took up residence in Cambridge just in time for the Communications Group meetings, in which he became one of the most active participants. Indeed, according to Brett Gary, over the next fifteen months as the group deliberated, it was largely Siepmann's influence that prevented the more propagandistically minded in the group from dominating, and led their final report, "Needed Research in Communication," away from its elitist, authoritarian tendencies and towards a model emphasizing a "two-way process of communication" between government and people, in which public discussion, counter-proposals, and consent are as important as the government's proposals and decisions (Gary 1996, 141).

This report, called by Peters and Simonson "the founding document of mass communication research" (2004, 136) declares itself to be based on two assumptions: "First, that events are obliging our central government to take on wider and wider responsibility for the welfare of the people. Second, that if the exercise of that responsibility is to be democratic, more effective ways of keeping the government and the people in communication with each other will have to be created" (2004, 137). However, events would soon push the seminar's participants towards the government side of the communications process. Though Siepmann, along with Lyman Bryson of NACRE and RF officer Joseph Willits, warned the group against the prospect of "moving their proposed research apparatus within the government" as war threatened, and cautioned a careful distancing from state agendas, this is eventually exactly what happened. As Gary concludes, "By the end of 1940, each of the established media projects had been tied into some security-related research" and new ones set up explicitly for cooperation with the war effort, including the Princeton and Stanford Shortwave Listening Projects (which would eventually be taken over by the newly established Central Intelligence Agency) (1996, 143). Nothing exemplifies the powerfully persuasive combination of foundation funding, government propaganda, and educational radio than the strange story of W1XAL, later known as WRUL, the "World Radio University for Listeners."

The Strange Case of WRUL

Frankly we have tried to imitate the British system which so many people in America consider superior to our own system, of wireless sponsored by advertising. Our venture is non-profit and non-commercial in character ... We have purposely changed our schedule so that the Sunday programs start at 5 pm EST rather than 7:30 pm so that British listeners can hear us and derive benefit from our broadcasts.[23]

—William Barber, Educational Director, W1XAL, 1935

[Thus] it happened that an American wireless station with an unsullied reputation for impartiality was, for many months during the most critical period of the war, unknowingly harnessed to the task of broadcasting British propaganda on a scale almost comparable in quantity of output with the BBC's Overseas Service.

—British Security Coordination (62)

As mentioned above, one of the Rockefeller Humanities Division's first mass media related endeavors under David Stevens and John Marshall had been to support the creation of the World Wide Broadcasting Foundation in 1935. This was a noncommercial organization founded by radio engineer, inventor, and IBM executive Walter S. Lemmon to extend the educational and cultural ends of US educational radio across the country and even beyond its borders, and to take an active role in broadcasting programs in English from other national systems, notably Britain and Canada; as *Time* magazine breezily put it, Lemmon "dips into his own pocket to broadcast New England enlightenment to the world," though those pockets were supplemented by the Rockefellers.[24] The programs were transmitted over shortwave station W1XAL in Boston from its studios in the Harvard Club, whose four frequencies gave it more than national reach, making it "the only station in the United States with national coverage that is devoted exclusively to educational and cultural programs" (Rockefeller 1938, 323–27). At first it broadcast only in English, with programs contributed by a consortium of New England universities, including Harvard, Tufts, Amherst, Yale, Columbia, Wellesley, Mount Holyoke, and Smith.[25] Later it added two more shortwave bands that allowed it to reach Central and South America with a power of 50,000 watts, and began foreign language broadcasts.

Buxton places Rockefeller support for this project squarely in the context of Marshall's effort "to establish closer working relationships between non-commercial entities in Britain and the United States, with a view to encouraging cross-fertilization," describing the station as a "'vest-pocket' American version" of the BBC (2003, 149). W1XAL producer Loring B. Andrews attended the BBC staff school in fall 1937, where he expressed interest in setting up a program exchange between the station and the BBC.[26] Later, the Canadian Broadcasting Corporation would also explore the possibilities for broadcasting CBC programs to the world via the station, including across the Atlantic to Britain. In 1938 its call letters were changed to WRUL, for World Radio University for Listeners; it was also known as "Radio-Boston" (Clements 1943).

A profound transformation began to take hold in 1940, however, as Britain engaged with Axis propaganda forces and struggled to bring the United States into the war effort. Only recently has the story of British Security Coordination (BSC) emerged (see Cull 1995). BSC was a secret agency set up by British Military Intelligence (MI6) under Canadian operative William Stephenson (later known as the "Man Called Intrepid" in books and a film) specifically "to coordinate the activities of British intelligence in America" (Ignatius 1989). Though a few high up American officials were aware of and condoned BSC's covert operations—including President Roosevelt, J. Edgar Hoover of the FBI, and William "Wild Bill" Donovan of the Office of Strategic Services, later to become the CIA—the agency operated entirely under cover, behind the façade of the "British Passport Control Office" located, tellingly enough, on floors 34 and 35 of the International Building at Rockefeller Center (the BBC's North American Service was on the 33rd). "BSC ran a vast range of covert operations which, in effect, became the foundation of subsequent OSS and CIA operations," according to CIA historian Thomas F. Troy (Ignatius 1989). In early 1990, former BBC director Sir John Reith was named head of MOI. Nicholas Cull describes Reith's mounting desire to press forward with propaganda efforts in America, despite objections from the Foreign Office that would see Reith replaced by Duff Cooper in May (1995, 66). The BBC's own Foreign Department appears to have mediated between the BBC and the MOI; only a few weeks after Reith's appointment, J.C.S. MacGregor, formerly of the Empire Service news division but now a member of MOI, inquired about the credentials of the station and was reassured by Cecilia Reeves of the Foreign Department that "You may indeed say the World Wide Broadcasting Foundation people are perfectly respectable."[27] There is some indication that Stephen Fry, a BBC employee with ties to the Foreign Office, may have been involved in WRUL's programming activity as well.[28]

Station WRUL became one of BSC's chief venues for placing false news stories designed to outrage US public opinion against the Axis forces, as described in the report finally issued in 1998 (Boyd 2006).[29] BSC money, passed through "cut-out" front organizations (presumably including the Rockefeller Foundation, and possibly the BBC itself) began to transform the ambitious but small-scale educational station into a highly effective propaganda outlet, aimed mainly at the peoples of North and South America to combat Axis propaganda and to incite intervention on the Allied side. As the BSC's report later described:

> Through cut-outs, BSC began to supply [WRUL] with everything it needed to run a first-class international programme worthy of its transmitting power and declared policy. BSC subsidized it financially. It recruited foreign news editors, translators and announcers to serve on its staff. It furnished it with material for news bulletins, with specially prepared scripts for talks and commentaries and with transcribed programmes. . . . By the middle of 1941, station WRUL was virtually, though quite unconsciously, a subsidiary of BSC, sending out covert British propaganda all over the world. (1999, 60)

Thus, in the report's own rather gleeful words, "it happened that an American wireless station with an unsullied reputation for impartiality was, for many months during the most critical period of the war, unknowingly harnessed to the task of broadcasting British propaganda on a scale almost comparable in quantity of output with the BBC's Overseas Service" (1999, 62). Help in the area of foreign language broadcasts was supplied by a group founded in the fall of 1940 by the British Foreign Office called the Inter-Allied Information Committee (IAIC), also headquartered in Rockefeller Center, comprised of representatives of the smaller Allied nations: Czechoslovakia, Poland, France, the Netherlands. The British Press Service and the British Library of Information (all, again, housed at Rockefeller Center) would provide the main cover. They worked closely with American interventionist groups (Cull 1995, 119–21). Soon they would be pulled together into a new organization, the British Information Service (BIS) (Cull 1995, 133). The BIS programmed WRUL, a fact unknown to most Americans.

Not everyone in the BBC knew about this undercover broadcasting project, either; initial steps prompted a surprised telegram in August 1940 from Gerald Cock, the BBC's current North American representative, who had apparently been kept in the dark:

LEARN PRIVATELY WRUL BOSTON WILL RADIATE EACH WEEKDAY STARTING AUGUST TWELFTH 19 AND 25 METERS 2200 BST SPECIAL FIFTEEN MINUTE CELEBRITIES DIRECTED BRITAIN STOP URGE LISTEN WITH VIEW OCCASIONAL REBROADCASTING SINCE THIS STEP ASTONISHING DEVEL-OPMENT STOP[30]

By the end of 1941, however, the US State Department was "contributing heavily to WRUL funds and had its own officials attached to the station, thereby exerting indirect influence on WRUL's policy" (*BSC* 1999, 63).[31] By 1941, too, WRUL founder and owner Walter S. Lemmon had become vice president of the National Defense Communications Board, presumably not for his purely educational work (Van Loon 1941, 23). The station, like all US short-wave stations, was officially taken over by the State Department in 1942; WRUL thereafter served as the primary North American transmitter for Office of War Information (OWI) programs (along with San Francisco station KGEI) and later for a time as principal outlet of the nascent Voice of America.

The development of American propaganda agencies themselves also drew heavily on British, and BBC, involvement. In April of 1941 a further initiative sent Lindsay Wellington to the US at the behest of the BBC and the British government, to work with the Americans to begin to develop an overt joint propaganda program directed this time not to Americans but to the rest of the world. Wellington had been seconded by the BBC to the MOI in 1940 at

Reith's behest, and stayed on after Reith departed. His letter of instruction from Sir Walter Monckton, MOI's Deputy Director-General, urged him to do all in his power to arrange "with the State Department, with the American broadcasters, and with us over here that broadcasting is used to the utmost in both countries to promote understanding between the two peoples and to increase the force of democratic propaganda from the two countries."[32] BBC Director Ogilvie concurred: "It would be difficult to exaggerate the value to the democratic cause of making arrangements so that broadcasting in and from our two countries may be used, and used soon, to the best advantage of both peoples."[33] However, as early as June 1941 it began to become apparent that the Americans were in the process of developing an agenda not entirely congruous with British plans; as Wellington wrote to Ogilvie, "The signs and portents . . . suggest that official America sees herself as the senior partner in any combine and proposes to pursue American policy in her use of the instruments of propaganda" (emphasis in original).[34]

It is impossible to know whether the Rockefeller Foundation knew of WRUL's secret mission; its support for the World Wide Broadcasting Project ceased in 1941, according to its own reports, but RF funding of other national security-related projects did continue through much of the war. Many recipients of Rockefeller support migrated to the Office of Facts and Figures (OFF, headed initially by poet and Librarian of Congress Archibald MacLeish) and its successor organization the Office of War Information (OWI) as the US entered the war, including Siepmann, who became an American citizen in 1942. Once again, he narrowly missed a major opportunity when the OWI Assistant Director post for which he had been considered vanished upon MacLeish's resignation as director and return to the Library of Congress.[35] Siepmann became a consultant to the OWI, writing several key studies, including *Radio in Wartime,* where he linked soap opera listening to child-like susceptibility to propaganda and described Axis broadcasters as "demented dentist[s]" using radio "as a drill to work on the decay in our wisdom teeth and drive through to the nerve ends of our morale. Belatedly we recognize that we must 'put away childish things'" (1942, 27).[36] His story will resume in the post-war period.

John Marshall continued his work with the Rockefeller Foundation until his retirement in 1970, becoming the first resident director of the Foundation's study and conference center in Bellagio, Italy. In 1945 Siepmann wrote to Harold McCarty of WHA regarding their mutual benefactor, "I haven't talked to John Marshall, except briefly, for some time. I have an impression (no more) that he has gone sour on educational radio and is absorbed in his new European reconstruction plans."[37] Indeed, though the Rockefeller Foundation would continue to support some aspects of educational broadcasting through its General Education Board, the Humanities Division turned its attention back to more traditional concerns after the war. Other foundations, notably Carnegie and Ford, would pick up the cudgels for educational broadcasting in the post-war period, with the emphasis on television and a far more contentious relationship with the federal government.

But the impact of foundation-supported educational radio was neither confined to a few university stations nor to the intelligence and information agencies of the war years. The attention that their criticism focused on the commercial networks in the mid 1930s, along with the spirit of commitment to the cause of democracy brought on by the threat of fascism, provoked a high point in innovative production in the years before the war. Once again inspired by British example, yet taken in a whole new freewheeling direction by American writers and producers, the rise of the dramatic documentary feature marked a high point in radio creativity—and the advent of a new form of radio nationalism in the public service.

Culture in the Public Service

It is now generally agreed that radio, medium of the fireside chat and the Martian panic, Pepsi-Cola jingles and the NBC University of the Air, can influence human thought and action in powerful ways. American radio uses the power chiefly for merchandising. Drugs, foods and tobaccos, chief financiers of the medium, fill many of the choicest listening periods with gag comedy and escape drama. But our radio also uses its power—more fitfully—toward pushing back the horizons of public knowledge and understanding. It is with this crucially important function, with "public service" radio, that the present volume is concerned.

—Erik Barnouw, *Radio Drama in Action* (vii)

NBC and CBS had always regarded the provision of certain kinds of high-quality educational programs as part of their public service obligation—to create favorable public relations and to keep federal regulators appeased, if for nothing else. One of NBC's first, and longest running, educational/public service programs was *The Music Appreciation Hour with Walter Damrosch* (NBC 1926). Organized, written, and announced by composer and music educator Walter Damrosch, scion of an influential German-American musical family and director of the New York Symphony Orchestra, it brought an hour of musical instruction every week to schools across America, Friday mornings from 11am to noon.[38] It ran until NBC was forced to divest its Blue network in 1942. The music was provided by NBC's house orchestra, called the National Orchestra. In the wake of the Communications Act of 1934 NBC raised its musical profile further by hiring world-renowned conductor Arturo

Toscanini and renaming it the NBC Symphony Orchestra, inspired by the long-standing BBC Symphony Orchestra.

NBC also took a page out of the BBC's operations when it brought opera to the millions with its *Metropolitan Opera Broadcasts* starting in 1931. A young Alistair Cooke got his first American broadcast experiences doing intermission filler between operatic acts in 1937. CBS debuted its *American School of the Air* in 1930 under the direction of its strong-minded public service director Judith Waller. But during these early years, while CBS struggled to survive, NBC led the way in the prestige programming department, inspiring John Reith's confidence in its role as the next best thing to a BBC and providing much worthy material for its annual reports to the Federal Radio Commission.[39]

In the wake of the compromise between commercialism and public service programming in 1934, a host of new sustaining efforts found their way onto the airwaves. Most were produced in a distinctly American way: by providing airtime to various groups who originated and planned the programs themselves, then drew on the networks' assistance in talent and production. Most of these were educational, civic, or religious groups, but cultural institutions such as regional orchestras, museums, and libraries, as well as state and federal government organizations, also contributed programs that the networks produced and aired. One important emphasis, in the years leading up to the war, was on public affairs and discussion programs. Here the American networks could act with more freedom than their counterparts in Britain: though balance and impartiality were important goals of such programs, a civic organization supported by university and foundation funds broadcasting over a private network could risk navigating political waters that a publicly subsidized monopoly organization could not. The most prestigious examples were the Rockefeller-funded *University of Chicago Round Table* (Red 1933) and *America's Town Meeting of the Air* (Blue 1935), produced by George V. Denny, Jr. and the League for Political Education. It featured not only a changing roster of experts on challenging issues of the day, but unscripted audience questions and comments (Goodman 2007b).

Its prestige extended across the Atlantic. In March 1939 NBC London representative Fred Bate informed John Royal, NBC's Program Director, that "Sir Stephen Tallents thinks that a 'Town Meeting of the Air' program is needed here. He would appreciate any and all detailed information which we could give them enabling them to plan."[40] This became the model for *The Freedom Forum*, a panel discussion on the North American Service sometimes moderated by Edward R. Murrow; nothing like it would be tried on the BBC national network until after the war.[41] The Mutual network had since 1928 distributed *The American Forum of the Air*, hosted by Theodore

Granik with a live studio audience, produced by its member station WOR-New York. CBS lagged behind, but in 1935 took a decisive step to correct that with the hiring of a young Edward R. Murrow as Director of Talks, a position patterned directly on the BBC model. Soon the CBS news department, under Murrow, would take the lead with a whole new emphasis on news and documentary, as will be discussed below.

Public Service Documentary Drama

In the arena of cultural programming, particularly drama, the British influence is clear, though it took the exigencies of the pre-war years for what we might call "public service documentary drama" to hit its peak. By *public service documentary drama* I refer to the rise of original works written especially for radio, mixing drama and documentary in creative ways, with a frequent emphasis on the idea of nation and national identity—history, issues and problems, concepts such as democracy and freedom—and an underlying aesthetic of factuality, even when scripted and performed by actors.[42] Often, in the US, such programs were produced in conjunction with educational and/or state and federal agencies. They might also be sponsored (underwritten by private businesses) but with public service—and public relations—goals in mind. An early commercial example is the long-running US series *Cavalcade of America,* which dramatized scenes from American history for over 18 years on NBC, sponsored by the DuPont corporation and produced by their advertising agency BBD&O.[43] Some of the US's most serious radio dramatists cut their teeth on *Cavalcade,* including Arthur Miller, Norman Rosten, Morton Wishengrad, Orson Welles, Peter Lyon, and Stephen Vincent Benet. More drama than documentary, and more conservative than liberal at least in its earlier years, it took its historical factuality fairly seriously, drawing on a board of historical experts that included Dixon Ryan Fox, President of Union College and the New York Historical Association, and Arthur M. Schlesinger of Harvard's history department.

Another early mix of fact and fiction that would influence the public service documentary dramas of later years was the innovative *March of Time* series, created in 1931 by Roy Edward Larson, general manager of *Time* magazine, also produced by BBD&O. It presented dramatized news events, at first in a 10 to 15 minute weekly program distributed free to stations as publicity for *Time* magazine. Later it would add commercial sponsors and expand to a half-hour. Narrated by "The Voice of Time" (variously Ted Husing, Westbrook Van Voorhis, and Harry Von Zell), it employed hundreds of actors to vocally impersonate actual figures in the news, from President Roosevelt and King Edward VIII to Benito Mussolini and Huey Long. The show prided itself on sticking meticulously to events "as they happened," with nothing fictionalized but, as the producers insisted, "re-created." Yet elaborate staging with music and sound effects blurred the edges of factuality, produced at lightning speed by a troupe of actors, musicians, and one of the most creative sound effects teams in radio (Dunning 1998, 436). During the war, however, as recording technologies improved, it began to bring in more actuality voices. In this it influenced, and was influenced by, other emerging actuality/news programs such as CBS's *We The People* and the BBC North American Service's *Radio Newsreel*. A film version of *March of Time* debuted in 1935, shown before feature films in theaters across the nation; both radio and film formats were wildly popular (Bluem 1965; Fielding 1978).

In Britain similar experimentation went on under the heading of the "radio feature," and in fact the BBC drama department under Val Gielgud formed a special Features unit in 1936, with Laurence Gilliam at its head. Gilliam made the distinction that "Features dealt with fact, Drama dealt with fiction" but, as Briggs points out, "[w]here fact ended and fiction began was never clear" (Briggs 1965, 168). D. Geoffrey Bridson worked with Gilliam in producing some early acclaimed features such as *The March of the '45* (1936)[44], an historical drama, and also experimented with a new technique of weaving scripted dialogue, performed by actors but based on actuality recordings gathered from real people, together with narration, music and creative sound effects into a dramatic documentary presentation. Sometimes non-actors would perform from scripts derived from their own dialogue but written and shaped by Bridson; more often professional actors would take on the roles. Bridson had pioneered this technique at the BBC regional station in Manchester before taking up his position in London.

It was also in Manchester that producer Olive Shapley took advantage of the new Mobile Recording Unit the BBC had just purchased to bring actuality recordings of real people and places into the mix, cut into programs without mediation by scriptwriters; this was a true innovation on British airwaves where the unscripted voices of everyday people were rarities. As Scannell and Cardiff claim, "It was Olive Shapley who first took the van all over the region to record people talking in their homes, at work and on the streets. Single-handed, she brought to maturity the use of recorded actuality as the basis of the radio feature in those last few years before the war" (Scannell with Cardiff 1991, 345).[45] Shapley's work consistently engaged with political issues as she documented the lives of workers and the unemployed in the North region, including its women, making a connection between actuality documentary and political engagement that would strongly influence the radio projects of the Library of Congress under Archibald MacLeish in a few years time (discussed below). The rise of the "dramatized documentary" in the late 1930s, already linked to public service and ideas of regional and national identity, became increasingly linked to politics, and from there, in wartime, to propaganda.[46]

For, as CBS producer Max Wylie stated baldly, "it must be frankly admitted [that] the documentary broadcast is a form of propaganda ... The facts presented have a curious way of adding up to a point of view" (Wylie 1939, 449). Already in the mid 1930s, the Roosevelt administration's numerous New Deal agencies and projects had become frequent users of informational/documentary radio, raising vehement controversy over government-sponsored programs that would eventually affect wartime agencies like the OWI (Sayre 1941). For instance, the Radio Division of the Federal Theater Project, created in 1935 by the Works Progress Administration (WPA) to give jobs to unemployed writers, directors, actors and stage workers, "probably produced more radio programs than any other single agency," employing more than 190 people at its peak focused on creating programs for commercial networks that could find sponsorship (Sayre 1941, 22–23). Though its efforts included non-controversial programs such as a Shakespeare series and *Command Performance*, a series of adaptations of great plays, more contemporary adaptations like Clifford Odet's *Waiting for Lefty* and Pietro di Donato's "searing working class novel" *Christ in Concrete* (Judith Smith 2002, 213) led to discontinuation of its funding in 1939 after vehement debate in both the press and in Congress (Sayre 1941, 23).

The US Department of Education had become involved in radio program production after the 1934 Act set up a Federal Radio Education Committee (FREC), headed by John W. Studebaker, the Commissioner of Education, whose explicit mandate was to work with educational and cultural groups to produce sustaining programs in the public service in conjunction with both commercial and educational broadcasters. With funding from the Rockefeller Foundation's General Education Board, FREC initiated the Federal Radio Project in 1935, "to present national educational programs over networks, and to promote education by radio on local stations and in schools" (Sayre 1941, 71). Besides employing nearly 200 educators, actors, writers, and other professionals by the time it hits its peak in 1940, it worked with "an elaborate interlacing of advisory committees" (72) to produce a total of 12 major network series. Though these included such diverse types of shows as children's programs (*Safety Musketeers*/CBS 1936), straightforward "talks" (*Education in the News*/NBC 1934–38; *Have You Heard?*/ NBC 1936–37) and even a domestic serial (*Wings for the Martins*/NBC 1938–39), the highest profile productions all experimented with documentary techniques in the form of the public service documentary drama (Stevens 1974). Addressing issues relating to America's immigrant heritage, the contributions of women to US history, the role of government in solving social problems, and the history of civil liberties in the US, programs such as *Americans All, Immigrants All* (CBS 1938–39), *Gallant American Women* (NBC 1939–40), *Democracy in Action* (CBS 1939–40), and *Let Freedom Ring* (CBS 1937) mixed real-life concerns with dramatic presentation, and in so doing engendered accusations that the Roosevelt administration was using its position to solidify ideological aims.

The Columbia Workshop

By the late 1930s, less politicized venues existed as well for the public service drama/documentary, as networks sought to differentiate their public service efforts from the numerous crime, comedy, and domestic drama series on both day and night-time schedules—though politics would soon catch up with them. These programs provided a launching platform for a whole new breed of writer/producer unknown before in the US, whose influences can often be traced to Britain and the BBC. CBS was the first to launch an experiment in original dramatic production in 1936, *The Columbia Workshop*, at the urging of Irving Reis, a studio engineer whose earlier visits to Great Britain and Germany inspired him to "try to do an American version of what he had observed abroad" (Blue 6). CBS had just hired William B. Lewis, a former advertising executive, as its new director of programs, to fill the role they had advertised in 1935 as "A BIG MAN for an important creative and executive post in RADIO BROADCASTING." One of this big man's talents should be "to take rough or complete ideas from others and build them into good shows."[47]

With Lewis in place Reis's ideas fell on fertile ground, and his engineer's interest in experimentation with new sound production techniques merged productively with the network's newfound interest in serious drama and culture in the public service. *The Columbia Workshop* offered both adaptations and original works in a sustaining, unsponsored setting, and soon became a training ground for new writers (or writers new to radio) such as William N. Robson—who became the series' director after Irving Reis's departure for Paramount Pictures—Norman Corwin, Orson Welles, Arthur Miller, Irwin Shaw, Pare Lorentz, Arch Oboler, Milton Geiger, Max Wylie, and Archibald MacLeish, whose "Fall of the City" in April 1937 marked not only that poet's radio debut but a high point in radio drama thus far. Its dramatic allegory of a fascist victory over a helpless city set the stage for the engaged political documentary drama to come. The production techniques pioneered in the *Workshop* not only brought the use of sound effects and music into a central role—the show's music director and composer was Bernard Herrmann, later to achieve fame in Hollywood as Alfred Hitchcock's musical collaborator—but allowed for a whole new form of radio expression, combining poetry, drama, actuality, performance, music, and sounds unhampered by concerns of genre or story or sponsor, free to "stand or fall by the impression made on a public of unbiased listeners" (Coulter 1939, vi). All of this was produced live, of course, in the studio, in a highly complex and innovative process that the *Workshop* helped to perfect.[48]

Its impact was transnational. The *Workshop* traveled to Britain in August 1937 and set up at the BBC; from there Val Gielgud directed an adaptation of Hilaire Belloc's "Death of a Queen" that was short-waved back to the States as it aired on the BBC.[49] Later that year, Gielgud introduced his own "Experimental Hour" to the BBC "modeled on the 'Workshop' of the Columbia Broadcasting System of America. The new program was designed to give producers an opportunity to try out new techniques, and was put on late at night since it was realized that the plays 'might not be to the taste of a large public'" (Briggs 1965, 163). Its first production was a British recreation of MacLeish's *Fall of the City*; the series was canceled, according to Briggs, "not because the public was uninterested—the audience was again bigger and more enthusiastic than had been anticipated—but because 'worthy material' could not be found in sufficiently large quantities."[50] Gielgud himself contributed to the *Columbia Workshop*, directing his own original mystery drama "Fours Into Seven Won't Go" from the CBS Studios in New York in April 1938, where he admired American ingenuity but deplored "the tyranny of the stopwatch" (Gielgud 1957, 38) characteristic even of unsponsored productions.

Another example of the transatlantic connections of this trans-genre form was a 1938 documentary series called *The Story of America* developed for the BBC by American producers in New York and recorded on sound film for rebroadcast in Britain. Its first episode, *Ecce Homo*, written by documentary filmmaker Pare Lorentz, premiered live on the *Columbia Workshop* on March 21, 1938, and its recorded version aired in Britain that summer under its British title *Job To Be Done*, where it was enthusiastically received. As Max Wylie, CBS's head of production, explained, "The BBC for years has been presenting documentary or 'actuality' broadcasts, but 'Ecce Homo', which presented a picture of American unemployment, was the first American experiment in this technique" (Wylie 1939, 448).[51] The *New York Times* described it as "an impressionistic study of unemployment, in which factories in a thousand American cities were suggested merely by the steady click of a time clock and the shuffling of feet on stone floors."[52] This was not documentary or actuality broadcast as we would later come to think of it, but a dramatic form that concerned itself with real-life issues and invoked actuality through poetic use of sound effects and scripted dialect. Other productions in the series included *Crosstown Manhattan* (written by Norman Corwin and

Travis Ingham), *G Men Against Crime*, and *No Help Wanted*, a program about unemployment and the WPA written by William Robson that proved too controversial to air in the US; its only broadcast was in England.[53]

Norman Corwin

The Columbia Workshop is also responsible for cultivating the talent of the American radio dramatist probably better known than any other, though his star faded fast after the war: Norman Corwin.[54] A reporter and film publicist in his early career, Corwin came to the attention of William Lewis at CBS via a program of his own devising on New York Station WQXR, called *Poetic License*—basically Corwin reading poetry and other short pieces interspersed with music.[55] He was hired as a director at CBS, working on various programs until the *Workshop* offered him a chance to direct an adaptation of Stephen Crane's *The Red Badge of Courage* (July 9, 1938). More *Workshop* productions followed over the summer and fall of 1938, until the young director was granted an extraordinary privilege: his own series, titled *Norman Corwin's Words Without Music*. Its debut program would be broadcast on the *Workshop* on November 3, 1938 (just a few days after Orson Welles' *War of the Worlds* debacle) as "Poetic License." *Words Without Music* had its first independent broadcast on December 4, a straight-forward, but well-received, poetry dramatization; his first original script, "The Plot to Overthrow Christmas," would debut a few weeks later, on Christmas day (Bannerman 1986, 35–36).

Corwin was launched. His next program for *WWM*, both written and directed by Corwin, entered the more political arena; "They Fly Through the Air with the Greatest of Ease" (February 19, 1939) portrayed a bomber crew oblivious to the destruction they cause on the ground below. This production, with its clear relevance to the threat of war in Europe, "brought him instant national recognition" as letters poured in and reviewers took notice. It also won the very first award for "best demonstrating the cultural, artistic, and social uses of radio" from the Rockefeller-funded Ohio State Institute for Education by Radio (Bannerman 1986, 43). Maintaining his *Words Without Music* and occasional *Columbia Workshop* commitments, he produced two additional series, *Seems Radio is Here to Stay* and *The Pursuit of Happiness* (best known for Paul Robeson's performance of "Ballad for Americans") as well as writing and directing a few episodes for commercial programs. In 1941 CBS rewarded him with his own original series. *26 By Corwin* was folded into the *Columbia Workshop* schedule; starting on May 4, 1941, Corwin wrote an astonishing 26 half-hour original programs over a six month period. Despite the overall acclaim and favorable critical reaction, Douglas Coulter, the new vice president for programming at CBS, let Corwin know in November that his contract would not be renewed (Bannerman 1986). Yet, on the brink of war, Corwin's greatest successes were yet to come. Once again, transatlantic influences would come into play, as American and British interests converged, in a story that will be continued in the final section of this chapter.

Best remembered now amongst the public service sustaining shows of the pre-war era is CBS's *The Mercury Theater on the Air*, created in 1938 as a vehicle for the talents of Orson Welles and his Mercury Theater company. Besides his better-known theatrical work, Welles had for years worked in radio as an actor, on shows including *The March of Time, The Shadow, The Cavalcade of America*, and *The Columbia Workshop*. This new project was intended to serve as a venue for creative adaptation of classic literary works, under Welles' direction with John Houseman as producer and lead writer, along with Howard Koch.[56] Houseman and Welles had worked together in Houseman's adaptation of an Archibald MacLeish play, *Panic*, and in the WPA Negro Theater Project. They formed the Mercury Theater when their controversial production of Marc Blitzstein's *The Cradle Will Rock* got them fired from the WPA. The story of the Houseman/Welles/Koch adaptation of H. G. Wells' *War of the Worlds* has become famous, and need not be repeated here, except to say that its notoriety brought an end to its sustaining days; it was picked up by Campbell's Soup and renamed the *Campbell Playhouse* in December 1938.[57] It would also propel Welles to Hollywood to make the equally enduring and controversial classic *Citizen Kane*. Houseman would go on to become the first Director of the US external broadcasting service Voice of America during some of the most desperate days of the war. Here he would draw upon his experience with the drama/documentary, working closely with talented writers and producers from both the US and the BBC, to craft an emotional appeal for the service's programs that would both inform and inspire (Houseman 1979; Shulman 1990).

The Library of Congress Radio Research Project

One more fruitful site for radio innovation before America's entry into the war was the Library of Congress radio project under the direction of Archibald MacLeish. MacLeish was one of the carefully chosen recipients of the Rockefeller Communication Seminar's final report; perhaps inspired by its findings he applied in 1940 for funding from the Rockefeller Foundation, at John Marshall's suggestion, to "conduct an experimental radio project for a year or two to determine how best to utilize the Library's resources for broadcasts" (Gevinson 2002, 100). MacLeish, as Librarian of Congress (and renowned poet and playwright), was convinced that "democracy can be saved by educating the people to value the kind of life democracy makes possible" and that libraries had a responsibility to perform this kind of "popular education" by reaching out in the form of, in Marshall's phrase, a "genuinely democratic propaganda."[58] The Foundation supplied the funds, and also recommended two young men, Philip H. Cohen and Charles T. Harrell, both fresh from Rockefeller Fellowships at the BBC, to work with MacLeish. MacLeish's staff consisted at that time of pioneering folklorist and musicologist Alan Lomax who, with his father John Lomax, had assembled the Library's Archive of Folk Song; and recording engineer Jerome Wiesner, who had worked with the Lomaxes in their musicological forays and who would go on to become president of the Massachusetts Institute of Technology.[59]

Philip Cohen had spent several months at the BBC in 1938, observing its documentary units both in London and in Manchester. On his return he worked in the New York unit of the Office of Education's radio project and directed its Radio Workshop at New York University. Upon joining the Library in early 1941, Cohen drew on his experience to propose what became the "Regional Series," designed to "portray various American regions and communities in terms of their cultural and historical diversity and of their individual formulations of the traditions they have in common" (Gevinson 2002). Cohen directed the project, working with writers Joseph Liss (another Rockefeller Foundation Fellowship recipient) and a young Arthur Miller; they set out in a van equipped with recording equipment, much as Shapley had, to tour the country in search of grassroots voices and concerns (Cohen 1941; Gevinson 2002). They also planned to draw on the Library's Archive of American Folk Song and its voluminous written records of American folklore, history, and social life. The series had big goals:

> We show how specific industries, land, the way of life and the culture of the people, contribute to democracy and at the same time if such be the truth show why certain communities or parts of communities lack either a traditional or historical or economic background for democracy and how such shortcomings may lead to the establishment of undemocratic procedures and influence. In short, we show . . . the real significance of the big-concept words such as democracy, liberty, and America by breaking them down into their everyday manifestations in communities or regions throughout the country.[60]

As with Olive Shapley's and D. G. Bridson's experiments in Manchester, recording apparatus was used to collect dialogue, performances, and background sounds. Due to the limitations of the disc-based recording technology available to the team, these collected sounds could not be cut and reassembled without considerable degradation and awkwardness. Rather, they were intended to be used as a basis for scripted roles to be voiced by actors, embedded in a narration and performed live, perhaps with a few recorded segments dropped in from recordings for effect.

A number of programs were scripted for this Regional Series, with titles like "New Orleans," "Williamsburg," "Nantucket, Ahoy!," and "Hudson Valley," but only one was actually ever broadcast—"Rebirth in Barrow's Inlet," written by Liss, which was produced on the *Columbia Workshop* in October 1942. A fellow writer later called it "one of the greatest documentaries we have ever had on the air" (Carson 1949, 70), but CBS declined to take any of the others on the grounds of being "swamped with national and international broadcasts which they, themselves, were preparing" (Gevinson 2002, 106). MacLeish asked the Rockefeller Foundation for $6,000 to produce a recorded version of the programs, but this was denied. Thus the raw recorded materials for this series exist in the Library of Congress, along with the scripts, but the documentaries themselves were never actually produced.

John Marshall by this time had grown concerned that the project was not moving in the right direction. He first asked John Grierson (by then head of the Canadian Film Commission, which had grown out of Marshall's Rockefeller initiative) to intervene with MacLeish, who, in Marshall's opinion, had given Cohen and his team "rather too free a hand . . . the boys are getting more engaged by the possibilities of outside recording. I guess that is all right, but I would like to be surer than I am that they aren't neglecting what is right at hand in the Library."[61] They had already embarked on a second documentary series, called *Hidden History*, which was broadcast live on the NBC Blue network on Sunday afternoons May 18 through November 9, 1941. This series returned to the narrated, talk-style format more familiar to listeners (and funders), investigating key moments of American history with an emphasis on disentangling myth from multiple and contested realities, and demonstrating as well the multiple heritages and ethnicities that make up the American people. It ended each program with an appeal for listeners to send any historical documents or information in their possession to the Library of Congress. And indeed listeners did, dispatching diaries found in attics, recounting historical fables and tales, relinquishing family letters from the Civil War period.[62] MacLeish himself narrated several of the series' episodes.

Even as the *Hidden History* programs were being produced live in New York from scripts written by the team in Washington, the "boys" had embarked on their most ambitious project yet. A new series, "America in the Summer of 1941" (sometimes referred to as "The Documentary Series"), put them on the road again, not only soaking up actuality sound and preserving it on disc, but pioneering a technique that allowed a radical innovation to emerge on the scene. Material from the recorded discs was dubbed onto celluloid tape, most likely using the Millertape system developed by American engineer James Arthur Miller (or something very similar). Millertape employed a mechanical method to etch sound onto film (Miller had worked at Warner Bros. during the transition to sound period).[63] It thus did not need to be processed and could be played back immediately, though it could not be reproduced easily except via re-recording (unlike discs, which could be pressed from a master in great quantities). British commercial producers, most notably J. Walter Thompson-London, had begun using the Millertape system in 1936 to record their programs for shipment and broadcast across the channel; the BBC began experimenting with it in 1937 but only in 1939 when the Overseas service took over the old JWT studios in Bush House did it come into more widespread use (Sean Street 2006, 131).

The advantage of this system is that it allowed sound recording, for the first time, to be edited like sound film but without photo processing, enabling producers to mix actuality sound with music and sound effects, then re-master the production onto a disc. Engineer Jerome Wiesner rented such a system in the summer of 1941, and the Library of Congress radio team immediately embraced its possibilities. Cutting together conversations, interviews, and background sound they recorded in settings such as migrant camps, hog killing grounds, folk festivals, shelters for flood evacuees, gas stations, trailer camps, city buses, shirt factories, shipyards, and other locations (mostly on the East Coast), they could mix in music both recorded on the spot and from LOC recordings, adding narration as needed but with primary emphasis on the actual voices of the people—unscripted, unrehearsed, recorded on the spot, one of the earliest uses of modern documentary technique in the US. The team produced six 15-minute documentaries over the summer and early fall of 1941, recorded on transcription discs. None were aired on network radio, although, according to Barnouw, "The programs were broadcast by some sixty radio stations in 1941, and were very popular in the South" (2003, 79). In May 1942 a fresh set of transcription discs were made and the series was distributed by the OWI to independent stations under the title *This Is History!*[64]

By this time, war had come to the US. Somewhat reluctantly, Marshall had in 1941 agreed to continue Rockefeller funding of the Radio Project for two more years, but when MacLeish was appointed to the OFF by President Roosevelt in January 1942, the project closed down. Philip Cohen soon followed MacLeish to the OFF, then the OWI; the other project participants worked for that organization in various capacities too over the course of the war. Before shutting its doors on Feb 28, 1942, the team completed a few other broadcasting projects at the OFF's behest. The most successful—and probably the single one remembered today—was "Mr. Lincoln Speaks to the

People and to the Soldiers," with Walter Huston relaying Lincoln's historical speeches as though they were addressed to the contemporary American public; Douglas Fairbanks, Jr. narrated. It was broadcast live on the eve of Lincoln's birthday, February 11, 1942.

Radio's politics and poetics of neutrality in the United States before its entry into the war were indeed productive. As a medium of original creative expression, employing sophisticated techniques to produce unique aesthetic experiences, and as a growing concern both to educators and to the state, radio's social centrality reached a peak between 1936 and 1941 that would fade all too quickly after the war. But the heyday of the public service drama, and public service radio, was yet to come. It had been seeded by Rockefeller funding, parceled out in bits and pieces around the nation, and drawn on educational broadcasters, government agencies, civic organizations, and commercial networks; now it was to find both a mission and a home in the domestic and international propaganda efforts of wartime agencies. There it would intersect with communication researchers and with its allies from across the Atlantic to produce some sounds unheard before in either the US or Britain, nor indeed around the world. The final chapter of this section takes up the story of transatlantic exchange and innovation during the height of World War II, when both nations were in it together.

CHAPTER 6

In It Together: Wartime Radio

"Columbus discovered America in 1492: America discovers Great Britain in 1942." So William Holt, a former Yorkshire weaver, said in a recent broadcast to the U.S.A. The American army is over here; and our broadcast programmes are over there.
—T. O. Beachcroft, *Calling All Nations*, 1943

Of course, the war began in Britain more than two years before America became involved. The earlier part of this chapter attempted to keep this in mind, dealing with British events mostly before 1939, and with US developments before the end of 1941, when America entered the war. However, some elements of the transatlantic story do not separate out quite this way; they are intimately involved with the fact that, during the intermediary period, some things were possible—and indeed necessary—based on the imbalance between Britain at war and America balanced on the edge of neutrality. We have already traced the tale of WRUL, and noted the influence of debates over national identity and ideology as reflected in the US public service documentary dramas of the late 1930s. Between 1939 and 1942, startling innovations would take place in radio practice. Broadcast news would develop as an important and inseparable part of radio's service on both sides of the Atlantic, bringing the war into homes around the world and shaping the news format that we take for granted today. The first British radio domestic serial would be originated on the North American Service as a propaganda vehicle designed to draw the US into the war, with far greater impact on British broadcasting than on American opinion. Significant careers would be built in the interstices between Britain and America, public service and commercial broadcasting, political involvement and neutrality, such as those of Edward R. Murrow, Norman Corwin, and Alistair Cooke.

Then, from 1942 until 1946, US and British broadcasting converged. With the advent of the US Armed Forces Radio Service (AFRS), and specifically the American Forces Network (AFN) based in England for the duration, Britain had American broadcasters directly in its midst, invading not only its airspace but its cultural domain. In the context of war this was perhaps not as dramatic a disruption as it might have been, but its effects would be lasting as the BBC re-established its autonomy after the war, reorganizing its structure and rethinking its public service mission—and eventually introducing commercial television. Similarly, being located on British soil and operating alongside the BBC affected how Americans thought about radio. Pressures to reform the American system would build up during the war and break out shortly thereafter, leading eventually not only to publication of the "Blue Book" (traced in Chapter 7) but contributing to later developments like the quiz show scandal, the rise of television news and documentary, and the evolution of educational broadcasting into an established national service under a whole new regime of foundation sponsorship.

New: News

> Ed Murrow of CBS['s] nightly broadcasts to America will for ever stand out as the classic day-by-day account of Britain at war. Wherever there was action or anticipated action Ed would be knocking at the doors of authority to be allowed to participate – whether it was in a bomber flying over Germany, or watching the cities of Britain burn, or a raid on the coast of France. . . . He remained in England for the duration of the war enjoying the friendship and complete confidence of Churchill, Cabinet ministers and Service chiefs while his nightly broadcasts gripped even larger listening audiences back home.
> —Ronald Tree, *When the Moon was High*, 1975 (188–89)

Today, when broadcasting is mentioned, one of its most prominent aspects is the provision of news programs, or entire channels, that keep nations and the world up to date on breaking events and public affairs. But as late as 1936 neither the American networks nor the BBC considered the provision of frequent, regularly scheduled coverage of breaking news to be one of their primary functions. Both had experienced a troubled history of conflict with newspaper publishers and wire services over their right to become news-gathering organizations, and both worked under institutional conditions that militated against the initiation of centralized news coverage. But even more, both the BBC and the major US networks regarded the provision of nationally networked news as one of the least significant parts of their service—not only was it difficult, in fact news presented a minefield of dangers for national networks, both public and commercial. Potentially disruptive and controversial, news coverage left a network open to charges of bias, sensationalism, and unfair competition for both content and (in the US) advertising. Further, with sound recording and transmitting technology cumbersome, bulky, and studio-bound, the kind of live coverage on location that we now consider obligatory simply was not possible.

In England, the BBC had fought against the severe restrictions imposed by the Post Office from the beginning, under pressure from the wire services, over how much and what kind of news they could provide, and at what times. Hilda Matheson established a News Section within the Talks Department in 1927 but was not allowed to develop it due to pressures from the powerful Newspaper Proprietors Association combined with the Post Office, whose income from wire service revenue was threatened. Though Reith and his producers in the Talks Department continuously pressed for greater freedom, as late as 1936 the reporting of breaking news was still limited to three five-minute broadcasts per day, in the morning and late evening (so as not to scoop the press).

However, as noted in the previous section, such restrictions did not apply to the Empire Service, and by the mid 1930s the BBC felt some pressure to provide news from a British point of view to compete with the shortwave broadcasts from Germany and Italy, among others. This time Reuters and the Post Office went along with it, and the first news bulletins went out on January 4, 1932 from Chelmsford, though not for domestic audiences (Briggs 1965, 383). A news department was set up within the Empire service in September 1934, under J.C.S. MacGregor, with three sub-editors under him. It grew exponentially, in several languages, as war approached.

At home, Charles Siepmann as Director of Talks after Matheson controlled a small News Section from 1932 to 1933. Under his aegis an experimental *News-Reel* program was tried out, in which "news and comment were welded into a continuous fifty-minute programme, with switch-overs to Manchester and Paris, gramophone and Blattnerphone [wire recorded] excerpts" covering not only news but sports, interviews, and historical topics—what we might call today a newsmagazine-style program. This groundbreaking experiment was produced by John Watt, from the Variety department, but lasted only from July to December of 1933; it was, as Briggs comments, "too expensive to survive in the conditions of 1933." It now seems oddly prescient of forms to come, but before its time. In August 1934 John Coatman, a former colonial administrator, was brought in as news director and as a conservative balance to what were perceived as Siepmann's left-leaning tendencies. According to Briggs, conflict between the two led not only to the establishment of a separate news division but also to Siepmann's banishment to the regions, as Director of Regional Relations (Briggs 1965, 146–47)—something one suspects Reith regretted once the "Charter of Regional Rights" landed on his desk.

Coatman built up the division by hiring experienced newspaper journalists R. T. Clark and Kenneth Adam, both from the *Manchester Guardian*. The BBC began to do some independent reporting, with Reith's full support and attention. As mobile recording units became part of the BBC's practice, on-the-spot news and coverage of important sports and news events crept delicately in, despite formal press restrictions. By 1938, with war impending, the BBC news staff expanded to 31 and again to 39 in 1939, providing 95 minutes of news time on National and Regional networks combined between 6 pm and midnight (Scannell with Cardiff 1991, 121), with two main newscasts now at 6 and 9 pm.

This commitment to news as a national public service is what Edward R. Murrow observed and admired as he pursued his career in England. Appointed CBS Director of Talks in 1935,[1] he was dispatched to London in 1937 to take over the role of Caesar Saerchinger, arranging interviews with celebrities and important officials, providing shortwave relays of significant events, and generally functioning "as a light entertainment impresario" (Persico 1988, 118). From the sidelines, he watched a serious news organization grow inside the BBC, one that contrasted sharply with the situation at CBS back at home, where radio journalism at the time he left consisted of "the facts in five-minute news capsules, the drama of pseudo-news through *The March of Time*, and analysis by a handful of commentators" (Persico 1988, 128). Or, as another Murrow biographer writes, "To a generation familiar with the worldwide operations of CBS News, the Columbia setup of 1935 would seem almost laughable—a handful of people, five or six at the most, including White, Murrow, Jap Gude, formerly of the New York *Telegram*, now doing publicity and news editing, an assistant or two, and Bob Trout as the voice on the air" (Sperber 1986, 86). Even in 1938, "There was no studio for news broadcasting at CBS, only a suite of offices on the seventeenth floor for the Special Events and Talks staff" (Sally Bedell Smith 1990, 170). But in London, Murrow witnessed what news could become. More important, his "on-the-job training" all came at the BBC. Murrow had no journalism background or experience whatsoever before coming to England; whatever he learned about journalism, he learned in England at the BBC. He would continue to draw on his BBC experience for the rest of his professional life. Charles Siepmann would become a particular mentor.

Much has been written about Murrow's groundbreaking albeit seat-of-the-pants coverage of the Nazi invasion of Austria: in Vienna to broadcast a boy's choir, he found himself on the evening of March 12, 1938, in the midst of the crisis, frantically found a telephone and called in reports to CBS. On Sunday March 13 at 8 pm the first American "news roundup" was pieced together by Murrow and his fellow reporters, consisting of "live reports from Murrow in Vienna, Shirer in London, and newspaper correspondents moonlighting as CBS broadcasters in Paris and Berlin" (Sally Bedell Smith 1990, 171). This multi-point live hookup did not become a regular feature of CBS news until the Munich crisis in September; both the America networks and the BBC recognized at that point that radio news had moved into a new era and began to expand their operations intensively.

Over the course of that fall and the spring of 1939, CBS head William S. Paley "authorized [Ed] Klauber and [Paul] White in New York and Murrow overseas to build a staff capable of covering the widening story" (Sally Bedell Smith, 1990, 172). By 1941, when Murrow briefly returned to New York, "the news floor was almost unrecognizable, transformed wholly from the small setup he remembered into the hub of a global news operation, with correspondents in Europe, North Africa, and the Middle East; Moscow and Chungking; the Philippines and the Dutch East Indies" (Sperber 1986, 202). Crisp, factual reports broadcast from their source, frequently featuring the voices of active participants in the events at hand began to replace, or at least to compete with, the measured pronouncements of commentators. News bulletins interrupted regular programs, and found a greater presence on their own in the broadcast schedule. By 1941 news made up nearly 10% of the schedule on both the BBC and the US networks.

The fertile interchange between the BBC news operation and the new breed of American radio reporters was nourished, and controlled, by a special organization set up within the BBC called the American Liaison Unit, under the direction of Roger Eckersley. This unit worked closely with the Ministry of Information's American Division and with the Foreign Office (Cull 1995, 42). Eckersley saw clearly the crucial role that radio would play, surpassing even that of the traditional press, in getting Britain's message to America. In a report reviewing the year 1939, he lamented that government officials "seem unable to get British conditions out of their minds" in terms of the prominence of radio in the US compared to Britain, and went on to say:

> We hope, however, that this Department has been on the whole successful in persuading Government departments to begin to realize that the American broadcaster in London, speaking as he does to so many million people with the human appeal of the living voice, carries far more weight than a paragraph written in an American newspaper, or a printed news item emanating from Europe, which

has been edited and altered by the time it reaches the American public to such an extent that the original is often scarcely recognisable . . . the problem of ramming home the British point of view to American audiences is one of extreme difficulty, and in the short time at their disposal the American broadcasters certainly do give a vivid picture of life in England.[2]

This "new breed" of newsman (and most were men, as in "Murrow's boys;" a few women, however, elbowed their way to the frontlines despite opposition[3]) possessed a greater ability to shape the news than ever before. The radio newsman possessed "a power in his own right . . . [able to] address a nationwide audience directly—no editors, no rewriters, no headlines shoved over his copy—beating the newspapers by hours, reaching millions otherwise dependent for their foreign news on provincial papers, a rising national figure with direct access to the vast American public that was beyond the reach of the great metropolitan dailies" (Sperber 1986, 131–32). This was also increasingly true in Britain, though ironically, since Britain was already at war and America not, US reporters could often supply news via shortwave across the Atlantic that was denied for security reasons to British audiences.

Though Murrow's experience with the BBC and with the exigencies of wartime reporting may have spurred and influenced the build-up of CBS's news department, most accounts credit Paul White, CBS News Director, with overseeing the development of the modern network news organization. It is the documentary and interview forms with which Murrow would primarily associate himself for the remainder of his career, and his innovations here should be placed in the context of the emerging drama/documentary practice discussed above, and continued below. Murrow's famed intimate style, his focus on the first-person conversational narrative, owed something to BBC influence: "Ed noticed that BBC reporters didn't write; they dictated their scripts to someone who would transcribe them. Ed, a former speech major, copied that practice and dictated a narrative to Kay Campbell, who then wrote his script" (Edwards 2004, 53). But Murrow also innovated in the arena of unscripted broadcasts from a variety of locations; before the war he delighted in bringing ordinary British voices onto the air in programs like "Saturday Night in the Spread Eagle Pub at Little Barfield, Sussex" and his first-person reports from various war locations remain unequalled. When Murrow and his reporters cooperated with D. G. Bridson on the developing use of "scripted actuality" in such programs as *Britain To America* (discussed below), a new aural form was born.

The flexibility of Murrow's staff and other American network reporters, mixing with and sharing ideas with BBC personnel but not bound by their institutional restrictions, had an effect on many at the BBC as well. A young

Richard Dimbleby innovated along the lines of this new type of radio practice; as Scannell and Cardiff claim, "The on the spot report, the use of recorded actuality sounds from the scene of the action, location interviews with eye-witnesses – these things which are today the very stuff of broadcast news were all pioneered by Richard Dimbleby who, more than any other individual in the BBC, laid the foundations of modern broadcast journalism" (1991, 123). In this he was influenced by developing American news practices. Both Murrow and Dimbleby placed as much emphasis on creating a vivid sense of place in the mind of the listeners through detailed description, including recorded actuality of sounds in the environment— such as the fabled air raid warning sirens and anti-aircraft gun barrages in Murrow's early broadcasts from London rooftops—and focusing on the interview with its edited bits of real-life dialogue. Murrow also participated frequently in the broadcasts of the North American Service, hosting *Freedom Forum* and producing *An American in England* (discussed below), giving him valuable experience with the interview/discussion and documentary formats that influenced his *Hear It Now* and *See It Now* programs in the US after the war.

In the spring of 1943, the very heart of the war, Murrow received an offer from Brendan Bracken, then Minister of Information under Churchill, to take a position with the BBC. Murrow's biographer A. M. Sperber describes it as the Director-General's job; according to him:

> Of the two director-generals now working there in tandem [Graves and Foot] the former was ill, his resignation imminent; the latter, onetime manager of a utility concern, unable to run a broadcast operation of his own. They needed, in short, a sort of deputy director-general to take charge of programming, responsible for everything relating to the content of what went out, worldwide, over the BBC. Churchill wanted to know: would Murrow take the job? (Sperber 1986, 221)

This seems a bit incredible; the BBC had only removed its prohibition on employment of non-British nationals a few years before; surely even the liked and trusted Ed Murrow would not be offered the director generalship. In Felix Frankfurter's account—Murrow turned to Frankfurter, then a supreme court justice but formerly Murrow's professor and friend, for advice as approved beforehand with Bracken—the post on offer is described as "the program directorship of the BBC" and clearly marked out as the one presently occupied by Cecil Graves, who was seriously ill. Whatever the post, Frankfurter wrote "that the British should ask an American like Murrow to take charge of the BBC is a very extraordinary thing and shows how far they have gone in their determination for collaboration" and advised Murrow to take it, at least for the duration of the war (Lash 1975, 256–57). But Murrow turned it down, concerned that, in Frankfurter's words, "when peace comes there may be real conflict of views between this country and Great Britain" (Lash 1975, 256). In this he was prescient, as we shall see.

Some of Murrow's most famous broadcasts, like his first-hand account from a bomber over Berlin and his wrenching observations from the Buchenwald concentration camp, followed this moment, as he continued in his usual duties, taking the field of documentary reporting from strength to strength. Murrow returned to the States in 1946 to take up the position of Vice President, not of News but of Public Affairs, at CBS, with the news department just one of his responsibilities. One of his first actions was to create a Documentary Unit at CBS, headed by Robert P. Heller. A contemporary critic described the venture:

> They set up a documentary unit which was given talented leadership, a budget, and time to do its work, time to carry into effect what Grierson calls the documentary's first principle, the mastery of "material on the spot," time for the dig-in period for coming "into intimacy" with the material . . . Not until the CBS Documentary Unit was organized under Heller did radio attempt systematically to use its medium in a grand design of large resources, great artistic skill, and the purpose of stimulating action. (Carson 1949, 70)

Murrow drew on his experience with the wartime drama/documentary but even by 1947 announced a break with some of its aspects. In an address to the Institute for Education by Radio, he contemplated a move in a new direction:

> I think that future documentary programs will be concerned rather less with production than is the case in most dramatic broadcasts. By that, I mean I believe we will place more emphasis upon the importance of the individual hearing and understanding what is said, rather than over-riding the voice with music or with sound effects of any kind. (Murrow 1947, 380)

The emergence of a pared down post-war aesthetic effectively sounded the death-knell for the radio drama/documentary form; the shift to television, despite its technological limitations, would soon obscure what had been accomplished. But the years between 1943 and 1947 mark a high point in radio creativity never to be surpassed, with the transatlantic relationship at its heart.

The North American Service: Transatlantic Programs

We have already traced the build-up of the North American Service. By 1943 it had offices in New York, Washington DC, Chicago, and San Francisco, and had just appointed a BBC representative to Canada, S. J. de Lotbiniere. The service had achieved considerable success in getting the programs onto regular US network airwaves in the 1940 to 1942 period, with the Mutual Broadcasting System the most receptive. Yet even Mutual began to let NAS programs drop once the OWI and other authorized war-related programs began to crowd domestic productions onto home airwaves. The NAS then astutely turned to America's independent clear-channel stations (*BBC 1944*, 90–94). Yet it became more and more difficult for the NAS to make an impact on America's crowded schedules .

One strategy to address this problem was to bring the two nations directly together, in programs produced jointly with the major networks and beamed across the Atlantic. This practice is distinct from the one discussed earlier, of each side picking up the other's broadcasts on an irregular basis; here were often elaborate attempts to create transatlantic participation in production, for deliberate purposes of bringing the national cultures closer together (often with a strong political subtext, as we shall see). Several of them were also continued experiments in using shortwave radio, an increasingly important aspect of wartime communications. One of the first of these was a joint BBC/CBC/NBC production, the "weekly tear compeller" *Children Calling Home* (*Hello Children* in the US) which featured shortwave trans-atlantic conversations between children evacuated to the US and Canada and their parents in Britain (Gorham 1948, 117). But most of the NAS programs were produced in England, sometimes with a degree of American partici-pation, and beamed to America entirely for North American consumption; aside from the few exceptions mentioned below, British audiences were excluded from hearing NAS programs until a few of them were added to the Light Service after the war.

It should be noted, however, that British audiences were provided with an increasing stream of programs about America throughout this period, which correspondingly were not heard in the United States. Besides the long-running *American Commentary*, as Sian Nicholas explains, "broadcasts of sympathy and support by Americans were hugely popular items in the BBC schedules" such as that conveyed by programs such as *Hi, Gang!*, a variety show hosted by three American personalities, Bebe Daniels, Ben Lyon, and Vic Oliver (2003, 223). Other series were underwritten by the Ministry of Information in the tense 1941–1942 period to help British listeners form a more nuanced impression of America, its culture and its politics than those available through more familiar venues like Hollywood films, such as *It's*

Different in the USA, America Decides, and *Let's Get Acquainted.* By the end of 1941, many American variety shows had begun to be aired from transcription discs to British audiences (with all advertising removed), such as *Broadway Calling,* which consisted of a series of top US comedy/variety programs like *Jack Benny, Bob Hope,* and the *Edgar Bergen-Charlie McCarthy Show* (Briggs 1970, 314–15). By late 1942, not only weekly episodes of Benny and Hope but special OWI-produced programs like *Command Performance* and *Mail Call* were transmitted as part of the regular BBC schedule, and many American stars and news of American events were heard on British airwaves. These were primarily aimed at entertaining the US and Canadian troops, though they were also perceived as contributing to mutual familiarity and understanding.

On the North American Service in 1942, with the US now gearing up for war, a new initiative seemed in order. Both John Royal of NBC and William Paley, president of CBS, visited London that June. They returned with ideas for two long-running programs. In July 1942 NBC agreed to broadcast a series produced by Laurence Gilliam of the BBC's Features department, called *Britain to America.* Narrated by Leslie Howard, known around the world for his role in the 1939 global blockbuster film *Gone With the Wind,* it employed the dramatic documentary format, bringing a distinguished cast of actors to the air relating the war-time experiences of "typical" Britons, scripted from actuality recordings by D. G. Bridson and interspersed with music provided by the London Symphony Orchestra, specially composed for the occasion (Bridson 1971, 92–93). The effect was powerful enough to convince listeners they were hearing the real thing. John K. Hutchens of the *New York Times* praised the program:

> They come to the microphone and tell their own stories – dock workers, soldiers, housewives, girls who have replaced men in the war factories – and in their very understatement is an almost heart-breaking gallantry. A Commando who took part in the raid on St. Nazaire discusses it as if it were an afternoon's boat trip on the Thames. A woman who operates an ambulance plane recalls an 800-mile round trip to rescue a wounded seaman as a mere incident which doubtless it was to her. (Hutchens 1942)

Careful scripting and inspired acting were required to create this impression. Bridson produced the first broadcast and supervised the remaining twelve, which were written by various members of the BBC Features Department. Though billed as a joint presentation of NBC and the BBC, in fact NBC's role consisted simply of giving the program airtime. As Maurice Gorham (then director of the North American Service) put it, "John Royal knew NBC would not stand for anything [too] ambitious so he asked the BBC to do a series for them . . . NBC were quite satisfied that they had got better value than Columbia without going to any of the expense" (Gorham 1948, 129).

CBS did go to the expense of devising a very ambitious program, dispatching Norman Corwin to England to make a series of documentaries based on his own observations and employing all the poetic license and dramatic technique he had honed in the studios of the *Columbia Workshop*. Corwin's career had risen to a peak of prominence that no other radio dramatist would ever experience in the US; as one historian puts it "Corwin was now considered radio's 'poet laureate'" (Dunning 1998, 165). One of Archibald MacLeish's first acts as head of the Office of Facts and Figures (OFF) had been to initiate, at President Roosevelt's behest, a special program celebrating the 150th anniversary of the Bill of Rights. Corwin was assigned to write and produce this effort, an unprecedented 60-minute dramatic documentary to be aired on all four US networks at once, scheduled for December 15, 1941. As it turned out, the attack on Pearl Harbor and America's entry into the war preceded the broadcast by barely a week, giving the program an éclat few others have ever experienced. *We Hold These Truths* featured James Stewart as the "citizen" whose thoughts held the presentation together as an amazing lineup of luminaries played historical and contemporary figures: Orson Welles, Lionel Barrymore, Walter Brennan, Walter Huston, Marjorie Main, Edward G. Robinson, and Rudy Vallee. Bernard Herrmann wrote the score for the New York Philharmonic Orchestra conducted by Leonard Stokowski. It was produced in Hollywood in the studios of CBS affiliate KNX; President Roosevelt said a few words by hook-up from Washington. It was as high-profile an event as American radio could muster. An estimated 60 million people tuned in (Dunning 1998, 165).

After this triumph, Corwin took on an even bigger task: a 13 week series called *This Is War!* again to be broadcast across all four networks, again initiated and underwritten by the OFF's Radio Division under the direction of none other than William B. Lewis, Corwin's former boss at CBS. Corwin wrote six of the episodes himself and directed twelve of them. It ran from February 14 to May 9, 1942, also featuring the writing talents of William Robson, Maxwell Anderson, Stephen Vincent Benet, George Faulkner, and Philip Wylie. Not all the episodes were well received, and the series as a whole seemed far too close to government-mandated propaganda for some, and for others too filled with hatred for an ill-defined enemy (Bannerman 1986, 100). However, one episode had been recorded, flown to England, and aired on the BBC, where the response was "electrifying." By June Corwin himself was on the way to Britain.

His transatlantic series *An American in England* has been regarded by many as an absolute high point of the public service documentary drama technique, American style. Edward R. Murrow, an old friend of Corwin's then at the height of his influence in England, served as producer and liaison with the BBC, who granted the production the world-renowned composer Benjamin Britten, leading the RAF orchestra. It was broadcast in the small hours of the morning—4 am—to reach the US East Coast at 10 pm, where it aired on the *Columbia Workshop*. A young American actor, Joseph Julian, narrated the series at Corwin's behest. Though the first broadcast "London by Clipper" failed to transmit properly,[4] the series took off as a success on both sides of the Atlantic—unlike most "transatlantic" broadcasts, it was also aired for British audiences two weeks after each transatlantic debut, via recording, running from August through September, 1942. Shortwave troubles continued to plague the series, however, so CBS proposed extending the series but producing it back in New York. Corwin spent several weeks traveling all over Britain making recordings and notes, then produced the final four programs back at home; they aired in December and are best known now because of the better quality of the recordings: *Cromer* (December 1, set in a fishing village in England), *Home Is Where You Hang Your Helmet* (December 8, a look at English families on farms and in cities), *An Anglo-American Angle* (December 15, a program that explored the contrasts and similarities between Britain and the US; it had been aired live earlier but with poor transmission), and *Clipper Home* (December 22, tracing Corwin's return to the States). They were praised all over; as the *New York Times* summarized, "Everything is done in little touches, but the cumulative effect is profoundly stirring. These 'good, average, unspectacular people,' are the decent people everywhere in what is left of the civilized world. They are heroes without heroics; and Mr. Corwin honors them by writing of them quietly, warmly, personally, with the intimacy and detail of a good travel letter that catches not only the moment but the vast implications behind it" (Hutchens 1942).

Not only British-American relations, and Corwin's reputation, were enhanced by this no-holds-barred approach to innovative public service drama production. CBS had already begun to articulate a strategy of loosening sponsor control over its network programs, using prestigious and reputation-enhancing series like *Columbia Workshop* and the various other public service dramas it would produce over the course of the war to build up its own production facilities and creative staff preparatory to restoring the network to its former creative role. NBC, by contrast, stuck much more closely to the commercial benefits of time-brokerage. We will pick up this thread a little later in the story. The same contrasting strategies can be seen in the next generation of cooperative programs wafted across the seas. By this time US troops had been stationed in Britain and the AFN had begun to set up stations across the country. Perhaps in preparation for the blast of direct

US radio that British citizens were about to be subjected to, the next set of transatlantic programs was received on both sides of the Atlantic as well as produced in tandem.

Transatlantic Call: People to People debuted in February 1943 on CBS and the BBC's General Forces Programme simultaneously, following a visit to the US made by Laurence Gilliam of the BBC (Gorham 1948, 132). Produced by his features department on the British side one week, then by CBS's station WABC in New York the next, it was "a radio program in which free men step to a microphone and speak to all the world about the life they hope to lead."[5] This time, it was closer to being true. D. G. Bridson again produced the first broadcast, and then turned the others over to Features Department producers under his supervision; Louis MacNeice wrote the first six shows from Britain. Edward R. Murrow loaned his reporter Robert Trout to the project. They first traveled to the Lancashire town of Oldham, where Trout conducted the interviews with local people that were shaped into scripts by MacNeice and Bridson but, in the turn towards increased actuality, spoken by the residents themselves from their own houses and pubs and broadcast live in a complex, carefully rehearsed choreography (Bridson 1971, 97). As Bridson later wrote a bit boastfully, rebutting CBS's suspicion that he had used professional actors, "the only professional thing about the shows was the way they had been produced" (98). This technique made a considerable hit at CBS, so it was continued for the whole series with BBC staff producers. Robert Trout and the Features unit traveled next to Wiltshire, where producer Jenifer Wayne brought residents from carpet makers to an Earl to the microphone; another show, produced by Marjorie Banks, featured the Cockney residents of Lambeth Walk in London. The broadcast closed with a few words from Charlie Chaplin, a former Lambeth "mumming bird" (street performer) himself, by telephone from Hollywood. By contrast, the first three US versions were written and produced by Norman Corwin, and met with criticism that "he has told too much of the story himself. The result has been that the US broadcasts have sounded like chapters out of Baedeker, while the English have sounded like themselves."[6] Corwin's more florid, poetic "playwright's" style now contrasted badly with the pared-down "performed actuality" technique of the British series (thanks, in part, to the new intimate style of reporting developed by Murrow and his staff).

But Corwin fell ill and had to step aside; after a search his role was taken over by former Library of Congress documentarist Alan Lomax. In attendance at the first show produced by Lomax in 1943, live from Philadelphia to celebrate the 4th of July, was D. G. Bridson, newly arrived in the US to produce yet another transatlantic series. As Bridson recalls, "In the first of [Lomax's] *Transatlantic Call* productions, American actuality came alive: he spoke the same language and sang the same songs as Americans everywhere.

More to the point, he was able to help them speak that language into a microphone, and to get the full flavour of their characters across" (Bridson 1971, 101). The series ran in both Britain and the US for the next three years, carried by over 180 stations at its peak. Bridson and Lomax became close friends; through his intercession Lomax produced a series for the BBC NAS in New York in 1944 called *The Martins and the Coys*, a "ballad opera" based on the "hillbilly" ballad by bandleader Ted Weems and featuring folk songs performed by Pete Seeger and Woodie Guthrie, narrated by Burl Ives. Later Lomax would come to London and, partly through Bridson's intercession, produce a series of acclaimed programs on folk music for the BBC Third Programme that not only familiarized British audiences with the American Folk Revival but helped to encourage the revival of British folk music—and the development of skiffle—in the 1950s (Gregory 2002).

Bridson made his own contribution to understanding in the other direction in the summer of 1943 with a series of documentaries about life in America produced for the BBC in cooperation with NBC. Here he returned to the scripted and acted technique of his earlier years. His first was "An Englishman Looks at Chicago," aired live in the US and by transcription back home. Bridson also looked at San Francisco, the Alaska Highway, and Brooklyn, among other destinations. In Brooklyn he returned to actuality as the basis of his production, studying the speech of Brooklynites, devising a script based on their dialect, and bringing them to the microphone to play "themselves." *Time* magazine described his approach: "When Bridson got around to Brooklyn last week, he was stymied . . . He gave the professional actors a rest and let the Brooklynites speak for themselves . . . Star of the program was an unreconstructed drugstore-lunch-counterman, who spoke his mind in profound Brooklynese regarding some of his more rugged customers."[7] One wonders what British listeners made of lines of dialogue like "So I say to him: 'Your idiocy is very refreshing.' So he gets sore and wants to fight. So I say to him nice and polite: 'Hey, bum,' I said, 'stop knocking yourself out. The door's open. Beat it.'" Even more entertaining is Bridson's own account of bringing the unruly members of a Brooklyn youth gang to NBC's Rockefeller studios to record their parts before a studio audience (Bridson 1971, 108).

Bridson's final production during this tour of the US was an ambitious project called *The Man Who Went to War*, which he conceived for an all-black cast featuring the writing talents of Langston Hughes, African-American folk songs selected by Alan Lomax, the acting talents of Ethel Waters, Canada Lee, and Paul Robeson, with Josh White as singing narrator and the Hall Johnson Choir providing music. This might very well have been "the most expensive Negro cast ever heard in a single broadcast" as Bridson claimed; all donated their services for a fraction of their usual fees. Bridson called it "one of the most popular broadcasts I ever had on the air, being heard in Britain by nearly ten million listeners on its first transmission alone." It was never heard on American radio, largely to avoid paying the performers the union rates that domestic broadcast would have mandated. And though recorded on disc, it was later destroyed by BBC engineers; no copy exists today of what must have been a stunning, and ground-breaking, program.

NBC's response to CBS's success with *Transatlantic Call* stuck to the glamorous world of entertainment. Debuting on January 1, 1944 and running until February 2, 1946, *Atlantic Spotlight* aimed at "introducing top talent from both sides of the Atlantic." Unlike *Transatlantic Call* it was "a two way show", meaning it was transmitted simultaneously on both sides of the Atlantic. Maurice Gorham recounts, "with unexpected timidity NBC thought this too risky and wanted to have the whole show coming from London one week and New York the next, but we got them to try it our way and had some novel stunts such as a singer in London accompanied by a band in New York, and Bob Hope in Paris talking simultaneously to Leslie Mitchell in London and Ben Grauer in New York" (Gorham 1948, 132). It aired Sunday at noon EWT, not the best time for an entertainment show in the US, but a fine time to suit BBC schedules. Though the BBC liked it, by 1945 NBC could hardly be bothered—but this relates to the next stage in US/British relations.[8]

Reaching Across, and Down

[T]he writer [should realize] that this material must appeal to an audience of relatively limited mentality, an audience who believes in thrillers, is not squeamish about an overdose of sentiment, and is almost completely credulous . . . I should like to add that it is an extremely responsive and faithful audience—an audience that has a real influence on North American opinion. Therefore, the job to be done strikes me as very worth-while.[9]
—H. Rooney Pelletier, BBC Overseas Service, 1941

Such programs as *Transatlantic Call, Britain to America,* and *Britain Speaks* represent the high profile aspects of North American Service programs during the war years. They were as much vehicles for national prestige and propaganda as for cultural exchange, and certainly encouraged the process of creative influence and innovation among radio professionals working at the higher echelons of the industry, such as Norman Corwin and D. G. Bridson, who are still written about today. Though employing the voices and venues of "working people," they were directed towards the sensibilities of the educated elite.[10] But planners at the NAS knew that, if the political ends that underlay the entire enterprise were to succeed—and in the crucial period before December 1941 Britain knew they had to succeed—another approach was necessary. Not only America's opinion leaders and intellectual elite had to be won to the British cause, but the vast American middle and working class as well—less Anglophilic than their upper class fellow citizens, not as well-educated, more likely to come from Irish or German or Italian ethnic backgrounds, much more likely to listen to radio serials or soap operas than to high prestige productions—not at all the audience whose tastes the BBC was accustomed to considering. In the spring of 1941 a novel experiment was tried, one that would lead more directly to changes in British broadcasting after the war than to any discernible effect on Anglo-American relations. In devising and producing its first ever domestic serial drama, *Front Line Family*, the BBC found itself negotiating not only differences between Britain and America, but between high and low culture, public service and commercial production, and hitherto unaddressed differences between the cultural interests of male and female audiences. I have told its story in depth elsewhere[11], but its outlines are interesting enough.

Front Line Family derived from a 1937 short series of comedy sketches, titled *The English Family Robinson*, by Mabel Constanduros, a writer and actress known for her *Buggins Family* skits on the BBC's *Children's Hour*. In the spring and summer of 1940 Gielgud's drama department commissioned another two six-episode runs of the series, as a way to represent the conditions of wartime trauma and the Blitz that English families were experiencing. They were so popular with home audiences, particularly women, that Ernest Bushnell, newly appointed program director of the NAS, proposed that a daily fifteen-minute "family life serial" based on the *Robinson* framework might succeed in reaching North American audiences in a way that other programs had not—in particular, the primarily female daytime radio audience almost completely untouched by previous NAS programs. Bushnell may also have been drawing on his Canadian experience: in Quebec the popular *radio-feuillitons* (serial dramas) had been employed by the CBC as propaganda vehicles to persuade the more reluctant French Canadians to support the war and the military draft. The idea behind the new serial was frankly propagandistic; as Bushnell later put it, "What we were trying to do was to drag America into the war."[12]

Never before had the BBC attempted the production of an American-style five-day-a-week fifteen-minute serial, constructed not to end after a short run but to carry on endlessly; never before had the BBC given much thought to attracting female audiences as a part of the public with distinct, and valid, tastes and interests perhaps quite different from the Oxbridge graduates populating Broadcasting House.[13] Above all, serial dramas seemed to represent all that was worst about American broadcasting, whose daytime soaps were reviled by many on both sides of the Atlantic. Val Gielgud, Head of Drama, had for many years adamantly resisted any notion of serial production on the grounds of its inferiority as a cultural form as well as the way that the demands of series production would disrupt normal BBC practices. But wartime demanded sacrifice. A writer, Alan Melville, was hired after producing a few scripts based on recorded examples Bushnell obtained from the US. By March 1941 *Front Line Family* was in production, scheduled for an April 27 debut on the North American Service. The shows were recorded rather than broadcast live, as was standard BBC (but not US network) practice. Thus the much loved Robinson family made their debut: Helen Robinson, family matriarch, played by Nell Ballantyne, husband John (Ernest Butcher), daughter Kay (Nancy Nevinson), and sons Andy (Tony Halfpenny) and Dick (Paul Martin), and eventually more than 60 ancillary characters over the show's 7-year career.

Reaction within the BBC to the program was at first surprisingly favorable. Laurence Gilliam proposed that the show might be suitable for the Forces Programme. "They are really first class programmes of their kind and a type which is new to broadcasting in this country, and if they were definitely presented as something we are telling our American audience about Britain, I think they might have a very high appeal."[14] Though this proposal was rejected, the Overseas Service considered it a significant success and added the program to the General Overseas Service in the fall of 1941, though little evidence could be produced as yet that it was having much of an impact in North America. However, by September Melville was feeling the strain of having to write, singlehandedly, five episodes a week of an increasingly populous and complex narrative. In addition, some within the Overseas service, notably Maurice Gorham and Ernest Bushnell, were concerned that Melville's serial, while perhaps very good in its own right, was not having the desired impact in the US, its primary target. Written in a style more similar to Carleton Morse's highly regarded weekly evening series *One Man's Family*, yet produced five days a week and shaped to fit daytime schedules (given US radio economics), it fell between genres and was not reaching the intended audience. Melville's need for a break prompted the "New York panel" of the NAS to advocate that a more authentically American serial be produced, written by an American writer with experience in the field—perhaps even a woman, as was typical practice in the US. Melville himself recommended that they consider Mrs. Ronnie Colley, an American woman living in London, married to an Englishman currently serving in the Forces, who had experience as a serial writer for J. Walter Thompson (one of the US's leading ad agencies in the field of radio production).

Colley was asked for a week's worth of sample scripts; she began the process with an analysis of *Front Line Family* in its current state, from the point of view of American soap production. On the grounds of accepted American techniques, Colley criticized much of *FLF*'s existing narrative structure and characterization: it must have a main character, preferably a female one, more focus on the family and their conflicts and less on outside events, more depth of characterization, more emotion; Mrs. Robinson must get out of the house and into canteen work; and finally, regarding Kay's "futile" fiancé, Bill, "I suggest that Bill meet, as soon as possible, with a fatal accident." Then, Kay might meet a young Canadian doctor, rise to a position of responsibility in the munitions factory where she worked, whence the factory head might fall in love with her: "These are the main threads only, in broad outline, to show how to carry on the story without conflicting with the established technique of serial writing, maintain the background of war but without constantly using bombs, etc."[15]

These suggestions fell like a bomb at BBC headquarters. Though Colley's proposals were strongly supported by Maurice Gorham and others in the North American Service, Val Gielgud disagreed equally strongly:

> My own view of these Colley scripts is that they are perfectly fright-ful. The sentiments may be unexceptionable but they are also almost unbelievably dull. There is no characterization worth a damn and this is surely an essential thing in a programme of this kind, because without it there is no reason why people should take an interest in the characters concerned, considering how flimsy the plots are bound to be. The dialogue is not only undistinguished, it is incompetent. As specimens these are simply not good enough from any standard. I quite realize that the propaganda motive must be paramount . . . But sheer dreariness cannot be propaganda for anything.[16]

However, Colley's contract went ahead, and by 23 December she had com-pleted fifteen scripts, three weeks' worth, which had proceeded to production and were scheduled to be broadcast starting December 29.

Yet on December 23, these plans came to a sudden, screeching halt based on a dramatic last-minute intervention from the show's producer, John Richmond (supported, perhaps, by the fact that Pearl Harbor had precipi-tated the US into the war a few weeks earlier). In a memo he passionately refuses to continue working with Colley, declaring "The time has come when I must say – I cannot produce this stuff." Two pages worth of reasons are given, among them, "Above all, they are cheap . . . If the early ones were on the level of the Boys' Own Paper, the latest ones received are on the mental level of Tiger Tim's Weekly . . . I cannot see <u>anything</u> to recommend them."

This provoked a crisis; meetings were called and reports were written; Colley was terminated and Melville temporarily brought back in, himself imposing the proviso that none of Colley's work be aired.[17] He would labor mightily to make up the difference. Colley protested strongly and eventually took her objections all the way to the Director General of the BBC, claiming that she had received nothing but encouragement yet had the rug pulled out from under her unfairly; here, she vanishes from our story. Melville took up the reins and the serial continued, but by February 1942 Melville's determination to leave his deferred job to join the RAF meant a search for a new writer. Once again some of the same conflicts surfaced. Now they are couched in more overtly gendered tones:

> It is becoming clearer that the right choice among the available writers depends on the future policy of the serial. If a domestic serial is wanted with human interest and inter-play of individuals within the family as the "leit-motif", then a woman writer may be the right answer. If the serial is to continue developing as a microcosm of Britain at war, embracing life in the Services, factories, etc. etc., a woman is automatically ruled out, and a dramatist who combines story-telling ability with reporting flair is wanted.[18]

Apparently in the eyes of the BBC, not only were storytelling and reporting male prerogatives, but no woman could possibly be equipped to tell the "real" story of Britain at war. (And, though it is left unstated, definitely not an American.) Indeed, once Mabel Constanduros was considered (largely, it seems, in light of her unattributed—and uncompensated—influence on the basic concept) and turned the project down, the bulk of writers for *FLF* would be male. Basil Woon took over from Melville, followed by Ronald Gow, Ted Willis, Donald Henderson, and Adrian Thomas. Two female writers hired in the serial's final years, Jonquil Antony and Lesley Wilson (another Canadian), would go on to become primary writers on *Mrs. Dale's Diary*, *FLF*'s successor.

However, *FLF*'s listeners no longer consisted of North Americans alone. Its addition to the General Overseas Service schedule meant that it now could be heard not only in the US and Canada (where it was being re-broadcast from recordings as part of the regular CBC schedule[19]) but also by British citizens living in Australia, New Zealand, most of Africa, India, Barbados and the West Indies, Malta, and South America, as well as through-out Europe. The BBC later claimed that "over a period of seven years, almost daily, 4,000,000 people in the British Empire followed the fortunes of this family with affection"[20]—still excluding domestic audiences, however. Their enthusiastic interest proved that not only Americans responded to the serial form and that even BBC-schooled listeners could find its message appealing and morale-raising. In May 1942, a special Listener Research study reported that "Front Line Family appears to have created more general interest than any programme other than the news . . . it appears that our audience feels unusually strongly about it."[21] Though the show had its adamant detractors (even more adamant than usual, eg: "It is a moronic entertainment"), a further study in August 1942 produced comments like:

> I don't ever remember listening to any play so full of human life, family squabbles and humour, as 'Front Line Family.' It is too great for words. I would rather miss my dinner than miss that. (Johannesburg)

> I would not miss it for worlds. It is so real and I hope it continues for ages. (Canada)

> There is no doubt that 'Front Line Family' is one of your most popular features. It is even closely followed by many of our coloured community. (Cape Town)[22]

The show was taken off the air in India and Africa briefly in early 1942 because of strong objections on the part of military officials; the fact that civilian populations (particularly women) appreciated the program and expressed themselves vociferously caused it to be reinstated. By June 1942 it had become so well established that, according to Briggs, "the Germans produced a programme called 'Our Version of Front Line Family,'" presumably as counter-propaganda (1970, 404).

On May 7, 1942, another proposal was made to add this popular show to the Forces Programme, the first time such a crossover would have occurred, but it was squelched the very next day by Gielgud's strong objections, this time delivered not just intra-departmentally, to his subordinate, but to Gorham and the Assistant Controller of Programmes:

> I was frankly quite appalled at the small beer and the middle-class dreariness of the whole thing. I know, as far as the series is concerned, it is my business to put it on and not to guarantee its standard, but I would like to be reassured that you are really convinced that the North American public is eagerly lapping up stuff of this kind . . . I do not pretend specialist knowledge on this point, but on the basis of quite normal human experience, I must beg leave to express the gravest doubts about it.[23]

Yet as the program stabilized and found a steady group of authors, it went from strength to strength. In 1943 an internal memo reported that Sir Ian Fraser, a member of the BBC Board of Governors, was an avid listener.

> When I was making my routine report to the Board on Thursday last Sir Ian Fraser made special mention of this regular listening to FLF. As a result of rather informal discussion I was asked to carry away from the Board Meeting a message of congratulation to all those concerned with this serial on its completion of two years as an unbroken series.[24]

It continued on the General Overseas Service through the end of the war, changing its name to *The Robinson Family* as the war receded and in July 1945 became one of the first shows to make the transition from the North American Service to the new Light Programme, scheduled to run from 2:45 to 3:00 pm, Monday through Friday, in American fashion. Finally, British audiences at home experienced their first continuous daily serial that reflected the family life of the nation, probably one of the last in the world to do so (except for English-speaking Canada). The program moved to 4 pm in March 1946 and earned some of the highest ratings of any BBC daytime program, with over three and a half million listeners. In 1947 its name was changed again, to *The Robinsons*.

The Drama department, in response to its popularity and perhaps also to Gielgud's continuing misgivings, established a special division to handle serial production. The success of its other long-running adventure-based serial *Dick Barton*, initiated in 1946, would make radio serials a part of everyday BBC, and British, life. Though Gielgud finally managed to persuade the Light Programme to kill off the Robinsons in 1948, they were immediately succeeded by the equally popular Dale family of *Mrs. Dale's Diary*, which in turn gave rise to Britain's longest-running radio serial *The Archers* in 1950, still on the air today. Though Gielgud remained adamant about the dangers of the serial form until his very last day as Head of Drama, the enduring tradition of British domestic serials had taken root. *Front Line Family*'s television successors *Coronation Street* and *EastEnders* have remained the top-rated programs on British television for decades, though it took wartime exigency and transatlantic propaganda to pry open a space for this deeply British tradition on domestic airwaves.

Another program that would become a popular favorite and succeed in carrying over onto the Light Programme after the war was *Transatlantic Quiz*. This show had started out as a feature called *Answering You*, which debuted in 1943 on the NAS supervised by BBC Talks producer Mary Adams. Along the lines of *Information Please!* and *The Brains Trust, Answering You* encouraged US listeners to send in questions about British life and culture, which were answered on the air by "every sort of talker from the ordinary housewife to the Speaker of the House of Commons" (Gorham 1948, 132). It was picked up by Mutual for its Saturday morning schedule. During its first year Alistair Cooke was brought in to host a few of the programs. As described in his biography, each program began with the announcer in New York stating "This is New York calling the BBC in London" followed by the reply "This is the BBC in London answering you ... Ladies and Gentlemen, through short-wave facilities we span 3000 miles of ocean to bring you the BBC's transatlantic discussion programme" (Clarke 1999, 189).

In 1944 the decision was made to try a two-way transatlantic shortwave version, with a panel of experts on both sides who posed questions to each other. Its title was changed to *Transatlantic Quiz* and it wafted across the war-torn airwaves for the first time on April 15, 1944, co-produced by the Blue network in the US and the BBC. It was hosted on the American side by Alistair Cooke, with Christopher Morley as the primary American expert partnered with a changing roster of guest panelists; on the British side Lionel Hale compered with panelists Denis Brogan, a Scottish historian, and actor David Niven, later replaced by actress Joyce Grenfell. As *Time* magazine described it in 1945:

> For ten months Manhattan's tweedy jack-of-all letters, Christopher Morley, and Britain's critic-historian (and authority on U.S. matters), Denis Brogan, with a partner apiece, have pitched "stumpers" at each other by short wave. The questions are designed to determine "who knows most about the other's country." The show's aim: to promote Anglo-American understanding with geniality instead of gags, and without benefit of cash awards.[25]

This format proved quite popular, prompting a move to the evening schedule and an increase in length from 15 minutes to a half hour on Tuesdays at 10 pm, US EWT (Eastern War Time). Like other NAS programs, only Americans could listen in; British audiences were excluded from this particular venue of Anglo-American understanding.

Though it faded out in September 1945 in the US, Maurice Gorham made the decision to pick the program up for domestic consumption in Britain on the newly launched Light Programme in July 1945. As he argued, "It seemed incongruous that a BBC programme with so much appeal to both sides should be heard only in America, and I jumped at the opportunity of scheduling it. It went on at a good time on Sundays and was a success from the start. It beat the Brains Trust in size of audience and became the most popular speech broadcast on the air" (Gorham 1948, 130). In 1946 a BBC television version aired briefly, and in 1947 it would be reconstituted on radio as the *Round Britain Quiz,* dropping its transatlantic emphasis in favor of challenging British national knowledge. Amazingly it still attracts audiences on BBC Radio 4 today. From 1996 until his death in 2006, it was hosted by longtime BBC journalist Nick Clarke, who is also the author of the only substantive biography of his 1940s predecessor, Alistair Cooke. Cooke himself would go on to develop his transatlantic personality and observations after the war, on both sides of the divide; his story resumes in Chapter 7.

By late 1943, the BBC North American Service had innovated so many successful programs, and had made such headway placing them on US stations, that a note of alarm was sounded in the American broadcasting industry, despite the pressures of war. As early as March of that year, John Royal of NBC sent a note to Frank Mullen, vice president in charge of operations: "You will be interested to know the activities of the British Broadcasting Corporation in America". He pointed to their expansion from one small office in the British Empire Building at Rockefeller Center to three floors in the International Building, the opening of offices in Chicago and Washington with more planned, and their enlarging circle of contacts, with more and more programs placed on independent stations, "all under the direction of the Foreign Office." By October Niles Trammell, the president of NBC, expressed a more direct threat:

> You will recall in the early days we had a gentleman's agreement with the BBC whereby we would not affiliate with high power commercial stations in France, Ireland and Luxemburg and they in turn would not attempt to exploit the local stations in America. This has evidently changed.

A few days letter, William S. Hedges, VP in charge of station relations at NBC, wrote directly to Colonel Edward Kirby at the War Department in Washington, reporting that the BBC was "making arrangements for some 100 radio stations in America to broadcast locally over their transmitters program which will be originated in London by the BBC . . . My reaction to this is that this is a job which should be done for Americans and by Americans."[26] This newly competitive attitude would play itself out ultimately in a venture that threw American and British broadcasters into direct contact, with contentious and lasting results.

Over T/Here: The American Forces Network

> By the middle of the war, the standing of the BBC had never been greater. All Britain and much of Nazi-occupied Europe listened to its news broadcasts. Yet at this high point in its history, the BBC spent months in an extraordinary attempt to stifle at birth a broadcasting service intended only for homesick American troops, the American Forces Network.
>
> —Patrick Morley, *This Is The American Forces Network* (xiv)

> The whole scheme is so alien to the tradition and practice of broadcasting in this country that to enumerate at this stage all the possible anxieties that may arise can only lead to wasted days and sleepless nights. I put forward, however, one consideration which, to my mind, transcends in importance any [other] . . . It is not unlikely that various parties who are interested in seeing a highly commercialised set up for British broadcasting after the war, may point to the American Forces Network as an example of a normal commercial chain and the programs it can produce, with accompanying disparagement of BBC output.
>
> —DPP memo, 27 April, 1943[27]

Whatever the trials and tribulations of transatlantic understanding in the build-up to the war, the events of December 1941 precipitated the nations and the broadcasting services of Great Britain and the United States into closer proximity than either had fully anticipated or desired. The long anxious years of careful British propaganda strategy had paid off; the Americans had entered the war and arrived on the shores of Britain itself, in the friendly invasion before the joint hostile one. Now what to do with them? Clearly one thing needed by the troops was entertainment, as the Forces Programme had established, but would British entertainment suit American troops? From the beginning the American answer was "no." American troops needed their own familiar radio service the same way that British troops needed the BBC.

The story of the American Forces Network in Britain—and its post-D-Day successor, the Allied Expeditionary Forces Programme—has been told in detail by Patrick Morley, among others,[28] but this chapter will focus on its peculiar moment marking both the greatest cultural convergence two independent nations may have ever willingly subjected themselves to, as well as their simultaneous—and inevitable—recoil and conscious divergence. Out of British and American cultural collision would come not only lasting and meaningful cross-connections that continue on to the present day, but a renewed effort to mark out distinctions and push back transnational influence, in both the political and cultural spheres.

The BBC had made a regular practice of broadcasting special programs for Canadian troops stationed in Britain since 1939. Ernest Bushnell, mentioned above, came to England originally at the behest of the CBC to coordinate such broadcasts, before his appointment to the North American Service. Limited to a few hours per week, such programs went out over the Forces network and were heard by troops and citizens alike. The Canadians had never pushed for more than this, despite the growing numbers of Canadian troops and civilians far from home. On the American side, as of early 1942 the OWI had not yet organized an overseas radio unit, though a precedent had been established early in 1941, when US soldiers stationed in Iceland to protect shipping lanes, "restive, fighting monotony . . . were constantly disappointed to tune in 'football' results from the BBC only to hear results of cricket and soccer matches. Could the War Department arrange to short-wave American baseball and football results?" (Kirby and Harris 1948, 15). This was achieved, setting a precedent for later broadcasts.

When the first American troops began to arrive in Northern Ireland in February 1942, US military authorities asked if a few programs couldn't be sent out over the BBC especially to suit American interests, but were turned down, on the grounds that a good number of US programs already took up scarce BBC airtime. A request to allow low power transmitters to be set up on US military bases also ran into both technical and bureaucratic problems. Fierce resistance broke out within the BBC and in other quarters; as Morley recounts, the British authorities felt they could not possibly give the Americans a privilege that had been denied to other non-British fighting units, notably the Polish forces in exile in Britain since 1939 (2001, 13). Besides, as they pointed out, to create a separate service for US troops would be to encourage their further insulation from British people and culture (Gorham 1948, 134). And, naturally enough, the idea of a foreign power broadcasting on domestic airwaves awoke not so much propaganda fears—as so much energy and attention had gone into bringing US and British political propaganda into coordination—but uneasy memories of the offshore commercial broadcasters before the war. Would the AFN work as a Trojan horse, smuggling commercialized broadcasting into Britain itself under cover of war?

But the formation of the Armed Forces Radio Service (AFRS) under the auspices of the Office of War Information (OWI) in early 1942 under the direction of Thomas H. A. Lewis, a former radio advertising man, meant that the Americans came to the table in the summer of that year with a considerable, and strongly backed, organization already in place, and an assumption that Britain was no different than the other places where US troops were stationed, and where AFRS radio stations were rapidly being established. Brewster Morgan of the OWI (formerly of CBS) was assigned as point man to negotiate with British authorities. Meeting with resistance, he was able to offer the BBC an agreement that, while not overturning their objections, at least offered some benefits in exchange. As reported by Morley:

> All programs on the 'troop network' (including the top US shows) would be offered to the corporation *first* for broadcasting in Britain. And the BBC would also have first choice when it came to the big American stars who were expected to cross the Atlantic to entertain the troops and appear on the new network (2001, 23).

This would allow the BBC to maintain its pre-eminence in providing entertainment programs and enable it to keep its hold on British audiences. Perhaps Laurence Gilliam expressed the dominant BBC attitude the most clearly:

> We cannot spend much of our limited output aiming directly at the American troops, though I agree that we should aim to get them listening to our stuff and liking it . . . generally speaking the ordinary American does not like British radio. It is going to be a very hard job to make him like it, but the attempt should be well worth making as it might result in the British listener liking British radio![29]

The popularity of American-style programs on the BBC would prove to be a double-edged sword in the debates over policy that would begin as early as 1943. Meantime, plans for the American Forces Network met with swift if somewhat grudging approval, under a series of limiting conditions.

The new network agreed to broadcast a substantial number of BBC programs, to conform to general BBC broadcast guidelines (including the elimination of commercial advertising), to confine transmitters to low power, and to install them only near military bases, well removed from population centers, so as not to interfere with British broadcasts. No transmitter would be based in London, even though all programs would be produced there, but special locations throughout the city were eventually wired for AFN reception, where service personnel could gather and listen. Later, exceptions would be made and transmitters located outside of Oxford, Bournemouth, and Bovington, only twelve miles northwest of London, because of heavy troop concentrations in those areas. But it was Britain's rural heartland and farther reaches—in the west of England, East Anglia, northwest England, and in Northern Ireland—that the AFN could be heard clearly by the local civilian populations, as well as by the nearly 2 million US servicemen and women eventually stationed there. Over 5 million Britons, it was estimated, began to tune in regularly.

The AFN made its debut broadcast on the Fourth of July, 1943. Most of its programs came from the AFRS in the form of recordings shipped from America, consisting both of "denatured" commercial network programs (with the advertising material removed and usually replaced by various kinds of announcements and advice to the troops) and AFRS original productions such as the high-profile *Command Performance* (featuring top Hollywood stars in a variety of genres), *Mail Call* (similar but focusing on comedy), and *Jubilee* (featuring top African American jazz and swing bands), along with news and sports by shortwave (Kirby and Harris 1948, 20). The AFN also began to produce its own programs, like the popular *Duffle Bag*, a musical request show DJ'd by Sgt. Johnny Kerr, and Corp. George Monaghan's equally popular *On the Record*. They became favorites of younger British listening audiences and had a great influence on the course of transatlantic popular music exchange after the war.

Other programs took on a more serious information task, such as *Combined Operations*, a kind of *Information, Please* with British and American servicemen asking questions of each other; *GI Tommy*, an interview with a British soldier just back from the front recounting his experiences; and *Weekend Leave*, a show that gave US troops suggestions for places to see on their short breaks from duty (and how to behave when they got there). The network also carried BBC programs, including *ITMA* (which most Americans found hard to follow) and a wide variety of musical and informational programs, though these made up only 25% of broadcast time "rather than the 50% hoped for" (Morley 2001, 50). Some debates cropped up over the less careful, more personal American news style compared to the BBC, but overall the AFN successfully served both its key audience—US troops—and its ancillary, unintended one, with few overt pitfalls.

Behind the scenes, however, the course did not run so smoothly. Many fears were expressed by BBC officials that the slick, glamorous, expensively produced American programs made the pared-down BBC operation sound dull and inadequate by comparison, as in the quote above, and ultimately would work to undermine the BBC's monopoly after the war. This was not helped by a certain amount of gloating from the American side. Even before the AFN debuted, *Variety* was shouting in 2-inch headlines, "BBC FACES PRESTIGE LOSS – Missing Out on Entertainment" and, while praising it as "not the least of the weapons that the Allies count on to win the war," making predictions that "the BBC is going to have a fight on its hands for its listening public when peace comes again."[30] *Broadcasting* magazine in September 1943 summarized a long article in Britain's own *Economist* predicting that competition in radio service, if not commercialism, would be required after the war.[31] Such predictions only intensified the reaction that had begun to set in within BBC itself against American-associated influences in the area of music, with certain crooners banned, "slush" and "over-sentimentality" barred from the air, and the "blacklisting" of certain songs and performers (Morley 2001, 46).[32] Meantime American broadcasters, threatened by the Roosevelt administration's investigation into network monopoly power, inveighed against "control by government" illustrated by the BBC in order to defend their own untrammeled enterprise (Paley 1943). The old rhetoric was reawakening.

But it was over the creation of the joint Allied Expeditionary Forces Programme that barely suppressed tensions came out. Morley tells the story of this program intended to serve Allied forces in Europe. The BBC was determined that Americans would not control this service, despite their much larger and better funded media machine; and though commanded from the very top to create a service equally representing, and produced by, British, American, and Canadian personnel, the BBC intended to sit firmly in the driver's seat, and to keep the Americans to their 50%, no more. Maurice Gorham was appointed to lead the effort, braced by his years of experience in the North American service, and with only two weeks preparation the service debuted on the day after D-Day, June 7, 1944. Programs mostly derived from the BBC Forces program and the AFN, but a growing number of original programs strove to bring the US, British, and Canadians together in a truly joint broadcasting effort. Morley demonstrates convincingly that, despite the disputes overhead, on the ground level a strong camaraderie produced inspiring and memorable programs that did their job of promoting cooperation and inter-allied morale. *Combat Diary* brought actualities of war experience from troops across the European theater. The popular two-hour daily morning program *Rise and Shine* presented top recorded hits co-spun by Ronnie Waldman of the BBC and Dick Dudley of AFN. As Morley describes the show: "They were the ideal Anglo-American combination, and their first words emphasized the two-nation approach: 'Hi fellers' from Dick Dudley, and 'Morning, blokes,' from Waldman" (2001, 97). Gerry Wilmot of the CBC subtly and skillfully negotiated the Canadian presence when opportunity permitted.

Yet the network identifier insisted upon by the British authorities—"This is the Allied Expeditionary Forces Programme *of the BBC*"—continued to alienate the Americans, even as—ironically—the many AFN programs carried on the AEFP meant that thousands of home listeners across Britain who had previously been excluded—including, finally, London listeners— could now get AFN programs on a self-proclaimed BBC channel, causing greater identity confusion issues for the BBC. As Gorham himself put it, "If this isn't inter-allied co-operation I don't know what it is—unless it's murder!" (Gorham 1948, 149). The AEFP continued until the end of the European conflict, shutting down on July 28, 1945. The AFN stayed on the air across occupied Europe, though its British presence ceased in late 1945. In Germany AFN would remain a resource for American troops (and young German audiences) until the early 1990s.

Part 2 Conclusion
Post-War Visions

It is an important continuing objective of British broadcasting that the programmes should be firmly British in character, and should, by reflecting our national environment and characteristics, have the effect of encouraging and consolidating listeners in their feeling for British speech, culture and institutions. This implies a steady, friendly resistance to foreign influences and particularly to the Americanisation of our programmes. During the war there has been a considerable infiltration of American entertainment, which as a temporary phenomenon is welcome and legitimate; and genuine American entertainment of the highest quality will always, I hope, be able to find a place in our programmes. But the by-product of this wartime vogue have not been so welcome – sham American entertainment produced in Britain, the unnecessary use of American slang, crooning in spurious American accents, and the pursuit of American idioms, sentiments, and rhythms. The reaction on our part should be positive and constructive, aiming at the establishment of authentic British entertainment, native idioms and accents and the best possible use of the richnesses of our own ways of expression. I would like all output departments to consider the problem and, where appropriate, make proposals.
    —William B. Haley, Director-General, 1944[1]

American radio is great and is emulated by practically every nation in the world save the dictatorships and England, because there is the competitive spirit and the incentive to excel. How England can harbor a free press and a kept radio is hard to fathom. It's one or the other.

—Editorial, *Broadcasting,* 1944

Already in 1943 and 1944 the shape of post-war broadcasting had begun to loom large, in both countries, inspired at least in part by the collision of ideas and practices brought about by the war. In the US, federal investigations had forced NBC to divest itself of one of its networks; the former Blue network became the American Broadcasting Company (ABC) in 1944. FCC Chair James Lawrence Fly, a Roosevelt appointee, won a second term in 1942 and continued his efforts to shake up the American radio status quo; in 1941 a young Clifford Durr would take a commissioner's seat and lead the way towards broadcasting reform in the years immediately after the war. These critics of the commercial system found support and inspiration in the British model and would foster close ties with the BBC in the decades to come. Yet even as reformers and educational broadcasters celebrated their newfound strength (soon to reach its apogee in the controversial "Blue Book" issued in 1946, as discussed in the next chapter), the broadcasting industry flexed its muscles, stockpiled its accumulated public goodwill, and prepared to roar back at strength, in radio, in television, and perhaps even into Europe. The BBC regrouped and restructured, re-dedicated itself to a national public service enterprise, and under a new director—William Haley, appointed in 1944—began to plan for its license review scheduled for 1946 as well as the many challenges it was sure to face in the post-war world. The cultural battle lines were being drawn. Dramatic changes would occur. Only this time, neither national cultures nor broadcasting practices would prove so easy to disentangle. Instead, a whole new era of contested interconnection would begin.

As early as summer 1943, Haley (in his initial post as "Editor in Chief"— perhaps the job first offered to Murrow?) showed his determination to move away from the wartime merger of US and British cultural interests and take steps to fend off challenges to the BBC's national public service mandate— and monopoly. In an exchange of memos devoted to the topic amongst top executives, the idea of the post-war tripartite structure first emerges— heading off the *Economist*'s suggestion that a rival corporation be formed by proposing a plan that kept competition "in-house." Some recommended more than three services (Cultural, Educational and Youth, Home and Family, General, and Light, in one proposal); some recommended exploring forms of sponsorship; some advocated greater exchange with American broadcasters; others emphasized a greater emphasis on regional broad-casting.[2] By December 1944 the tripartite, "taste pyramid" structure had emerged victorious, with the Home Service resuming its central position, the

Forces Programme becoming the Light, and a Third, more exclusively highbrow service in preparation, designed to head off any complaints of "Americanisation" or dumbing down.

This rhetoric of "re-nationalization" also shows up in American industry discourse asserting the superiority of the American commercial system, with the trade press reporting that "the British public, having heard our kind of radio, wants it"[3] and "National advertisers in Great Britain are deeply interested in use of radio on a commercial basis."[4] Returning Americans like Arthur Feldman, who had worked within the BBC's North American Service, predicted that "despite opposition from various directions— Brendan Bracken, British Ministry of Information head, and of course the BBC itself—commercial radio in Britain is likely to develop after the war."[5] Yet as America's first national educational service emerged out of the fruitful convergence of private foundations, government agencies, and educational institutions after the war, they would turn to the BBC once again for inspiration, training, and programs in a process that may have had a greater impact in the long run on British broadcasting than its outright rivalry with commercial networks—at home as well as abroad.

And, of course, on both sides of the Atlantic the new medium of television both promised and threatened. The BBC's television service, the first in the world before the war, resumed under difficult financial conditions. Soon the debates over commercialization would move to this potentially rich new arena. In the US, the enormous manufacturing capacity devoted to military technology and equipment would re-gear itself to produce not only millions of new FM-equipped radio receivers but thousands of television sets to kick off a new media era.

Television, Trade, and Transculturation, 1946–1975

The viewer has got to realize that his television set should not provide him with an endless succession of pictures which he can switch
on to drug his mind whenever he feels like it . . . I believe that the
new viewer whether child or adult must learn from the first to make
a date with television and not to expect something that he likes to
be there whenever he wants it.[1]
                    —George Barnes, Director of BBC Television, 1951

I always think the BBC is my best business friend and drives more
young people into the cinema than anything else in the country.[2]
                    —J. Arthur Rank, Head of Rank Film Studios, 1946

If there is any degradation of television service . . . it will come from
TV film producers and the vault of Hollywood.[3]
                    —David M. Sarnoff, President of NBC, 1956

By the time the war drew to a close and even before all troops had returned
home, speculation was on about television. The BBC had begun television
service from Alexandra Palace outside London in 1936, and by September
1939 when it closed down abruptly in the middle of a Mickey Mouse cartoon, BBC Television daily transmissions could boast more than 100,000
viewers. Television service in Britain resumed June 7, 1946, with old NAS
hand Gerald Cock at its helm. Though the number of television-equipped
households increased steadily, Britain's economic hardships in rebuilding a
war-torn country ensured that radio would hold its central place in British

culture even as television developed gradually. Radio's continuation in Britain as a national service, enlarged and enhanced, continuing after television's introduction well into the present time, marks a significant contrast to the United States. It allowed for continuities in programs, personnel, and policies that persist to this day, allowing pre-television forms such as drama, comedy, documentary, and discussion programs to continue to prosper in their aural forms despite television's inroads on the national audience. Popular music, however—which quickly became the only viable alternative for American radio as commercial networks turned their whole attention to television—would prove problematic for British radio especially as the "youth revolution" wrought its changes in the 1960s.

In the US, though NBC trumpeted television's imminent arrival at the 1939 World's Fair, only an experimental service available to a few hundred television-equipped homes existed before the war, which quietly shut down in 1942 with barely a ripple of notice. In 1946 a total of six stations crept back on the air, and close to a million brave households purchased an expensive early set, but expansion to a nation-wide service was slowed by the FCC "freeze" on station licenses in 1948, brought about by disputes over technical standards and frequency allocations. The number of stations on the air numbered only 34 in 1948, and had crept up only to 107 by 1952 when the freeze was lifted, providing television service to most major cities but leaving large swathes of the country still primarily reliant on radio. Not until 1953–55 would the true television revolution occur as the number of stations on the air quadrupled, changing the nature of American radio radically and forever.

It is often forgotten that, besides television's rapid growth, this period also witnessed an enormous expansion of the number of radio stations on the air in the United States, due in large part to FCC re-organization of its frequency allocation procedures in a move to encourage local broadcasting. From a little more than 800 stations before the war, AM expanded to over 1000 by 1947 and then more than doubled to over 2600 by 1955. Meantime, the burgeoning field of FM radio, despite its travails (see Keith and Sterling 2008), numbered 150 stations by 1950, growing to more than 650 by 1955. Many of these were non-profit public service stations in 20 reserved frequencies on the FM band, set aside finally in 1942 as educational radio groups had been recommending since the 1920s. The relationship between educational broadcasters and the BBC would survive and thrive through this exponential growth, creating a boom in program exchange and co-production for both radio and television that would profoundly affect broadcast culture on both sides of the Atlantic, and resonate around the globe. Though the debut of television dominates historical memory of the post-war era, in fact for at least a decade after the war's end, and in many nations far longer, national radio held and even strengthened its place at the heart of national culture, woven deeply into the fabric of everyday life.

While television's potential was frequently praised as a "window on the world" that would bring peoples and nations closer together, in fact television's limited transmission capacity introduced a kind of re-territorialization of the spectrum, especially when compared to the enormous footprint that shortwave radio had developed during the war. With a maximum reach of 70 miles from the typical transmitter, television became, like early radio, a primarily local endeavor, necessitating carefully directed high antennae to get clear and trouble-free reception. Of course, stations located close to national borders could extend over such virtual barriers, but not very far. Networks, both public and commercial, were immediately employed to link such local stations together into national grids, but television's wider bandwidth made special cable networks necessary. Not until 1951 was the US cabled coast to coast, and many areas of the country remained unreached by television due to distance or land-mass interference, giving early rise to local cable television operations that relayed distant signals into homes by wire. During television's first decade, then, while much of what was on the air went out live, its reach was limited and its address was a mixture of the local and the national. Not until the sale of filmed series came to dominate TV's textual system did anxiety over transnationalization again raise its head.

Television's advent brought decisive changes to the relationship between cinema and broadcasting. Film studios and producers watched the new medium's development with interest on both sides of the Atlantic. Though the major Hollywood studios delayed their move into television (largely because of trade and talent union disputes and re-organization brought on by the 1948 Paramount decision), a host of independent television producers sprang up seemingly overnight. Filmed series soon became the backbone of the new medium, despite an earlier period of much-vaunted live single-play production, driven by the economics of the new industry (Hilmes 1990). As control over programming shifted from the sponsor to the networks and production companies, the ability to sell programs both domestically and internationally became nearly as profitable as selling time to advertisers. In Britain, where profit-making did not (yet) drive broadcasting—and where the production of nationally specific culture remained a central mandate— the BBC continued to value live television far longer than did its American counterparts, giving the US an initial advantage in global distribution and global influence that it would take decades—and a burgeoning practice of US/UK co-production—to remedy.

The Coronation of Queen Elizabeth II in 1953 introduced television as a social form to British society, but the careful arrangements of the BBC were disrupted by allegations of disrespectful treatment by American commercial television. Yet even as J. Fred Muggs became the symbol of the dangers of transnational commercialization, the tables suddenly turned, and Britain found itself with its first privately produced, advertising-based broadcasting service, bypassing radio and heading straight for television. ITV's birth also marks the union of film and broadcasting interests in Britain, something that had never occurred with radio. The revival of an indigenous film industry during the War years had brought new players into the field and allowed the expansion of established companies, such as the Rank Organization and Hammer Films. It also encouraged the growth of American production in Britain, as the establishment of the Eady Levy in 1950 (taxing box office receipts to fund British film production) and the tightening of import quotas (40% in 1949, reduced to 30% in 1950), as well as ongoing currency restrictions, meant that for Hollywood studios, opening up production facilities in England, Hollywood's second largest market, made economic sense. Most major studios opened up or expanded London-based subsidiaries, and many independent producers moved overseas, some additionally impelled by the increasing pressures of Cold-War witch hunts and the burgeoning blacklist. British cinema, which had kept itself largely separate from radio broadcasting (unlike Hollywood), would craft a new and vital relationship to television (Holmes 2005; Mann 2008; Sarah Street 2009)—and not just at home; as Hollywood studios held back, British films found far larger American audiences on TV than they ever had in theaters.

From the mid-1950s on, a period of highly productive interchange between British and American producers left lasting marks on television around the world. With Independent Television's (ITV) contested debut in Britain in 1955, a new kind of transatlantic program emerged in response to economic and political conditions in both nations, most prominently exemplified by the career of US producer Hannah Weinstein and her stable of refugees from the Cold War blacklist, producing filmed television programs in Britain both for domestic consumption and for export abroad. ITV developed rapidly, demonstrating a model of commercial television linked to regional rather than national service and keeping sponsor influence firmly out of programming decisions—something American networks viewed with envy, and would later turn to their own advantage. The debut of American educational television in the 1950s, building on radio's success and backed by a new globally powerful benefactor, the Ford Foundation, brought a new player into the field of international and domestic broadcasting, pursuing television as a field of international cultural exchange. The BBC adapted itself to the new commercial situation in a variety of ways: forging strong links with American educational broadcasting, taking on a newly aggressive profit-centered role in television exports and co-productions, and eventually bringing it in-house by hiring Canadian producer Sydney Newman away from commercial television in 1960 to open a fresh chapter in the history of BBC television drama. There would be no turning back the tide of transatlantic transculturation this time—though, in a move to resist creeping "Americanization," in 1964 a much-coveted second channel went to the BBC rather than ITV, enabling continuation of minority-interest production on BBC Two as well as BBC One's more popular fare.

In the US, the post-war decade opened with a new round of transatlantically inflected policy disputes between a reformist FCC and a resurgent commercial radio sector with the publication of the admonitory "Blue Book," authored by none other than Charles Siepmann, formerly of the BBC. The Blue Book re-awakened some of the dueling rhetoric of the 1930s, and led to Siepmann finding his work strategically deployed not only in the US but in both the 1951 Beveridge Report in Britain and in the Massey Commission report in Canada, sometimes in contradictory ways. Commercial broadcasters responded to public service expectations by looking again to the BBC model, with the Ford Foundation-produced experimental program *Omnibus*, hosted by Alistair Cooke, the most eminent. US educational broadcasting went through a fallow period in radio, but received a boost as the focus turned to television, due to frequency set-asides negotiated by the FCC's first female commissioner, Frieda Hennock, and the increased interest by US foundations such as Ford and Carnegie. A well-established system of co-production between the emergent National Educational Television network (NET) and both the BBC and ITV would ensue.

By the mid 1960s and into the 1970s, cultural exchange between the US and Great Britain reached a peak. British programs aired on American prime time television, and vice versa; each had become the other's most important trading and co-production partner. In the US, President Johnson's Great Society initiative along with longtime educational broadcasting supporters such as the Ford Foundation ushered in the first American national public broadcasting service, focused on television but with radio thrown in as an afterthought, thanks to the quick work of a few wily educational radio lobbyists (Mitchell 2005). The new Corporation for Public Broadcasting (CPB) and its Public Broadcasting Service (PBS), financed by a combination of federal, state, and foundation dollars along with corporate underwriters and individual donations, continued the tradition of co-production with the BBC and ITV that had begun in the 1950s—to the extent that some wags quipped PBS actually stood for the "Primarily British Service." Alistair Cooke would rise to public prominence as the host of one of PBS's main outlets for both British and American dramatic series, *Masterpiece Theatre*, as the new service suffered through political controversy, funding crises, and the tumultuous growth of an American public arts sector that slowly worked its way into the mainstream. This section ends as a whole new era of satellite-distributed cable television not only opened up the American television landscape, but accelerated the process of the spread of American programs and popular culture around the world, ushering in the era of "globalization" as we know it today.

CHAPTER 7

Disentangling and Differentiation, 1946–1955

Britain's Bid to Rule the Air Waves: A sharp contrast to American radio, the British Broadcasting Corporation, a government monopoly, today is aggressively blanketing the world with programs that are designed to get people to think British as well as buy British . . . [O]ne of the things the war did [was] to transform the BBC from a domestic-entertainment monopoly into a far-flung instrument of British national policy, with world-wide operations that are still growing . . . In its own way, the BBC out-Hollywoods Hollywood.[1]
—*Saturday Evening Post*, 1946

There is a demand in the US for more serious programmes which the BBC is well qualified to produce, such as the dramatic presentation of historical events, plays, and readings with first-class actors and the exposition of current affairs. Apart from the commercial networks which have shown interest in the possibility of the BBC producing television films for the US, an 'educational' television network is being built up in the US with the assistance of the Ford Foundation. Such 'educational' stations have already made approaches to the BBC and are certain to look to the BBC as they do in sound, to provide a considerable part of their programmes.[2]
—Report "Establishment of Overseas Television Service"
Oct 22, 1953

The [American] programmes are almost all within the field of what we would call Light Entertainment, although with a wider range . . .

In this connection, I remember clearly the bewilderment caused by
my official BBC title. One man asked me 'Do you mean that you also
have a Head of Heavy Entertainment?'[3]
—Ronald Waldman, Report on American Television, 1953

The immediate post-war years—1946 to 1955—are significant both for
television's introduction and for a resurgence of critical thinking about
broadcasting, not only in the US and Britain but in countries around the
world. Radio had played such an important role in summoning nations to
war, relaying wartime events, and recruiting both victorious and defeated
peoples to the cause of democracy (or, in many nations, to Soviet-sphere
communism) after the fighting was over, that the idea of simply returning to
"business as usual" once wartime operations ceased seemed a betrayal of
radio's powers.[4] Radio had proven its worth on the national and international stage, and placing it back into the hands of meretricious advertisers,
in the US, or to a complacent monopoly, as in Britain, hardly seemed
possible, much less desirable. Reform, restructuring, and re-imagination
formed the order of the day.

On July 29, 1945, the BBC returned to peacetime status. The Forces
Programme switched off and the new duopoly of Light and Home signed
on, with the Third Programme on the horizon to debut September 1946.
Luxembourg's commercial service got a two months' head start over its
highbrow rival, however, resuming in July 1946 and continuing its barrage
of "Americanized" programs from offshore, to ever larger audiences despite
the Light's new lighter, brighter touch under the direction of Maurice
Gorham. The resumption of television service and the demands it made on
the now inadequate license fee brought renewed attention to the issue of
commercialization, which could at least help to pay for things despite the
threats not only of cultural vulgarity but of increased American influence.
The BBC's charter was due for renewal in 1946, but it received a temporary
extension until the next big inquiry could be organized. That occurred in
1949 under the direction of Lord Beveridge whose Report, appearing in
1951, roundly endorsed the public service status quo. Comparison with
American broadcasting once again emerged as crucial to the debate, especially as the question of television became more acute.

In the US, the years immediately following the war witnessed the most
organized effort to reform American broadcasting along British lines that
US regulators had ever attempted, in a climate of criticism based on radio's
national public service role during WWII. Appearing in 1946, the FCC's
report on "Public Service Responsibilities of Broadcast Licensees," better
known as the "Blue Book," both sparked and responded to a growing
national debate on just where the power over broadcasting standards lay in

the American system. Could the FCC use its power over license assignment and renewal to bring about significant change, stipulated and controlled from Washington and enforced on a station-by-station level, as the original Communications Act had envisioned? Or was the commercial sponsor the true force behind US radio? What about the networks, dominant now in ways that earlier regulators could not have envisaged as television added to their empires? The attempt by the "Blue Book" to answer that question would end up having more impact in Britain than in the United States.

The "Blue Book" and the Revolt Against Radio

> I start from the premise that the [American radio] system is basically sound, much of the output good, some of it the best in the world. But is it good enough? Good enough for an America which is newly emerging as a world power, and whose people must know, if they are not to perish, what that means – what it means in terms of our own national life, in terms of the problems of other nations, in terms of peace or war for us or our children?
> —Charles Siepmann, Radio's Second Chance, April 1946 (x)

In the United States, commercial radio quickly returned to pre-war status, with big plans for the anticipated wave of post-war prosperity. Television might loom, but radio networks remained confident of their centrality and dominance both in American life and for American advertisers. NBC executives met in September 1945 to discuss a two-year forecast put together by top management. All agreed that tighter network control over programming was imperative; that international news and political commentary would probably command less audience attention though national and local news might take up the slack; and that "networks and stations will be under increasingly heavy pressure from the FCC to broadcast more public service programs." Overall, however, an aura of complacency reigned. After a string of reports in trade publications boasting "American Radio Sets World Pattern"[5] and "American Radio Best, Europe Trip Shows"[6] it is perhaps not surprising that NBC executives concluded that "there will be no radical changes in commercial programs" and could confine themselves to more whimsical recommendations as "Stunts and trivialities, such as singing mice, will be disregarded."[7]

But those who had envisioned radio as a medium for service to the nation held on to their conviction that more than singing mice were at stake. One of those people was FCC Commissioner Clifford Durr, appointed by President Roosevelt to the FCC in 1941. Durr was an Alabama-born lawyer who had attended Oxford on a Rhodes scholarship, where he won a "blue" in rugby and a degree in jurisprudence.[8] His previous experience had been with one of the New Deal agencies, the Reconstruction Finance Corporation, through the intercession of his brother-in-law, then Senator (later Supreme Court Justice) Hugo Black. He had little knowledge of radio, but had become interested in broadcasting after reading transcripts of Axis propaganda broadcasts and attending one of the Ohio State Institute for Education by Radio conferences. Convinced that commercial broadcasting should not be allowed to dominate such an influential medium, Durr championed the cause of a frequency set-aside in the new FM band for educational stations, which passed in 1942. He would later work with the first female FCC Commissioner, Frieda Hennock, to make sure that a similar system of reserved educational frequencies got applied to television, with far-reaching consequences (Brinson 2002).

Joining the Commission just after the 1941 Report on Chain Broadcasting had taken to task the dominant status of the major networks[9] (leading eventually to NBC's forced divestiture of its Blue Network, which became ABC), Durr's experience through the lengthy appeals and debate in Congress over implementation of the new rules convinced him that what regulators needed was a better yardstick for assessing which stations were performing in the public interest and which were not. He proposed that the FCC should do a study of license renewal promises versus practices, and come up with some concrete standards and guidelines. FCC Chair Paul Porter approved the project; to do the job Durr brought in a young Canadian researcher from the FCC Economics division, Dallas Smythe,[10] as well as Durr's own neighbor Charles Siepmann, with whom he carpooled into Washington each day.[11] Siepmann was appointed as a special consultant to the FCC in July 1945 and wasted no time getting down to the task. As Durr later recalled, "instead of this study dragging on for a couple of years, in a month it was ready and that really baffled [the FCC]."[12] Besides Smythe and Siepmann, Durr's assistant Edward Brecher and Washington lawyer Elinor Bonticue assisted in the effort. Their report, officially titled "Public Service Responsibility of Broadcast Licensees" appeared in March 1946; it became known as the "Blue Book" due to the color of its cover.[13]

As Durr well knew, Siepmann had the critical perspective and depth of experience with radio that Durr and his young staff lacked. Over the course of his participation in the Rockefeller Communications Research Group, his three years lecturing on radio at Harvard, and his stint with the OWI's West Coast office, Siepmann had become actively involved with the leading educational radio organizations, attending their conferences and publishing articles in educational radio journals (Siepmann 1940, 1941a). A few of his articles had reached wider audiences, including one published in *Public Opinion Quarterly* in 1941, another entitled "Radio's Big Chance" that appeared in *The New Republic* in 1942, and an essay included in Paul Lazarsfeld and Frank Stanton's 1943 volume *Radio Research*. He was quickly becoming one of American radio's best-known academic critics. The furor that ensued over the Blue Book not only confirmed that status but led to his appointment as chair of the Department of Communications in the School of Education at New York University, where he would remain for the rest of his career.

Long before the report itself emerged, uneasy rumors of Durr's employment of Siepmann rumbled through the industry press. *Broadcasting* magazine, in particular, stirred the pot in tones reminiscent of the 1930s debates. "Is there a move afoot to BBC-ize American broadcasting?" asked a July 30, 1945 article, under the headline "BBC Expert Probes Procedure for FCC." Noting that Commissioner Durr "lists to the portside in his social philosophies" and "believes there is too much commercialism in American radio," it recited the brief facts of Siepmann's BBC, Harvard, and OWI career. After a survey of his published work it concluded, moderately (on the second page) "Mr. Siepmann is an alert, able and persuasive man. . . . He seems to like American programs. But he appears to feel he would like them better without sponsors."[14] A second article by the same author on August 6 repeated many of the same concerns, adding an element consistent with one strong BBC attitude: "Woven through Mr. Siepmann's articles is a lament against daily serials. He believes that such escapism as they provide does not promote a better world."[15] This is a note Siepmann would return to strongly in his own writing.

On August 13 the gloves came off. In a blistering editorial entitled "The Great Program Hoax," editor Sol Taishoff made the case that recent FCC initiatives rested on nothing less than an elaborate plot on the part of the US government to abrogate the First Amendment by setting up its own radio network. At the heart of the plot was revealed "Charles I. [sic] Siepmann, ex-director of program planning of the government-owned BBC, until 1939 a resident of London." In case these facts failed to alarm readers sufficiently, Taishoff emphasized "He was with BBC, which loathes the competition it suffered when our brand of radio was introduced in England for our GI's, and on which the British public eavesdropped to the point of almost ignoring BBC schedules."[16] Many more such insinuating articles and editorials followed, extending suspicion of Siepmann to the BBC itself, accusing it of "an inordinate desire . . . to spread the influence of state-operated radio" in Europe and around the world, and claiming that its government-subsidized transcribed programs were replacing domestic production in places like Australia and New Zealand, hurting US program sales, even as it attempted to block the return of commercial broadcasting to Luxembourg and Normandie.[17] Perhaps even the most jingoistic in the industry felt that resurgence of this sort of rhetoric after a proud record of wartime co-operation went too far; speculation died down in the intervening months as Siepmann turned in his report and left Washington for his farm in Vermont. Or perhaps the 300 stations that had received only temporary renewal of their licenses while the new guidelines were being formulated thought better of kicking up too much of a fuss lest their chances be jeopardized.

When "Public Service Responsibility of Broadcast Licensees" finally made its appearance on March 7, 1946, the barrage resumed but at first without the xenophobic tone. No one could deny that some radio stations had abused their license privileges through a surfeit of commercials and refusal to carry network sustaining programs. Many in the industry felt some relief at having license renewal requirements spelled out so clearly. After surveying numerous instances where a station's performance failed woe-fully to live up to the promises made in its license renewal application, the FCC declared its intention to weigh practice, not promise, against a set of four obligations owed by broadcasters to the public: a well-balanced sche-dule that contained a sufficient number of sustaining programs, including network sustaining programs; a commitment to local live programming; more programs devoted to the discussion of important public issues; and finally—the provision that hit the industry closest to its heart—the "elimination of advertising excesses" (FCC 1946, 75).

Though *Broadcasting* predictably attempted to whip up reaction against the "F(ederal) C(ensorship) C(omission)"[18] in the usual ways, arguing for broadcasters' First Amendment rights and against government interference in business (even likening the actions of the FCC to those of Goering and Goebbels under Hitler), most in the industry accepted their regulatory upbraiding as the cost of doing business and made new plans accordingly. And one branch of the industry positively glowed in the recommendations of the Blue Book. *Variety* took out a full-page ad in its own March 27 edition for the purpose of quoting approvingly from the report:

> Says the FCC: 'The reviews and critiques published weekly in VARIETY afford an illustration of the role that independent criti-cism can play; newspapers and periodicals might well consider the institution of similar independent critiques for the general public. . . . Responsible criticism can do much more than mere promotion; it can raise the standards of public appreciation and stimulate the free and unfettered development of radio as a new medium of artistic expression. The independent radio critic, assuming the same role long occupied by the dramatic critic and the literary critic, can bring to bear an objective judgment on questions of good taste and of artistic merit which lie outside the purview of this commission.'[19]

The networks themselves saw discretion as their best response; already they were positioning themselves as responsible caretakers of the public airwaves in contrast to maverick station owners and sponsors—a strategy that would soon show up in popular press articles and pay off ten years later as the "quiz show scandal" threatened government intervention once again.

This period of thoughtful reflection was brief, however: when Siepmann's own critical missive, *Radio's Second Chance*, appeared on bookshelves only one month later, the flames of industry resistance and resentment again rose high. Siepmann had clearly put the months since July to good use, drawing on his work at the FCC for one-third of the book and writing the rest at his farm in Newfane, Vermont.[20] The cover promised "A hard-hitting analysis of the service and profits of radio broadcasting, showing its failures and possibilities as the most important means of communication in a democracy". Siepmann went to some lengths in the opening pages to emphasize his loyalty both to his new American citizenship and to the American system of broadcasting:

This book is in no sense a comparison of British and American systems of broadcasting. I do not advocate or anywhere imply that the United States would do well to adopt the British system. We certainly should not. American broadcasting stands on its merits. Our commercial system, whatever faults it may have, is the most efficient and, with due care, democratically the safest system functioning anywhere in the world. (1942a, viii)

These caveats made little impact on *Broadcasting* and its fiery editor Sol Taishoff, who once again led in turning attention away from the actual content of both Siepmann's work and the Blue Book with editorial invective that evoked an attack on America's national interests: "The Blue Book was conceived in the minds of men of Government. . . . It was written in great part by a man practiced in the Governmental radio art of Great Britain. . . . We are opposed to the tactics which produced it. We are opposed to the way of life it portends."[21] The journal also, as Chad Dell points out, buttressed these attacks by publishing a series of articles criticizing the BBC itself, with titles like "Freer BBC Desired"[22] and "BBC May Consider Going Commercial" (Dell n.d.)[23] The Manichean rhetoric of the 1930s had made another appearance, this time with a hint of the red-baiting to come thrown in, as *Broadcasting* asked of Durr, "the FCC's knight errant": "the banner he bears high – is it the white of purity, or is there a hint of pink?"[24]

Siepmann spoke up in his own and the Blue Book's defense. He debated Justin Miller, president of the NAB, at an NAB regional meeting in April, and stood up to Sydney M. Kaye of BMI, the industry-run rights organization, at an ACLU meeting in June. He published an article in *The American Mercury*, titled "Storm in the Radio World," in August (in which he called the Blue Book "an extremely able work") and in December 1946 in *The Nation* exhorted readers concerned about radio to speak up against the license renewal of a particularly notorious offender, station WBAL in Baltimore, owned by the conservative Hearst group. "The greatest weakness in our system of broadcasting is the indifference of the public to the possibilities of radio service," he claimed (1946a); in a later article he expressed particular disappointment in the failure of educational groups and the non-profit broadcasting sector to speak out in an organized way in favor of the FCC's attempts at reform (1948, 45). He might also have been discouraged by the lack of outspoken defense emanating from the FCC itself; deeply divided along political lines, only Durr himself stood up for Blue Book principles in public over the subsequent months.[25]

By 1947 the furor had died down and the Blue Book's careful arguments were already fading into the past. The rush towards television and towards getting hundreds of new radio stations on the air, in both the AM and FM bands, meant that backed-up license renewals and applications were approved with the same lack of close scrutiny that Durr, Smythe, and Siepmann had deplored, usually with Durr as the lone dissenter (Dell n.d.). Too, some of Siepmann's own recommendations, while not explicitly evoking the BBC, had a distinctly BBC-ish tone that did not win them adherents, even among those favorably inclined. His disdain for soap operas and their female audiences, whom he characterized as "addicts" with a "morbid frame of mind" and "pitiable credulity," born of "low IQ and many other attributes which, from the standpoint of vigorous democratic health, mark it as a social liability" (Siepmann, 1946b, 58–59) reflected an inability to consider such programs on their own merits or to take the needs and interests of a large portion of the audience seriously—even while he argued for a need for more programs catering to "women's interests".[26] His definition of "minority programs" retained a Reithian focus on the culturally uplifting, far more concerned with the wealthy, highly educated "minority" than on America's racial, ethnic, and regional groups, who had finally begun to find the foothold on the airwaves that had been denied them so long (Barlow 1999; B. Savage 1999). Even Llewellyn White, in his philosophically very similar critique, found Siepmann's volume "hortatory in style" and "given rather more to pietism than to specificity" (White 1947, 253). The fact was that American radio was changing, from a national medium of broad-based programming to the localized, music-dominated, recording-driven niche medium that it would become. Television quickly emerged as the new focus of public service expectations.

Yet many of Siepmann's recommendations would bear fruit in the world of educational broadcasting, as we shall see in subsequent chapters. His call for "a production center for public service programs" supported by universities and foundations (1946b, 270) would materialize as the Educational Television and Radio Center (ETRC) in 1952, funded by the Ford Foundation. It began producing and distributing cultural and public affairs programs for non-profit stations and established a distinct identity through importing BBC programs, a practice that would continue as the ETRC became the National Educational Television network (NET) and later morphed into PBS. Siepmann continued to play a role in this sequence of developments, as we shall see; for him the Blue Book episode was only a beginning. Clifford Durr, by contrast, left the FCC and the field of radio reform for good in 1948, not only in disappointment over the neglect of his program for reform of radio, but in protest against the rising tactics of the Red Scare that would have forced him to sign a loyalty oath to keep his position. He went on to defend many against HUAC accusations and other charges, returning to Alabama in the early 1950s to become a respected activist in the civil rights movement where he represented Rosa Parks in her suit against the Montgomery bus system, amongst many others.

However, it was not just Siepmann, Durr, and their associates who had begun to speak out against commercial radio in the post-war years. As radio slid from its heights of wartime service and high-flown cultural programming into boom years of expansion and heightened commercialism, critics gathered their barbs based this time not only on a hypothetical public service model (represented previously by the powerful but distant example of the BBC) but on actual experience during the war with a different kind of broadcasting in the service of the nation—both at home and abroad. The publication in the summer of 1946 of Frederic Wakeman's scathing novel *The Hucksters*, with its portrayal of the world of radio advertising as culturally bankrupt and morally inert, fed the flames. It was picked up by both *Reader's Digest* and the Book of the Month Club to become one of the bestselling novels of 1946. Wakeman spoke out on *America's Town Meeting of the Air* in December 1946, throwing down the gauntlet to the very medium giving him a voice by declaring:

> Since advertising's chief interest is in products, it should not be permitted to control the program material of radio, whose chief interest must be not in customers but in listeners . . . you radio people should take back your programs from the hucksters. Take back your networks. Take back your stations and do your own programming without benefit of what any sponsor thinks any program should be . . . commercials can then be sold to the advertisers

on a dignified, properly controlled basis that will protect the program, not destroy it. It works with newspapers and magazines – why
not with radio?[27]

MGM released *The Hucksters* in a movie version in 1947, evoking little
remark in the advertising world but prompting NBC executives to consider
a sweeping retaliatory broadside against not only Wakeman but the entire
Hollywood movie industry (Havig 1984). A resurgent consumer movement
linked radio advertising to a host of post-war social woes (Newman 2004).

Nor was the critical movement confined to radio. In 1942, through a
grant made to the University of Chicago by Henry Luce, founder of the Time
Inc. media empire, a Commission on the Freedom of the Press had been
formed much in the spirit of the Rockefeller Communication Seminars, "to
consider the freedom, functions, and responsibilities of the major agencies
of mass communication in our time: newspapers, radio, motion pictures,
news-gathering media, magazines, books" (White 1947, iv). Often referred
to as the "Hutchins Commission" after its chair, University of Chicago
chancellor Robert Maynard Hutchins (see Chapter 8), its board members
included several figures also active in Rockefeller Foundation projects, such
as Harold Lasswell, Archibald MacLeish, Beardsley Ruml, Arthur M.
Schlesinger, and John Grierson. The group organized in 1944 and by 1947
had produced their two best-known works, *A Free and Responsible Press* and
The American Radio.[28] The latter volume was authored by Commission
assistant director Llewellyn White, and covered much of the same ground
first plowed by the "Blue Book" and Siepmann's study. Each volume had
been heavily reviewed both by the Commission and by outside readers in the
industries concerned; each set out a careful analysis of the history and
problems within each media sector and laid out proposals for reform. All
were respectfully received. Yet for most, as a 1948 reviewer summarized,
"*The American Radio* and all the effort that went into it appear, at this date,
to make up a lesson in futility" (Carson 1948, 910). No direct initiatives of
note emerged from their prodigious efforts.

Yet a persistent drumbeat of criticism began to accumulate around US
commercial broadcasting and its sponsor-based practices. *Fortune* magazine,
hardly an anti-business venue, titled a March 1947 article "The Revolt
Against Radio" and proclaimed in large type, "A loud minority is disgusted
with American broadcasting" (101). While giving considerable space to
critiques such as Wakeman's, which it quoted as above, it also noted (presciently) the "fundamental unreality" of his proposed reform: "if programming reverted from the advertising agencies to the networks, the slick
agency wizards who now set so much of the tone of radio might simply
revert with it" (102). Yet to many, including such influential radio critics as

Jack Gould of the *New York Times* and John Crosby of the *New York Herald Tribune*, the sponsor and its agency were the problem, the networks and stations the potential solution. Crosby wrote a lengthy essay in the January 1948 issue of *Atlantic Monthly* simply entitled "Stalled," arguing that since radio seemed mired in the same old way of doing things, "more leadership by the broadcasters and less control by advertisers" (29), would be required for the new medium of television. Along the same lines, Gould attempted to sweep aside "the veil of anonymity which always has enshrouded the advertising agency" in the production of radio programs in an April 1948 article, urging them to take responsibility for their actual role as "trustee of national values . . . trustee of standards in entertainment, in taste, and in thinking." He recommended that the ad agency be openly credited for its role in production, the same way a publisher or film studio is, and looked to television as a medium that might "set matters aright in the world of broadcasting."[29] Others, such as famed commentator H. L. Mencken, laid the blame elsewhere; in a letter responding to the *Fortune* article, he wrote, "The real villain, only too obviously, is the public taste . . . I believe that, in part at least, it reflects a serious deterioration in the American stock, perhaps mainly due to long-continued dysgenic breeding."[30] All of these notes would soon be sounded not only in the pages of America's quality press, but across the Atlantic in the Houses of Parliament and the reports of government committees. As Britain turned her attention to the future of broadcasting, the critique of American broadcasting made by Americans themselves would become key to defending the BBC's monopoly franchise.

The Beveridge Report and the American Other

'A Note On U.S.A. Radio' is, I think, a correct record of fact. It is not, however, a fair picture and overall appraisal of broadcasting in the United States.
—Charles Siepmann, *Beveridge Report, 1951* (293)

The monopolist broadcaster cannot concentrate on his proper business of pleasing the greatest number of people; he is compelled to do the direct opposite—to concentrate on offending the smallest number of people. He is forced to be timid, and mediocre, and dull. Since every bright colour is displeasing to some raucous interest, he can use only grey.
—*The Economist*, November 1944 (565)

The massive post-war inquiry into the future of broadcasting in Britain that culminated in the Beveridge Report, released in January 1951, may have contrasted strongly with the Blue Book in its scope and basic assumptions but was destined to meet with very much the same fate. Firmly endorsing the BBC's monopoly over both radio and television, the report relied strongly on negative assessments of American broadcasting to make its case, now gratifyingly coming from American critics such as Gould and Siepmann as well as observers from overseas. But within two years its complacent re-affirmations would be pushed aside in a rapid scramble towards commercial television that would permanently change the British broadcasting land-scape.

As early as 1943, American trade periodicals began circulating reports that the BBC was under pressure to change, predicting that the "BBC is going to have a fight on its hands for its listening public when peace comes again."[31] A survey done by the Incorporated Society of British Manufacturers in 1944 showed that the majority of respondents planned to use commercial radio advertising after the war, at home in Britain if it was available or, if not, offshore.[32] Rumors of American involvement in constructing offshore commercial stations in Ireland, France, Andorra, and even Iceland began to circulate just as they had in the 1930s, often with the familiar name of Leonard Plugge attached to them. In fall of 1944 the well-respected British business magazine *The Economist* published a series of articles that came out strongly against the traditional BBC monopoly—calling it a "disastrous mistake" caused by "inadvertence and absence of mind"[33]—but also pleading against the usual simple dichotomy of regarding a public service monopoly or an unregulated private commercial system as the only two options. Rather, "a system that would avoid the manifest defects of these two" was necessary. FM and wired radio presented two intriguing possi-bilities, with local radio a distinct option for the first time, perhaps even "a 'network' on the American pattern—that is, one or two or three chains of local stations."[34]

The incoming Labour government in 1946 rejected out of hand both the concept of commercial radio in Britain as well as any *Economist*-like notions of multiple corporations. A few members of Parliament persisted in raising the question, however, and on June 26 the issue was debated in the House of Lords, enlivened the very morning of the debate by an excoriating letter in the *Times* from former BBC Director-General Sir Frederick Ogilvie that may have had more impact on public opinion that the debate itself. In it he argued:

> What is at stake is not a matter of politics, but of freedom . . . monopoly of broadcasting is inevitably the negation of freedom, no matter how efficiently it is run, or how wise and kindly the boards or committees in charge of it. It denies freedom of choice to

listeners. It denies freedom of employment to speakers, musicians, writers, actors, and all who seek their chance on the air.[35]

This sudden broadside prompted a general backing away from any attempt to determine such heated issues at such a transitional time, leading to an agreement that the BBC's charter, due to expire in December, would be renewed for five years only, and an independent commission formed to reconsider more coolly and deliberately.[36]

This commission was appointed in 1949 under the leadership of economist William H. Beveridge (Lord Beveridge), already a household name due to his shaping of the British social welfare program structure after the war, most notably the National Health Service. The selection of Beveridge as chair set the investigation off on a somewhat predictable course; as someone whose career evinced "the central moral and political assumptions of the postwar social order" (Rodgers 1998, 494) it was highly unlikely to lead to radical change in the direction of free-market economics. The committee was composed of ten representatives of the great and the good: four were members of Parliament, five had titles affixed to their names, one was a trade unionist and three were connected with the field of education. They began to solicit comments from members of the general public, which arrived in the form of individual letters as well as memoranda from organized groups. Despite the *Economist*'s call to avoid the traditional dichotomies, American commercial broadcasting was destined to play a central role yet again as the foil for those who wished to defend the BBC's monopoly status—though this time the examples of Canada, Australia, and New Zealand would also factor into the debate.

It is significant that Lord Beveridge's first action as chair was to prepare "A Note on U.S.A. Radio" in September 1949; clearly, the comparison with the United States would form the fundamental argument, for good or bad, about the future of broadcasting in Britain (Great Britain, *Report*, 1951, 289–96). To do this he drew on "books and documents available in this country" (289): primarily Charles Siepmann's *Radio's Second Chance*, Llewellyn White's *The American Radio*, and the FCC's "Blue Book" itself. In addition, when contacted by Beveridge for additional information, Llewellyn White recommended that Beveridge consult *New York Herald Tribune* critic John Crosby, who could fill him in on more recent developments. Beveridge sent his "Note" when completed to Siepmann and Crosby for comment. Both replied with a number of objections to the way in which their work had been construed.

Sounding a note that would often recur when American critics found themselves embroiled in British debates, Siepmann stated that, although as a factual statement of the structure of US broadcasting Beveridge's "Note" was fairly correct, "It is not, however, in my judgment, a fair picture and overall appraisal of broadcasting in the United States" (1951, 293). He pointed out that his book had been more concerned with enumerating and correcting the weak points of American radio than in praising its many strong elements, including the enormously greater number of stations, amongst them educational broadcasters; the vital and long-standing role of local radio; and the variety and quality of news and public affairs programs (293). Crosby, too, made several amendments to the chair's report. He disagreed strongly with the report's assertion that US radio had "fail[ed] to bring important public issues to public notice" (294). He argued that "the commercials on our radio are not nearly so offensive to most radio listeners as to you British who aren't used to them or to our own intellectuals who listen to the radio hardly at all anyway." He also pointed out that the networks had recently been moving in a direction to take back control over programming from the sponsors: "There has been increasing recognition that the abdication of responsibility by the networks to the advertisers was a grave mistake. The broadcaster is trying not to repeat it in television" (294). Beveridge summarized and quoted parts of Siepmann's and Crosby's responses in Appendix G as part of the report (293–95). Significantly, however, he did not amend his "Note" before he shared it in its original form with the rest of the committee preparatory to their assignments; they set out on their task under the assumption that his disputed assertions were matters of accepted fact.

The second part of Appendix G (287–327) consists of the accounts of four of these committee members who traveled to the US and to Canada that year, in teams of two: Brigadier (later Baron) John Selwyn Lloyd, a Conservative MP, and Mrs. Mary Stocks (Baroness), principal of Westfield College, in August 1950; and Lord Elgin, Earl of Elgin and Kincardine—a Scotsman (descended from Robert the Bruce) and later member of the BBC's Advisory Council—with Alderman J. Reeves, a Labour MP, the following month. Their accounts would form a large part of the body of knowledge about American radio and especially television that the committee would draw on. They each set out with a set of questions prepared in advance, and their responses, in pairs, were included in Appendix G of the final Beveridge Report, along with more detailed individual reports.

Agreement was unanimous that the American system of sponsored broadcasting was to be avoided, and generally American radio suffered by comparison with the BBC, especially since the observers were there for less than a week and did not get to hear a full range of US programs—nor have a chance to become accustomed to radio advertising techniques. All were struck with the speed and urgency of American presentation, and the overwhelming variety of stations and programs. Reeves and Elgin came out strongly against American radio generally: programs were "positively ruined by obtrusive and objectionable advertising matter" (298) and "few programmes would compare" with the BBC's (299). Stocks and Selwyn Lloyd gave far more lengthy and nuanced reports. They admitted a few advantages—the amount and quality of news, "greater flexibility and freedom of discussion" (302), the variety of stations from which to choose, the ability to afford high-profile performers, the existence of local community stations. Selwyn Lloyd even noted something rarely mentioned by the BBC or anyone else in Britain: that US commercial radio had innovated a number of programs which, when adapted to British broadcasting by the BBC, became some of the most popular programs on the home airwaves. He also included detailed lists of the music broadcast over a 24-hour period in New York City on five different stations, along with a breakdown of programs generally and the time devoted to "serious" issues (306–15). Overall, though, both expressed anxiety at the influence of sponsors and advertising agencies over the content of much of network radio.

Reeves, sometimes with Elgin, investigated the arena of educational radio, and also inquired into issues having to do with labor unions and broadcasting. He reported on educational stations in Cleveland, Ohio; Madison, Wisconsin; and the University of Chicago, as well as network affiliate and independent commercial stations in Chicago and New York. He found, not surprisingly, that most educational broadcasters were highly critical of US commercial radio, and echoed one of Mary Stocks' observations: "American radio provides little in the way of entertainment for the professional class listener" (303). After visiting the CBS headquarters in New York and finding them impressive, Reeves concluded "We were convinced that they could have rendered magnificent public service if they had not been so dependent on the finances of commercial undertakings" (318). However, he was balanced enough to express surprise, when inquiring about the "famous Town Hall program" (*America's Town Meeting of the Air*), that it was in fact sponsored—by a labor union!—and observed that "it rather looks as if one of our well-known discussion programs is copied from America" (319).

These reports were pulled together in a conclusion that, while acknowledging that American radio had its strong points (and its own native detractors) and that British and American broadcasters had much to learn from each other, nonetheless expressed a conviction of "the importance of maintaining for Britain the present system of financing the costs of broadcasting either wholly or predominantly by license fees paid by the listeners rather than by advertisement revenue derived from sponsors" (320). Observations that followed of radio in Canada, Australia, and New Zealand did nothing to change this conclusion. The BBC's sole franchise on both radio and television in the UK was confirmed, though regional broadcasting received new emphasis. However, a minority report by Selwyn Lloyd pointed far more presciently to the system that would, in fact, develop within a few short years, and also to the primary rhetorical strategy by which Britain would reconcile itself to the idea of commercial television: the separation of sponsorship from program control (201–10).

For a time, then, the public service spirit existed on both sides of the Atlantic in troubled conjunction with commercial forces that would soon dominate and lead to sweeping changes in both US and British broadcasting. Reformers drew on critical analysis taken from both Britain and the United States, strengthening the bonds between advocates of public service broadcasting that had been forged in the transatlantic initiatives of the Rockefeller Foundation before the war and extended by wartime broadcasting exchange. In the US, attempts at reform would continue to have a British accent, as momentum slowly built towards the establishment of an American public broadcasting service. A new set of players began to emerge in the early 1950s.

Building Transnational Exchange: "Ivory Towers Sound" and Vision

At long last educational broadcasters have discovered that they are not faint, isolated whispers in the broadcasting world. They have discovered for the first time that they are a part of something of great significance in America.[37]
—Robert B. Hudson, NAEB, 1951

Since its inception, the NAEB has been in contact with the BBC . . . [R]ebroadcasting of British material by NAEB has become an important item in the activities of the North American Service . . . Respect for the Third Programme has amounted to something like veneration by certain persons associated with the NAEB.[38]
—H. Rooney Pelletier, BBC North American Service, 1952

With the fading of the wartime imperatives that once motivated trans-Atlantic exchange, new types of relationships began to emerge. On the British home front, William Haley's determination to return BBC radio to its most British roots, rejecting American influence and re-dedicating the organization to national public service, reached its apogee in the Third Programme. While the Home and Light Services catered to the mass audience's need for entertainment and basic information, the Third pursued the notion of cultural uplift and the education of taste to such an extent that even Lord Reith found its frankly highbrow disregard for all but the elite audience "objectionable." His statement in the Beveridge Report said of the new service: "It is a waste of precious wavelength" (Great Britain, *Report*

1951, 364). Yet intellectuals, critics, and public broadcasters around the world hailed it as a model and a global resource. Here the tide of popularization would be turned back, with attention to the arts, classical music and opera, literary discussion, poetry, and creative drama and features produced not with the mass audience but with creative excellence in mind. In America it immediately drew the attention of educational radio advocates and public interest-minded reformers, and strengthened their commitment to producing similar change in the US. Educational radio broadcasters, who had aired BBC programs since the 1930s, began to draw on the offerings of the new channel, aided by the establishment in 1946 of the BBC Transcription Service, dedicated to "the projection of Britain by good radio" (Briggs 1979, 506).

In 1946, nearly fifty hours per week of BBC radio programming could be heard on US airwaves, with an estimated audience of 3 million. The largest transmitters were independent commercial stations such as WIP Philadelphia and WLW Cincinnati, but educational radio stations were becoming an ever greater part of the service. The BBC estimated that in September 1946, 16 educational stations regularly broadcast British programs, counting for more than 11 hours of the total. Furthermore, as Warren MacAlpine, North American Service Director, put it, this was the "quality" audience most likely to appreciate what the BBC had to offer: "[T]hese stations afford our main outlet for material of the more serious, expository character . . . we are getting economical coverage through these stations for the kind of British programme we should get across to the type of Americans who are most likely to relay what they hear from us."[39] As the nature of US commercial radio began to shift away from set programs towards music and news formats, educational stations became more and more important as links to British radio culture. Simultaneously, imported programs from Britain became more and more important to US educational radio, as well as to educational television as it developed.

The National Association of Educational Broadcasters (NAEB), whose origins were traced in Section 2, had been revitalized with the 1945 FCC decision to set aside 20 channels in the FM band for educational radio, as well as by the experience many of its members had during the war with radio as a public service and a national priority, both at home in the US through the OWI and overseas through the BBC. Their vision was bolstered as well not only by the example of the BBC Third Programme but by the movement towards international public service broadcasting, exemplified in such efforts as the Prix Italia, established in 1948 by Radio Italiana to recognize the best in international radio broadcasting, and the revitalization of L'Université Radiophonique Internationale (International Radio University, or URI) founded by the joint efforts of UNESCO and

Radio France. Plus, with educational television on the horizon, the NAEB knew that its success in utilizing the FM frequency set-asides would have a direct bearing on any movement to achieve a similar status for educational television.

Yet new FM stations were slow to develop, television's future remained unclear, and one of educational radio's strongest backers, the Rockefeller Foundation, had largely withdrawn from the field. It did, however, intervene one last time to organize and fund two groundbreaking conferences in 1949 and 1950 held at the University of Illinois' Allerton House with the goal of considering "the nature of public service radio, the validity of the idea of mass communication . . . and the distinctive responsibilities and opportunities of non-commercial broadcasters."[40] Bringing together broadcasters from universities around the country as well as representatives of the BBC, the CBC, and other international public service broadcasters, the basic organizational structure for a newly expanded and centralized kind of educational broadcasting, for both radio and television, was hammered out. For radio, these consisted of plans for a central facility for sharing programs, leading eventually to an educational network and a "well-financed program-producing center" (Hudson 1951, 243). The NAEB would take leadership in this area with a grant from the Kellogg Foundation in 1951 that established its new headquarters in Urbana, Illinois and initiated a program exchange center under the direction of Robert Hudson, formerly of the Rockefeller-funded Rocky Mountain Radio Council. Programs from the BBC and from Canada would form the backbone of this exchange, with repercussions on both sides of the Atlantic. This story will be taken up below.

For television, the prospect was less clear. The growing dominance of US commercial television worldwide, especially in the English-speaking nations of the Commonwealth like Canada and Australia, augured a need for the development of continued British outreach in television as well as radio, despite the difficulties that this brought with it (see S. Potter 2011). As early as 1950 the Overseas Service had received a plea from Sir Archibald Nye, the British High Commissioner for Canada, for British-produced television programs to counterbalance American influence on Canadian airwaves: "Our challenge must come now, or the web spun across the border will become too strong to be loosed. Television is a major and dynamic force tending to draw Canada away from the United Kingdom and the Commonwealth . . . Every day that passes without the United Kingdom being able to offer what is needed adds to the strength of the US in Canada. This is a problem which cannot wait."[41] A report in 1953 stated it succinctly:

> The prestige of the United Kingdom (and of British trade) will suffer in the long run unless British programmes on film are

available soon to the television services of the rest of the world. Production for television is a costly business and as each new country introduces television services it will look abroad for supplies of television films to supplement its domestic programmes. At the moment such supplies in appreciable quantities can come only from the United States and unless early action is taken the US will in the course of time dominate television, particularly in the English-speaking countries of the Commonwealth, even more than it does the dilemma at present. The United Kingdom High Commissioners in Canada and in Australia have drawn attention to the dangers which such a development involves.[42]

Yet the problem, as always, was money. The BBC had always resisted producing programs on film, for reasons discussed below. Programs that would compete with American material would be expensive, and it was unclear, as well, who should be in charge of their production: the BBC or another sector of the British state. Discussion dragged out through 1954 between the BBC, the Foreign Office, the British Board of Trade, and the Central Office of Information (COI).[43] Though an Overseas Television Service would begin to address this gap in 1954, not until 1957 did British productions made explicitly for non-profit public policy export begin to circulate widely, produced mainly by the Overseas Information Service, a consortium combining the efforts of all these groups but dominated by the COI (Kaye 2007). By that time, the experience of Independent Television had proven to all that a whole separate sector of commercial exports and co-productions could also be highly profitable.

In the US, while commercial interests rushed to obtain licenses for the new medium, educational broadcasters held back, hampered by a lack of organization, poor funding from educational institutions struggling to respond to the dramatic GI Bill-induced expansion of higher education, and new FM opportunities. Their saving grace came with FCC's "freeze" on the assignment of new television licenses in 1948, which created an opportunity for educational broadcasters to organize and intervene in the commercial station goldrush. The appointment in 1948 of Frieda Barkin Hennock to the FCC, its first female commissioner, also helped the cause; though Hennock had no previous background in radio she had been influenced by Clifford Durr and had attended the Institute for Education by Radio conference in 1948 where she became convinced of the importance of non-commercial broadcasting. Her dissenting opinion in the FCC's proposed allocation plan in 1949, arguing against the majority for a 25% reservation for education television in both the VHF and UHF bands, has been called a "history-making plea" that "provided the legal and moral platform on which the educational establishment was subsequently to act" (Hull 1965, 340; see also Brinson 2002).

Final hearings on the subject were scheduled for December 1950. In the nick of time—on October 16, 1950—the NAEB in conjunction with the US Office of Education assembled all the major American groups concerned with this new field to form a cohesive group to lobby with Congress: the Joint Committee on Educational Television (JCET). With a grant from a new and barely organized player in the field, the Ford Foundation, the JCET was able to pull together contributions from educational broadcasters and make decisive interventions at the hearings, against strong opposition from commercial interests, which secured frequency set-asides for educational television. They were placed on sharp notice, however, that these allocations were only temporary and could and would be revoked unless noncommercial institutions made concrete plans for using them quickly and decisively, within a year.

Now an enormous task faced educational television in the US: essentially, to create something like the early BBC from the ground up, with no public funding or direction, out of the scattered and ill-funded group of noncommercial radio broadcasters and educational groups, for a new medium in which none had training and for which little expertise or infrastructure existed. No ready supply of programming existed either. In August 1953 the NAEB Advisory Committee expressed its frustration:

> [T]he educational TV station approaches its first day on the air not only without the operating experience and physical resources of the commercial station it is expected to surpass, but with the immediate necessity of doing in quantity what the commercial station never does—initially producing all its programs without benefit of a network source of local programming experience. At the same time, the public will expect from the educational TV station not only routine programs of an educational nature, but outstanding offerings. In other words, super-normal performance is expected from an educational TV station with subnormal fiscal and operating conditions.[44] (emphasis in the original)

Fortunately for educational broadcasting in America, a new power stepped in, to assume and to exceed the Rockefeller Foundation's place in radio in the 1930s and 40s.

It is impossible to overstate the crucial role played by the Ford Foundation and its Fund for Adult Education (FAE) in the history of American public broadcasting, or indeed in American cultural history in the second half of the twentieth century, with impact on cultural, scientific, and political organizations in virtually every nation around the world. As the Rockefeller Foundation had dominated the interlocking worlds of education, broadcasting, and politics in the 1930s and 40s, so the Ford Foundation stepped into that role in the 1950s and after.

Organized in a small way in 1936, the Ford Foundation came into its own after Henry Ford's death in 1947. For inheritance tax purposes the bulk of his estate went not to his heirs but into a charitable trust, whose astonishing net worth of over $400 million by 1950 suddenly thrust it to the forefront of American philanthropy. Under the titular direction of Henry Ford II, but guided more closely by 1950–53 president Paul G. Hoffman, the Ford Foundation determined to dedicate itself to "the advancement of human welfare" and "solving humankind's most pressing problems" across a wide field of activities (Macdonald 1956). One of those fields was education, and the Foundation's Fund for Adult Education (FAE), established in April 1951, quickly became its single largest effort.

Less well remembered today is the Ford Foundation's connection to the world of Cold War politics and international economic policy.[45] James Schwoch nominates the Ford Foundation as a key node in the network of "high level government and philanthropic leaders work[ing] in concert to aim the vision of the field of international communications and media studies through the single lens of Cold War psychological warfare" (2008, 64) and points to Paul Hoffman as one of its prime operators. Hoffman, a native of Illinois, attended the University of Chicago briefly before leaving to get into the automotive industry. He became President of the Studebaker Corporation in 1935, and in 1942, along with William Benton, founded the Committee for Economic Development (CED), an influential business-oriented public policy think-tank, still in existence today, that aimed to assist in the transition from a wartime to a peacetime economy and helped muster support for the Marshall Plan after the war. In 1948 President Truman appointed Hoffman head of the Organization for Economic Cooperation (OEC), the body in charge of administering the Marshall Plan in Europe. He served in this post for two years before agreeing to head up the Ford Foundation in 1950.[46]

Working under Hoffman at Studebaker was a young Australian, Cyril Scott Fletcher, in whom Hoffman had taken an interest; in 1942 he appointed Fletcher Executive Vice President of the United China Relief Fund, an organization formed by Hoffmann and Henry Luce, president of Time-Life (another organization soon to become significant in these pages), to raise money for America's Chinese allies. After the war Fletcher joined Hoffman at the Committee on Economic Development, where he became an Executive Director and Trustee. Here Fletcher (whose story will be taken up below) worked closely with William Benton, founder of the Benton and

Bowles agency known for its early involvement in commercial radio. It is worth following this cast of characters a little further, to point at the numerous ways that the birth of educational television in the US was tied to the interlocking circles of power and privilege that became a political as well as a cultural force in the post-war era.[47] The names of Hoffmann, Benton, and Hutchins figure centrally (with Luce on the sidelines), along with their chief lieutenant, "Scotty" Fletcher.

William Benton had attended Yale University, where he became a close friend of Robert M. Hutchins. Hutchins, previously discussed as chair of the Hutchins Commission on Freedom of the Press, had a startlingly brilliant academic career: having earned a law degree at Yale University in 1925, he was appointed to its faculty immediately upon graduation and in 1927, only 27 years old, became its Dean. Three years later, at the ripe age of 30, he took on the post of President of the University of Chicago—the university founded by the Rockefeller family. At Chicago he developed and implemented his philosophy of education, not only in University of Chicago policies but in his partnership with Mortimer Adler, among others, in promoting the Great Books of the Western World approach to learning (see Beam 2008; Rubin 1992).

Hutchins stepped down from the Chancellorship of the University of Chicago in 1951 to become head of the Fund for the Republic in 1952—an organization created and funded by the Ford Foundation, yet kept at arm's length in what critic Dwight Macdonald wittily called a "wholly disowned subsidiary"—whose mission was to resist McCarthyite challenges to constitutional freedoms and "to educate Americans about civil liberties and civil rights" (McCarthy 1987, 282) which it did effectively enough to find itself under investigation by HUAC (Kelly 1981). One of the main instruments of the Fund's mission would be the mass media, particularly television. Hutchins' later career took him out of the limelight and into semi-retirement in Santa Barbara, California, where he published a number of books and served as Chairman of the *Encyclopedia Britannica*'s Board of Editors from 1943 until 1974.

Hutchins' involvement with the *Encyclopedia* stemmed from his decision in 1945 to bring his old friend William Benton, co-founder with Hutchins of the Committee for Economic Development, to the University of Chicago as a vice president. Here Benton worked with George Probst on the *University of Chicago Round Table* and became sympathetic to the cause of educational media, whether in the form of book series, films, radio, or television. When the University of Chicago was offered the opportunity to purchase the *Encyclopedia Britannica* organization from Sears Roebuck in 1937, Benton helped raise the purchase money and became president of the company. Though his name is not as widely recognized as those of

Hutchins or Hoffman, Benton's career is an astonishing one. Originally from Minnesota, Benton attended Carleton College and then Yale, graduating in 1921 and moving into the thriving advertising industry. With Chester Bowles in 1930 he formed the eponymous advertising agency Benton and Bowles, one of the earliest to move heavily into radio. Benton and Bowles produced a number of highly popular commercial programs in the 1930s and 40s, including *The Maxwell House Showboat*, the crime serial *Gang Busters*, and comedian Fred Allen's *Town Hall Tonight*. But tiring of the commercial world, determined to use his talents to improve it instead, Benton retired from business and soon took up the post at the University of Chicago at the behest of his Yale friend Robert Hutchins.

In addition to espousing the cause of educational radio with his involvement in *The University of Chicago Roundtable*, Benton also led the University into the arena of educational film with the purchase of the ERPI Classroom Films division and the Eastman Teaching Films subsidiary; Benton consolidated them into a subsidiary of the *Encyclopedia* business called Encyclopedia of Britannica Films, Inc. Benton appointed "Scotty" Fletcher to the post of President of this company in 1947.[48] Benton's links to Britain went further than the *Encyclopedia* enterprises, however. As co-founder of the CED, at the top of Benton's agenda was the consolidation of America's economic and political alliance with Britain. He traveled to England in the summer of 1943 "to study the possibility of a friendly and profitable economic policy between the two nations,"[49] returning to write up several reports on Anglo-American trade relations that were widely published and influential. These activities led to an appointment as Assistant Secretary of State in 1945 under President Roosevelt. Here he helped to found the US Information Agency (USIA) and UNESCO, still espousing radio and film as key elements in an Anglo/American-dominated world system. He became a US Senator from 1949 till 1952, where in 1951 he famously introduced a bill denouncing red-baiting Senator Joseph McCarthy, then at the height of his influence. Benton returned to the *Encyclopedia Britannica* in 1952, and established the Benton Foundation to support this and other educational efforts.

Together, Hutchins, Benton, and Hoffman, along with Henry Luce (president of Time, Inc.), played crucial roles in the powerful circuits linking American liberal politics, higher education, publishing, business, and international communication during the Cold War. All three shaped the education, career, and outlook of the younger man who would become the guiding force behind the next chapter in American educational broadcasting and its international relationships, Cyril Scott Fletcher. When Hoffmann became head of the Ford Foundation in 1950, he immediately appointed Robert Hutchins to the Board of Directors; one of their first decisions was to name the "short, wiry, super-energetic" Fletcher the director of Ford's Fund for Adult Education.[50] Under Hoffman and Fletcher, radio and television, but especially the promising new medium of television, represented the most important venue for adult civic education available at a moment when America's new global role and the political threats to democracy from both within the country and from the Soviet Union made education vitally necessary. Like John Marshall at the Rockefeller Foundation in the 1930s, "Scotty" Fletcher determined not merely to fund and work through existing organizations but to intervene directly and decisively "to make educational television a reality" by creating new ones (Blakeley 1979, 85). As its first venture, to test the thesis that a well-done cultural program could attract commercial sponsors, the FAE set up its own Television-Radio Workshop in October 1951 and plunged into program production with the BBC-inspired *Omnibus* (discussed below); further transnational programming initiatives would follow with the Broadcast Foundation of America and INTERTEL.

But educational television needed to be created from the ground up—or to be more accurate, from the airwaves down. The FAE's very first grant, of $15,000, founded the Joint Committee on Educational Television and launched its crucial intervention into television frequency allocations. Thanks to the JCET's focused organization and testimony before the FCC, the "Third Notice" passed in March 1951 gave educational broadcasters a grace period of one year to come up with a plan to get educational television underway. The FAE granted another $90,000 to the JCET in April to mobilize the planning and lobbying process; between April and October "838 statements or exhibits of support or requests for additional reservations were filed with the FCC by colleges, universities, public school systems, state departments of education, and voluntary organizations" (Blakeley 1979, 89). Without such Ford-funded mobilization it is highly unlikely that the FCC's "Sixth Report and Order" in June 1952 would have reserved the 242 television channels (80 VHF and 162 UHF) for "exclusive noncommercial educational use by schools, colleges, universities, and nonprofit educational television corporations" (Hull 1965, 343).

But the clock was ticking, loudly. As FCC Chair Paul A. Walker told an educational assembly at Pennsylvania State University in July 1952: "These precious television assignments cannot be preserved for you indefinitely. They may not even be reserved for you beyond one year unless you can give the Commission concrete, convincing evidence of the validity of your intent. . . . Time began to run out the minute this Report was issued . . . I fear you will find this year of grace the shortest year of your lives" (quoted in Blakely 1979, 90). Here again Scott Fletcher entered directly into negotiations with the FCC, making a private national foundation a party to license allocation decisions in a way that was unprecedented in the history of American broadcasting. Too much was at stake on both sides, and too much remained to be done, for the business of building educational television from scratch to be left in the hands of the educators. The FCC needed assurance that the frequencies would be used, justifying their decision; the Ford Foundation needed to know that if they succeeded in their ambitious plan the channel reservations would indeed become permanent, justifying their multi-million dollar investment.

At a meeting in May 1952, after FCC Chair Walker laid out to the Foundation's directors the urgency of the situation, "Fletcher explained to Walker the Fund's plan: to stimulate applications, to aid station activation financially, and to establish a national program exchange center" (Blakeley 1979, 91). The Ford Foundation approved over $4,500,000 (nearly $40 million in today's dollars) to be used by Fletcher and the FAE to achieve these goals, and at a dinner in Washington in October of that year Fletcher put their proposal to the entire assembled Commission: matching grants to build stations, the creation of a national program production and exchange center, and the formation of a national citizens' committee to bring whole communities, not just educational institutions, into the field of public service television. In effect, Fletcher had set himself up at the helm of a whole new, independent broadcasting organization—a "fourth network," as some later called it—that promised to unite the scattered efforts of educational radio and television into a system funded not by advertising but by private funds drawn from the non-profit sector.

A year of feverish work and the expenditure of over $700,000 by the FAE culminated in the triumphal "First National Conference on Educational Television" in Washington DC on May 4, 1953, at which speakers from twenty-one states reported on the progress they had made towards getting their stations up and running; one week later, the FCC confirmed the educational channel reservations as permanent. Though many bumpy years followed, the first two educational television stations went on the air in 1954 and by 1961 another fifty stations had joined them, thanks to over $4 million in Ford Foundation construction and facilities support. It is doubtful that any of this could have been accomplished without Ford Foundation funds, or even more importantly without Fletcher's and Hoffman's political connections at a time of Cold War crisis.

But now came the next challenge: these 52 stations needed something to put on the air, besides the programs they could produce themselves, as did the 175 educational FM radio stations beginning to take their places on the 88–92 MHz band across the nation. Again Fletcher and the Ford Foundation stepped in, working with a special committee of the NAEB in which Rockefeller-supported, BBC-trained radio figures played a lead role on the advisory committee: George Probst, Robert Hudson, Seymour Siegel,

Richard Hull, Harold McCarty, and Parker Wheatley. Their Educational Television and Radio Center (ETRC), established in November of 1952 with Fletcher as temporary director, set its goals as "facilitating the production and exchange of programs in the four subject areas [of] international affairs, national or political affairs, economic affairs, and the humanities" (Blakely 1979, 102). These four aspects of adult education were the main concerns of the Ford Foundation's FAE, as opposed to programs to be used in schools or to provide direct training. Rather than produce programs itself, the ETRC encouraged the production of programs by its member stations, provided the means to distribute them to others across the country, and also sought to procure programs, both radio and television, from other sources for distribution throughout the network. Here acquisitions and co-productions with both the BBC, the CBC, and eventually British commercial broadcasters as well, became particularly important, and a vital but controversial relationship quickly developed that would embed British Commonwealth culture in the heart of American public broadcasting, and entwine BBC economics and aesthetics deeply around its American counterparts.

By September of 1952, with the ink on the Sixth Report hardly dried but with Ford Foundation funds in their pockets, an NAEB delegation consisting of Siegel, Probst, and William Harley, program director of the Wisconsin State Broadcasting System, set off for Europe, first stop the BBC. A ready supply of radio programming presented the most urgent issue, and the BBC was eager to participate. As the BBC's Rooney Pelletier reported it:

> The object of the London meeting was: (a) to show the NAEB officials as much of the BBC operation as possible; (b) to discuss all possible methods of mutual co-operation. A complete fortnight of Third Programme output was recorded and sent to NAEB 'for information' before the arrival in London of their representatives.[51]

Issues of rights and royalties, currency exchange, and commercial commitments would complicate BBC and NAEB cooperation, but *Broadcasting* magazine reported on the NAEB trip under the headline "Educators Find Radio, TV Vines Strong," not only with the BBC but with Italian television as well, from whom they commissioned a series on Italian art and history.[52] Radio programs from France, Italy, and Britain were added to the NAEB library.

And the exchange went both ways. The Ford Foundation intended that American noncommercial broadcasting should rise to the level of its European public service counterparts. With an FAE grant of $300,000, the NAEB formed a production unit under the direction of William Harley to produce three documentary programs that would demonstrate that "radio programs could be both educational and appealing."[53] This effort resulted in *The Jeffersonian Heritage* starring Claude Rains; *Ways of Mankind*, a 26-episode cultural anthropology series funded by the NAEB but produced by Andrew Allan at the Canadian Broadcasting Corporation; and *People Under Communism*, made in conjunction with Russian scholars at Harvard University and again produced in Canada. Both would air in Canada and in Britain on the BBC. But such efforts could not compete with the increasing number of British programs on educational radio schedules. In 1953 the BBC sent a young Charles Parker, later to become well known for his innovative radio ballads, on a tour of US and Canadian stations. His report on "The Wisconsin State Broadcasting Service" noted that BBC radio programs, obtained through the NAEB tape service, were held "in very high regard. At least one full-length classical drama is used each month, plus such series as the Reith Lectures, some music of a distinctive quality (such as British Cathedral music) and some of the outstanding features." The station, and its state-wide radio network, also aired BBC North American Service programs on a regular basis.[54]

A factor that made British radio programs attractive but also limited their usefulness was that they were all but free. The British government under-wrote distribution of overseas programming through the Transcription Service and also subsidized the duplication of such programs onto tapes for stations in the US, which had only to pay for shipping fees. However, with the limited funds available, only seven hours a week of English language radio programs could be offered. In 1952, the BBC's young Assistant Controller of Overseas Services, Hugh Carleton Greene, proposed that the NAEB might change this by subscribing in the amount of $56,000 per year to the BBC Transcription Service, affording a longer list of titles to be made available. As the report noted, the BBC broadcast more than 250 radio plays at home each year but could only provide 14 for overseas distribution under its current funding. The NAEB recommended that the NETRC, its distri-bution arm, raise the funds to do this; in return, the BBC promised that it would provide at least one full-length drama and two shorter talks, dis-cussions, or readings per week, to be duplicated and distributed by the NETRC on behalf of NAEB. The NAEB would retain the right to broadcast these programs on any of its member stations for three years, so that they could be distributed serially to participating members and aired more than once if desired. Rights issues complicated the airing of programs containing musical material, with some requiring additional payment to British musical rights organizations.[55]

As the NAEB, the NETRC, and their funding organizations squabbled over responsibilities and dragged their feet,[56] the BBC continued to provide programs but insisted on distributing them themselves, without using the NAEB as an intermediary. A twelve-spoked "bicycle" system was designed, with the BBC's New York office duplicating Overseas offerings and shipping them out to twelve "point" stations, who then sent them along a chain that might consist of six to eight additional stations; the last one receiving the tape returned it to the BBC. This cumbersome method—used for most NETRC programs—kept costs down but created enormous scheduling difficulties and prevented any kind of nationally consistent program from being established until the late 1950s, as discussed in the next chapter.

From the initial visit of the NAEB delegation to the BBC in 1952, television exchange was very urgently on the agenda too. The NAEB expressed great interest in several existing BBC programs as well as in commissioning others; however, the BBC at this point still considered US commercial broadcasters better prospects for program export and had an agreement with the William Morris Agency to distribute BBC television in the US. This marks the beginning of the idea of program export as a profit center for the BBC; though commercial exploitation of publicly funded production at home was forbidden in the terms of the license, any monies that such programs could make through foreign distribution could only help the BBC's bottom line and mission overall. Hugh Carleton Greene, from his position in the Overseas Services, may have been the first inside the BBC to see this potential clearly. In 1953, in an article entitled "Television Transcriptions: The Economic Possibilities" which appeared in the *BBC Quarterly*, he presciently predicted the course that BBC exports to the US would take. Noting that "Kinescopes of BBC shows will not, except very occasionally, be seen in America until non-commercial educational television . . . finds it feet" he predicted, "Then, assuming that all union problems are satisfactorily settled, the day for BBC kinescopes may be expected to dawn" (1953, 218).

But in the meantime an opportunity existed that would not last for long: "American television does not want kinescopes: it does want films specially designed for television—specially designed for American television. It wants them in large numbers and it wants them now" (218). Showing an unusually detailed grasp of the economics and structure of American television, he proposed "a transcription service producing films tailored for American television, films of the right length and the right tempo, with the right stories and the right voices and accents."

> And by 'right' I do not mean pseudo-American. . . . One reason why British television films would be welcomed in the United States is that they could provide something fresh for the jaded viewer. . . . The streets of London, the English countryside, the old market

towns, the country houses, the cathedral and university towns provide the scene for hundreds of stories which would be an immense attraction for the American viewer—and (which is what really counts) the American sponsor. (Greene 1953, 219)

Such shows would also hold appeal in Canada, Australia and New Zealand, he argued, and "If the opportunity is not grasped by this country it certainly will be by others, particularly by the United States, and, in Asia, by Japan." This was an opportunity not taken by the BBC in the 1950s, though ITV would soon answer the call. In 1960, one of Greene's first actions as Director-General would be to set up BBC Television Enterprises for just this purpose, under the direction of Ronald Waldman.

For American educational television in 1952, lacking its own production center as yet, the purchase of programs of almost any kind from the BBC represented the best chance for a viable national service. Interestingly in light of later developments in co-production, the Americans seemed to envision the BBC as a source of commissioned productions: a kind of off-shore production company for hire. Val Gielgud, now head of television as well as radio drama, put the situation in his usual succinct way:

[T]hey were very anxious to have a list of suggestions of subjects which would make half-hour television feature shorts in which they might interest the Ford Foundation, and which as a result they might be able to invite us to make for them over here. ... The trouble is that the Americans have already been and gone after their usual vigorous and athletic fashion, so I think it is really a question of firing a list of hypothetical notions into the blue.[57]

And in fact the delegation came away with a commitment on the BBC's part to produce a thirteen part series on British culture (or on "BRITISH WORTHIES," as Pelletier put it). This would eventually result in a ten part series, *Art and Artists*, which would air on US educational stations in 1956. A host of problems with currency restrictions, performers' union contracts, and BBC finances kept British television programs off US airwaves in any significant amount for several years. Too, at the point of the NAEB visit, only one educational television station was actually built and on the air: WOI-TV in Ames, Iowa. By 1954 there would be 10 more, including WHA-TV in Wisconsin, along with powerhouse producing stations that would forge a new relationship with the BBC: WGBH-Boston, KQED-San Francisco, and the forerunner of New York's WNET. In June 1954, Scott Fletcher stepped in once again to kick-start the stalled relationship with a visit to George Barnes, Director of BBC Television Broadcasting, who outlined a series of potential projects and scheduled a visit to the US in July.[58] By the late 1950s, as Britain adjusted to commercial television, American public broadcasting would emerge into a new era, with British programming one of its main staples and also one of its main points of controversy. However, the influence of British broadcasting on American television was not confined to direct import of programs.

Alistair Cooke, the Ford Foundation, and *Omnibus*

In the early 1950s, as radio in Britain soared to new heights and US educational broadcasting got its long-awaited second wind, it seemed as though even American commercial broadcasters felt the pull towards public service. Many had served in the OWI or the AFRS during the war, and sustained strong feelings about broadcasting's central role in mobilizing and motivating citizens in a cause larger than selling toothpaste. Sylvester "Pat" Weaver at NBC was one of these; having produced *Command Performance* for the OWI, he returned to his pre-war employer, the Young and Rubicam advertising agency, convinced that television should take a different path from radio. In this he sounded positively Reithian:

> For some time I had been disturbed by the question of whether advertisers and their agencies should exercise so much control over what went on the air. . . . Only the networks, it seemed to me, were in a position to help television fulfill its promise. . . . If properly developed, [television] could raise the educational and cultural level of the entire nation. It could enrich the common man—make him the uncommon man. (Weaver 1994, 164–65)

Weaver recognized, too, that television would be far more expensive to produce than radio, potentially straining the resources of the single sponsor system. Weaver first approached William Paley of CBS with his ideas, aware that CBS had moved ahead of NBC in pursuing network responsibility for programming. As early as 1936, CBS had begun to articulate a philosophy of network-originated sustaining production, with Norman Corwin and the *Columbia Workshop* as its signature, and had also pioneered in the production of its own package shows before the war (Boddy 1990). When Paley failed to respond positively, Weaver turned to NBC, where "they weren't much interested in my vision of television's future, but it soon became apparent that they were interested in me" (Weaver 1994, 167).

Hired as Director of Television Programs, he departed from previous commercial radio practice by putting together an in-house programming department and began the effort to convince sponsors, agencies, and General David Sarnoff that the future lay with network control over programming and a "spot advertising" system for sponsors. In this he was doubtless influenced by the need to please the FCC as station license applications were being evaluated, but the idea of the network not merely as time-broker but as a center for creative production also served key network objectives, as Vance Kepley notes: not only did high profile programming help to line up and retain affiliates during a competitive period, it pointed in a direction that would give control over the entire programming schedule to the networks, who could use it to build audiences and ratings more effectively than they were able to do under the sponsor system (Kepley 1990, 50).

Weaver's "Operation Frontal Lobes" at NBC achieved these objectives both through high-quality documentary/actuality series, like *Victory At Sea, Project XX*, and *Wisdom*, as well as NBC's much-vaunted "spectaculars," one-time prestige event programs an hour or longer that would feature literary adaptations, original dramatic works, or stage presentations. All of these were unsponsored yet played a key role in NBC's overall commercial strategy. "We get them coming for the caviar, and they stick around . . . for the bread and butter," an NBC spokesman explained, in a neat reversal of BBC programming philosophy (Kepley 1990, 47). It may have worked but it also put NBC-TV deeply in the red by 1953. CBS, meantime, focused on sponsored live anthology drama programs like *Studio One, Playhouse 90*, and *Climax* as well as on news and documentary from its prestigious Public Affairs department under the direction of Edward R. Murrow. The networks were determined to prove that, under their direction and control, commercial television could produce public service programming of a quality higher than that produced by any self-interested sponsor or struggling educational station—while also raking in their accustomed profits.

But as the Cold War burgeoned, the Ford Foundation was not content to sit back and let others experiment with television in the public service, nor to confine itself to purely instructional programming; it had larger goals that reflected the philosophy of the networks more closely than that of educational broadcasters. As noted above, in 1951 it formed the Ford Foundation TV-Radio Workshop, underwritten by $1.2 million in foundation funds, with the specific mission of demonstrating "that television programs with educational and cultural content can achieve audiences of a size and character—and at a cost—commensurate with the requirements of commercial sponsorship" (Ford Foundation 1953, 61). They had been advised on this matter by James Webb Young, formerly of J. Walter Thompson and an old friend of both Hutchins and Hoffman (1953). The Foundation named Robert Saudek, a Harvard-trained former ABC documentary producer and public affairs vice president, as director of the Workshop. Saudek himself described his mission as "creating programs which would attract a mass audience large enough to interest commercial

sponsors in programs which contain values of information and enlightenment calculated to help raise not only television's program standards but also
the general level of American taste and interests" (Saudek 1952). Out of these
aims grew the central concepts of *Omnibus*, the program that brought
Alistair Cooke to television and to national prominence in the United States,
presaging the role he would assume on PBS in the future.

Omnibus was conceived as a kind of cultural and informational magazine
of the air, a format that renowned critic Walter Lippmann had suggested to
Saudek (Clarke 1999, 267). As Saudek and the Ford Foundation planned it,
the program would be presented live, consisting of four or five separate
features of varying content and length, some live, some on film, over the
unusual period of 90 minutes, to maintain "the two principles of 'freedom
of time' and 'freedom of frequency'" that US broadcasting so rarely displayed
(Saudek 1952). It would not interrupt the features with advertising; ads
would appear only in "natural breaks" between the program's segments.
Most importantly, Saudek declared, "the character of 'Omnibus' is firmly in
the hands of its producers"—emphatically *not* the sponsors who would be
kept at arm's length. Its producers, Saudek included, were Ford Foundation
employees, numbering more than 30 by 1955 (about one-sixth of Ford's
New York-based workforce) (Macdonald 1956, 96). CBS agreed to air the
program on Sundays at 4:30, and sponsors including Willys-Overland
Motors and Greyhound Bus signed up. The role of the host was key: the one
element recurring every week, giving the show its public face and personality, requiring someone who could demonstrate expertise across an
incredibly wide cultural spectrum yet who remained capable of reaching out
to the vast masses of the American viewing public; falling, as Alistair Cooke
himself put it, "between Somerset Maugham and Milton Berle."[59]

Saudek had met Alistair Cooke before, but it was at the annual Peabody
Awards presentation in spring of 1952, at which *Letter From America* won
the prize for "Radio's Outstanding Contribution to International Under-
standings during 1951," that he realized he'd found his host (after a rebuff
from Laurence Olivier). Not only had Cooke perfected a friendly, unpre-
tentious on-air persona, he looked the part of the genteel and cultured
Englishman: tall, smooth, well-groomed, and with an accent distinctly
British though of a kind Americans would have no trouble understanding
(Macdonald 1956, 88). Publicity for *Omnibus* centrally featured Alistair
Cooke's persona and presence. As the promotional brochure claimed "He
will pace and unify and set the character of the whole show. He will be the
Good Companion, always welcome in your home for his fresh and witty
slant on the doings of the human race" (Clarke 1999, 268). Though Saudek
(and eventually co-producers Fred Rickey, William Spier, and Mary V.
Ahern) made the content decisions, Cooke's ability to ad-lib, live and under

pressure, made an enormous difference to the way the show ultimately appeared to its audience. Saudek later wrote, "I had the highest hopes for Alistair in his untried role of host, but I must say that in ease of manner, clarity of expression, deftness of wit and the unusual ability to flatter an audience into feeling sophisticated themselves, he soared above even my hopes" (Jones and Walworth 1999).

Alternating original drama with classics, dance with documentary, history with current affairs, opera with jazz, the program lived up to its name. Its debut on 11 November 1952 presented an abbreviated version of *The Mikado* starring Martyn Green of the British D'Oyly Carte Opera Company; a short original drama by Maxwell Anderson, "The Trial of Anne Boleyn," with Rex Harrison and his wife, Lilli Palmer, in the lead roles; a sketch by William Saroyan; a film featuring Haitian voodoo dance, "The Witch Doctor"; and a reflection on Armistice Day narrated by Cooke himself. In its mixture of these elements—drama, documentary, the arts, discussion, history[60]—the program encapsulated not only a BBC-inspired vision of middlebrow culture but an attempt very much along Canadian lines to incorporate a national sensibility within a cultural framework dependent on a transnational other: in this case, the tradition of British cultural heritage that has remained so evident on American public service television (Jarvik 1999; Jones and Walworth 1999). As time went on, the British elements would remain but the American ingredients would become stronger. In 1956, for instance, the program undertook a three-part dramatization of the foundations of the American Constitution, written (with Harvard historian Richard Hofstadter) and narrated by Joseph N. Welch, the Boston lawyer who had defended the Army against the red-baiting charges of Joseph McCarthy a few years earlier.[61] This type of program harked back to the public service drama/documentaries of the war years, themselves forged in transatlantic artistic convergence, and took a "safely" cultural program onto contested political ground—very much in line with the objectives of the Fund for the Republic.

Perhaps because of the chances it took, *Omnibus* also holds the distinction of being one of the few programs to air sequentially on all three major networks. Starting out on CBS from 1952 through 1955, it moved first to ABC from 1956 to 1957, then went to NBC from 1957 to 1961. NBC had tried to get it as early as 1953, while Pat Weaver was still in "Operation Frontal Lobes" mode, for its high public service profile as well as the respectable ratings it was generating: a 28.9 in February 1953.[62] In fact, to court the original show NBC agreed in the fall of 1953 to broadcast a second Ford Radio-TV Workshop program, *Excursion* (1953–54), aimed at younger audiences (Ford Foundation 1953). But in 1957 the Ford Foundation withdrew its support, not out of disappointment but because its intention had always been to launch the program, then let it flourish on commercial sponsorship. Several corporate "subscribers," as Cooke preferred to call them, had underwritten the show to the tune of nearly $6 million over five years (with Ford supplying more than $3 million additionally).[63] Ford's withdrawal prompted Saudek to continue with the show on his own, forming Robert Saudek Productions, Inc. with several partners, including Cooke; they declared themselves "architects of commercial programs of quality."[64] During its last season on the air, *Omnibus* picked up a new sponsor, Aluminium Ltd, a Canadian Corporation that mandated that each week's show premiere on Canadian television before its US debut. So, as the *New York Times* reported, "It may well be the only television program produced on tape in the United States, exported to Canada for an initial showing there and then 'imported' for use in this country."[65] Canadian audiences viewed the program, which had been taped a week in advance, on Monday evenings over 45 stations, before its broadcast the following Sunday afternoon on NBC.

However, this would be *Omnibus's* last season. Though it attracted considerable critical praise, its determinedly middlebrow sensibility alienated those who would have preferred more of a "Third Programme" approach; Dwight Macdonald noted that it "has a disturbing habit of falling flat on its face when it tries to soar" (1956, 90). Yet, in going after an audience large enough to attract advertisers, Jack Gould of the *New York Times* found that "regular commercial television often runs rings around the workshop in cultural accomplishment" and also that "'Omnibus' has grown notorious for its pliant susceptibility to commercial promotional gimmicks".[66] Macdonald cites an example of a visiting expert on housing problems, Charles Adams, who found himself asked to read a script endorsing prefabricated aluminum houses made by Aluminium Ltd.—something his recent report had explicitly criticized. By 1961, too, the networks' public service plans had turned more decisively in the direction of news and documentary (Curtin 1999). Meantime, educational television had picked up steam with continuing support from the Ford Foundation. The next few years would see a gradual bifurcation in programming, as educational and cultural fare became the territory of NET and its eventual successor PBS, and the commercial networks narrowed their vision to entertainment programs plus a continuing commitment to national and local news. But the British-American relationship in the cultural programming sphere would not fade, and at most of its key moments, Alistair Cooke would be there.

The post-war years in Britain and America found both nations eager to move ahead with the new technology of television, tied closely to demands for reassertion of national identity and for reform that built on wartime experiences. Radio continued to dominate until the mid 1950s; Britain diversified its service into three distinct channels based on "taste," with the highbrow Third Programme quickly becoming "the envy of the world" (Carpenter 1996). In the US radio held on to its dominant position for a few years even as the networks shifted their emphasis to television and music came to dominate the airwaves one again. Both the Blue Book and the Beveridge Report focused their attention on that medium, each nation drawing on the example of the other to advocate for regulatory change, in the case of the US, and the maintainance of the status quo, in the UK. Charles Siepmann, the BBC man turned US policy analyst, played a key role at the heart of both major investigations. The fading out of the Rockefeller Foundation from the broadcasting scene left the field wide open for a new player with deep political connections to forces of Cold War era liberalism, the Ford Foundation, which under the leadership of "Scotty" Fletcher almost single-handedly gathered the scattered forces of educational radio and television into a coherent whole in the early 1950s. During this early period, the exchange of radio programming across the Atlantic increased as US educational radio stations found a secure home on the FM band set aside for them. But television's international role remained unclear, as Britain dragged its feet in the production of television programs for export, while the US moved swiftly into filmed production that would soon be marked worldwide, as the next chapter details. However, the influence of British forms and culture could be clearly detected in the Ford Foundation-produced magazine program *Omnibus*, hosted by Alistair Cooke in a role he would soon develop on America's budding public television network. In both nations, television became the new field of national and transnational anxiety, The rivalry of radio's early years and the conflicted cooperation of wartime gave way to a new struggle for world dominance, as these two mighty network nations became empires of the air.

CHAPTER **8**

New Directions and
Disputes, 1955–1964

There never has been and never will be any majority demand for sponsored TV in Britain; it is something dreamed up by a group of interested politicians and it is utterly alien to the British way of life.[1]
—Jonah Barrington, *Daily Sketch*, June 8, 1953

We can improve TV, Mr. Minow! Culture can be popular and Shakespeare a hit on TV. It has happened here in Washington where the kings of England appear to be giving Bat Masterson and Wyatt Earp quite a bit of competition.[2]
—Josephine Ripley, *Christian Science Monitor* 1961,
reviewing *Age of Kings*

Between 1955 and 1964, television on both sides of the Atlantic began to take the shape it would hold for the next thirty years. Commercial television was introduced in Britain, after an extremely bumpy process during which a comical chimpanzee sidekick on an American morning news program briefly became the symbol of all that was wrong, and furthermore simply *not British*, about the whole idea of commercial broadcasting. The advent of Independent Television created an opening and a demand for a type of "mid-Atlantic" production that combined British and American interests in popular entertainment programs which also provided shelter to blacklisted American film and radio writers and producer refugees from the cold war. Such series, as well as the rhetoric around sponsored television in Britain, proved equally useful in the American networks' strategy to take back control over their programming from the powerful sponsors in the wake of the quiz show scandal. In the US the Ford Foundation continued to build up the "fourth network" of National Educational Television, drawing for inspi-ration and also increasingly for programming on its public service counter-parts in Britain and Canada (including ITV), even as British broadcasters contemplated their own version of educational television, based on the American model, leading up to the Pilkington report, which would harshly criticize ITV's performance.

Through the critical lens that a transnational view offers, it is possible to observe the anxieties produced by the capabilities of live television as it became a part of national life, creating a new kind of public space that projected into hitherto private places and occasions, now no longer pro-tected by the traditionally controlled public life of nations but open to the world's sometimes unsympathetic gaze, charged with Cold War tensions. Yet transnational exchange became an even greater ingredient of national culture as the demand for programming on channels around the world exceeded what could be produced live at home and created a new sphere of internationally circulating filmed programs, produced by multi-national production teams and finding audiences in national spaces far from their points of origin, once again dominated by Britain and America. Their discursive construction of "the other" continued to figure large in policy debates, whether for good or bad—a situation made more complex by the emergence of non-commercial television in the US and commercial television in Great Britain. As Britain and the United States continued to take a leading role in producing and distributing programs for the millions of TV viewers around the world, their own operations and economics became ever more closely entwined, yet also more firmly differentiated, especially as America's burgeoning educational television system began to rely more and more heavily on "quality" British programs, and as selling its programs internationally became more vitally important to an expanding BBC as well as to its commercial rivals.

The Queen, the Chimp, and Commercial TV

On June 2nd, the NBC Radio and Television networks will bring the British Coronation ceremonies to the American people, under the sponsorship of General Motors Corporation. The Coronation, rich in pomp and pageantry, promises to be truly memorable viewing and listening fare. It is probable that many of us will never again know its like in our lifetimes. ... The pages which follow will outline for you a number of exploitation approaches which should prove of value in this connection.[3]
—Coronation: NBC Exploitation Manual, 1953

Sirs: I read with horror in "The People," a British newspaper, the account of the relaying in your country of the coronation of our beloved Queen. . . . We are shocked to read America should belittle and humiliate our Queen and the religious and solemn coronation service in our Abbey. . . . Believe me, this insult, not only to our Queen but to the British people will be remembered for a long time to come.[4]

—Letter from Mrs. H. E. S—, Somerset, June 8, 1953

In 1951, when the Beveridge Report was published, it was anticipated that the eagerly awaited coronation of Queen Elizabeth II in June 1953 would serve as confirmation of the rightness of the decision to preserve the BBC monopoly. Between 1951 and 1953, however, the Labour government that had dominated since the war was voted out, the Conservative party came in, and in May 1952 a new White Paper put commercial television back on the table, after heated debates in Parliament.[5] The BBC's renewed Charter came into effect in June 1952—under a new Director General, Sir Ian Jacob—as debates raged around it. It began to seem even more politically expedient that the upcoming royal event, already hailed as the sign and symbol of Great Britain's post-war renaissance, be displayed to the nation and to the world via the new medium of television the way that only the BBC could be trusted to do it.

The BBC itself spared no effort in planning a truly regal occasion. The Coronation would not only be British television's finest hour; the BBC fully intended that it should be shared with world broadcasters to fulfill the many predictions of television's service to mankind and Great Britain's pre-eminence in the field. Preparations began early in 1952 for the June 2, 1953 event. Massive studies of logistics and technical requirements for transmitting the entire procession and ceremony live as it took place, with ample commentary and explanation, fill multiple folders today at the BBC Written Archives.[6] Frequent releases were made to the press, who followed the preparations with close attention. All six outside units of BBC Television would be pressed into service for the Coronation coverage, which would run from 10 in the morning to 5 at night, with the heart of the event, the coronation service in Westminster Abbey, occurring at about 12:30 pm.[7] Camera crews would be moved into place successively as the procession made its way through the streets of London, and would be installed as unobtrusively as possible in the Abbey itself. Broadcast relays would be used to beam the coverage to stations throughout Europe. For more distant viewers, the plan was to kinescope the coverage (film the live broadcast off the television screen in a special studio) as it aired live in Britain, then fly the films to destinations around the world. In the US, all three major networks made competitive plans to get the footage first.

The BBC and the US networks began discussions in January 1953 on how the coronation footage would be handled once it arrived on US airwaves. American networks agreed that no commercials would interrupt the actual service in the Abbey, and that advertising during the rest of the long day's coverage would generally "be kept down to a minimum and would be in good taste." According to later BBC statements, they also agreed to limit advertising to "public service sponsorship" announcements, "in which only the advertiser's name is given and in which there is no interruption during a programme to sell or to urge the merits of a product."[8] NBC agreed, in writing, to "keep all sponsor identification entirely away from the religious part of the program" and pledged that "public service sponsorship of the Coronation will be in the greatest dignity and good taste, and . . . will be consistent with our coverage of the recent inauguration of President Eisenhower."[9] To ensure this, the network hired Paul Gore-Booth of the British Information Service to monitor the coverage all morning and advise NBC engineers as to when a commercial break might be appropriate—or not.[10] CBS similarly assured the BBC that "the Coronation religious service will be completely excluded from implications of sponsorship."

However, US networks' idea of what constituted "public service sponsorship" would certainly have raised eyebrows at the BBC. For example, a script prepared by General Motors' agency in May included such announcements as "Complete NBC coverage of the Coronation of Britain's new Queen, both radio and TV, is being brought to you by General Motors, maker of Chevrolet, Pontiac, Oldsmobile, Buick and Cadillac, GMC Trucks and Coaches, and Frigidaire Home Appliances."[11] In Britain, this would read like an outright advertisement. The BBC might have grown uneasier still if they could have seen the brochure NBC distributed to its television and radio affiliates in May 1953. Titled "Coronation Exploitation Manual," it made suggestions for attention-getting program tie-ins like "Queen Interviews— Have one of your news men do on-the-street tape interviews with women on the subject: 'Would you like the job of being Queen?'" And had BBC representatives read the accompanying memo, in which it was noted that "General Motors will sponsor eight six-minute segments of TODAY on June 2" with its somewhat off-hand closing sentence "A cluster of GM commercials around the religious portion of the Coronation is to be avoided,"[12] they may have felt some warning of what was to come.

The pump was primed for international misunderstanding. In the weeks leading up to the event, US newspapers covered the competitive jockeying of the networks to be the first with Coronation coverage. US news cameras and commentators would be set up along the procession routes to record their own filmed footage, but only BBC cameras and reporters were to be allowed inside the Abbey. The BBC would transmit live to Alexandra Palace, where kinescope films would be made of the broadcasts, developed, and heli-coptered to Heathrow for transport via Canberra jet bomber to Goose Bay, Labrador, at three different points in the day, the first carrying films from the morning procession, the second with the footage of the Abbey ceremony, and the third with kinescopes of the final procession from the Abbey to the Palace. From Goose Bay the kinescopes were to be flown to Montreal by jet fighter plane for the Canadian Broadcasting Corporation (CBC) broadcast.

In the US, the ABC network opted simply to re-transmit the CBC feed to its stations.[13] But NBC and CBS made far more elaborate arrangements to scoop each other. Using prize-winning jet pilots flying P-51 Mustangs, each network planned to rush its own set of BBC kinescopes from Goose Bay to Boston, where special transmitters had been set up at Logan Airfield. Meantime, the networks both chartered planes—NBC a DC-6 and CBS a Stratocruiser, stocked with video recorders, editing equipment, and network news reporters—to fly their own footage taken in London directly to Boston, processing and editing the film and adding commentary en route. Even further, NBC secretly planned to stage a coup, hiring a Canberra jet to speed its own kinescopes of the BBC coverage directly from London to Boston, bypassing the Goose Bay stop and reaching network transmitters first. But their plan was thwarted when the plane developed fuel system problems two hours out and had to turn back. The network was then forced to rely on the CBC feed, same as ABC, for the first part of the ceremony; only later did its own filmed coverage arrive.[14] Until the filmed coverage could reach US shores, the live radio feed, beamed via shortwave, could be heard over numerous radio and television stations, often accompanied on TV screens with still photos of the ceremonies transmitted by facsimile.

It was a hectic day for all. At the end of it, at first, reaction to coverage of the Coronation was laudatory on both sides of the Atlantic. British viewers, who had seen the ceremony live as it occurred, praised the BBC's respectful and informative handling of the event. David Sarnoff sent a telegram to Sir Ian Jacob, the new BBC Director General, later that day:

PLEASE ACCEPT MY WARMEST CONGRATULATIONS TO YOU AND YOUR ORGANIZATION ON THE SUPERB ACHIEVEMENT OF THE BBC. THROUGH YOUR RADIO AND TELEVISION COVERAGE, MILLIONS OF PEOPLE IN THE WESTERN WORLD WERE ABLE TO SHARE IN BRITAIN'S DAY OF SPLENDOR. MY COMPANY HAS FELT IT A PRIVILEGE TO PARTICIPATE WITH YOU AND THE CBC IN BRINGING THE CORONATION TO OUR GREAT AUDIENCE IN THE UNITED STATES AND WE REGARD THIS EVENT AS ONE OF THE HIGH MARKS IN OUR LONG AND FRUITFUL ASSOCIATION WITH YOU.[15]

In the best American fashion, both NBC and CBS took out self-congratulatory ads in the *New York Times* on June 3 (which they must have prepared far in advance), praising their own skillful handling of the event. CBS proclaimed the day "a triumph of the whole television industry" and reminded readers "the best medium to stage a spectacle is the best showcase for a product. There's crowning success for both on television's most popular network."[16] NBC boasted that its television coverage "topped all networks."[17] Even the General Precision Equipment Corporation got into the act, pointing out the role that its "GPL Video Recorders" and "Rapid Film Processors" had played in the event.[18] Similarly, critic Jack Gould's same-day review in the *Times* proclaimed "today marked the birth of international television" and praised the BBC's coverage as "exceptionally fine documentary reporting – detailed, dignified, and authoritative."

Yet more ominous notes were already being sounded. For the US networks Gould had some sharp criticism:

> Both CBS and NBC television provided their own special touches, not all of which were very attractive. CBS permitted a commercial that was in the worst possible taste, a description of a car as the 'Queen of the Road.' In the morning, when the radio coverage was picked up at the time of the coronation, NBC television program called 'Today' broke in and out of the religious ceremony with spot announcements and a scene of a monkey. Those responsible should be ashamed.

Despite these charges, Gould concluded on an upbeat note: "Yesterday's fruitful partnership between British and American television should be continued on a sustained and active basis."[19]

But across the Atlantic, organized opposition to any such idea found its golden opportunity. The National Television Council, headed by Labour MP Christopher Mayhew and other influential figures such as Lord Simon of Wythenshaw and Lady Violet Bonham Carter, had been working since early spring on a pamphlet entitled "Dear Viewer," a vehemently argued broadside against commercial television. The group had already determined to launch its campaign on June 4, immediately following the Coronation, with a letter to the *Times* that argued "commercialization—now imminently threatened—is fraught with dangers to those spiritual and intellectual values which the BBC has nobly striven to maintain" and hoping that the government would decide, "even at this last moment, to remain true to the principles which have given us the finest broadcasting system in the world," accompanied by a mass mailing of the pamphlet.[20] Though the letter and the pamphlets went out too soon to take the events of the Coronation into account, the group soon had the best supporting ammunition it could have wished for delivered into its hands, from an American no less.

In his longer Saturday recap column on June 7, Gould repeated his criticisms of US Coronation coverage, citing the networks' "astonishing lack of discernment in the handling of commercials" and condemning their "callousness in the injection of commercials that defied description." Even Edward R. Murrow's *See It Now* summary was, Gould lamented, "not immune to the placement of commercials at the most inopportune moments."[21] In Britain the Socialist newspaper *The People* immediately picked up Gould's criticisms and ratcheted them up a few notches. "One showman actually broke into the religious ceremony with a picture of a so-called human chimpanzee and questioned whether there are queens and coronations in the monkey kingdom," its report fulminated. "And there were other plugs for soap, salad oil, jewelry, race tracks, three dimensional films, and cars."[22] Though the first part of this charge was not entirely accurate,[23] and the second part, referring to other moments of the lengthy coverage, well within the agreement that the BBC and US networks had made, Reuters news agency picked up this coverage and spread it further.

On June 8, a firestorm erupted in both British and American Sunday papers. The London *Times* repeated Gould's complaints, taken from the Reuters coverage, and charged that both CBS and NBC had "refused to make any statement in reply." The *New York Times* reported that the New York office of the BBC had made a complaint to NBC regarding its lapses in discretion and noted "the main burden of the BBC's protest . . . was said to have been directed against the appearance of a chimpanzee on the [Today] program."[24] The *Daily Express* in London picked up on the story, quoting the Gould articles at length on its front page, as did the *Daily Herald,* the *Manchester Guardian,* and the *Daily Mail.*[25] The *Daily Sketch* took the implications of the episode one step further, asking, "Has the BBC's magnificent achievement in televising the Coronation put paid to the Government's plans for introducing sponsored TV in Britain next year?" and claiming baldly, "There never has been and never will be any majority demand for sponsored TV in Britain; it is something dreamed up by a group of interested politicians and it is utterly alien to the British way of life."[26]

Over the next few days charges and counter-charges flew across the Atlantic, with BBC representatives defending the "gentleman's agreement" they had made with the US networks and accusing them of having broken their word. CBS and NBC denied this indignantly, declaring their handling of the coronation to be entirely consistent with the terms they had mutually agreed upon. According to NBC, "At no time during the showing of the BBC telefilms (kinescope recordings) did NBC interrupt the religious ceremonies or permit commercial messages to be connected thereto."[27] CBS's Sig

Mickelson likewise claimed that the network had "scrupulously observed its gentleman's agreement with the BBC" though he did have to admit to airing one commercial for a Willy's Motors car as "Queen of the road"—though not during the religious part of the broadcast.[28] The *Daily Herald* came closest to getting it right: "On Coronation Day the BBC sound broadcast of the service was put out by the National Broadcasting Corporation [sic], accompanied on the television screen by excellent still photographs but also by advertisements for soap and shots of an interview with a chimpanzee."[29]

A symbolic simian star had been born: the *Today* show's resident chimp, J. Fred Muggs. As readers all over the world soon knew, J. Fred Muggs served as *Today* host Dave Garroway's comic mascot and occasional foil; as this magazine-style morning news and talk program cut to and back from news segments, in this case radio coverage supplemented by photographs of the Coronation, viewers saw the baby chimp sitting next to Garroway at the host's desk. Thus, indeed, might a chimpanzee have been juxtaposed with images of Britain's new Queen. Though the American networks had apparently observed the letter of their agreement with the BBC, it was clear that any proximity of chimpanzees or commercial products with images of their Queen completely violated the British interpretation of their intent, no matter what careful agreements the BBC and US networks had made. The situation was not helped by the generally casual, offhand American reaction, summed up by *Variety* in its usual pithy manner in a headline that read: "Webs on Liz Biz: 'Oops, Sorry.'"[30]

In Britain, however, Muggs quickly became the very symbol of all that commercial television portended for an uneasy nation. "<u>This</u> is Plug-TV" declaimed the *Daily Herald*, "That advertiser's chimp they call J. Fred Muggs, who popped in and out of the American Coronation relay and annoyed the BBC so much, is only part of it."[31] "America ashamed of its TV" another article asserted, again citing "a chimpanzee in connection with an advertisement." "Plugged TV: the crowning insult" read another headline, as the *Daily Herald* asked, "After this demonstration of commercial TV, do we really want advertisers (linked with American interests) to decide what the British public should see on television?"[32] As Britain's Parliament prepared for release of its Television Advisory Report in late June, both sides of the commercial television debate attempted to use the incident to support their cause. For those who opposed commercial television, as the American magazine *Time* later reported, the Muggs incident "did more than any other argument to fan fears of US-style 'television vulgarity.'"[33] Commercialism itself could hardly be condemned outright—plenty of British businesses sold Coronation-related products; even the British Information Service used the occasion to promote itself by selling "official" souvenirs of the event.[34] The

British tabloid newspapers themselves were heavily laden with advertising, most of it in even more dubious taste than the American television commercials, and in even closer proximity to pictures and coverage of the Coronation. But the particular insult of bringing a chimpanzee into visual relationship with the Queen provided the element of outrage necessary to condemn commercial television, and indeed to heighten anxieties over how this new medium could be controlled. Proponents of commercial TV were forced into lengthy defensive explanations that, despite Muggs, British commercial television would remain fundamentally British and hence resistant to American foolishness.

For the BBC, the controversy was a mixed blessing. Initially BBC officials, particularly those in its New York office, had led the charges of tastelessness and impropriety. Peter Black of the *Daily Mail* noted that "The BBC is making no pretence of its indignation over the reported US breaches of taste" and went on to speculate "Its complaints must be related to the fact that the Government is about to study the report, to be published this month, of the Television Advisory Committee on Sponsored TV."[35] But with US networks contending that the BBC had in fact agreed to their treatment of the event—and when reports from the British embassy in Washington asserted that the matter had been blown out of proportion to what had actually occurred[36]—officials at the BBC began to back away from the fracas, perhaps under duress. On June 12 NBC newsman Merrill Mueller, according to a confidential NBC memo, "received a call from a friend of his with the British Embassy in Washington, who said he wanted to tell him, officially, that the British government was not disturbed by our Coronation coverage. . . . Furthermore, he said, the government had passed the word to the BBC to stop "stirring up the issue" in the British press. Mueller was also told that the New York offices of the BBC have been instructed to 'lay off.'"[37] Even Jack Gould, whose criticisms had provided the basic ammunition for the fight, began to "take exception to being quoted as exhibit 'A' in the controversy between proponents and opponents of commercial television in Britain" and backtracked from his initial claims.[38] By late July, George Barnes, the BBC's Director of Television Broadcasting, could write to Davidson Taylor of NBC, somewhat misleadingly, "As for the Coronation broadcast in America, I am sure that what happened or did not happen is best forgotten. The anti-American press in this country played up the reports. . . . Thereafter the situation got out of control and everyone used the chimpanzee for their own ends—except the BBC!"[39]

However, others sprang into action. On June 10, the National Television Council seized the opening the incident had created to send a copy of their "Dear Viewer" pamphlet to every Member of Parliament and to every daily newspaper, with a warning that if advertising were permitted on British airwaves, "British TV will quickly become Americanised."[40] J. Fred Muggs, or related simian representations, became a permanent feature of the commercial television debate. When the victorious Tory government published its White Paper setting out plans for commercial television in November 1953, several editorial cartoons appeared in British newspapers depicting commercial television as "the monkey in the room." One, in the *Manchester Guardian*, entitled "Broadcasting House Takes a Paying Guest," showed a chimpanzee seated at a boarding house table, slouching and waving a spoon over its head, while figures representing the various BBC services and the Post Office look on in displeasure.[41] Another *Guardian* cartoon showed a stuffed chimp, labeled "Commercial TV Man—Missing link between homo sapiens and a vastly superior being" examined by a group of gowned academics, amongst them Lords Reith, Simon, and Halifax, who exhibit rejection of this claim under the caption, "Another Fake?"[42]

Despite the correlation of commercial television with the less-than-human, or at least with the relatively un-evolved American treatment of the Coronation ceremony, the debate over commercial television reached a rather hasty conclusion. The November 1953 White Paper produced by the new Tory administration—only 7 pages in length but marking a complete reversal of the Beveridge report—provoked a two-day perturbation in the House of Lords, with what the *New Yorker* called "the biggest turnout of peers since the American-loan debate in 1946."[43] While some peers, like Lord Simon of Wythenshaw, argued that "his study of commercial television in the United States had convinced him it was evil," supporters of the measure responded by asserting one key difference: "British traders and industrialists are not at all unscrupulous and irresponsible, nor are British advertisers,"[44] unlike, apparently, Americans. The Tories won the measure by a margin of 70 votes out of 234. The House of Commons debate in December also passed the measure forward, by a narrower margin. Commercial television was slated to arrive in Britain in two years time, by September 1955.

Yet the version of commercial television that won the day in Britain differed substantially from its American counterpart, in a way that would eventually rebound to affect broadcasting across the Atlantic. The deployment of J. Fred Muggs had achieved a result. Primarily, what the Conservative government devised was a system that created a commercial competitor to the BBC while still retaining a maximum of control over the program providers and advertisers. Rather than sponsorship on American lines, by which advertisers themselves devised and produced programs, British commercial television would separate sponsors from program control from the outset; as the report declared, "There is a vast difference between accepting advertisements and sponsoring. The Press accept advertisements but they remain responsible for their own news and editorial columns. Cinemas show advertisements in the intervals, but their programmes are not sponsored by advertisers" (Great Britain 1963, 4). This separation was accomplished by keeping the actual infrastructure of television under public ownership through the creation of a second public broadcasting corporation, the Independent Television Authority (ITA), charged with the mandate to "build and operate television transmitters across the country, to award licences to regional programme companies, and supervise programming and advertising" (Johnson and Turnock 2005, 18).

Between 1954 and 1962 the ITA funded and built a series of regional stations in locations designed to cover the entire country, thus creating an alternative to the London-centric national bias of British broadcasting by providing genuinely regional and local perspectives. Private companies applied for a license to operate and program these regional stations on an exclusive basis, promising to provide a "mixed program schedule" very much along the lines of the BBC, with careful attention to serving all sectors of society. The private broadcasting companies would support themselves and reward their shareholders through the sale of "spot" advertising only, with no involvement of the advertiser in program production whatsoever, and no more than six minutes per hour of commercials (this would later loosen a bit). The ITA would oversee and regulate the operations of the private companies and their advertisers but, unlike the BBC, would have no direct hand in the provision of programs itself.

The Television Act passed in July 1954, creating the ITA. The first franchises were awarded in 1954–55 in the major population areas of London, The Midlands (Birmingham), and the North (Manchester), with eleven more eventually added over the next eight years for a total of fourteen covering all of England, Scotland, Wales, and Northern Ireland. Each of these franchises was further split into weekday and weekend concessions. In London, Associated-Rediffusion, partly owned by Associated Newspapers, the *Daily Mail*'s parent company, received the Monday through Friday franchise, with the London weekend assigned to Associated TeleVision (ATV), a venture between Norman Collins, former head of BBC television, and Lew Grade, a powerful talent agent active in the British film industry. ATV also gained the weekday Midlands concession, so in other words provided programs to two separate areas of the country: London on weekends and the Midlands during the week. Film interests also backed ABC Television, formed by the Associated British Picture Corporation (APBC), a consortium of British film producers and theater companies, including Pathé News, whose director, Norman Thomas, became head of the company. A large proportion of the shares of ABPC were owned by the American film studio Warner Bros., and ABC used as its London base the former Warner Studios in London. ABC was granted the franchise for both the Midlands and the North on weekends, so operated studios in Birmingham and Manchester as well.

The final "big four" original ITV company was Granada, again linked to the film industry through ownership by Granada Pictures founders Sidney and Cecil Bernstein, with the weekday North of England franchise and studios in Manchester. The big four would soon be joined by Scottish Television (Scotland), Southern Television (South of England), Tyne Tees Television (North-East England), Anglia Television, Ulster Television, and others in the West, the Channel Islands, and several more. Many would drop out, reform and regroup over the next several decades. All the companies collaborated in the operation of the Independent Television News (ITN) service, which provided national news coverage throughout the system. London's commercial service beamed into operation first, on September 22, 1955. Despite the fact that the regional structure of the new service was intended to encourage a strong basis in regional program production, the ITV companies soon began to share programs in various ad-hoc network formations; eventually prime-time schedules across the nation would show almost as much conformity as US networks or the BBC. Over the years, too, the number of private companies would reduce considerably, as advertising economics provoked consolidation. By 1963 ITV had captured 70% of the television audience from the BBC, and had provoked enormous changes in its rival as well. And despite a de facto quota that held imported—read American—programs to approximately 14% of the weekly schedule, many of these changes held close associations with American television.

Men in Tights: Mid-Atlantic Filmed Series

> Sooner or later, the BBC will be forced to start producing filmed television series on the American pattern. There are two main reasons for this: (1). It is the easiest type of programming with which to maintain quality, and keep up long hours of output. (2). The opposition will tend to rely on this type of programming and the BBC will find it very difficult to break the viewing habit by means of the one shot programme, unless through 'spectaculars' . . . [F]or the sake of our prestige alone, if not for any other reason, I cannot help but feel that the BBC ought to contemplate series production, and see whether MCA, or some other body would be willing to consider cooperating in a documentary, drama, or situation comedy series.[45]
> —Aubrey Singer, BBC New York Office, March 4, 1955

In both Britain and the United States, the early years of television were marked by an emphasis on live program production. Though the BBC had made far greater use of recorded radio programs than had the US networks, recording for television presented greater difficulties. In the period before videotape's invention, film was the only medium that could preserve both sound and visuals. But the sheer expense of film production, as well as the fact that reliance on film threatened to bring with it dependence on the film industry, kept US television stations and networks as well as the BBC away from this shift in production methods for television's first decade.[46] Plus, most television producers and managers came from the field of radio, bringing years of experience honed on live studio production into the new field. Thus, early television carried over from radio not only the medium's basic and distinctive characteristic of seriality—a system of episodic programs recurring on a regular weekly or daily basis (a relatively recent development in Britain)—but its emphasis on live studio-based production as well.

Yet radio series, produced live, were limited by their audio-only nature to relatively small casts, reduced situational complexity, and short episodic duration. It is when broadcasting's seriality met the possibilities inherent in film's visuality and permanence that television programs as we know them today began to take shape.[47] Filmed serials for television opened up a lucrative new market, giving broadcast programs a fixed and highly salable form relatively new to the medium. It also extended broadcast programs' lifespan in syndicated sales far beyond the original network broadcast, not to mention a new transportability through space that would begin to build television beyond live radio's national scope towards a new international field of distribution, such as film had long enjoyed. Time, too, could be expanded since filmed series could easily be repeated, reviewed, and revived. And in contrast to live production which required network studio space, filmed programs could be produced anywhere, opening television up to what would later be called independent or "package" production. Televisual seriality thus brought with it a new aesthetics—an aesthetics centered on familiarity, repetition, and the everyday, placing new demands on narrative structure and visual representation—that many found wholly vulgar and antithetical to accepted artistic traditions (Allen 1985).

By the time that commercial television debuted in Britain, television in the United States, though still dominated by live programs, had begun the switch to Hollywood-based film production that would become the hallmark and mainstay of American TV, and eventually television around the world. Some farsighted independent producers—and even a few major players, such as the CBS radio network and MGM studios—had already ventured into recorded "package" productions for radio in the 1940s, building on a change in the US tax laws that allowed creative artists such as radio and movie stars to incorporate themselves as small businesses with considerable tax advantages. Companies such as Ziv, Four Star, and Desilu built programs around major radio personalities, selling them as a "package" (with star/writer/producer bundled together around a particular dramatic property for a run of 13, 26, or 52 episodes) both to single sponsors via their ad agencies or, increasingly, directly to the networks themselves. These productions were usually, though not always, recorded onto transcription discs, so that they could be marketed widely not only to networks but syndicated to stations as well; they could also be preserved and sold over time in this recorded format, airing not just once but repeatedly where it suited station schedules. New players began to see the advantages of the package production business, particularly talent agencies like Lew Wasserman's MCA in the US (see Gomery 2007). And as previous restrictions on the playing of recorded material were loosened, both networks and studios expanded into the music business, starting or purchasing major labels— again, on groundwork that had been laid as early as 1939, when major radio interests formed their own music rights organization, Broadcast Music Incorporated, to compete with ASCAP in signing new musical talent and distributing royalties.

Innovative independent production companies like Desilu were the first to perceive the emerging opportunity in filmed series production presented by television's voracious schedules as the new medium emerged in the early 1950s. Desilu quickly came up with the innovative "three camera film" style of production that took the basic three camera set up of the live TV studio but used film cameras to produce footage that could be edited in post-production. They were soon joined by the first wave of filmed television producers, such as Jerry Fairbanks Productions, Hal Roach Studios, Ziv Television, Jack Webb's Mark VII Ltd., and many more, along with a few of the more prescient studios like RKO and Columbia's Screen Gems division.

The movement towards filmed series production also permitted the emergent medium a far greater degree of transnational circulation than live radio and television had ever enjoyed, which prompted both opportunities and anxieties. The BBC, with its head start in television, contemplated as early as 1948 the possibilities in selling kinescoped programs to the rapidly expanding US market. A report on "West Coast Television" commissioned by Norman Luker of the BBC from former North American Service adviser Sam Slate concluded that there was great interest in BBC programs for American television at the present but "This will not be true two years from now"[48] (emphasis in the original). He was right; by the time the BBC began to think about filmed or taped series programs, independent "mid-Atlantic" series had flooded the market—even as the Independent Television bill wended its way through Parliament. With the advent of commercial TV, it became clear that while publicly funded filmed television production might struggle to compete in the popular sphere, there would still be a need for high quality productions for public and educational broadcasters, in the nations of the Commonwealth as well as the US (See S. Potter 2011). This topic will be taken up in the next section.

On the commercial side, the story of Hannah Weinstein's Sapphire Productions illustrates the transnationality of early filmed television, and brings it into conjunction with the politics of the Cold War.[49] During the era of the blacklist, as the US House Un-American Activities Committee and publications like *Red Channels* hounded many established Hollywood writers, directors, and actors out of the business, "runaway" productions overseas provided a productive refuge. By 1952 a group of astute blacklisted Hollywood artists were living in Paris. Amongst them was a young political activist named Hannah Weinstein, who had little experience in the film industry but had been active in left-wing Hollywood organizations; by 1947 she had become executive secretary of the Hollywood branch of the Independent Citizens Committee of the Arts, Sciences and Professions (HICCASP), a group that would soon be denounced as a "communist front organization" by the House Un-American Activities Committee. After producing a short film on the French resistance that she sold to American television, as she later recalled, "I began to look for other material and came up with some offbeat English mysteries which we went to London to make because it was cheap at that time."[50] In 1952, she produced a three part series, *Colonel March of Scotland Yard*, in partnership with Boris Karloff (who starred in the program), based on the novels of John Dickenson Carr. Production took place at Southall Film Studios in West London. These three episodes were later combined and released as a feature film, *Colonel March Investigates* (1953); 22 more episodes were produced in 1954 and distributed in the US in syndication by Official Films; later they would be broadcast in Britain (Neale 2003). What makes this series memorable today is not so much the content of the programs themselves, but their production credits. Many were written by "Leslie Slote"—actually the "nom de blacklist" (among others) of two well-known Hollywood writers, Walter Bernstein and Abraham Polonsky. Unable to get the kind of work they were accustomed to as "A" list writers in Hollywood films, they contributed their considerable talents to the new field of filmed television, an arena of creativity that would never have been able to afford them without their political misfortunes. Exiled Hollywood talent contributed in many ways to the British film and television industries in the 1950s and early 1960s.

However, it was the advent of commercial television in Britain that turned Weinstein's one-off production unit into a small transnational television empire. When his first bid for an ITV franchise was turned down, talent broker Lew Grade—no doubt fully aware of the role played in American television by agency-based filmed program "packagers" and independent production companies—formed the Incorporated Television Programme Company to provide programs to those who did succeed in winning regional licenses. However, when Associated TeleVision (ATV) proved financially incapable of carrying out the Midlands service it had been awarded, the ITA rethought its earlier rejection and invited Grade's company, now renamed ITC (Independent Television Company) to join with ATV. Grade eventually came to dominate the ATV company, maintaining ITC as a separate production arm that provided programs not only his own franchise but for others as well, including American networks.[51]

Grade purchased the *Colonel March* series and ATV aired it with favorable ratings in 1955. Based on that success, he invested in Hannah Weinstein's new production company, Sapphire Films, with the objective of producing adventure series in Britain for ATV that could also be syndicated in the United States (Neale 2005; Tankel 1984). Sapphire's big advantage was that it could draw on blacklisted talent of a far higher quality than television production could count on normally, making its shows stand out on both sides of the Atlantic. Sapphire's first hit was the series *The Adventures of Robin Hood*, which did well not only in the US and Britain but around the world, including Canada, Australia, Japan, Norway, Italy, Mexico, and Argentina. Its pilot was the work of Oscar-winning screenwriter Ring Lardner, Jr. (*Woman of the Year*, 1942; *Laura*, 1944) who with Ian McLellan Hunter (*A Woman of Distinction*, 1950) wrote most of the series' episodes under a variety of pseudonyms such as Lawrence McClellan, Oliver Skene, Robert B. West, Eric Heath, Ian Larkin, and many more. Other exiled writers for this and other series included Waldo Salt, Robert Lees, Bernard Gordon, Norma and Ben Barzman, and Donald Ogden Stewart, to name only a few (Neale 2003, 247–48). Several of the episodes were directed by another blacklisted American, Joseph Losey.

Sapphire produced several subsequent series, including *The Adventures of Sir Lancelot* (1956–57), *The Buccaneers* (1956–57), *Sword of Freedom* (1958–60), and *Four Just Men* (1959–60). Besides giving work to blacklisted Hollywood talent, the advantage of filming these series in England included getting around broadcast import quotas and taking advantage of British tax incentives designed to encourage indigenous production. They were produced at Nettlefold Studios in Walton-on-Thames but found their largest audiences in the US and internationally. Such series were true cultural hybrids, drawing on distinctively British historical legends and fictional characters to tell stories that often seemed to relate strongly to the American politics that so concerned many of their writers. As Ring Lardner, Jr., was later to note, "*The Adventures of Robin Hood* gave us plenty of opportunities for oblique social comment on the issues and institutions of Eisenhower-era America . . . perhaps, in some small way, setting the stage for the 1960s by subverting a whole new generation of young Americans" (Lardner 2000, 141). Here the filmed seriality of television intersected with politics and policy to create a program written by political exiles from Hollywood, produced in Britain with British talent, for a company funded by both US and British investors. Though unique in many ways, the story of Sapphire Films marks the arrival of the filmed dramatic series as television's dominant narrative form, both domestically and internationally, that would serve as the reliable base of film studio economics for decades to come.

But Sapphire, though unique in its talent roster, was not alone in the business of "mid-Atlantic" television. A lively independent production sector had sprung up in Britain even before ITV's advent, some founded and financed by American producers as with Sapphire Productions, some home grown but taking advantage of US-style filmed production techniques and facilities, most of them selling to American as well as British broadcasters. A survey done by the British Board of Trade in 1953 came up with a list of fourteen companies then producing filmed television series in Britain.[52] One of the first was Douglas Fairbanks Ltd, owned by Hollywood star Douglas Fairbanks, Jr., who had relocated to the British National Studios at Elstree to produce his prime-time filmed anthology series *Douglas Fairbanks Jr. Presents*. Fairbanks hired both American and British writers for this series focusing on adaptations of short stories; many of them would go on to considerable success in British television. Companies like Fairbanks' served as training grounds for many writers and directors from the British film industry who had never before worked in the new medium, as Dave Mann explains (Mann 2008). Another firm was launched by the American brothers Edward and Harry Danziger, who had begun as small-time producers of B movies in the US, featuring titles like *Babes in Baghdad* (1952) and *St. Benny the Dip* (1951), both directed by Edgar G. Ulmer. Moving to Britain, they set up operations at Riverside Studios in London to make an anthology crime series, *Calling Scotland Yard* (1954), which was released in the US as *Adventure Theater* (NBC 1956). Their next series was *The Vise* (ITV 1954–57; ABC 1954–57), starring Donald Gray as detective Mark Saber, later expanded into the related series *Mark Saber* and *Saber of London*. Blacklisted American director Joseph Losey served as script editor. Other Danziger titles included *Man from Interpol* (ITV 1960–62; NBC 1960), *The Cheaters* (ITV 1960–62; US syn. 1961), and *Richard the Lionheart* (ITV 1961–65).

Some small TV companies grew out of the British film or commercial radio industries. Merton Park Studios, for instance, was a producer of "B" films since the 1930s located in South Wimbledon. In the 1950s they produced the series *Scotland Yard, The Edgar Wallace Mysteries,* and *The*

Scales of Justice. Another was Towers of London, a production company started by Harry Alan Towers, who had gone from the BBC to supplying radio programs to Radio Luxembourg and other commercial stations, and had in fact brokered the original arrangement between Grade and Weinstein.[53] At Highbury Studios outside London he produced several series for ITV, including anthology series *Theater Royale* (ATV 1955–56), *Television Playhouse* (ATV 1955–63), and *Tales from Dickens* (1959), as well as the series *The Scarlet Pimpernel* (ITV 1955–56; US syn. 1958). Interestingly, many British series, especially those that did not get picked up overseas, were repackaged into three-episode "movies" that were released in theaters as pre-feature attractions, usually under different titles. Occasionally one of these "mid-Atlantic" productions was picked up by the BBC, as with the series *Fabian of the Yard* (BBC 1954–56; CBS 1955, under title *Patrol Car*), produced by Trinity Productions and based on the real-life cases of Scotland Yard detective Robert Fabian. This was very much along the lines of the long-running US series *Dragnet*, and indeed Susan Sydney-Smith points to the fact that *Dragnet* aired on ITV in 1955 and had a certain impact on later British crime series (Sydney-Smith 2002, 100).

By 1958, the volume of "mid-Atlantic" productions had grown to such an extent that ITA felt obliged to come up with a new set of guidelines for determining what would count as a British production. The Television Act of 1954 had stipulated the "proper proportions of the programmes shall be of British origin and of British performance," but it was left to a kind of "gentleman's agreement" what proportion of the schedule that should actually represent. A rule of thumb emerged that no more than seven hours of a 50-hour broadcasting week, or about 14%, should consist of "imported film"—for all intents and purposes, programs from the United States. But what constituted a British production? And how to achieve the goals of "giving full opportunities to British talent and enterprise . . . making this country a thriving home of film production for international markets, and the contribution that can be made by international talent" while limiting the influence of foreign investment that was vitally necessary to make this happen? The ITA's October 1958 memorandum attempted to negotiate this with syntactical subtlety:

> Normally, the Authority will not necessarily require a film series made in British territory to be counted as 'imported' if:
> (a) one of the leading performers is not British,
> (b) the executive producer or the producer or the director (but not more than one of these) is non-British,
> (c) a non-British, as well as a British, script editor or supervisor is employed,

(d) up to one third of the writing has come from non-British writers.

The whole of the rest of those engaged in all parts of the production should be British.[54]

This definition had the advantage of not basing itself on the actual money behind the series—a series wholly funded by American investment could still count as British, as long as significant proportions of the creative and below-the-line staff were themselves of British nationality. A form had to be completed for each episode of each series, and submitted to the ITA.[57] Despite these safeguards, by 1958 the IBA reported that ITV stations transmitted on average 11 hours of "mid-Atlantic" programs per week, mostly in "peak time," along with a further 9 hours of programming imported directly from the US. As Jonathan Tankel argues, "The result [was] a peak-time schedule dominated by programs and program forms not uniquely British, nor particularly regional" (1984, 80). Yet they were popular, drawing in audiences that boosted the advertising revenue that supported ITV and its more regional and more "British" productions.

By 1960, Anglo-American productions had become a significant form of entertainment on both sides of the Atlantic. Programs such as *The Avengers*, *Danger Man*, *The Saint*, and *The Prisoner* would achieve popularity in the US as well as in Britain. Even the BBC had ventured into mid-Atlantic waters, with its production of *The Third Man* series in 1959–60. In partnership with National Telefilm Associates, 20th Century-Fox's television arm, it was filmed half in Hollywood, half in Britain, and aired in both countries. Ronald Waldman was the executive producer on the British side, and his experience would convince him that co-productions could work to the BBC's advantage. Another co-production venture involved the BBC, the Canadian Broadcasting Corporation, and the Australian Broadcasting Corporation and resulted, somewhat less successfully, in the 39-episode series *RCMP*, an adventure series about the Royal Canadian Mounted Police. It aired in those three countries and had a brief syndicated run in the US.

Yet it may be less in terms of programming and more in terms of industry structure that ITV had its greatest impact on United States broadcasting. In the early 1960s the American commercial networks would use British-inspired rhetoric to finally rid themselves of the domination of the sponsor, against whose power many had chafed since the 1930s. The result, producing the classic three-network system of television's most profitable decades, 1960 through the early 1980s, combined the centralization of control long associated with the BBC with the drive for profits behind ITV to produce a result that made few critics and regulators happy. The Pilkington Report in Britain, conversely, made use of American educators' rhetoric to support a critique of commercial broadcasting while preparing the ground for a new era in US-British cultural relations.

De-commercialization and a Network for Eggheads: TV Reforms, 1955–1964

A number of thoughtful people have written in, asking how they can help push for the establishment of . . . a 'BBC.' But if this would be too big a break with our habit . . . I suggest we simply consider that other type of TV network developed by the British: the BBC's commercial rival, known as the Independent Television Authority.[56]
—William H. Stringer, editor, *The Christian Science Monitor*, 1959

The British system is so extreme that it is impractical to believe it could be superimposed on ours . . . We must find a way to blend the two into a system that is both economically sound under our competitive system and morally justifiable on the grounds that it represents an honest effort to present the best possible balanced schedule. This can be achieved on a practical basis by tailoring the British system of schedule control to our current and acceptable sales practices.[57]
—*Report of CBS Special Committee*, March 3, 1959

As we have noted above, American networks had begun to chafe under the domination of the sponsor as early as the late 1930s, themselves proposing and producing shows like *The Columbia Workshop* not only to fulfill public service obligations but to allow the network's identity to emerge as an originator of programming. During the war years, the networks produced an increasing percentage of their sustaining programming, working closely with government agencies and the military. After the war CBS, in particular, ventured into "package" production of recorded programming, created and/ or commissioned by the network itself, often aired at first on a sustaining basis until it attracted a sponsor, whose advertisements—later to be called "spot" ads—could be inserted at standard intervals. The network retained both creative control and ownership, so that a sponsor's departure only meant that another would have to be found; it eliminated the risk that a program could be pulled from the network and taken to a rival.

Television's debut, however, forced the networks to back up a few steps. Television production was expensive and its audiences still developing, so that sharing the costs with sponsors and the risks with advertising agencies seemed a sensible hedge. Thus the single sponsor system dominated early network television, despite efforts to dislodge it, notably by Sylvester "Pat"

Weaver at NBC. As early as 1953 NBC proposed its new "magazine concept" of combining multiple sponsors for a single program, and allowing them to advertise throughout the schedule. *Fortune* magazine presciently predicted, "Probability: sponsors will lose influence over programming, and those on multiple-sponsor shows will ultimately have no more to say about content than magazine advertisers do about the articles published alongside their ads."[58] However, the other networks resisted this notion, along with the sponsors and especially advertising agencies, who stood to lose the most. By October 1954, *Sponsor* magazine might well wonder "Are Agencies Earning Their 15% on Net TV Shows?" Yet noting the rise of network-produced shows and spot advertising, the trade journal still came down on the side of agency importance, detailing "some of the 48 steps [an] agency must take" in getting an advertising message out on TV.[59] Several scholars have discussed the shift in control from sponsor to network that took place in the 1950s (Boddy, Stole, P. Wilson, Kepley).

By 1958, though sponsors still owned and managed close to 40% of prime time programming, networks already insisted on buying ownership rights from those programs they purchased from independent producers—most of the remaining 60%—and furthermore demanded retention of syndication rights in perpetuity (unlike most sponsors, whose only interest was in one-time broadcast of a program, leaving syndication rights to the producers) (Boddy 1990, 171). Yet, when what would soon be called "the quiz show scandal" broke in 1958, networks saw to it that the sponsor attracted most of the blame, thus removing the last impediment to the kind of control over their whole schedules that they had desired since the 1930s. This development also sounded the death knell of live television programming; with increased reliance on the licensing of filmed series with their lucrative syndication rights, network programming of the 1960s and 1970s enters what we might, after Bordwell, Staiger, and Thompson's analysis of the classic Hollywood system, call the "classic network system" for its highly systematic and rule-bound mode of production (Bordwell, Staiger, and Thompson 1985). This would have happened even without the quiz show scandal—quiz shows, after all, obtained a good part of their drama from their live production and thus might be seen as occupying the preferred end of the live/filmed hierarchy—but it was their typically close association with a single sponsor that allowed network spin control, aided by the calumny heaped on the sponsor in the British television debates, that won the day.

Quiz shows had become an increasingly important, if always contested, part of the television schedule since the late 1940s. In many ways they suited the demands of the economics of popular commercial television almost perfectly: inexpensive to produce, live and participatory, creating cliffhangers that encouraged tuning in next week, unlikely to offend by taking on controversial topics that might offend either advertisers or viewers. By 1956, the year that the first rumblings of dishonest practices could be heard, there were fifteen game shows in prime time across three US commercial networks, ranging from those that emphasized "high-culture and factual, often academic, knowledge" such as *The $64,000 Question, Dotto,* and *Twenty-One* (Hoerschelmann 1994) to those demanding specialized information or puzzle-solving (*Name That Tune, I've Got a Secret, What's My Line*) to comedic or human interest shows, like *You Bet Your Life, Queen for a Day,* and *Do You Trust Your Wife?* Even more could be found on daytime schedules. Many of them had made the leap across the pond to Britain, where their names might be changed but their format remained the same— *Name That Tune* became *Spot That Tune; Tic Tac Dough* became *Criss-Cross Quiz.* Another difference was that the British prizes were smaller, often amounting to no more than recognition or a token gesture. L. Marsland Gander, regular TV columnist for *The Daily Telegraph,* wrote in the *New York Times*: "The biggest prize offered was in 'The $64,000 Question' but it was shillings, not dollars, roughly the equivalent of $9,000. The top 'Treasure Trail' prize in Hughie Green's 'Double Your Money' here is about $2,800."[60] A total of five of the cash-reward quiz shows aired on ITV; the BBC offered one, an adaptation of *What's My Line?* with only a certificate as a reward.

Quiz shows had always attracted a certain amount of suspicion, from radio days on. But their low costs of production and widespread appeal made them preferable in many sponsors' and networks' eyes to the crime dramas and westerns that dominated the schedules, with their violence and dramatic excess. The high profile and big prizes of the prime time shows no doubt exacerbated the pressures felt by all game show producers since the dawn of the genre, and furthermore made it almost inevitable that their by no means unprecedented practices, such as the coaching of contestants and manipulation of the questions, would be revealed. Several isolated complaints were heard from disgruntled contestants over the course of the 1950s, but not until 1958 did the famous face-off between *Twenty-One*'s Herbert Stempel and Charles Van Doren blow the lid off the quiz show industry (though it was Edward Hilgemeier's affidavit submitted to the FCC in July detailing his treatment on *Dotto* that got things started; see K. Anderson 1978). Over the summer and fall of 1958, the American public learned the techniques used on most of the major shows:

> Suspense was maximized and outcomes pre-arranged with a kind of mock innocence. To 'control' began with picking contestants who were attractive and preferably, but not necessarily, competent. They would then be warmed up in 'playback' sessions in which trial questions were asked them; if they answered wrongly, they would

be given the correct answer. For contestants selected to defeat their rival on the air, these same questions would be used. The controllers would also teach contestants how to close their eyes and bite their lips as they pregnantly paused before exploding with the answer (Real 1995, 5).

In October, a grand jury convened in New York to hear the charges, calling one witness after another from the networks, production companies, ad agencies, and sponsors, all of whom denied guilt and pointed the finger at others. By the time the trial was over, not only had game show cheating been made illegal, but other "false" industry practices like coaching studio audiences, the use of canned laugh tracks, and even Edward Murrow's rehearsing of guests on *See It Now* and *Person to Person*, had been called into question.

Many factors contributed to the scandal. In 1958, a widely forgotten but sharp economic downturn sent network, station, and sponsoring industries' profits into a decline. The ABC network, which had trailed behind the CBS and NBC in number of affiliates and in ratings, had made a turnaround in 1956–57 and began to compete more heavily with the dominant nets. The FCC had begun an investigation of network practices in 1955, which led to the recommendation early in 1958 of the abolishment of option time, threatening the primary building block of network operations. And the rising tide of packaged film serial programs made in Hollywood had begun to dominate prime time schedules, pushing many of the critically valued programs of television's first decade off the air. In particular, the live anthology dramas produced in New York with theater-based talent had begun a sharp decline, from a high of twenty-five in 1953 to only ten on the air in 1958. And, as a harshly critical article in *Fortune* magazine noted in 1958, that fall the percentage of filmed program for the first time exceeded live programming, comprising 55% of CBS's and 54% of NBC's schedule, threatening to turn television, in *Fortune*'s works, into "an electronic comic strip." Once again, it was the networks' weakness in the face of sponsors' demand for high ratings that received the blame; said *Fortune*, quoting a CBS executive, "The sponsor-rating relationship has been responsible for the standardization of programming. If a big show is a success, the advertiser and his agency say 'I want one of those.'"[61] All of this riled those who had invested their energies and critical analysis in the public service rhetoric so dominant during television's first decade; here was the disappointment of commercial radio happening all over again. Where was the responsibility and public service the networks had promised?

In fact, their very disappointment was a marker of the fact that the networks had been trying for some time to assert themselves as responsible parties and good citizens, even as they relied heavily on their sponsors, for reasons that were as much economically self-interested as civic-minded. Despite the chastisement they were about to receive from the new FCC chair, Newton Minow, in 1961, both CBS and NBC, and even struggling third-place ABC, devoted a considerable amount of time and energy to public interest programming over the course of the 1950s; only by 1958 or so had the economics of commercial programming become well enough established—and had network radio declined sufficiently as a competitor for sponsor dollars—to create the kind of over-commercialized situation the quiz show scandal so abruptly pointed up. Besides participation in such foundation-supported experiments as *Omnibus*, discussed in the last chapter, both CBS and NBC had built up their educational and public affairs departments considerably since the war. CBS led in the development of documentary programming and news, and though Edward R. Murrow's tenure as head of the news and public affairs division was fleeting (he resigned after one year, out of dislike for administrative duties and the strong wish to return to reporting), CBS continued to pride itself on the strengths and innovation of its News Division, with programs like Murrow's *See It Now* and an active schedule of news broadcasts led by talented reporters such as Howard K. Smith, Eric Sevareid, Walter Cronkite, Charles Collingwood, Harry Reasoner, and Robert Trout.

Though in 1958 Murrow anticipated Minow by addressing a scathing challenge to the Radio-Television News Directors Association, he was deploring a situation that had only recently emerged:

> I invite your attention to the television schedules of all three networks between the hours of 9 and 11 p.m., Eastern Time. Here you will find only fleeting and spasmodic reference to the fact that this nation is in mortal danger. There are, it is true, occasional informative programs presented in that intellectual ghetto on Sunday afternoons. But during the daily peak viewing period, television in the main insulates us from the world in which we live. (Murrow 1947, quoted in Edwards 2004, 132)

Indeed, 1958 marks not only the year that *See It Now* was removed from its long-standing prime time slot, but, as Michael Curtin points out, the year that the CBS news department moved from being a sustaining service of the network into an "operating division" that "now was expected to generate a positive cash flow" (Curtin 1999, 125). What these charges point up, however, is the fact that, up until 1958, there had been indeed been public affairs and news programs in prime time, and many more in daytime and weekend slots.

At NBC, a flourishing Public Affairs division under the direction of Davidson Taylor from 1952 onwards oversaw the production of network programs in three different areas: news, sports, and public service programs. Though both news and sports attracted sponsors, the public service category comprised religious, dramatic, educational and public affairs talks/discussion offerings, nearly all non-commercial, for both radio and television. Margaret Cuthbert headed up the general public service division until 1952, when Edward Stanley took over; Doris Ann oversaw religious programs such as *The Catholic Hour, The Eternal Light* with Morton Wishengrad, and the compelling-titled *Conversations with Distinguished Elderly Men* (1952–55), whose ranks included such notables as Bertrand Russell, Carl Sandburg, and Frank Lloyd Wright. Under Cuthbert's aegis Theodore Granik had brought both *American Forum of the Air* (1950–57) and *Youth Wants to Know* (1951–58) to NBC, both public affairs discussion programs. Some of the most notable programs to come out of NBC's Public Affairs division in the early to mid 1950s were *Meet The Press* (carried over from radio), the prime time compilation documentary series *Victory at Sea* and *Project XX*; a quiz show called *Who Said That?* which asked contestants to identify recent quotes in the news; *NBC Theater*, a dramatic anthology program for radio produced by Wade Arnold; and *Wide, Wide World*, globally focused documentaries that aired once a month as part of the *NBC Producers Showcase* anthology, one of Pat Weaver's "Operation Frontal Lobes" projects. The vast majority of the programs did indeed air in the Sunday morning ghetto, but a few found prime time slots, as did the ever-increasing number of network news programs. Some were sponsored, some were non-commercial, but all attempted to direct attention to important political, social and cultural issues and to fulfill public service obligations.

In 1957, even as the quiz show scandal brewed, NBC joined forces with the educational broadcasters and embarked on one of its most ambitious projects ever, in the previously underdeveloped area of educational programming. Edward Stanley had succeeded Margaret Cuthbert as the manager of public service programs at NBC in 1952. In 1956 his assistant, Marilyn Kaemmerle, floated the idea for a live educational series that would fill a regular time slot, five days a week, with a different topic assigned to each day. The advantage of such a structure would be flexibility within a fixed framework, since, as she claimed, "all studies of viewing habits have long confirmed that the viewer is interested in change and variety providing, and only providing, that he is aware of the framework in which it is happening."[62] Since the expense of such a series would be greater than a stand-alone production, NBC took the idea to Harry Newburn (Robert Hudson's successor) at the Educational Television and Radio Center, proposing that they split the costs. NBC would produce the series in consultation with ETRC, using its own production personnel and facilities, and distribute it live to ETRC affiliates, with NBC permitted to offer it to affiliates by kinescope in markets where no educational station existed. For the ETRC, it promised an attractive alternative to the recorded, locally produced programming that made up the bulk of the schedule, and its live distribution at NBC's expense promised to link educational television's scattered affiliates together in a tighter, more coherent way than had ever before been possible. This would be, as NBC trumpeted, "the first time the twenty-five Educational Television stations will be interconnected for live programming, a great milestone in American education."[63]

Named the Educational Television Project, it kicked off in spring 1957 with five 13-part series aired not during the Sunday ghetto but on the fringe of prime time, from 6:30 to 7 pm EST. On Mondays, *The American Scene* devoted itself to American literature, with a noted author interviewed in each episode; Tuesdays brought *Geography for Decisions*, Wednesday *Mathematics*, Thursday *American Government: Pursuit of Happiness*, featuring politicians and public figures; and on Fridays *Highlights of Opera History* employed the talents of the NBC Opera Company. Both NBC and educational broadcasters were pleased enough with the results to renew for a second season in fall 1957 with another five 13-week series (*The International Geophysical Year, Camera on Washington, Arts and the Gods, Mathematics,* and *Survival*) and again in the spring of 1958, this time with only three programs, *Decision for Research* and *The Subject is Jazz* on Mondays and Wednesdays at 6–6:30 EST, and *Briefing Session* on Tuesdays at 10:30.

However, once again, as with the networks in the 1930s, these schedules were not reliably maintained. Constant network pre-emptions of the stated live broadcast times, in favor of news and sports events or commercial programs, threw off ETRC affiliates' schedules. The shows themselves received lukewarm reviews, criticized for sticking too closely to the classroom lecture/talking heads model of educational TV. Though the partnership was renewed in late 1958 for one more series, of just two programs, by the end of 1959 several significant changes had taken place. The ETRC, with encouragement from the Ford Foundation, had eased Harry Newburn out and replaced him with a new director, John F. "Jack" White, who had a new vision for educational television. White determined to set the ETRC in a more centralized and coherent direction as a program provider. Claiming that, because of pre-emptions, only three or four stations were taking the NBC shows live, and that "none of the programs were topical, and both talent selections and production have been uneven," he dissolved the relationship with NBC.[64]

By this time, the quiz show investigations had produced the effect that commercial networks had hoped for since the late 1930s: a demand that the networks take back control over their programs, banish the sponsors from direct influence, and in fact become more like an American BBC in terms of centralized control—or at least, more like a British independent television company. Pundits from Walter Lippmann to Robert Lewis Shayon, publications from *Fortune* to *Harpers, Life,* and the *Christian Science Monitor,* and the heads of all three networks held up the British independent television system as their new model—with many a side glance at a BBC-inspired educational network as an additional goal. Lippmann stormed,

> Television has been caught perpetrating a fraud which is so gigantic that it calls into question the foundations of the industry. . . . The alternative, which is practiced in one form or another in almost every other civilized country, is competition—competition not for private profit but for public service. The best line for us to take is, I am convinced, to devise a way by which one network can be run as a public service with its criterion not what will be most popular but what is good.[65]

On the front page of the *Christian Science Monitor,* William Stringer, the Washington bureau chief, described the ITV system in some detail, as one "distinctively different from the American networks in this vital point: there are no sponsors! . . . The link of commercial consideration between those who plan programs and those who pay for them is totally sundered."[66] *Fortune* magazine agreed, "British commercial television sells time for commercials and the total of such sales pays for all the programs without giving any advertiser control over any program. Such a system deserves careful consideration here."[67] Even *Sponsor* magazine, the trade journal for those now being blamed for all TV's ills, weighed the US against the British system and, though doubting that the ITV commercial monopoly had applicability to the American situation, nonetheless found things to admire: "both the non-commercial British Broadcasting Corp. and the commercial Independent Television Authority have in their program schedules a better balance of shows appealing both to the majority and minorities."[68]

But in this matter, the US networks were far ahead of their critics. CBS had convened a special committee in March 1959, well before the press outcry, whose conclusions embraced the idea of network control over programming but rejected the ITV system of handling advertising sales: "Such a sales system exists in Great Britain as a result of the monopoly under which their commercial networks operate. The economic demands of a competitive environment make it quite doubtful that such a sales system can be effectuated in this country."[69] NBC had been pushing for such a "magazine concept" since the Pat Weaver days, and strenuously denied any wrongdoing on its part in the quiz show debacle; and as for ABC, as *Variety*'s cynical dissenting voice pointed out, that struggling network had, by necessity, more magazine-style spot ad-supported programs on their schedule than any other network. "Does the more prevalent magazine concept on ABC-TV make the programming level of that network superior to that of CBS-TV?" it asked, referring to ABC's widely disparaged line-up of violent actions show and situation comedies. "Patently, not so." Or, as its headline succinctly declared: "Magazine Concept a Panacea for Program Evils? Hardly".[70] The key ingredient missing from the American formulation, of course, was public ownership of stations and a central regulator keeping close watch over a well-defined programming remit. This concept rarely won US adherents, even among commercial television's most vehement critics.

As the networks clearly perceived, the "ITV-like" magazine concept, American style, held real advantages as commercial television came of age. Over the next five years, for reasons having more to do with advances in audience measurement techniques—enabling spot ads to emerge as more effective at targeting key consumer groups via specific programs—and with the networks' increasingly oligopolistic control over the spot ad market as well as the program procurement process, an era of maximum network profitability, centralization, and standardization of television programming would emerge, along the lines that *Variety* had predicted: the classic network system. The ITV-influenced rhetoric of "sponsors out" had achieved its purpose, divorced from British-style public oversight, to the benefit of the now more powerful commercial networks. But in the short term, two notable developments marked the early 1960s. The first, well-documented by Michael Curtin among others, brought about a dramatic increase in the prime-time documentary, produced on film, on all three networks, from 1961 through 1963, as well as the expansion of network news operations. In documentary, none of the hesitation about employing film and film practices that existed in the realm of dramatic production applied; television documentary built happily on the film tradition in an extraordinary flowering that would move to NET and PBS once the networks had established their dominance in the commercial arena.

The second, ironically, gave a boost to the cause of educational television. The first harbinger of this surprising phenomenon can be seen in a memo from the files of the BBC, written by Derek Russell, BBC representative in New York, to Sir Beresford Clark, BBC director of External Broadcasting, in January 1960, as the dust of the quiz show scandal was beginning to settle. He reported on a meeting with Allen Cooper, Director of Corporate Planning for NBC, who was "drawing up the pros and cons of a theoretical 'Fourth Network'".

Cooper argued that NBC was failing in its first duty – to its stockholders. It was not making enough money, and at the same time it was being assailed by a minority of 'eggheads.' One possible answer lay in the creation of a fourth 'network for eggheads' financed by government grants and/or Foundation money . . . Cooper spoke again of stockholders' irritation when NBC public service programs lead to reduced audiences. He implied that he would like to see all such programs shifted into the fourth network, leaving NBC free to compete with ABC and CBS.[71]

Russell reported that Cooper "thought that BBC experience might help" and quizzed him on how such a public service network might operate. Russell opined that "the whole project seems quite unrealistic" and more a measure of NBC insecurity in the wake of the scandals than a realistic scheme. However, just such a system would come to pass before the decade was out: the creation of a government-funded national non-commercial broadcasting structure that would allow the commercial networks their most profitable, purely commercial decades.

The tenuous, struggling enterprise of American educational television was to have a further unforeseen impact on television's transnational emergence, though its effects were fleeting. In 1960, with the expiration of the ITA's first ten-year term due in 1964, and with the BBC's license renewal up in 1962 (extended to 1964 as well), the British government formed its first investigative committee since the introduction of commercial television, headed by Sir Harry Pilkington. The commercialization—and Americanization—of British television was clearly the major subject at hand: with the BBC's audience share at only 30%, with no BBC programs in the top ten, and with three of those programs, including the top two, American imports (*Riverboat, Cimarron City,* and *77 Sunset Strip*),[72] the ITV companies knew that their performance would be heavily scrutinized. At stake was not so much their continued operation—the British public had clearly voted with its tuning dials—but the disposition of a potential "third channel" in Britain using UHF frequencies. Both the BBC and the ITV coveted this channel, and both clearly perceived that the make-up of the Pilkington Committee (Richard Hoggart was one of its most vocal and influential members) and the tenor of the times would mandate emphasis on the educational and public service uses of television to counterbalance its turn, on both channels, to Americanized entertainment programming.

Thus it is not surprising that both the BBC and various ITV companies developed a new interest in American educational television in 1960. The BBC issued a statement in 1961 that attempted to pre-empt any criticism that comparison with America's frankly educational programs might inspire:

BBC has surveyed the American education TV scene in relation to its own operations: it has concluded that . . . the BBC fulfills its education obligations under the Charter through its programs as a whole . . . that all serious broadcasting as well as many programs conceived primarily as entertainment serve educational purposes, and that its first duty is to maintain standards of excellence in all its output. Fifty percent of BBC TV during prime evening time is of educational value in the sense that it makes a demand upon the intelligence of the viewer. (emphasis in original).[73]

However, plans were announced to develop more expressly educational ventures; more explicitly, "BBC looks forward to the development of its own second nation-wide TV Network. This will enable it to provide two complementary TV services, each of which would contain a balanced proportion of light and serious programs, and would enable minority interests to be met."[74]

This sort of declaration spurred ITV companies, both collectively and individually, to explore the field of adult education in 1960 and 61. Tony Bartley of Associated-Rediffusion wrote to Basil Thornton in June 1960, looking into co-productions with NETRC in light of their new Educational Advisory Council's request for more drama and news programs.[75] Another letter, from George Wedell, secretary of the Independent Television Authority, proposed a more ambitious project and linked it directly to Pilkington:

We are trying to clear our minds about the whole question of educational television with a view to deciding what to say on this subject to the Government Committee which is now considering the whole future of broadcasting in this country. Naturally, we are bound to rely for a very large part of the background material for the formation of our views on your experience in the United States . . . What we want is material about the objects, organization, finance control and operation of educational television services with particular reference to adult education.[76]

Thornton sent him a copy of one of NETRC's booklets, "The 4th Network: What it is – How it operates" and Wedell later wrote asking for 15 more copies to circulate to the whole ITA. By early 1962 ITV interests, spearheaded by the Earl of Bessborough, one of ATV's directors, had proposed to set up an Institute for Educational Television. Bessborough was not the only one to schedule a trip to visit White and the NETRC headquarters that winter; George Wedell arrived in February, followed by Lord Gladwyn and Norman Collins. Such a procession of distinguished visitors prompted ETRC executive Basil Thornton to express his amusement to Hugh Carleton Greene, by then BBC Director-General, in early 1962, "For what it is worth, it looks as though ITA and the commercial boys are going to make a great fuss about educational TV, and as this can have some impact on the assessment of their holiness and fitness, I thought you might like to know." Greene responded, tongue in cheek: "Smart wear for commercial television lobbyists this year will consist of academic gowns and mortar boards—and dog collars too for that matter."[77]

Broadcasting in the United States would play as great a rhetorical role in the Pilkington report and debates as it had for Beveridge twelve years before, this time regarding television. Once again a delegation of committee members visited the US to observe television there, and once again, as Jack Gould put it, the final report was "studded with assorted and, for the most part, unflattering reference to United States video." Newton Minow's oft-repeated criticisms from his NAB speech were reproduced at length, and the FCC's inability to regulate the content of television programming was deplored (small details like the First Amendment notwithstanding). Educational television in the US was viewed as a worthy though inadequate and under-funded attempt to correct the shortcomings of the commercial system, something with which US educational broadcasters themselves would most likely have agreed.

In the end, as most had predicted, the Pilkington Committee report was read as a scathing indictment of commercial television and as a defense of the BBC. As the *Guardian* commented:

> The Pilkington Committee finds that good broadcasting and the sale of advertising time do not mix. 'The objectives do not coincide: the secondary objective has been realized; the first has not.' This is the core of the Pilkington Report. The main recommendations stem from it. The BBC should have the third television channel. Commercial radio is rejected. Independent television should be decommercialised (the Pilkington Report is not guilty of the word; but the politics of the day suggest it).[78]

The 1963 Television Act awarded the BBC its second channel, opening up a new era in British broadcasting as it went on the air in 1964. The ITV companies were required to institute a series of reforms, levying a tax on their advertising revenue and strengthening requirements for balanced provision of minority and majority programs. Yet even as commercialization was decried at home, the BBC had already entered into a period of change under Hugh Carleton Greene that extended its global marketing of programs in order to support production across two television channels as well as three radio services. Now that the BBC could schedule against itself, it felt freer to popularize its programs on one channel while its other channel provided more serious fare. These changes will be taken up in the next chapter.

Transnational Exchange and Co-Production: 1955–1964

One continues to be embarrassed when foreigners visit the world's richest country only to find that even its educational television system is devoid of the American performing arts and artists. In fact, ETV relies upon foreign broadcasting systems for much, if not most, of its great drama.[79]
—Hartford Gunn, station manager WGBH-Boston, 1958 (148)

In the United States, though it is noncommercial at home, the British Broadcasting Corporation engages in business with the elegant rapacity of a nobleman chasing an heiress.[80]
—Donald Mainwaring, *Christian Science Monitor*, May 12, 1963

While commercial television established itself in both the US and, a bit later, in Great Britain, they were the anomalies; other countries focused on building up their national public service systems. Across Europe, the countries of the Commonwealth, and throughout the Middle East and Asia, television rolled out slowly but inexorably across the 1950s, driven as much by Cold War propaganda anxieties as by the opportunities for national and international cultural exchange that the new medium promised. Given the bandwidth required for television transmissions and their relatively limited geographical reach, transnational live broadcasts remained difficult —though of course cross-border signals could not always be blocked—but until the development of satellite transmission, no equivalent of shortwave radio existed to facilitate international television exchange. However, important advancements in recording technologies after the war, though less glamorous and widely heralded than live television, opened up a new era in transnational communication and exchange far more effectively than broadcast TV itself, until the introduction of satellite transmission in the 1970s.

Magnetic tape recording had revolutionized sound recording and radio production in the late 1940s, as discussed in Chapter 7, and shortwave radio drew on lessons learned during the war to expand enormously in the 1950s, mostly driven by Cold War propaganda initiatives. Another new technology came along in the mid-1950s that changed radio's cultural role forever: the vinyl record, and especially the 33⅓ rpm LP that could hold up to 25 minutes of sound on each side. In 1956 the BBC became one of the first national broadcasters to see the vinyl LP's potential for international exchange, embarking on a program to distribute its radio programs on the far cheaper, lighter, and more durable recording medium, offering them not for rent but for sale to individual stations worldwide. This new phase of the BBC Transcription Service allowed stations around the world to build up a library of programs that could be scheduled at will and repeated as desired, from an extensive catalogue that offered choice and variety. By 1956 about 700 programs a year were offered this way. Each station had to subscribe, for $5 per year, to the BBC's printed program catalogue, from which it could place an order and receive the programs by mail about two months later, for a nominal fee (since the Transcription Service was still operated as a government-subsidized extension of the Central Office of Information, not as a money-making venture). Offerings consisted of single dramas, drama series, and musical performances, most of them recordings of BBC domestic programs.[81] They found radio play not only in the US but worldwide, especially in English-speaking nations of the Commonwealth such as Canada and Australia. Other national broadcasters also began to adopt the new technology, particularly France and Italy, and to offer programs for international exchange.

For television, though film provided the preferred medium of the commercial sector, it was expensive to produce and, during an era when so much of television production took place live, only offered the possibility of kinescoping, or filming live programs off the screen—never a high quality visual option. Not until the late 1950s did magnetic video recorders become reliable and affordable enough to allow live transmissions to be preserved on tape. Telerecordings, as they were called, did not need to be processed and were more portable than film, though they remained bulky. Telerecordings not only became the backbone of early television exchange but soon gave the BBC, which had rejected Greene's call to produce on film, a product to rival Hollywood.

All of these new technologies, combining live transmission with recorded production and distribution in the fields of both radio and television, along with the new international imperatives of post-war economic development and Cold War political jousting, awakened interest around the world in the utopian possibilities—and dystopian threats—in international intercultural communication, facilitated by a host of organizations that sprang up after the war to encourage it. Some were the external, or propaganda, arms of national governments such as the BBC Overseas Service, the Voice of America and other programs run by the United States Information Agency, Radio France Internationale, and their ilk. Others stemmed from the initiatives of non-governmental international agencies, such as UNESCO's radio service, the European Broadcasting Union's Eurovision and its Eastern counterpart, Intervision, and the International Radio and Television Organization (OIRT).

In the US, no non-governmental national institution existed to facilitate this new kind of exchange, until the Broadcasting Foundation of America was founded in 1955 with the backing of the NAEB and of the Rockefeller and Ford Foundations. On its board were the familiar figures of George Probst, formerly of the *University of Chicago Round Table* and now at WBGH Boston; Seymour "Si" Siegel, long-time director of station WNYC; Lewis Hill, the innovative founder of KPFA and the Pacifica Foundation; and a long list of scholarly notables. Chloe Fox served as Executive Director. The Broadcasting Foundation of America conceived of itself as an antidote not only to the lack of a centralized American broadcasting organization that could take a leading role in international radio exchange, as most national broadcasters in other countries did (and American commercial networks did not) but as a non-partisan alternative to the highly politicized offerings of the U.S. Information Agency services abroad: Voice of America and Radio Free Europe. These services, BFA argued, were "designed as a weapon of psychological warfare, not of communication" and furthermore operated on shortwave, while most radio listening was done on long wave via existing terrestrial stations.

Instead, the BFA proposed to "nurture an international conversation" by sponsoring the exchange of radio and television programs that displayed the worlds' cultures, not its politics. They claimed to have support for their mission from some within the USIA itself, as well as from the Senate Committee on Overseas Information Programs.[82] In fact, they might be considered as one of the "cultural front" organizations that James Schwoch describes as increasingly important in USIA's Cold War program of "indirect information activities . . . in which the source of the material or funds is concealed but which would not, if the source were revealed, involve serious damage to the prestige of the American government" (Schwoch 2008, 66). This is the story that Frances Stonor Saunders lays out in her history of covert CIA support for "the world of arts and letters" during this period, though she neglects the role of radio. The BFA itself claimed, perhaps over-defensively, "None of these programs will contain propaganda."[83]

In January 1957 Seymour Siegel, on behalf of the BFA, applied for funding from the Rockefeller Foundation. He met with John Marshall to make his case, and though the Rockefeller Humanities Division had largely detached itself from educational broadcasting, Marshall was already convinced of the value of transnational radio programs from his own listening to WNYC. A Cold War cultural context contributed too:

There are now in the United States, mainly in New York, the representatives of some 18 foreign broadcasting systems, all of them, of course, national governmental operations. One of their principal duties is to try to get radio and television time for programs originated by their companies. They know from experience that overt propaganda programs have little appeal and as a result are satisfied, and hope to produce for American hearing, programs of the highest possible quality dealing particularly with the arts.[84]

Marshall noted as well that airing such programs in the US would "encourage foreign broadcasting companies to give more time to comparable programs from this country." He approved Siegel's proposal to undertake a survey of European radio in order to make a concrete assessment of the possibilities for working together, focusing on the members of the Université Radiophonique Internationale and the Prix Italia "under two program headings: Intercultural Understanding and Radio as a Means of Access to the Humanities."[85] Seymour and Probst headed across the Atlantic as radio ambassadors from America, a role that the commercial networks had abdicated. In Britain they met not only with Hugh Carleton Greene, by this time Director of Administration of the BBC, but also with Geoffrey Bridson, head of the Features Department, and with Basil Thornton, who had left his post as the BBC's North American Representative for another within the organization back in London.

One result of their visit was luring Thornton back to the US as Executive Director of the BFA, a move that advanced its international profile a great deal and, given Thornton's extensive international connections, helped to ensure its success, especially in terms of its credibility with the BBC. He took up this post in late 1957, just as grant from the Ford Foundation allowed the BFA to set up a duplication and distribution center in New York. By 1959 it was providing eighteen hours of cultural radio programming a week to 200 member stations, both commercial and noncommercial. Though programs from France, Italy, India, Greece, Turkey, Austria, Korea, Japan, Israel, and Norway were included in its service, each with anywhere from two to five available series or single programs, the BBC represented its largest supplier by far, contributing "the whole of the BBC Transcription Service Library, some 300 different programs and series covering drama, concert music, light music, documentaries, children's interest, religion, talks, and variety."[86] Though NAEB member stations made up the single largest group of subscribers, the BFA also distributed its programs to commercial radio stations and networks needing high quality sustaining programs. Later BFA would be absorbed into the Educational Television and Radio Center's operations, with Thornton at the helm of an International Division handling both radio and television.

Meantime, US educational television, rolling out slowly but determinedly, required a source of programs. The Educational Television and Radio Center (ETRC), established with a grant from the Ford Foundation in 1952 and set up in Ann Arbor, Michigan under the direction of Harry Newburn, focused mostly on domestic production. Along the lines of the decentralized vision of Hoffman and Fletcher, the ETRC did not itself produce programs but funded and facilitated production by its member stations and other organizations. Negotiations to acquire kinescoped programs from the BBC began in 1952, after the NAEB delegation's visit, but problems regarding reproduction rights from the Actor's Union and the Society of Authors impeded the process, much to the Americans' dismay. Robert Hudson, ETRC program coordinator, wrote to Hugh Carleton Greene in 1954: "Since we have rather urgent need for programs of the character and quality of BBC drama, we should appreciate your redoubling efforts to solve the problem."[87] In 1955, after more postponements, he wrote again, "I have never known a project with more characteristics of mirage than our negotiations with you for the BBC drama kinescopes."[88]

Finally, in 1956, rights issues began to settle and a mutually beneficial period of transatlantic cooperation could begin. One of the first projects was the *British Art and Artists* series, produced by John Read of the BBC Talks Department with funding from the ETRC, in a spirit of friendly cooperation and perception of benefit on both sides. Memos from the period show that, typically, BBC producers shared their proposed program ideas with Hudson and others at the ETRC, who indicated the topics that most interested them. Questions about comprehensible accents or use of certain phrases occasionally arose, with those at the BBC end willing to accommodate American suggestions, though equally willing to forgo a sale to ETRC if they felt a particular program was important to BBC schedules and audiences. Leonard Miall, BBC Director of Talks, wrote to Harry Newburn, president of the ETRC, in July 1956, reflecting the unconflicted cooperation of this era:

Now that the *British Art and Artists* series is completed, we should like to express our appreciation to you and the Center for the understanding co-operation which you have given us. We have, on occasion, had to change our plans and offer you alternative subjects, and we are grateful for your latitude on this point, and also for the complete freedom we have enjoyed in preparing the films once the subjects were agreed. It has been for our part, a most happy association.[89]

That same year, too, the ETRC was finally able to enter into a contract with the BBC's Overseas and Foreign Relations division for kinescopes of drama programs at a rate of $500 per half-hour of programming. Furthermore, the BBC authorized the ETRC to act as its distributor in the US for these programs to non-affiliated educational and commercial stations "in areas where there is no educational television station," taking a 70/30 split in fees from such stations.[90] For the BBC, this arrangement promised to provide an extra stream of income at very little extra cost or trouble to themselves. For the fledgling American educational network, it was a godsend.

During this period relationships between American educational broadcasters and those involved in television and radio exports at the BBC became quite warm and friendly. Many visits were exchanged; first names were employed. Robert Hudson, head of programming at ETRC, and George Barnes, director of the BBC Television Service, became particularly good friends, staying in each other's homes on frequent trips to London or Ann Arbor. By 1958, when Hudson made a trip to London to line up future programs, he reported back enthusiastically on a long roster of interesting possibilities amongst BBC productions cleared for export, including the *World Theatre* series of classic and modern drama, a number of serial adaptations of novels like *David Copperfield* and *Kenilworth*, and documentary specials and series such as *Transantarctic Expedition, Half the World Away*, and *Buried Treasure*. Hudson noted, however, that the exchange remained somewhat one-sided: while ideas for future co-productions involving American creative contributions were discussed, "very little actual headway was made"; and though the BBC expressed some interest in the potential of taking ETRC-produced programs it did not commit to any specific plans.[91] At this point export to the US fell under the supervision of the Overseas Service, and specifically remained the concern of Cyril Conner, Head of Overseas and Foreign Relations, as a subsidized government activity more about international relations than profits. This was soon to change, altering the whole tenor of BBC/ETRC relations.

The appointment of Jack White as President of the NETRC in 1959 also affected US/BBC relations. One of White's main priorities was to make the idea of a "fourth network" a reality: developing the quality and quantity of programs available to educational television stations, through acquisition of existing programs from international and domestic sources and through the funding of original programs, both via affiliated stations and directly by the NETRC. Inevitably, since the BBC remained the single largest source of quality programs for the new NET network, the transatlantic connection took on even greater importance. A series of events, all occurring in 1960, changed the course of BBC/US relations in a new, sometimes contentious but highly productive, direction.

First, the addition of the "National" to the National Educational Television and Radio Center in 1959 along with its move to New York City signified, as Robert Blakeley put it, "that the center had embarked on a new course of large-scale planning and bold action" (1979, 128). With a fresh $5 million from the Ford Foundation, White hired the center's first full-time professional staff in both station relations and program areas. With a new emphasis on quality programming, the proportion of station-produced programs fell from 73% to 40% of NETRC's output between 1960 and 1962, with a corresponding rise in productions by contract and by acquisition via film and the new potentiality of video recordings (Blakeley 1979, 129).

Second, in 1959 the NETRC—realizing that many of these acquisitions would have to come from overseas—joined the European Broadcasting Union, and with an extra $500,000 from Ford in 1960 acquired the Broadcasting Foundation of America, creating a new International Division under the direction of Basil Thornton (Thornton later referred to it as "something of a shotgun wedding," with the Ford Foundation holding the gun[92]). The Center next jettisoned its radio operations, making them the province of the NAEB, to devote itself fully to television.[93] Even more controversially, it moved away from what would henceforth be termed "instructional programming," programs aimed specifically to provide educational credit in schools, leaving that for the future in the hands of its affiliates and their parent institutions.

Finally and most prominently, White pledged to pull together the national educational television schedule in a way that had never before been attempted, introducing the concept of a "prime-time" lineup of programs that all stations would be expected to carry from 7:30 to 10:00 pm each Monday, Wednesday, and Friday, starting in September 1961. Monday was international night ("Perspectives"), Wednesday focused on people in the news ("The Light Show"), and Friday featured "Festival of the Arts" (Blakeley 1979, 131–32). Many in the educational broadcasting fold objected strongly to this adoption of "commercial" methods and techniques, though others—particularly the larger urban stations—endorsed it wholeheartedly. In 1963 White would drop "radio" completely from the organization's name, and it became simply NET, the National Educational Television network. White's other primary initiative was to do away with the confusing welter of programming produced and distributed under the NET name, creating two primary divisions, public affairs and cultural programs, under a new vice president for programming. Though the hard-hitting and increasingly critical public affairs documentary programs produced under the direction of William Kobin became a hallmark of the new network, bringing it recognition and controversy that would later contribute to its downfall (Brooks), it quickly became apparent that, on the cultural side, NET's programming success would depend heavily on its British partners.

Yet this relationship was complicated by the fact that, during this same period, the BBC had embarked on a program of expansion of its commercial export operations and a change in its profile in the world. On June 29, 1960, the BBC's new $45 million Television Centre opened in Shepherd's Bush, billed as "the largest, best-equipped, and most carefully planned factory in the world" by BBC Director of Television Gerald Beadle in a North American press release. He went on to say:

> The BBC is an enormous producer of electronic programs—without a doubt the greatest in the world. Just as Hollywood is the principal world center for photographic programs, so the BBC Television Centre is the principal world center for electronic programs. Television, for economic reasons, will always be mainly international. Few television stations will be anywhere near self-sufficient in program material. Most of them will buy heavily from America and Britain. Britain has, or soon will have, the electronic program ball at her feet.[94]

His words not only marked out a clear distinction between American and British television production, but placed the international export of television programs on a new footing as a money-making operation that would compete with commercial suppliers around the globe. The process had already been initiated with the appointment of Ronald Waldman as Business Manager, Television Programmes in 1958 (Briggs 1995, 712), who immediately began pursuing a plan of mid-Atlantic co-productions with commercial US and Canadian companies (as discussed above). In 1960 a new department, Television Promotions, was established with Waldman as director. In 1961 this was absorbed into a new Television Enterprises division for which Waldman served as General Manager. Denis Scuse became the Television Enterprises division's North American representative.

This went hand in hand with a general rethinking of the BBC's role in the world, prompted by the appointment of Hugh Carleton Greene as Director-General in January 1960. Greene would remain in that post throughout the tumultuous decade of the 1960s, presiding over great changes in policy and programming. He is frequently hailed as "one of the last giants of British broadcasting, a man of exemplary vision" (Vahimagi in "Greene, Sir Hugh (1910-1987)") and credited with making "the decisive shift from the conservatism of the 1950s to the more radical, irreverent, and . . . permissive 1960s" (Waymark 2006, 13). Asa Briggs deems his impact "as significant in BBC history as Reith's role during the formative 1920s" (1995, xix). A striking figure, 6′7″ tall with thick dark-framed glasses, brother of the novelist Graham Greene (and cousin to Felix Greene), Hugh Carleton Greene was educated at Oxford and worked as a journalist before joining the BBC as head of its German Service in 1940. He remained in the External Services division until becoming Director of Administration in 1958 and the Director-General in 1960. Greene was critical of the hidebound, Oxbridge-dominated culture of the BBC, while remaining fiercely loyal; as he claimed:

> I wanted to open the window and dissipate the ivory tower stuffi-ness which still clung to some parts of the BBC. I wanted to encourage enterprise and the taking of risks. I wanted to make the BBC a place where talent of all sorts, however unconventional, was recognized and nurtured. (Greene 1969, 13–14)

One area of change involved the relationship with the United States and with the new commercial television environment more generally: Greene moved the BBC onto the world stage as a commercial competitor while maintaining "an unshakeable belief in the virtues of public service broadcasting as exemplified by the corporation" (Waymark 2006, 33). Most immediately, changes in his External and Overseas territory were on the cards.

In September of 1960 the BBC's old New York office in Rockefeller Center closed, even as Television Enterprises opened theirs. In 1962 the North American Service, founded with so much urgency in 1940, ceased operating. This was not due to a lack of success; according to the 1963 *BBC Handbook*, 1962 had been the most successful year ever for re-broadcasts of BBC pro-grams by American stations, nearly 14,000 hours (70). Instead, it represents a rethinking of the BBC's international role more generally, in the wake of Suez, the Cold War, and decolonialization. A restored and reorganized General Overseas Service continued to broadcast British news and culture to the world on a 24-hour basis, now targeted not to the outposts of Empire, nor as a propaganda vehicle designed to rally nations to the British cause, but to "the listener who understands English but is not of British descent."[95] As Briggs enigmatically reports, "Unfortunately, the citizens of the United States, the largest group of English speakers outside Britain, did not figure directly in the picture after the closing of the North American Service" (1995, 692). A new era of private markets had emerged, though in radio the BBC Transcription Service would continue to operate on a subsidized basis. In television, however, the competitive international game was on.

The objective of Greene's new BBC Television Enterprises, as Scuse stated it bluntly in a letter in 1962, was "to sell [BBC programs] in the open markets of the world . . . to earn profits, which could be ploughed back into the Television Service, to meet rising costs and improve domestic produc-tion standards."[96] To assist with these efforts the BBC contracted with an American commercial distributor, Peter M. Robeck, who would later merge his company with Time-Life Films to become an influential presence in the growing economy of transatlantic co-production in the 1970s (Chapter 9). Ronald Waldman expressed the BBC's new vision in even more ambitious terms than Greene's 1953 statement, only two years after the triumphant opening of the Television Centre: "My main concern in this general area remains the gradual replacement of American-made film series, on our screens and the screens of most of the world, by high-quality British-made series inspired and directed by BBC Television."[97]

To accomplish this, Waldman maintained, two vital changes in BBC policy were necessary: programs must be produced on film, as Greene (and Aubrey Singer) had argued ten years earlier, and co-productions with American commercial companies must be actively cultivated. Beadle's vision of the BBC as the world capital of live television production, while a good place to start, simply would not suffice in the long run. In an extraordinary memo marked "confidential" directed to Kenneth Adam, whom Greene had installed as Gerald Beadle's replacement in the fall of 1961, Waldman developed his vision at some length.

> If BBC Television fails to add photographically-produced series to its own output, if it fails to use photographic methods for those of its own programme ideas that so badly need them, then it must continue for ever to rely on the Americans to provide this important programme element in its output. And this, I deeply and sincerely believe, would be a disastrous abdication to American programme thought and American programme judgment. If the British cinema industry was able (as it amazingly and triumphantly was) to combat and at very least to equal in this country the domination of Hollywood, then surely the British Television industry can? I am simply not prepared to believe or accept that we have no alternative but to surrender to the Americans and leave this element in our programmes entirely to them.[98]

Waldman recognized that money, as usual, impeded the BBC's ventures in this direction, and also that producing only for British consumption could never provide a sufficient economic base. Though Europe and the Commonwealth nations were important markets, the biggest would always be the United States, which had both the funds and the experience with filmed production that the BBC needed:

> We need some of their money and we need some of their skills. To adjust and lengthen a well-worn phrase, then, 'if you can't beat 'em, join 'em, learn from 'em and then beat 'em at their own game.' This

simple, even crude, method is, of course, 'dignified' by the resounding name of 'co-production.'[99]

Noting that the BBC had already partnered with American producers for two series—*the Third Man* and *RCMP*—neither of which had proved a strong success, Waldman pointed to the fact that, although they had been intended as an equal partnership in both funding and creative input, the Americans had dominated on the creative side. This was due as much to the BBC's inability, or unwillingness, to devote sufficient personnel and resources to the projects as it was American insistence, and Waldman envisioned Television Enterprises entering into a new era in which "we shall be in a position to dispense with American 'help' and do the job on our own." He recommended moving towards hour-length, rather than half-hour, productions based on British popular literary properties, and mentioned a proposed project based on the Horatio Hornblower series to be undertaken with MCA, but with the BBC firmly in charge:

[W]e are going to make C. S. Forester's 'Hornblower' and not Jules Stein's 'Hornblower.' However much Lew Wasserman, Taft Schreiber and Co <u>may</u> want us to make 'Wagon Train' at sea, the entire series (if there is one) will be made in this country under the control of Collier Young and ourselves.[100]

In fact the BBC collaborated with Collier Young, an American producer under contract with MCA, to produce a single play, "Hornblower," for the *Alcoa Premiere Theater* in 1963. Donald Wilson, Director of Serials under Sydney Newman, did the adaptation; it was filmed in Hollywood with a British cast but an American production crew. It did not, however, lead to the new era in series production that Waldman had hoped for. Waldman left the BBC in 1963 to become the director of VisNews, a highly successful television "wire" service later incorporated by Reuters. His vision for the BBC remained, though it would be taken in unexpected directions.

Certainly Waldman's and Greene's emphasis on commercial sales became the BBC's priority, coinciding profitably for a brief time with American commercial broadcasters' chastened behavior following the twin threats of the quiz show scandal and Newton Minow's admonitory regime at the FCC. The effect, however, was to leave their long-time educational partner the NETRC out in the cold. Even before Waldman articulated his plans, in February 1961 the BBC steeply increased the rates charged for its drama programs, from $500 to over $3,000 per half hour, on top of a new provision that would take away the exclusivity that NETRC had previously enjoyed for the markets in which an affiliate aired a particular program. The NETRC argued for concessions, arguing that "the typical BBC production, which is generally not in commercially exploitable series, nor tuned to the taste of the American mass audience, is much more acceptable to NETRC than to any other American organization."[101] But the BBC had embarked on an aggressive marketing campaign, targeting not only commercial stations but going after direct sales to NET affiliates as well, cutting out the NETRC. A few NET affiliates began to see opportunities in dealing directly with BBC TV Enterprises, reasoning that they could cherry-pick desired programs for less than their NETRC affiliation fees—acting to weaken NETRC's function as a network. This prompted NETRC to threaten to withdraw from its previously comfortable relationship with the BBC altogether in August 1961, and again in 1962.[102]

NETRC's position was undercut, however, by the spectacular success of a BBC import, the *Age of Kings* series of Shakespeare plays, debuting October 5, 1961 in the Friday "Festival of the Arts" slot. *Age of Kings* gained more praise from critics, viewers, and station managers than any previous NET offering, becoming "public TV's first unqualified national success, a smash hit" (Stewart 43). Brice Howard, one of White's new professional program executives, spearheaded the acquisition, aided by one of the first instances of corporate underwriting, by the Humble Oil Company (later renamed Exxon) to the tune of $400,000. This fifteen-part series, made to mark the debut of BBC Two (see below) strung into a single series the Shakespeare's series of plays focusing on Richard II, Henry IV, Henry V, Henry VI, and Richard III, "effectively presenting a chronological history of British royalty from 1377 to 1485" (Brooke 2009). This was one of the most expensive and ambitious dramatic ventures undertaken by BBC television to date, directed by Michael Hayes and produced by Peter Dews, featuring, among other notables, a young pre-Bond Sean Connery as Hotspur and pre-Dame Judi Dench playing Katherine of France. Its "schedule friendly" segmentation into 60 to 75-minute episodes no doubt took the American market into account, and in fact two US commercial stations, in New York and Washington, DC, purchased the series and aired it in 1960, the same year of its broadcast in Britain.[103]

For its national debut on NET, Frank Baxter, a University of Southern California English professor who had hosted a CBS Shakespeare series earlier, introduced each episode. It received more favorable notice in national publications than any previous educational broadcast, at least in part due to promotional efforts also underwritten by Humble Oil at the urging of yet another one of White's professional hires, Nazaret "Chic" Cherkezian, NETRC's first full-time publicist. Such demonstrations of the superiority and popularity of the BBC's programs over more homespun efforts irked many within the educational television field, even as they perceived clearly that such series gave NET the kind of identity and attention (and funding) it sorely needed—a full reversal of the way that many in Britain viewed the utility of American commercial entertainment programs. And it worked, as well, to convince the BBC that a lucrative market existed for their productions in America. Dennis Scuse wrote to Jack White even before NET's national debut reporting that the advertising agency BBD&O had expressed interest in packaging *The Age of Kings* for sponsors in 14 markets across the US.[104]

Later, NET programmers would look back nostalgically on the days when BBC programs like *The Age of Kings* could be had for a relatively low price. They had acquired exclusive rights for 3 years (for non-commercial screenings in cities where an educational affiliate existed) for $3,100 per episode; Baxter's introductions and closings done at KQED, by contrast, cost $35,000 to produce.[105] By the time the next offering of a high-profile series—this time *The Spread of the Eagle*, a nine-part series based on Shakespeare's Roman cycle, comprising *Coriolanus*, *Julius Caesar*, and *Antony and Cleopatra*—occurred in 1963, the BBC's asking price had gone up to $40,000 to $50,000 an episode. Dennis Scuse reported to Basil Thornton that they were "confident they would get a [commercial] network" to pay this price, and if not could achieve it in commercial syndication; further, "this has been talked over at the highest level in the BBC and the prospect of obtaining this kind of money in the USA is an integral part of going ahead with the project: They have to get it." Thornton concluded, "It means there will, in future, be very little drama available to us from the BBC" and that "as a long term project, we ought to be getting into production ourselves."[106] By May of 1963, NET was informed that a package of BBC dramas would not be made available to the educational network at all, since it had been placed in the hands of Peter Robeck for purely commercial syndication; however, educational stations were welcome to bid for the package individually if they could meet the price.[107] Some within NET suggested that they might do well to form their own "runaway" mid-Atlantic production company, to produce literary adaptations on videotape in England using British talent, as so many of their commercial counterparts had done.[108]

In fact, though British programs would enjoy their highest profile ever on American commercial television in the early to mid 1960s (mostly from ITV companies, however), the next phase of American-British television relations would shift yet again, to bring US educational broadcasters—now part of a new public television system—back into a close network of co-production that would prove both profitable and contentious on both sides of the Atlantic. This will be taken up in the next chapter, as the Pilkington's creation of BBC Two brought deep changes to British broadcasting and as the Carnegie Commission and President Johnson's Great Society programs brought public television, finally, into the center of American cultural life.

However, another twist in the US/British relationship during these transitional years came in the form of one of the most ambitious efforts at international documentary production during this period, partnered not with the BBC but with one of its commercial competitors. It was Britain's Associated-Rediffusion (A-R) that came up with the idea, approaching NET in September 1960. In a letter to Basil Thornton, Anthony Bartley, head of A-R's International Division, explained that since the advent of the Independent Television Network, A-R had taken on the responsibility of providing a series of one-hour public affairs features for distribution across the ITV regional schedules. He proposed that the scope and content of such programs could be enhanced and expanded if an international partnership could be formed between his company, the Canadian Broadcasting Corporation, the Australian Broadcasting Commission, and NETRC.

> Each member of this co-operative would produce, and make available to the others, a predetermined number of programmes. . . . The number of episodes made by each, and the topics, would be a matter of common agreement, but there would be no restriction placed on the producing members as to where or how they should make their programmes. . . . A valuable contribution could be made to closer international relationships within the English speaking world, through the medium of visual journalism.[109]

The idea suited NET's priorities very well, as they began to develop their reputation in the public affairs programming area. Yet, another stipulation was that the resulting programs be shown in prime time; this meant a high standard of production that put stress on NET's limited resources. A partner, the Westinghouse Broadcasting Company, was brought in to share the burden, under the direction of programming VP Richard Pack.[110] This meant that the project, soon named INTERTEL, would air not only on educational stations but also on WBC's five commercial stations.

The whole project was a daring mix not only of nations but of types of broadcasting systems: ABC and CBC were national broadcasters while the others were private; A-R, Westinghouse, and the CBC were at least partially commercial while the ABC was state-funded and NET funded by the Ford Foundation. Their purpose was to produce a bi-monthly series of documentaries, alternating between partners, in which "no nation may contemplate itself. Each must look over its horizons and seek to draw some conclusions about a changing society elsewhere."[111] Thus, for the first season, the NET/WBC partnership produced *Postscript to Empire*, a look at contemporary life in Great Britain, while A-R created *America Abroad,* exploring the impact of American citizens and organizations working around the world. A-R also produced *Living With a Giant,* an investigation of Canadian culture under the shadow of its enormous neighbor, while in 1963 the CBC turned its gaze on the American South, with *One More River,* an attempt to negotiate the treacherous territory of racial integration. Other productions explored life and politics in other nations around the world, including Vietnam (*The Quiet War,* A-R 1961), *Heartbeat of France* (A-R 1961), Mexico (*The Unfinished Revolution,* NET/WBC 1962), *Where Is Cuba Going?* (CBC, 1962), and *Tahiti: Pacific Cocktail* (ABC 1963). As a glossy brochure produced in 1963 put it, "Each of the four member countries send a team of cameramen and writers into *other* nations, to report on their critical issues— and capture history as it occurs—for the television viewer. This is international television at a depth and objectivity never before possible— designed for an audience of 280,000,000 English-speaking people. This is INTERTEL."[112]

And this could be controversial. NET/WBC's production *Britain: A Postscript to Empire* was its first attempt, written and produced by Michael Sklar, who had previously worked under Irving Gitlin in CBS's news and documentary division. In a neat harking-back to the early days of radio documentary, Rodney MacLeish, nephew of Alistair MacLeish and head of the foreign desk at WBC, introduced the program; and Joseph Julian narrated, as he had so often for Norman Corwin during the war. Robert Hudson at NET and Richard Pack at WBC supervised the production, and lest anyone think that WBC intended to be a silent underwriter, the production file is full of lengthy memos of ideas and criticisms from Pack, who also facilitated introductions and logistics in numerous ways. Sklar spent several months in England, finally determining to focus on two communities that to him embodied the show's theme, "Britain in transition": Stevenage, a "new town" representing the present, and Cubitt Town on the Isle of Dogs in London's East End, representing the past. Predictably enough, when the documentary was aired in Britain in January 1962, Cubitt Town residents objected strongly to their designated role, drafting a petition against the documentary signed by the members of the Cubitt Town Residents Association.[113] Its Honorable Secretary, R. E. Gayler, wrote plaintively, "But oh; after much publicity, with every Islander watching their television, there was a great let down . . . a more fabricated & untrue picture of life was never made. . . . My conclusion is that your journalist must be mentally deranged with eyes pointing in different ways presenting a Picaso [sic] type of picture instead of a true understandable one."[114] Michael Sklar later summed up the British critical reaction as "half the British press, the better half, thought it a good show, one quarter found it dull and the rest found it 'scandalous, full of lies."[115] Transnational documentaries tread on dangerous ground, filled with sensitive toes that might be trampled on.

Similarly, the CBC's *One More River* (1964), looking at the story of racial integration in the South, raised considerable controversy amongst NET affiliates, especially its Southern ones. Described by its producer Douglas Leiterman as "a report on the mood of the Southern States, as we found it," it was accused of focusing too heavily on the views of civil rights "extremists" like Malcolm X but also for allowing unregenerate Southern racists to speak their views. In attempting to be even-handed, the Canadian producers gave screen time not only to well-educated middle-class African Americans, but also to the poor and illiterate who seemed to confirm the prejudices of the racists, causing some viewers to conclude that the film hurt the case for integration.[116] Both WBC and NET, separately, refused to air it; it won an award in Canada. And when the CBC delayed the release of its first film, *Where Is Cuba Going?*, because "CBC management was concerned with certain elements," speculation was rife that the elements were political, not technical as implied, especially in the wake of the international controversy caused by Chris Marker's controversial *Cuba, Si!*, released earlier that year.

At other times, the sheer pace of production—the series was meant to air once a month on Mondays, as part of the "Perspectives" series—meant that the planned documentary could not be shown and another, usually from the designated producer's regular schedule, would have to be slotted into its place. This caused considerable unevenness in output, so that the number of productions fell to six a year almost immediately. It also meant that the idea that the partners would all approve of each documentary fell by the wayside; *One More River*, for instance, had been produced for the CBC's regular public affairs series and simply slotted into its INTERTEL offerings without consultation with its international partners. Reactions amongst the partners' audiences were generally favorable. Associated-Rediffusion reported that the first season offerings each received an audience percentage well over 70%, with the exception of *Postscript to Empire* (they explained that it had been scheduled opposite a major football match on the BBC).[117] In the US it aired regularly on 55 NET affiliates and the 5 Westinghouse stations. The INTERTEL partnership would hold up until 1970, though its output dropped to just a few productions a year. By this time NET had been absorbed by the emergent PBS, and partnership in both dramatic and documentary production had become a hallmark and a mainstay of both British and US television.

Thus the years 1955 to 1964 mark a transitional time both in the United States and in Britain, in both radio and television and for both commercial and public service broadcasters, setting the stage for post-1964 developments that would carry television into the modern era. After the rocky transatlantic moment of the coronation of Queen Elizabeth II, commercial television got off to a strong start in Britain with a system that attempted to avoid American evils, notably the influence of the sponsor. In America the "quiz show scandal" reorganized US commercial broadcasting along British lines and set up expectations for reform which were partly met by the Ford Foundation's continuing support for NET. Ford's directives set the terms for Jack White's vision of a nationally unified American public system, leading to the establishment of a long-awaited "fourth network." It laid the groundwork as well for the Carnegie Commission on Educational Television and eventually to the construction of a national public service system that would finally find permanent governmental support in 1967.

Britain's ITV brought a new set of possibilities to the transatlantic relationship, encouraging a new kind of filmed, "mid-Atlantic" program that would achieve even greater success in the following decades, as well as collaboration in more serious educational and documentary fare that found a home on NET. 1964 marks the year that BBC Two came online, thanks to the pro-BBC Pilkington report, changing the balance of British programming and its relationship to its transatlantic competitor. And the BBC's new director Hugh Carleton Greene, under pressure to expand its worldwide presence, established its Television Enterprises division under Ronald Waldman to compete not only with its Hollywood counterparts but with its US educational allies as well.

One theme running through this period was the reluctance of broadcasters, particularly within the BBC, to expand into filmed production despite the advocacy of many within its own organization as well as the example of the ITV companies. The single play, produced live and telerecorded, remained central in the British television universe.[118] The next section will see the reversal of this attitude, as filmed series become the staple global commodity of British television, both BBC and ITV, in close connection with the United States as its single biggest market and frequent coproducer. It is interesting to speculate about the reasons for the BBC's emphasis on live production of the single play. Some scholars, such as John Caughie, point towards the deep debt that British radio and television owed to the theatrical tradition, with the values of the theater providing a hallmark of "quality" and seriousness of cultural intent that was nurtured and encouraged both in British critical discourse and in broadcasting policy (Caughie 2000). Though the famous "Nats go home" moment rejected the particular kind of theatrical naturalism that dominated both the British stage and British screens up to that point and argued for a less restrictive, more inherently visual approach to television drama, I would argue that it was the negative example set by Hollywood filmed production, in both cinema and television, that set the opposite pole along very similar lines as those William Boddy describes for American television during the earlier period. Thus resistance to film became a form of resistance to popularization and all the Americanizing influences that implied. Though individuals within the BBC, and many involved with ITV, argued for a turn to filmed series and serials as an important sector of television production—whether for commercial or aesthetic reasons, or a combination of both—in fact it was not until the adaptation of literary works, produced in filmed series form, became a staple of programming on ITV, BBC, NET and PBS in the late 1960s and 1970s that the live single play faded away—only to be replaced by the made-for-TV movie and mini-series. The move towards filmed television, combined with new recording technologies and the radio-inherited seriality of broadcasting, opened up television to international exchange and a new globalization of culture, as Britain and American both struggled to retain their pre-eminent positions. The next chapter takes up these developments.

CHAPTER 9

Transatlantic Partnerships, 1964–1975

There's domestic television and there's American television. In every territory in the world that is how it divides.
—Antony Root, President, Granada Entertainment USA; Steemers 2001 (104)

There is a lexicon of phraseology that seems to be reserved for American television imports . . . one often waits for the following epithets to follow on any mention of American television programmes: 'mindless', 'glossy', 'shallow', 'junk,' 'inane,' 'pap,' 'bilge', 'bland, brainless, and boring'.
—Geoffrey Lealand, *American Television Programmes on British Screens* (69)

In the mid-1960s both British and American broadcasting entered new eras, a little ahead of the general social revolution that would soon sweep across the globe. Now established in the structures that would persist into the early 1980s, a period of relative stability and profitability ensued in both nations, as television became a settled part of the national culture, and as television systems established themselves across the globe drawing on both British and American models and programs to guide and sustain them—as well as to alarm and infuriate many sectors of their populations. Yet within these stable structures, surrounding social and political pressures prompted changes in both rhetoric and practice from within. The advent of BBC Two in 1964, along with the rise of public broadcasting in the US culminating in the formation of the Public Broadcasting Service (PBS) in 1968 and National

Public Radio (NPR) two years later, shifted the priorities of all involved institutions and led to an era of mutual cooperation and involvement unprecedented except in wartime, with many of the same kinds of tensions operating underneath the surface.

During this period the global market for filmed programs and the emerging practice of what would later be called "format sales," or the sale of rights to adapt a program in another national context, became well-established characteristics of television worldwide. In effect, these practices worked to embed elements of specific national cultures, most often American, squarely in the center of everyday life in national contexts both closely linked and widely distant. A new spate of worries about the Americanization of culture, this time not only in Europe's affluent and "culturally proximate" (Straubhaar 2002) countries but far and wide, began to generate the strand of media scholarship associated with theories of "media imperialism" and of cultural imperialism more generally (Mattelart 1979; Schiller 1976; Tunstall 1977). Terms like "cocacolonization" and, later, "Dallasification" mark the tenor of these times, sparked by the much-cited 1974 UNESCO report by Kaarle Nordenstreng and Tapio Varis, *Television Traffic: a one-way street?* which in turn contributed to the explosive 1980 UNESCO-sponsored MacBride Report (actually titled *Many Voices One World: Towards a new more just and more efficient world information and communication order*) that led to the New World Information and Communication Order controversies and eventually prompted both the US and Great Britain to withdraw from UNESCO for the better part of two decades.

Though most fingers were pointed at the US, as in the quotes above, Great Britain, France and Germany figured as dominant world suppliers as well despite a wide gap between their exports and those of the US, with Britain well in the lead. As the 1974 report stated, "The BBC is second only to the United States as a major distributor of TV programmes" worldwide (Nordenstreng and Varis 1974, 34). This is also remarkable for a single institution's prominent position; though the US share of world imports amounted to between two and three times more than that of the BBC's Television Enterprises division,[1] it was divided between several hundred distributing organizations, the largest of which were Viacom (formerly owned by CBS),[2] Worldvision (formerly owned by ABC), National Telefilm Associates (formerly part of NBC), Screen Gems (Columbia), MCA, and 20th Century-Fox. In terms of a single corporation's dominance over the global market, the BBC established itself as the largest in the world.

During the 1960s the trading relationship between Britain and the US remained somewhat lopsided. Though the US represented by far the largest supplier of non-domestic programming on British networks, Britain ranked fourth in terms of US sales by dollars earned, after Canada, Australia, and Japan. This would change as the 1970s progressed, with American imports gaining a higher profile on British prime-time schedules, in part due to the end of government regulations over the number of hours British stations could broadcast per day. By the late 1970s, Britain was the United States' single largest customer for television exports.

The US became Britain's most lucrative customer earlier, at the end of the 1960s (Nordenstreng and Varis 1974, 34), mostly via sales to NET/PBS and through syndication to stations (not network sales); before that, the Commonwealth nations had dominated as purchasers of British programs. In 1974, nearly half of British exports to the US were shown on educational stations, and though a few programs made an impact on the commercial networks, they were more significant in terms of their creative influence in the US than to market share in Britain. Not until the 1980s would US cable channels and the new Channel 4 in Britain make the two nations each other's single largest trading partner, a situation that remains to this day, especially if not only program sales but co-production agreements are taken into account. In fact a whole range of dialogic practices mark the transatlantic cultural economy during this period, from direct import to adaptation to transnational co-production, weaving the project of both British and American broadcasting more tightly together than ever before, despite continued controversy and even denial, as the quote above demonstrates.

Anxiety over the terms of this transnational dialogue was evident on both sides of the Atlantic, with US television threatening the "Dallasification" and "dumbing down" of British culture, and the struggling American public broadcasting service open to charges that it had become too dependent on British production, unable to assert a distinctly American "quality" aesthetic in either documentary or drama. These tensions necessitated a system of cooperation that was both overt and covert; it becomes useful here to think about the distinction made by film scholar Mette Hjort between "marked" and "unmarked" transnationalism (Hjort 2010, 13–14).[3] When transnationalism is *marked*, the attention of the viewer is directed towards recognition of the various different national components that went into making it, in terms of the subject matter, style, location, or nationalities of the production personnel involved, both on the screen and behind it. When *unmarked*, surface appearance and ostensible subject matter might reflect or invoke a single national context, despite transnational cooperation in its conception, financing and/or production. These attributes vary according to reception context as well, and may function to completely obscure the transnational roots of a given program, effectively domesticating and "de-nationalizing" it despite production circumstances.[4] Thus in the United States Hannah Weinstein's *The Adventures of Robin Hood* would be marked as British, therefore transnational—though its American (or "un-American") roots, hidden behind false credits, went unmarked. In Britain, however, it appeared as a domestic production, its transnationalism completely unmarked, as its surface appearance and accent were entirely British and few would have cause to realize its American (or "un-American")-influenced provenance. INTERTEL's documentaries, on the other hand, were explicitly and prominently marked as transnational, from the outset, wherever they aired; this was precisely their objective and their appeal. Most programs fell somewhere in between these two poles.

The balance between marked and unmarked transnationalism is an important factor in considering the directions that British-American exchange took in the 1960s and beyond. Typically, British programs in the American context were decidedly and enthusiastically marked as British (and still are), since that designation added cultural value. In the 1960s, when England's "swinging" image held a special appeal for the younger generation, imports on commercial channels like *The Avengers* and *The Prisoner* (and later, *Monty Python's Flying Circus*) were "cool" precisely because of their marked transnational qualities (as Greene had predicted): distinctly British, but recognizable and assimilable in the American context. However, in the 1970s the commercial network practice of adapting a different kind of popular British program unmarked into an American version, such as *All in the Family* or *Sanford and Son*—usually with little or no acknowledgement of its roots—began to compete with the longer tradition of marked Britishness now receiving an even higher profile on PBS, which itself had become controversial in terms of the lack of quality domestic production. On the emergent public broadcasting network, Britishness was more apt to be marked in some genres and contexts—such as drama— than in others, such as documentary. Often this degree of marking corresponded to the extent and nature of American participation: in those cases where American dollars funded an essentially British production, with little or no American creative or intellectual input (ostensibly, at least), its very value lay in its marked transnationalism. Americans were willing to pay for a certain kind of Britishness for a host of reasons, some of them practical, some of them symbolic. Their British origins were marked, the extent of their American-ness was left unmarked—just as with *The Adventures of Robin Hood* two decades before.

In Britain, where the issue of American influence on British culture remained contentious, the marked American-ness of popular imported programs could not be hidden and in fact was frequently exploited for audience-building purposes on both the commercial network and the BBC (though downplayed before regulatory bodies and the critical press). American-ness had its disadvantages as well as its advantages. Thus, though

American Westerns achieved almost as much cultural impact in Britain as in the US, with shows like *Wagon Train* and *Rawhide* highly popular on regional ITV schedules for most of a decade, this was certainly not a fact to be trumpeted aloud and most official and unofficial histories make little mention of it.[5] In the sphere of co-production—the more typical transnational situation that Hjort has in mind—American involvement typically went unmarked, or in fact was concealed. As we have seen, rarely were British adaptations of American programs acknowledged as such—in fact, often considerable effort was expended to deny or downplay the idea of such roots, as with Howard Thomas' recollection of the origins of *The Brains Trust*. And as American funding began to underwrite an increasing number of high-profile British drama and documentary co-productions in the late 1960s and early 1970s, controversies arose within the halls of both the BBC and ITV as to where the lines of American participation should be drawn, and how the public should be encouraged to understand this un-marked American influence at the heart of British television.

However, sometimes a marked North American influence could be advantageous in both the commercial and the public sphere, especially if it derived from Canada rather than from the US. This chapter begins with a discussion of just such a Canadian, Sydney Newman, one of the leading figures in the development of British television drama in the 1960s. His influence has been identified by a number of historians as well as by critics at the time as central to the changes that took place in the early 1960s in Britain's television culture—though more often than not Newman's decidedly "marked" presence conceals the considerable Canadian contingent of producers and directors active in British television in the 1950s and 1960s, as will be discussed below. The surge of popularity of British imports on American screens in the 1960s, along with the resurgence of an American-style address to female audiences with the domestic serial form in Britain, presents a complex mélange of both marked and unmarked transnationalism in the second section. Meantime, the United States finally installed a public broadcasting system in its cultural sphere, marked by some distinctly American characteristics as well as a renaissance of British programming in the US. Finally the transatlantic culture of co-production, still in vibrant operation today, found its place on the world stage.

Sydney Newman and Transatlantic Drama

Sydney Newman had taken up his appointment just over a week beforehand . . . I thought, like everyone else, that he looked like a second-rate character actor playing Tennessee Williams, or a suburban hairdresser . . . Sydney's revolution was very simple. He industrialized the making of television drama, and he did it in the simplest possible way, by setting up the situation he had himself had at Armchair Theatre, which had itself been borrowed from the practice of the film industry.

—Don Taylor [BBC Drama Producer] (169, 190)

Sydney Newman's career is a product of what Richard Collins has termed the "North Atlantic triangle" (Collins 1990a, 212), that circuit of cultural influence that runs between the US, Canada, and Great Britain. In television, it has produced key programs and practices that have circulated worldwide. As the previous chapters have begun to demonstrate, cultural relationships in the "North Atlantic triangle" are complex and deeply intertwined. Both Canada and the United States share a fundamental historical relationship with Britain that ties them to that nation's culture even in the face of extensive linguistic, racial, ethnic, and social variation. The BBC was influential in the formation of the Canadian Broadcasting Corporation (CBC) through the efforts of its representative, Felix Greene; the CBC's first general manager was the Canadian-born former director of public relations for the BBC, Gladstone Murray (see S. Potter 2011). Canada and the United States have a long-standing shared tradition of commercial radio and television (among many other cultural, political, and economic relationships). Both the BBC and American public television, as well, form a central part of the Canadian cultural experience, received by direct broadcast or cable in millions of Canadian homes; Canada is an (often unmarked) contributor to many programs on both British and American radio and TV. Britain and Canada have direct ties as members of the Commonwealth. Canada has frequently served as a source of cultural influence in Britain linked to American practices and values but also more closely tied to a public service aesthetic. In English-speaking Canada the legacy of British identity has served as a bulwark for a large section of the population against both the French culture of Quebec and Americanizing influences from across the border. It is in this complex triangulation of cultural influence that Sydney Newman's career was shaped and in which the full impact of his influence must be understood.

Born in Toronto, the son of Russian Jewish immigrants who ran a shoe store, Newman studied graphic arts and animation in a technical school, never attending university (a factor contributing to the disdain with which he was greeted by many in the BBC, as in Taylor's quote above). Newman's earliest aspirations took him to Hollywood in 1938, where he was offered a position as an animator at Disney Studios, but lack of a work permit returned him to Canada, where he took up a position as film splicer at the National Film Board of Canada under famed British documentarist John

Grierson (Vahimagi in "Newman, Sydney (1917-1997)"). Grierson took Newman under his wing, promoting him first to film editor and then to director of wartime training films; eventually he became producer of the prestigious wartime series *Canada Carries On* (Goetz 1977, 73). In 1949 the CBC, preparatory to starting up its television service, sent Newman to the NBC studios in New York to observe and report on television production methods, "where he closely observed the new wave of play writing for television."[6] In 1952 he was appointed CBC Director of Features, Documentaries, and Outside Broadcasts, and in 1954 became Supervisor of Drama.

In this capacity he had the opportunity to put his New York experience into action as producer of the *Ford Television Theatre, General Motors Theatre, Graphic,* and various other sponsored live anthology-style shows delivering not high-brow literary adaptations but the more "topical and commercial" programs popular with broad audiences, modeled on American programs (M. Miller 1987, 188).[7] Newman's experience in the world of commercial broadcasting is often "written out" of accounts of his career; most refer only to the CBC in recounting his history, without noting that it was on the commercial side that Newman chiefly labored, producing programs modeled closely on their American commercial counterparts—hardly surprising, since they were sponsored by the same American corporations. Exceptions to this include John Cook, who concludes "When it came to TV, above all else, he was a commercial animal" (2000, 121) and Helen Wheatley, who gives credit to commercial television for providing certain key hallmarks of the work Newman was to produce for *Armchair Theatre* at ABC, such as "a certain intimate mode of address . . . and a deep concern with the colloquial and the everyday" (Wheatley 2007, 37).[8] That Newman's connection to North American commercial television was something to be downplayed in Britain at the time can be seen in an ad taken out by ABC in *World's Press News* in November 1958, soon after Newman's debut at that company. Asking the question, "How British is British television?" ABC asserts, "Our current schedule for *Armchair Theatre* is virtually one hundred per cent British – in writing, in acting, in production," noting also that "British standards of television production and the British way of life are spread internationally by our sale of telerecorded *Armchair Theatre* productions to stations in North America and other parts of the world."[9] The overt presence of too many Canadians, particularly those trained in North American commercial television, might have disrupted these claims. However, transatlantic connections were numerous, particularly in the ITV companies.

John Caughie notes that it was the BBC's purchase of a series of *General Motors Theatre* productions that brought Newman to the attention of Howard Thomas of ABC in 1956 (2000, 73). ABC hired Newman in 1958, where he found former CBC colleague Ted Kotcheff already putting some of Newman's own innovations to work in *Armchair Theatre*, ABC's high profile live anthology drama series (Cooke 2003, 39). According to Irene Shubik, several other directors trained under Newman at the CBC soon joined them, including Leonard White, Ron Weyman, Alvin Rakoff, and Henry Kaplan. Other ABC directors, like David Green, John Moxey, and Charles Jarrott, had previously worked either in Canada or the US (Shubik 1975, 45). Another group of former CBC personnel joined what one participant called "the Canadian mafia" at Granada under Harry Elton, himself a Canadian trained in the US, including Silvio Narizzano, who became Newman's counterpart as Granada's head of drama (Forman 2003, 34). As an explanation for this strong Canadian presence at many of the ITV companies in the 1950s, a co-worker offered, "One of the problems at the beginning was the shortage of experienced TV directors. There were very few in Britain, and the BBC had most of them under contract. Not being able to compete with American salaries, Granada did the next best thing and hired half a dozen Canadians, who were as experienced in television drama as anyone in the world" (Wildeblood 2003, 133). A few Americans were hired as well; Tim Kiley and David Low both came to Granada from CBS, though they soon returned (Lancashire 2003, 43).

Newman is credited with two accomplishments at ABC that reflect his North American background: the inflection of BBC dramatic output with a down to earth, hard-hitting, populist approach to drama, revitalizing the single play tradition; and the innovation and encouragement of the production of popular series, like *The Avengers* and *Police Surgeon*. *Armchair Theatre* became one of the highest rated programs on the air during Newman's tenure, specializing in contemporary, original drama that reflected the concerns and experiences of its audience, as opposed to the literary adaptations and high-flown drama that had preceded it. Inspired both by the "angry young man" currents in British theater as well as the working class realism of American and Canadian live television drama, Newman introduced young playwrights like Harold Pinter and Alun Owen to television. He is also credited with encouraging a more flexible, filmic visual style, emphasizing a moving camera, and bringing more attention to pacing and to realism in set design (Caughie 2000; Jacobs 2000). Newman introduced the role of story editor to the production process, long a feature of US and Canadian commercial radio and television production, hiring Irene Shubik "to go out and find suitable material that could be turned into plays and/or to discover and develop new writers" (Cook 2000, 122).

Newman's success brought him to the attention of Hugh Carleton Greene, newly installed as Director-General of the BBC, which had watched its hold on the public erode steadily since ITV's debut in 1955. Greene offered him the position of Head of Drama in 1962 "at a salary somewhat above that of the television chiefs with whom he was working,"[10] though Newman did not actually join the BBC until 1963, after his ABC contract expired. Now he was responsible not only for all drama programs on the original BBC channel, but also for the new service, BBC Two, scheduled to start up in 1964. This was an enormous task, an effective doubling of the BBC's previous output, and Newman responded by immediately re-organizing the producer/director-driven drama department into three sections: Plays, Serials, and Series, each with its own head and production staff. This effectively ensured that, even though the single play would remain an important keynote of BBC drama, serials and series held equal weight and would no longer be regarded as second-class forms in the BBC schedule. Furthermore, the three sections were broken down into 14 small units, each responsible for a single program, consisting of one producer, anywhere from two to six directors, and one or two story editors. Each production unit was matched with a similar dedicated group in "programme servicing" (sets, costumes, etc) and engineering.[11] Never before had the BBC drama department been so tightly organized. But it needed to be: when Newman joined the BBC in January 1963 the entire drama staff consisted of about 170 employees. By October it had expanded to 260 and would eventually reach 350 personnel in total. These and other innovations in institutional structure and practice, again modeled on commercial production, would be sharply criticized by many inside the BBC.

Much has been written about Newman's impact on the BBC, not only in the prestigious *Wednesday Play*, which restored the BBC's reputation as a leader in serious drama, but also in the popular series developed under him such as *Doctor Who*, *Z Cars*, and *Adam Adamant Lives!*[12] However, this hardly gets at his impact on the culture of the BBC; as Cook comments, "Newman's arrival at the Corporation in 1963 was nothing short of a political earthquake" (2000, 120). This excerpt from an internal planning memo from 1964 gives some impression of how Newman's vision must have shaken up the stolid BBC:

In relation to audiences, the following will be taken into account:

a) we haven't enough programmes which have <u>strong appeal for women</u> and we certainly don't have enough programmes which specifically <u>appeal to the young</u>—that is, up to 30–35. Part of this stems from the preponderance of material in which our heroes are never young nor attractive to emulate. We must recognise the specific needs of the young working couple in which the man is likely to be in the skilled-worker class in new industries like

      plastics, electronics and so on. In short, the new modern con-
      sumer type that Commercial television sets out to get.

b)   we must rectify the imbalance of too much period stuff—it
      gives BBC a fusty look. We must not forget that even DR.
      FINLAY'S CASEBOOK, SHERLOCK HOLMES and KIPLING
      are period as well as the Chuzzlewits and Madame Bovaries.[13]
      (emphasis in the original)

This willingness to go after sectors of the audience not normally recognized by the BBC and to take an approach frankly modeled on commercial television produced excellent audience numbers for Newman's shows but generated enormous controversy within the BBC.

Accused of "dumbing down" the BBC through such practices as creating a "branded", regularly scheduled live drama series (*The Wednesday Play*), alternating "serious" contemporary drama with mysteries and romances to hold the audience, undermining the autonomy of the director as the creative element in drama, introducing streamlined "commercial" practices and imposing a "house style," Newman suited the goals of the new BBC management but not the old guard in its ranks. As Newman himself admitted, "bringing in the new people because of the expansion of BBC Two was one of the major factors in my success. I often wonder what I would have done if I hadn't been able to infuse the staff with new people and bring some of the kids up" (Cook 2000, 131). In return, his years at the BBC represent the peak of Newman's career as a producer. He returned to Canada after his five-year contract expired, and though appointed to a series of prestigious positions—Director of Programmes at the Canadian Radio-Television and Telecommunications Commission, Chairman of the National Film Board of Canada, Director of the Canadian Broadcasting Corporation—never again would he exercise the profound transnational effect on global broadcasting that he did through his triangulated position during television's formative decades. Shaun Sutton, whom Newman had appointed Head of Serials in 1966 and who succeeded him in the Head of Drama post would become influential in the transatlantic co-production arena in the 1970s.

Newman's career demonstrates the utility, perceived both in the ITV companies and in the BBC, of transnational influences at times of technological and institutional change. By bringing an innovative North American producer in-house, a productive engagement of North American styles and techniques with concerns and genres firmly rooted in the British context produced not only creative work but institutional innovation that suited the changing conditions of British television. However, by the mid 1960s, with the unstoppable rise of filmed television programs as global commodities, transnational exchange shifted into a higher gear. Britain and America came increasingly to rely upon each other as the most significant trading partner each possessed, and the exchange of programs took center stage. With increased exchange of programs—produced now in national environments that, while still distinct, showed increased similarities of concern—came a far more unified broadcasting culture, a sphere of shared cultural experiences and references that permeated not only television but, most notably in the 1960s, popular music and consumer culture as well.

The Transatlantic Popular

They give us things we don't do easily ourselves—especially cheap, slick, escapist material such as cop and adventure shows. Sometimes it looks as though we are programming for morons but there is no reason why people can't have escapism; the stuff to relax in front of at the end of the day. American programmes are easy stuff but necessary for the right mix—to provide for diverse television.
            —Leslie Halliwell, buyer for ITV; Lealand 1984, 19

We became terribly British. A car is a car, and not an automobile. A lift is a lift is a lift and never an elevator. It is this Britishness that fits the fantasy world so appealing to the Americans.[14]
            —Brian Clemens, writer for *The Avengers*

A quick look at top-20 program lists in both Britain and the US in the late 1960s and 70s would not leave the impression that transnational television exchange occupied a very large part of the national consciousness in either nation. This is partly a result of how viewership tends to be measured—emphasizing prime-time schedules over other parts of the day, national over local, regional, or specialized preferences—but also a misunderstanding of how transnational influence worked within two highly developed systems of national broadcasting. Between 1964 and 1980 transatlantic circuits of influence hummed as never before, with the actual marked presence of British programs on American screens and American programs on British screens only the tip of the iceberg. The products of this hyperactive exchange became the new media culture that circulated around the globe, triggering the first wave of "media imperialism" anxieties and leading to still greater global dialogues and disputes.

In the US, the traditional kind of British presence—literary, highbrow, marked "quality"—could most easily be seen on public television screens; this topic will be taken up in the next section. But in the popular realm, the tastes and interests of the baby boom generation drove a new kind of popularized transatlantic culture most obvious in the realm of music and fashion but also to be heard on the airwaves and seen on TV. There has been surprisingly little written on this history of transnational cultural influences in television—while transatlantic currents in music and film, on the other hand, have received numerous studies. One of the few remains Jeffrey Miller's *Something Completely Different*, which thoroughly and engagingly recounts the history of British television programs on American commercial network airwaves in the 1960s and 1970s and theorizes their cultural impact. As the book jacket notes, it "casts a new light on traditional discussions of American cultural imperialism," but it is an illumination not much employed in subsequent studies. When Jeanette Steemers wrote her in-depth study *Selling Television: British Television in the Global Marketplace* in 2004, she had many works to draw on that theorized the extent and impact of global communications since the 1970s, or that analyzed streams of media dominance in macro terms, but very few that attempted to take a detailed historical examination of specific instances of exchange and influence in the US, Britain's largest market; in fact, she draws on Miller. Only recently has the opposite side of the equation found equivalent discussion, in the form of Paul Rixon's *American Television on British Screens*, which focuses on the current period but does include some discussion of earlier patterns of exchange, while developing a productive analysis of specific strategies and tactics of transnational influence, such as the way that broadcasters actively mediate the tension between the national and the transnational through promotion and scheduling. James Chapman's study, *Saints and Avengers: British Adventure Series of the 1960s*, while primarily focused on the shows as texts within the British context, also makes it clear how fundamentally transnational these programs were, and how much that aesthetic appealed on both sides of the Atlantic.

One further scholar whose work has centrally concerned British and American interrelationships for several decades is Jeremy Tunstall, whose sociologically oriented studies first argued that *The Media Are American* in 1977, at the height of the media imperialism moment, and later focused more narrowly on *The Anglo-American Media Connection* in 1999. Both books cast a wide-ranging view over all the different forms of media, from advertising to music to journalism, revealing important industry patterns, economic consequences, and policy implications; both basically conclude that Britain comes out the loser in this relationship, and that "Britain is a net importer of media entertainment, fiction, and dreams" from the United States (1999, 264). I hope in this section (and the next) to illuminate some of the more complex factors that a narrowly economic focus cannot reveal. Extending the type of humanities-based cultural analysis typically applied to literature and the arts enables an exploration of transnational flows of authorship, creativity, textual forms and practices, cultural influence and reception. Such cultural flows have existed throughout the history of nations, and work to reinforce, extend, and revitalize local and national cultures, in patterns that are multivalent and productive.

If the presence of programs produced in one nation and shown on the screens of another is our marker of transnational television exchange, a perspective looking beyond the top-20 reveals a good deal of cross-influence on both British and American screens in the 1960s and 1970s, though the US-to-Britain tale dominates.[15] As noted in the previous chapter, British program producers began to circulate their wares in the US television market from the very earliest days of television in that country, in the form of movies distributed in particular by J. Arthur Rank and in the "mid-Atlantic" programs discussed in Chapter 8. In the UK, starting in 1955, the fledgling ITV companies relied on American imports to build up their audiences, quickly surpassing the BBC. Such programs made up a consistent 14% or so of British TV schedules (limited to this proportion by regulatory expectations), were often scheduled prominently in prime time, and frequently figure in listings of the year's top-rated shows. Clearly they played a large role in British television culture. Yet very little British scholarship has traced this influence, on television practices or on the culture as a whole; in the multi-volume history of ITV written by Bernard Sendall (vols. 1 and 2) and Jeremy Potter (vols. 3 and 4), the barest mention is made of actual American programs on the air or their impact on trends in British programming. Often the phrase "foreign material" stands in, though it is readily apparent that this virtually always means "American material," and even direct adaptations of American shows—game shows, most notably—are very rarely identified as such: a good example of strategic "un-marking." However, for the earlier period, Sendall (vol. 1) does admit that shows such as *Dragnet*, *I Love Lucy*, and *Wagon Train* made an impact. And the very frequency and vehemence of phrases like "cheap American rubbish," or dismissive summaries like that quoted above from ITV's chief buyer of imported programs, Leslie Halliwell, indicates that a considerable level of cultural influence is being felt—too considerable for comfort.

This is a history that still needs to be written, one that is difficult to cobble together from existing sources. But according to those available, in 1956 four American imports showed up in the list of the 20 top-rated shows in Britain: *Dragnet, Assignment Foreign Legion, Gunsmoke* (titled *Gun Law* in Britain), and *Frontier Doctor*, all on ITV; no BBC show appeared in the top 20 that year (in fact, from 1955 to 1961, ITV shut the BBC out of the top 20 completely). In 1958, *Wagon Train* became the second most popular show in Britain, after the first place show *Dotto*, one of six British adaptations of US game shows highly popular over a number of years: *Twenty One, Spot That Tune* (*Name That Tune* in the US), *To Tell the Truth, I've Got a Secret*, and *Criss Cross Quiz* (*Tic Tac Dough* in the US). In February of 1958, one Western was screened every night in Britain, most of them second-string pot boilers like *The Cisco Kid* and *Rin Tin Tin*, but also including quality series like *Wyatt Earp* and *Wells Fargo*, both on the BBC (Harbourd and Wright 18). By 1960, that roster included *Rawhide, Bonanza, Cimarron City, Bronco*, and *Riverboat* and had been joined by a British version of *Candid Camera*, along with the crime drama *77 Sunset Strip*.

By 1962 the BBC under Hugh Carleton Greene's direction had begun to build itself back into popular prominence, and to take as innovative an approach to programming on home schedules as it did to program production for export. A judicious use of American imports helped—including *Perry Mason*, a show Greene insisted on after both the BBC and ITV had previously turned it down (Waymark 2006, 36) and *Dr. Kildare*, to compete with ITV's *Ben Casey*—but it wasn't American programs that finally moved the BBC into the top 20. Those were, besides *Royal Variety* and *Miss World 1962*, the BBC-produced mystery series *Maigret*, based on the French novels by Georges Simenon, and in fact adapted by him to the screen, and in 1963, *Steptoe and Son*, which would soon make a reverse migration via adaptation. In 1965, when ITA launched an investigation of the domination of ITV's 8 and 9 pm time slots by imported "crime and westerns," it was found that the BBC itself was scheduling "a western on Mondays and crime series on Tuesdays, Wednesdays, Thursdays, and Fridays" (Sendall 1983, 226–27).

By this time, too, a general popularization of programming genres and styles had occurred, most visible in the rise of the long-running serial drama, discussed below. These genres and formats might have American roots—or at least might have been blamed on American influence in former decades—but shows such as *Coronation Street* and *EastEnders* represent the final frontier of a truly popular British television culture, at last allowed to unleash itself (McNicholas 2004). However, US imports continued to form an important part of British schedules; a few of the most highly rated and longest-running (more than 100 episodes aired) through the 1960s and 1970s include *The Beverley Hillbillies, Bewitched, Big Valley, The Bionic Woman, Charlie's Angels, I Dream of Jeannie, Ironside, Kojak, M*A*S*H, The Man From Uncle, Mission: Impossible, The Muppet Show, My Three Sons, Police Woman, The Six Million Dollar Man, Star Trek*, and *Starsky and Hutch*. About half of these aired on the BBC, and half on ITV. None receive the briefest mention in either Sendall's or Potter's accounts, and only a few in Briggs'.

But direct import, or direct format adaptation as with game shows, is only the most visible tip of the transatlantic iceberg. Throughout the 1960s and 1970s, and indeed into the 1990s, while the number of direct British imports on the American commercial television screen remained relatively small, their influence exceeded their overt presence. On public television quite the opposite was true, as discussed in the next section. Looking only at direct imports, much distorts the actual impact of British TV in the US, and vice versa. Both the "mid-Atlantic" program—shows produced in the UK with the American as well as the domestic market in mind—and the adaptation of British shows into American versions became important contributors to US TV culture. For the mid-Atlantic programs, it is with the advent of the "international thriller" genre exemplified by such programs as *The Saint* (ATV 1962–69; NBC 1967–69), *The Prisoner* (ITV 1967–69; CBS 1968), and most successfully of all, *The Avengers* (ABC-UK 1960–69; ABC-US 1966–69) that a "marked," popular Britishness hit its peak on US commercial television. These programs, like the earlier *Adventures of Robin Hood* and its counterparts, also occupied a prominent role in the economics and schedules of British commercial television, though occasionally export to the United States drove the engine of mid-Atlantic production over the demands of British exhibition. *The Champions,* for instance, was produced by ITC in 1968 and aired on NBC that same year, well in advance of its debut before British audiences (Bignell 2010).

As Bignell points out, such programs were transatlantic creations from the beginning, "hybrids for American and British distribution" (2010, 34) produced in Britain but already influenced by the broader currents of transnational flow. To exemplify this process through one key example, *The Avengers* (by far the greatest transnational success, both critically and popularly) in its initial version (Keel/Steed) had originated at ABC-UK in 1960 as one of Sydney Newman's attempts to streamline and popularize series production with a program influenced by such stylish North American crime thrillers as *77 Sunset Strip* (ABC 1958; ITV 1960) and *M-Squad* (NBC 1957–60; ITV 1958–60). It launched on ITV in January 1961, produced not on film but on video, using the live production methods still predominant in Britain and not intended for export. Meantime, in the fall of 1960 ITC (the company formed by Lew Grade in 1954 to produce *Robin Hood*) launched production of *Danger Man* (ITV 1968–69; CBS 1961), arguably the first international secret agent series, starring Patrick McGoohan. It aired on CBS briefly in 1961. This success led directly to ITC's commissioning of its next successful export, *The Saint,* which starred a young pre-Bond Roger Moore—already familiar to American audiences as James Garner's British cousin, Beau Maverick, on occasional episodes of the Western series *Maverick* (ABC 1957). It was sold into syndication in the US in 1963.

These successful exports prompted a reworking of *The Avengers,* which in its second season on ABC-UK discarded Dr. Keel in favor of a female protagonist, Kathy Gale, played by Honor Blackman as "a widowed, leather-clad, martial arts expert with a Ph.D" (Luckett 2004, 197). The show continued in Britain through 1963 and into 1964, when suddenly the transatlantic spy thriller burst onto the global scene, inspired by the James Bond phenomenon (Bennett and Woollacott 1987). The first in the series of feature films starring Sean Connery, *Dr. No*, had been released in 1962 and the second, the international blockbuster *From Russia With Love*, in 1963. That same year Ian Fleming, author of the *James Bond* novels, himself contributed to the creation of the popular American spy series, NBC's *The Man from UNCLE* (NBC 1964–67; BBC 1965–68), which debuted in September 1964. And when the third Bond movie, *Goldfinger*, was cast in 1963, *Avengers* star Honor Blackman was tapped for the lead character Pussy Galore. Her departure, along with union disputes concerning the network's desire to move the production onto film, caused a year's hiatus in the television series.

But strong interest by the American network ABC prompted a third incarnation of *The Avengers*, the one best remembered today. Diana Rigg as Mrs. Emma Peel replaced Blackman, in very much the same mode but now captured on film and ready for export. It debuted on ITV in October 1965 and on ABC-US in 1966. By this time the "British invasion" had captured the American imagination, and as Luckett points out (and the quote above demonstrates) the show was able to retain a highly "British" tone and focus and still remain strongly appealing to US audiences. In 1965, even before the *The Avengers* aired in the States, ABC rushed a series of its own into production, based on the "Peel phenomenon" (*Honey West* (ABC 1965–66), starring Anne Frances). The new *Avengers* also contributed to the revival of ITC's *Danger Man*, now in an hour-long filmed version. This incarnation was purchased by CBS in 1965 and broadcast under the title *Secret Agent*, whose memorable theme song became an international hit on its own. Like *The Avengers*, *Danger Man* demonstrates the key role that the US market played in its production by the fact that later episodes were produced in color, two years before color television would be introduced in the UK on BBC Two and four years before ITV would roll it out.

The impact of this transatlantic dialogue can be measured not only in terms of ratings, which were generally modest, nor their impact on home audiences, which Miller convincingly explicates on the American side, but on the continued genre and stylistic development that took place on both sides of the exchange. To follow our tale of international back-and-forth a little further, 1965 marks the height of the second wave of transnational filmed series. Even the BBC, to replace its hit import *The Man From UNCLE* in the summer of 1966, waded into the fray with *Adam Adamant Lives!* (BBC 1966–67), a series that combined the concept of action-adventure with time travel (a detective frozen alive in 1902 who revives in the midst of Britain's swinging 60s), very much in the tradition of the earlier series *Dr. Who*. Sydney Newman commissioned the program and put Verity Lambert, *Dr.*

Who's producer, in charge. As Chapman points out, this was seen as an antidote to *The Avengers* and its more fantasy-driven counterparts, instead developing an aesthetic that used "a realistic, at times almost documentary-like style to present unlikely events" (Chapman 2004, 136).

A variety of further iterations of transnationally inflected spy adventures followed, including well-known series like *Mission: Impossible* (CBS 1966–74; ITV 1967–73), *The Prisoner* (ITV 1967–68; CBS 1968), and *I Spy* (NBC 1965–68; ITV 1967–69). Less well-known efforts include *Man in a Suitcase* (ITV 1967), a British production that actually starred an American, Texas-born Richard Gill playing an ex-CIA agent, produced by a primarily British team headed by Sidney Cole (Hannah Weinstein's main producer) but with an American story consultant (Stanely R. Greenberg, a former writer for *The Defenders*). Another ITC show, *The Baron* (ITV 1966–67; ABC 1966), also featured an American protagonist; clearly produced with the US market in mind, it aired on ABC-US before it debuted in the UK, like *The Champions* in 1967. Taking this strong form of trans-Atlantic marking even further, *The Persuaders!* (ITV 1971–72; ABC 1971–72), which Chapman describes as "the most ambitious and expensive of Sir Lew Grade's international action adventure series" (2004, 225), put American star Tony Curtis and rising British icon Roger Moore increasingly together as playboy crime fighters under associate producer Terry Nation, who had cut his teeth on *Dr. Who*, written for *The Saint*, *The Baron*, and *The Champions*, and would follow up writing and editing scripts for the last seasons of *The Avengers* (later, now in Los Angeles, he would also contribute to the series *McGyver*). However, *The Persuaders!* all-star team proved a greater hit in Britain and in Europe than in the US (it aired for only one year on ABC, scheduled against the highly popular *Mission: Impossible* on Saturday nights).

By this time the trend had begun to slow. *The Avengers, The Prisoner, and The Saint* were all cancelled in 1969, and though other shows drawing on the spy adventure tradition—including parodies, like *Get Smart!* (NBC 1965–69)—continued to be made, most analysts conclude that by the early 1970s not only this genre, but the effort of British television producers to break into the American commercial market, had faded. Yet a new trend had started: 1971 saw the debut of the classic sitcom *All In The Family* in the US, an adaptation of the BBC series *Till Death Us Do Part* (1965–75), followed by *Sanford and Son* in January 1972, based on *Steptoe and Son*, also a BBC production. It was innovative American independent producer Norman Lear who saw the potential in both of these critically and popularly acclaimed British shows, at a time when American television was just about to go through a transformation. With the passage of the Financial Interest and Syndication rules (usually known as Fin-Syn) and the Prime Time Access Rules (PTAR) in 1970 (and their gradual implementation from 1972 to 1979), the networks were forced by the FCC to relinquish the power over their program procurement and distribution processes that they had won in 1960 after the quiz show scandals. The rules forbad networks from owning (taking a financial interest in) more than a small proportion of the programs they broadcast, and thus returned ownership along with syndication rights to the production companies. With PTAR also prohibiting affiliates from filling up the first hour of prime time with network programming, a vital new market was created for independents, and Lear's Tandem Productions proved one of the most successful in moving into the new opportunities these regulations presented. This resulted in a series of programs that productively combined the transatlantic sitcom format with a more political and social-realist approach to comedy developed by the British tradition, giving rise to the "era of relevance" in the American sitcom—and to Britain's first all-black-cast comedy.

Both *All In The Family* and *Sanford and Son* took a familial conflict defined in the British originals along class, race, generational and political lines that could not have played out understandably in the American context, and translated them into versions that sparked a new mode of comedic confrontation on American television. *Till Death Us Do Part* featured Alf Garnet, a politically conservative, racist, working-class ranter, his put-upon wife and politically left daughter and son-in-law. Unlike Lear's adaptation, few non-white characters were introduced to the cast to provide a response to Alf's racist diatribes, leading to heavy criticism of its ultimate effects on social attitudes. *Steptoe and Son* focused on a white father and son "rag and bone" men in London, locked in struggle with each other and their circumstances. Lear took both shows and upped the racial component by, in the case of *Sanford and Son*, casting black actors in the leading roles. Comedian Redd Foxx played Fred Sanford and Desmond Wilson his son, Lamont, as junk dealers living in the Watts district of Los Angeles (the scene of significant racial riots in 1965). This was the first show with a primarily black cast to air on US television since the ill-fated *Amos 'n' Andy* in the 1950s. *All In the Family* took the emphasis off class—though Archie was a working-class man, his son-in-law Mike Stivic played an upwardly mobile graduate student, unlike Alf's son-in-law Mike, a laborer—and put it squarely on race and ethnicity, along with the generational divide. Mike Stivic was frequently berated as a "Polack" by Archie and forced to respond to a barrage of insults to his and many other ethnic identities, while Lear moved a black family, the Jeffersons, right next door. With George and Louise Jefferson and their son Lionel, amongst others, in frequent dialogue with Archie, able to respond directly to his offensive proclamations and attitudes, the show's potential for offense—and perhaps also for sharp political statements—was reduced compared to its British inspiration, though by no means eliminated.

It resulted indirectly in Britain's first black-cast comedy as well. *The Jeffersons* (CBS 1975–85) was spun off as its own series in 1975, as was *Maude* (CBS 1972–78), a comedy centering on Edith Bunker's liberal feminist cousin whose housekeeper, Florida Evans, became the center of a further primarily black-cast spin-off, *Good Times* (CBS 1974–79). Though the character of Florida's son J. J., played by Jimmie Walker, evoked controversy for conforming to a host of derogatory black stereotypes, the show also focused on less humorous and more socially relevant topics like "evictions, gang warfare, financial problems, muggings, rent parties, and discrimination" (Deane 2010, 1012). Both *Maude* and *Good Times* were adapted for British television, *Maude* as the short-lived *Nobody's Perfect* (ITV 1980) and *Good Times* as *The Fosters* (ITV 1976–77), featuring a black British family living in a south London housing complex, a first for British television. The ITV may have taken this adventurous step under pressure from the continuing mono-racial quality of British television. A study done by the BBC in 1972 on "Non-Whites on British Television" showed that fewer than 2% of speaking characters on British television were non-white, with 60% of those characters on imported American programs.[16] Clearly this was not a satisfactory situation, and the debate over representing Britain's non-white minorities would escalate as the assignment of a fourth television channel surfaced in the 1970s.

Along with increasing numbers of adaptations over direct imports, another factor affecting the role played in Britain both by American imports and by transatlantic programs was that they had been overtaken by a new wave of popular domestic production, with roots perhaps in past transatlantic exchanges but now firmly planted in the British social environment and deeply re-nationalized. Launched under duress in 1941 with *Front Line Family* and continued on radio with *Mrs. Dale's Diary* and *The Archers*, not until December 1960 did the open-ended domestic serial drama form make its debut in Britain in the form of Granada Television's *Coronation Street* (1960–).[17] Such programs demonstrate, among other things, a new attention to the female audience sparked by ITV's commercial mandate and the need to reach the female consumer, long the backbone of commercial broadcasting. They quickly came to occupy a spot in the yearly lists of top programs that no other genre could dislodge.

Set in Manchester, on a street at first name Florizel by its creator Tony Warren, *Coronation Street* followed a group of working-class neighbors through the trials and tribulations of everyday life. "It eschewed glamour and sensationalism and concentrated on trapping the knobbly yet snug ambience of North-Country working and lower-middle-class life" (M. Richardson 1965, 13). Aired twice a week in an early–evening time slot, *Coronation Street's* enormous success led directly to the first American experiment with a serial drama in prime time—*Peyton Place*, adapted from a best-selling novel by Grace Metalious and aired on ABC twice or three times a week from 1964 to 1969. In Britain the evening serial drama continued on ITV with *Crossroads* (1964–88), *Emmerdale Farm* (1972–), *Brookside* (1982–2003) and finally the BBC's long-delayed venture into the form with *EastEnders* (1985–), all set in regionally specific areas, mostly focusing on working- and lower-middle-class characters, in contrast to their American daytime and night-time counterparts. It was a form that would influence the introduction of the mini-series later in the 1970s on US commercial television—though not before PBS had taken up the serial literary adaptation imported from Britain in a big way, as discussed in the next section.

PBS: The Great Society and the "Primarily British Service"

> Without British product in those early days . . . critics and viewers would not have embraced NET as the source for quality. Having forsaken its educational mission, I wonder if, without the Brits, PBS could have survived the 70s on Big Bird alone. Built of several hundred parochial fiefdoms, PBS was and is without the singleness of purpose essential to the production of great programs. PBS is where it is today because of talents from without the US, most notably the British. So put me in the "thank God" column when it comes to British programming. Sorry, I can't express the same enthusiasm for the royal family or BP!"[18]
>
> —Betty Cope, Director, WVIZ-Cleveland

> As I look back on over 30 years as a public/educational broadcaster in four different states, it appears to me that we might well credit our UK programming with establishing our image as elitist. The snob appeal of British programming, especially the earliest ones that seemed to fit our educational goals, not only helped us gain an audience but also helped us gain a reputation we're still trying to overcome in the press and Congress.[19]
>
> —David Leonard, PBS-Hawaii

The years 1964 and 1965 mark a dramatic shift in American conceptions of national culture, though in the company of so many other turbulent events this particular moment often goes unrecognized. Shaken to its core by the assassination of popular, charismatic President John F. Kennedy in November 1963, facing an escalating conflict in Vietnam, and with the struggle for civil rights throwing into question some of the basic, unresolved contradictions of US-style democracy, the American public cast its support behind an unprecedented set of initiatives that, in the space of five years, created not only a national public broadcaster but the establishment of a network of federally funded institutions to define and support American culture, for the first time, on a national scale. Though many of the initiatives had begun under Kennedy, it was the landslide Democratic victory of 1964 that enabled President Lyndon B. Johnson to enact his extraordinary set of "Great Society" programs. These encompassed a number of crucial political and social reforms—the Civil Rights Act, voting rights legislation, changes in immigration laws, the "War on Poverty" programs, the extension of Medicare and Medicaid, and enormous advances in educational and environmental policy—but no less momentous in the cultural sphere was the founding of the National Endowment for the Arts (NEA) and its companion, the National Endowment for the Humanities (NEH), in 1965.[20] These two federal agencies, along with the (private, nonprofit) Corporation for Public Broadcasting (CPB) founded two years later, would usher in a new era of American arts and culture, adding a national public source of funding and direction to the older dichotomy of private commercial and foundation support—and drawing American culture ever closer to its British partner.

In broadcasting, NET entered its third and last phase—before becoming subsumed by PBS—with the largest grant yet from the Ford Foundation. Yet this support came with considerable strings attached, some of them strung by none other than Charles Siepmann, who enters our story again in 1963 as a special adviser appointed by James Armsey. Armsey, a stolid Midwesterner with a background in higher education administration and no great liking for, nor experience with, any form of mass media, had taken C. Scott Fletcher's place at the Ford Foundation in 1962. Though his tenure at the helm of Ford's educational broadcasting division would be brief, it would have a lasting impact.[21] One of his first actions was to hire Siepmann, now retired from his post as professor of media and education at New York University, in an effort to assess what the Foundation was getting for its considerable, continuing investment. Siepmann spent a year, beginning in November 1963, studying NET's programming and reporting weekly to Armsey. In June 1964, as NET prepared to ask the Ford Foundation for more than $6 million to support its next year's operations, Armsey called a meeting with NET staff intended "to review the Ford Foundation's position on television policy" and to set the terms under which any further monies would be granted.[22]

Notes taken at the meeting show that it quickly became confrontational. Declaring that "he and Dr. Siepmann would do all the talking," Armsey made it clear that no grant would be forthcoming unless NET gave serious consideration to Siepmann's review and changed its ways. Siepmann proceeded to deliver a scathing indictment of NET's entire schedule and operations, calling its programming frequently "lousy" and accusing it of lacking professionalism and any sense of a "grand design." Specific programs were deemed "a disgrace," "a mess of pottage," "a model of sheer ineptitude," "a poor replica of a commercial program," which taken all together showed, over and over, "no picture of a philosophic grasp of design or strategy." "Let's have a plan that can justify the Ford Foundation investment," he concluded, noting that too heavy a reliance on producers from abroad reduced NET's ability to set its own course, even though, as he also pointed out, foreign programs bested NET's own by far in terms of production values.[23] This is a conundrum that would continue to haunt NET and its successor, PBS.

Though obviously stung by these criticisms—and pointing out that much of what Siepmann had viewed dated from before NET's 1963 initiatives—White and his staff also leapt at the meeting's major message: Armsey, backed by Seipmann, strongly recommended that NET redefine itself as primarily a centralized national program-producing and -acquiring organization—a full reversal of Fletcher's original philosophy of dispersed, localized production.[24] White was charged with preparing a grant proposal that would not only supply a more coherent organizing philosophy and plan for implementing it but sketch out the programs that NET would both produce and acquire for the next three year period, through 1966. This White did, submitting a lengthy memo on program plans plus a booklet entitled 'N.E.T. Program Philosophy and Purpose: A Guideline for Staff Planning."[25] Now, as one historical account puts it, "NET would contract for programs by the best producers they could afford to hire and would acquire the most professional programs they could afford" (Carlson 1967, 140).

NET received its funding that year, with promises of more to come—perhaps at least in part because Armsey stepped down as head of Ford's educational broadcasting division a few months later. But the conditions he attached to the 1964 grant would bring NET to its highest level of national prominence yet, while also sowing the seeds of its destruction. The Foundation insisted that at least 50% of funding be spent on incisive, hard-hitting public affairs programs—the category most likely to offend local station managers, Congress, and the public – with the other 50% having to cover all other programs: cultural, scientific, and children's: the categories most popular with audiences. This challenge prompted White to hire a professional staff, as described above; by 1965 the triumvirate of William Kobin as Vice President of Programming with, under him, former commercial network news reporter Don Dixon as head of the public affairs division, and Curtis Davis as head of the cultural division, began the process of building NET into a national presence, a "Fourth Network". Carolyn Brooks has traced the history of NET's activated public affairs division, arguing that the inception of PBS might have come at least in part from the desire to stifle the strong national political voice that NET soon developed under Kobin and Dixon. Less has been written about the career of Curtis Davis, who embarked on an ambitious schedule of cultural programs, launching the *NET Playhouse* as a vehicle for both original and imported productions. These consisted mostly of adaptations of plays and short stories, but also included imported feature films such as Roman Polanski's *Knife in the Water* and Antonioni's *L'Avventura*. By 1966, 10 out of 40 of *Playhouse* offerings were original NET productions. But most of the rest, nearly 30 out of the 40, came from the BBC, Granada, Rediffusion, and the CBC.[26]

However, as these plans developed, even before NET's new philosophy could be put fully into effect, other forces were pressing towards a place for educational broadcasting more in line with Great Society plans for the arts and humanities. In December 1964, the NAEB under the direction of C. Scott Fletcher (who had retired from the Ford Foundation only to be drawn back into the field he had built) led in the formation of a commission to study the future of educational broadcasting, funded by the Carnegie Corporation. Throughout 1965 and 1966 the Carnegie Commission, chaired by James Killian, president of MIT, held meetings and interviews with hundreds of organizations and individuals involved in the field, visited stations, conducted surveys, and sought out information on the public broadcasting systems of other countries. Carnegie Commission members David Henry, Hyman Goldin, and Gregory Harney visited the BBC in July of 1966[27], and it also commissioned a report from television critic John Crosby, who found almost everything to admire and virtually nothing to dislike (aside from Lew Grade's transatlantic series) in the combined BBC/ITV system of 1966.[28] By now, word was out that "work is well along on a foundation-primed BBC-type television system for the United States."[29]

But the proposal that the Carnegie Commission put forth eschewed the centralized BBC (and new Siepmann- and Armsey-inspired NET) model in favor of a revival of the dispersed, locally based system that would eventually become the Corporation for Public Broadcasting (CPB) and its two network arms, the Public Broadcasting Service (PBS) for television and National Public Radio (NPR).[30] The fate of NET in these arrangements was an ironic one: encouraged by the Ford Foundation to become a national program production and distribution service (via videotape duplication; live net-working plans remained in abeyance[31]) and subject to all the criticism and controversy such a central position entailed—from NET stations, Congress, the general public, and the Foundation itself; from right, left, and center— its very success lost it the chance to take on that role in the new, federally funded organization that emerged. Despite all Jack White's best efforts, NET's experience was used against it, and those backing the formation of PBS were able to turn dissatisfaction with its hard-won accomplishments into a mandate for a new organization—even though CPB/PBS would soon replay exactly the same trajectory that NET had traced, as indeed any centralized public television network would have. As White said in a later interview, "They will never get away from it" (Robertson 1993, 222). Seeing the writing on the wall, White stepped down from his post in 1969, just as plans put in place by the Public Broadcasting Act of 1967 coalesced into the Public Broadcasting Service.

White's successor, James Day, described NET's scapegoat role in the founding of PBS in stronger words:

> I was blithely unaware that NET was being used as a bargaining chip in political games being played out in Washington. Years later it would be revealed (through files released by the Freedom of Information Act) that at the time I was preparing to take office, the Corporation for Public Broadcasting was preparing to jettison NET to win points with the Nixon White House (Day 1995, 170).

However, for the next few years NET continued to operate as a primary supplier of programming to the new network. Though in October 1970 it would effectively cease to exist—merged with a formerly commercial New York station to become WNET[32]—it may be best remembered for the event that kicked off the next phase in the relationship between American and British public broadcasters: its acquisition in October 1969 of *The Forsyte Saga* from the BBC.[33]

This 26-episode adaptation of John Galsworthy's series of novels had been produced in 1967 as a major dramatic event to encourage British viewers to convert their televisions to UHF frequencies, in order to be able to receive BBC's second channel, which had debuted in 1964 (Cooke 2003, 83). The series gained its greatest audience when re-run on BBC One in 1968. It was one of Sydney Newman's last contributions before he returned to Canada, under the immediate direction of Donald Wilson, former Head of Serial production under Newman. Its success, not only in Britain where it became "a national obsession," but around the world contributed, according to Cooke, to the resurgence of the "quality drama" as a "heritage export" (2003, 84). Though the BBC produced the series, it had to negotiate with American movie studio MGM for the rights to do so—MGM had acquired rights from the Galsworthy estate when producing *That Forsyte Woman* in 1949, starring Greer Garson and Errol Flynn—and MGM retained distribution rights outside the Commonwealth (Briggs 1995, 525). NET, operating in its capacity of program provider to the public network, purchased rights to air the 26-episode series from MGM in 1968. US audiences were among the last in the world to see it; it had already been aired in Malta, Zambia, New Zealand,

Finland, Sweden, Taiwan, Norway, Belgium, Hong Kong, and the Soviet Union, to enormous enthusiasm.[34] Though the fledgling public system already enjoyed a rising profile that shows such as *Sesame Street* and Julia Child's *The French Chef* had brought it, *The Forsyte Saga* took it to new heights; the series "inspired tea-and-crumpet parties among loyal viewers, catapulted Galsworthy's novels from recent obscurity to prominent display in bookstores, and became one of public television's most widely recognized programs" (Ouellette 2002, 156).

Despite this impact, it remains an orphan event in the history of American public television. One cannot help but conclude from reading official accounts of the era that the success of this British import remains to this day something of an embarrassment to the fledgling public service, despite the enthusiasm it sparked in the nation's audiences. Because of the Ford Foundation's insistence on original programming, NET had to raise separate funds to buy the series (for a bargain price, it is claimed) and consequently had very little interest in publicly taking credit for the program. White stepped down before it aired. James Day, NET's president during the show's first, second, and third runs, inherited the wildly popular series with little enthusiasm. His memoir barely mentions the show, outside of this grudging footnote:

> I was in office less than a month when my NET colleagues persuaded me to stop over in London on my way to an international meeting in Florence and interview the entire cast of *The Forsyte Saga*. The resulting films were cut to fill out the oddly timed episodes to an even one hour in what can only be viewed as an exercise in husbanding limited production dollars (Day 1995, 383, f2).

Shortly after it aired, NET effectively ceased to exist and PBS embarked on its own contested struggle with the production of original programming, soon to result in the well-documented showdown with the Nixon administration that nearly cost the fledgling service its life. This was hardly the time to point to a British import as the network's greatest achievement. On the side of the emergent victor organization, CPB president John Macy reported that "some of us gagged at its advance billing as a 'British Victorian soap opera'", and admits only reluctantly that *The Forsyte Saga* brought to PBS's debut "the largest adult audiences attracted up to that time" (Macy 1974, 58).

Thus it is not entirely surprising that it was not PBS but one of its member stations operating independently that picked up the Forsyte torch and transformed it into an enduring institution, one that would revitalize and institutionalize the long-standing British/US cultural relationship. *Masterpiece*

Theatre, still a fixture (under the new name *Masterpiece*) on public televi-sion today, got its start at WGBH-Boston. Many people have taken credit for its inception in the various accounts that exist. Christopher Sarson, a British-born producer who had worked at Granada before coming to WGBH, recalls that when PBS decided to follow up on *Forsyte*'s success with the documentary series *Civilisation* rather than a drama series, it "seemed a terrible shame."[35] He was not alone in feeling this way; Frank Gillard of the BBC—a frequent consultant to US educational television – claims to have discussed the concept of a US showcase for BBC drama serials with Stanford Calderwood, WGBH's new director, at a Boston Pops concert in the summer of 1970 (Stewart 1997).

Calderwood himself states that the idea came to him on a June 1970 trip to London with his wife, even before he had officially accepted the WGBH post. According to Laurence Jarvik's account, Calderwood, remembering *Forsyte*'s success and thinking about what he could do to advance WGBH's profile, simply picked up the phone and called the BBC to see what other worthwhile British dramas might be available. He ended up speaking to Robin Scott, head of BBC Two, whose interest was piqued by two factors: first, having finally made the switch to color production in 1965, the BBC had a backlog of four years of high-quality literary serial drama for sale very little of which had screened in the US, despite all their best sales efforts. Second, the BBC had just made a shift in its handling of foreign sales and co-productions; now, instead of all deals having to go through BBC Enterprises, individual programming heads were empowered to deal directly with potential buyers or partners around the globe.[36] Scott met with Calderwood and sent him back to the US with 16mm kinescopes of several BBC drama productions, as well as a few nature documentaries (Jarvik 1999, 32). Though the BBC had a long-standing agreement with Peter Robeck, now president of Time-Life Films, to distribute its product in the US and to broker co-production deals (see next section), Calderwood's idea was to buy unsold BBC backlog at cut-rate prices, using such programs both as a kind of promotional trailer for BBC programming in the US (as he argued to Scott) and as a way for WGBH to attract audiences, underwriters, and other funding in Boston (as he argued to his colleagues back at the station). As Jarvik recounts Calderwood's argument to Scott: "Look, I said, that good stuff sitting in the can is like a hotel room unsold—it's worthless. Why not give us some cut prices and use it as a loss-leader?" (1999, 32). Further, approaching Robeck back in New York, Calderwood advanced the idea that "if he let us have the programs cheap, it would be like getting paid to run what in effect would be commercials for his library of BBC programming" (1999, 35).

Thus with the BBC, Time-Life, and WGBH on its side, Calderwood brought the idea both to PBS (now under the direction of Hartford Gunn,

WGBH's former president) and to the potential underwriter, Mobil Oil, aided by his contacts in the business world built in his previous career at the Polaroid Corporation. Herb Schmertz, Mobil's vice president for public affairs, had observed the publicity potential gained by public broadcasting underwriters such as Xerox (*Civilisation*) and Humble Oil years before (*Age of Kings*), and liked the idea of creating an image "franchise" on public TV. Laurence Jarvik describes in detail the negotiations that led to the debut of what came to be titled *Masterpiece Theatre*, complete with British spelling, just a few months later in January 1971, with Christopher Sarson in charge of production and, crucially, with Alistair Cooke as the series' host and public face. And Laurie Ouellette provides a thorough critique of the broader social context of Mobil's decision to become a major PBS underwriter, linked to the oil crisis and its need for some uplifting public relations work (Ouellette 2002).

In the years between his role as host of *Omnibus* and his new and enduring role on *Masterpiece Theatre*, Cooke had risen to prominence as a reporter on US politics and culture both for the BBC and for the *Guardian* newspaper. He retained some presence on television in the 1960s as host of the UN-produced news program *International Zone*, which aired on various commercial stations in the Sunday morning public affairs ghetto, and as a commentator on US news shows. In 1965 he undertook a world tour, reporting back in *Letters* not just from America but from locations around the globe, turning the adventure into a book, *Around the World in Fifty Years*, that combined present-day reporting with a history of each place he visited. Cooke had authored several books over the years, beginning with two early works on film—*Garbo and the Night Watchmen*, a collection of essays, and a monograph on Douglas Fairbanks. More recently, he had contributed an account of the Alger Hiss case in *A Generation on Trial*, and had pulled his *Letters from America* into several collected volumes. As the plans for *Masterpiece Theatre* began to come together in the Fall of 1970, Cooke was already involved in writing the BBC series *America* (see next section) that would be published as *Alistair Cooke's America* and rise to best-seller status in the mid 1970s.

Thus, Jarvik reports, Cooke was not initially anxious to take on the role of host for what looked to be a showcase for BBC literary adaptations. His identity was as a cosmopolitan observer of the contemporary American and global scene, not a stock Englishman purveying dusty classics to a minority audience. Yet his undeniable mid-Atlantic persona made him the ideal broker for the series, capable of persuading millions of middle-class Americans that British literature and history had a relevance to their lives that they might not have previously suspected. For this shoestring operation—far from the public broadcasting institution that it would become—Cooke provided transnational "marking" of just the kind this series required. It was a way for the BBC to bring in additional income to support its own domestic production, selling already-produced programs to an American outlet that would not attempt to alter or influence them, with an ex-pat British showman to give these British cultural productions their proper respect in a non-commercial setting (though the sponsoring presence of Mobil Oil did raise some eyebrows eventually). For WGBH, it was distinctive programming, entertaining yet marked "quality" by its British origins; for PBS, it represented an arms-length endorsement of an audience-building series hosted by a familiar mid-Atlantic figure that the beleaguered network needed even as its public face turned towards original production.

The opening sequence first devised for the show reveals the value its marked British origination held: as the stately, suitably classic strains of Jean-Joseph Mouret's *Rondeau* plays (chosen by Sarson, who had heard it at a Club Med in Palermo!),[37] the flag of Great Britain completely fills the screen, then the camera pulls back to reveal it attached to the "P" in "Masterpiece" as to a flagpole. As it fades out, a voice with a marked British accent—not Cooke's—intones, "Masterpiece Theatre is made possible by a grant from the Mobil Corporation" over the single word "Mobil" on the screen. A cut brings us our host, a bit older but still recognizable from his *Omnibus* days, clad in a dark suit and tie, sitting in a carved wooden chair with books and a framed photograph on a table next to him. "Good evening" he says, "I'm Alistair Cooke," and so the series begins. Cooke's introduction promises a season filled with the works of "Balzac, Henry James, Dostoevsky"—no British authors mentioned, though they would be by far the most numerous as the program progressed.[38] And, as Asa Briggs points out, no BBC credits were ever rolled before or after any of the episodes; WBGH "happily took the credit for itself" (Briggs 1995, 713). Mild, Americanized Britishness held value; emphasis on the actual British origination of the programs did not, within PBS's embattled cultural economics.[39]

In the later, more familiar version, overt Britishness is downplayed—no more Union Jack—even as its more subtle yet suitably transnational indicators are emphasized: the camera pans over what seems to be crowded tabletops in a plush Victorian parlor. It brushes first over the leather spine of a book with the show's title picked out in gold, then glides over framed photographs, rows of classic novels by Trollope, Hardy, Thackeray, and James, marble busts and knick-knacks, war medals, miniatures (one portraying Henry VIII, another Elizabeth I), a magnifying glass, and, surprisingly, a crystal glass containing a martini complete with olive. Perhaps that is what we are supposed to imagine the sequence's closing image, a seated Cooke, sipping as he introduces us urbanely to the evening's installment. Here is a program clearly, strongly marked as "British" but in a way designed to smooth such potential "foreignness" into something as familiar as assigned readings from high school English class, as cozy as a parlor in an Agatha Christie novel. What is more "American," after all, than a fondness for all things traditionally and quaintly British?

The tactic did not work so well with PBS's critics and regulators—nor with the BBC's. Despite *Masterpiece Theatre*'s iconic status as the face of public TV today—along with the heavily British co-produced series it inspired such as *Nova* (documentaries) and *Mystery!*—its initial path was not entirely smooth. The economics of import and co-production made sense, and audiences enjoyed the programs, but was the central mission of American public television to bring British culture to the masses? Jarvik makes a point of disputing Christopher Sarson's later claim that WGBH intended to "gradually introduce American-made productions. That was a very important part. The idea was not just to stay on this importing line, it was to encourage American production," pointing out that Sarson could not substantiate this claim and no one else he interviewed ever mentioned such a plan (1999, 43). Yet within the ethos and history of early public broadcasting this made sense; British imports had always provided relatively inexpensive quality programs that allowed ill-funded public broadcasters to divert scarce funds to original production elsewhere.[40] This is exactly the way that American programs worked in British broadcasting, though the definition of "quality" differed considerably.

At any rate, the content of *Masterpiece Theatre* remained unrelentingly, and unrepentantly, British. *Variety*, always critical and contemptuous of public broadcasting, consistently referred to the program as "the BBC's 'Masterpiece Theatre'" and ran headlines like "BBC Grinds Out Classic Dramas Like Soap Operas."[41] Its premiere series, *The First Churchills*, was carefully chosen for its American connections and appeal, and the series that followed—*The Spoils of Poynton, The Possessed, Père Goriot, Jude the Obscure, The Six Wives of Henry VIII*—might not always have been of British origins (even a few works of American authors, such as *The Last of the Mohicans* and *The Golden Bowl*, were aired in the first two seasons), but they were always produced in Britain with a British cast. Not all the series were adaptations, nor was the BBC the only supplier; independent television too sold programs to WGBG, most notably the highly popular *Upstairs, Downstairs*, an original drama created by Jean Marsh and Eileen Atkins and produced by London Weekend Television. It ran over several seasons on *Masterpiece Theatre*, from 1973 to 1977, repeated in 1980. Only in 2000, thirty years after its premiere, did PBS—as part of the series now called simply *Masterpiece*, with the British-inflected "Theatre" dropped—introduce its "American Collection" of US-made adaptations of American writers—a long-deferred development.[42]

By September 1971, *Masterpiece Theatre*—and the other important PBS/BBC project, Kenneth Clark's *Civilisation* series—had become such a defining symbol for the still-nascent and struggling PBS that John W. Macy, CPB president, made his first trip to Britain to consult with the BBC—noting with tongue in cheek:

> In the development of American public television the BBC is cited so frequently as a model or prototype that a first-hand visit to that institution in London has become an essential mission for all of us. I consider it an exercise of great restraint that my visit did not occur until the 27th month of my CPB tenure.

One of the first things he discussed with Huw Weldon, Director of Television, was the BBC's acquisition policies, notably whether there was any possibility of "more direct dealing between American public broadcasting and the BBC without the intervening presence of Time-Life." To this proposition Weldon gave a decided no, indicating his "complete satisfaction" with Time-Life and Peter Robeck.[43] This was about to change, a marker of the next stage of transatlantic relationships in an expanding field.

A more jaw-dropping marker might be found in a letter from David Webster, the BBC's US representative, to David Attenborough, now Director of Television Programmes, dated March 8, 1972. In it he reports on a long discussion he had with Wallace Edgerton, Deputy Chairman of the National Endowment for the Humanities, now in its fifth year of sustaining the best of American scholarship and culture. Edgerton proposes that the NEH might actually grant funds directly to the BBC for television production, possibly disguising the transaction with "a proper production partner" in the US. As Webster reports:

> They find themselves in a situation where they have a lot of money they don't know quite what to do with and this money is accumulating. They would like to be able to encourage film and television activity of what they call a meaningful nature. To this end, Wallace Edgerton has been talking to me about how they might go into business with the BBC in order to underwrite the cost of some of our more serious and thoughtful programming. . . . In retrospect, they would have wished to have been able to invest in Civilisation.[44]

This is rather astonishing, given the existence of PBS and its member stations, all striving for the funding to produce "meaningful" programs, and it testifies both to the BBC's prestige and PBS's lack thereof in the minds of

America's cultural establishment. Webster points out the obvious, which somehow must have eluded Edgerton: "there would be great difficulty in having a direct relationship with a governmental body" such as the NEH. Dennis Scuse, in a subsequent memo, sums up the BBC's reaction well:

> [A]n association of this sort might well produce embarrassments in the long term. There is enough implicit and explicit criticism about American influence as it is. Involve a US government agency—and one can see the letters in the Times![45]

Surely the letters in the *New York Times* would have been equally outraged: an American government agency supporting another nation's public broadcaster! Yet in fact the NEH had already provided funding to help distribute the *Civilisation* series to schools, and in 1973 it would underwrite PBS's acquisition of the BBC/Time-Life co-production of *War and Peace*.[46] By that time, Time-Life-distributed BBC productions had been nominated for eight Emmys, all but one shown on PBS, and had won two Peabody Awards. Was the best of American culture British? And what was that notion doing to British culture at home?

Co-Productions: If you can't beat 'em . . .

> I think one of the points we have to accept is that a co-production is no longer a BBC programme. It is a joint programme with some other party and the other party's interests have also to be given considerable weight.[47]
> —John Stringer, head of BBC co-productions, 1970

> The advantages to the BBC were obvious. To give one example: the BBC was determined to make Tolstoy's 'War and Peace' for television. On our own we would probably have shot it on location in Scotland (and prayed for snow). With Time-Life's co-finance it was possible to shoot it in Yugoslavia and to make use of a large part of the Yugoslav Army.[48]
> —Synopsis for General Advisory Council paper on Co-Productions, June 4, 1979

Inevitably, as many had predicted, the innocuous sale of off-the-shelf programs—programs produced with the needs and interests of the British public first in mind, with sales to others a distant bonus—gave way rapidly in the seventies to a different kind of situation, as PBS grew and as the US cable market developed, and as the BBC and its commercial competitors faced technical challenges and financial difficulties. As Elke Weissman convincingly demonstrates, the continuing demands of running two separate networks, the cost of converting to color transmission, pressure from an increasingly unionized workforce, and the failure of the license fee to keep up with rising expense of production left the BBC by 1971 in desperate need of funds, a situation that would persist throughout the decade and beyond (Weissman 2009). Despite two license fee increases, in 1971 and again in 1975, the BBC fell increasingly into debt. Commercial television felt the same pressures, especially after restrictions were lifted in 1972 on the number of hours per day that television was permitted to broadcast, expanding the daily schedule and creating a need for more programming.

This mandated an emphasis on program sales abroad. Commercial companies started up their own international divisions and contracted with foreign distributors, Thames, London Weekend, and Granada most prominently. BBC Television Enterprises succeeded in selling its programs in 1968 to more than 80 countries, bringing in nearly 2 million pounds. Sales of *The Forsyte Saga* led the pack, but the BBC's racially retrograde *Black and White Minstrel Show* was the most popular color title (it was never sold to the US, however). That year the United States became the BBC's single largest customer, purchasing 2,840 programs, though the Commonwealth nations put together represented an even larger market with 5,543 while European sales amounted to 2,125 (BBC *Yearbook* 1969, 26–27). 1971 was an even bigger year, with foreign sales up 30%, supplying over 11,000 hours to 80 nations and bringing over 2 1/2 million pounds into the BBC's coffers. The BBC's in-house reports always shy away from revealing the exact amount that US sales represented—since the potential influence of its largest customer was once again becoming contentious, as we shall see—but its 1971 *Yearbook* sounded a nearly boastful note: "Now that the distribution agreement with Time-Life Films has become fully effective the United States is the major outlet for BBC sales.... At long last it seems to have been recognized that high quality drama and prestige documentary programmes can be as commercially successful in the United States as thrillers, and that there is a growing demand among American audiences for programmes made by the BBC" (BBC *Yearbook* 1971, 30–31). By the middle of the decade BBC Enterprises, via Time-Life, was selling a wide variety of programs to American networks and stations, both public and commercial; highest profile sales included *The Six Wives of Henry VIII* (CBS 1971), *Elizabeth R.* (PBS 1972), and not least, *Monty Python's Flying Circus* (PBS 1974; ABC 1975).[49]

However, monies derived from program sales supported the BBC but did not necessarily get channeled back into programming. As Shaun Sutton, Sydney Newman's successor as Head of Drama, put it, "Any money over after Enterprises have hived off expenses can go to any project, from Pebble Mill [the BBC's new Birmingham studios] to a new uniform for the night-watchman at Ealing."[50] But, as the previous sections have indicated, another system had begun to develop in the 1960s that enabled the BBC to plan more ambitious and securely financed programs: co-production. Co-production income was negotiated either before or during production of a program and went directly into the programming budget, with Enterprises out of the picture until the project was finished and sale of the completed product to other takers became available. For program makers, co-production had huge advantages. Quoting Sutton again: "The profits from sales are not large, and the rewards from co-productions can be immense. And every penny goes on to the screen" (emphasis in the original).[51] Additionally, co-production funds were not taxed, whereas program sales revenues were (Pilsworth 1979–80). The term "co-production" became increasingly fraught with tension; anticipating many of Hjort's later distinctions, the BBC began to struggle internally with the meaning of that term beginning in 1969, as its internal re-organization began to take effect.

What was a co-production, and what did that practice entail? How could domestic priorities be balanced against pressure from outside? An internal document, one of the first to address the issue in its new significance, defined it broadly: co-production consisted of "pre-production deals, usually with other broadcasting organizations but sometimes with sponsors by a) sharing facilities b) financial contributions."[52] But almost immediately, a section on the "Dangers" inherent in such arrangements opened with a familiar theme: "a) Programmes may become Americanised or otherwise distorted to suit overseas market." Following up on this, Shaun Sutton's memo from August 1970 shows a national public broadcaster struggling with the new transnational market and the more highly commercialized situation in which the BBC now operated. It is worth quoting at length. A distinction between true co-production, in which partners all contribute to the end product, and co-financing, by which a partner simply contributes funds and stays out of the creative process, begins to emerge.

> [W]e are at present manipulating our first tentative drama co-productions. We are at a most experimental stage, and are un-ashamedly trying to learn. The idea of co-production is immensely attractive in theory, and absurdly simple on the surface. Early discussions are easy and courteous; most potential co-partners begin by giving the impression that they merely wish to be co-financers. . . . I have found however, that, as things progress, the demands of the co-partners increase. Script approval, participation in casting, the inclusion of their own actors, their own directors, slow whittling away of the artistic control that is essential to the

BBC. Yet, curiously, it is this artistic excellence and technical know-how which first attracts the partners—they then proceed to do away with the very qualities they have admired.

This situation was particularly true when the partners were North American; the familiar discourse of "dumbing down" once again emerges.

> Drama-wise we are so much closer to Europe than to the States and Canada; the Europeans do not grow pale at the sight of a script that might possibly play only to a minority audience. American T.V. drama is run on sparkling, lush, polished tram lines and the majority of it is totally mediocre. Moreover, the aim of the American co-partner is not to bring himself up to European standards, but to bring us down to his.

During this period the BBC had achieved some success with sales to commercial networks, and American public broadcasting had not yet found its footing. Sutton's memo reflects this situation, which was about to change, as he notes, "N.E.T. may offer possible outlets, but for the most part co-production with the States, on a large scale, seems to mean a fall in artistic standards, certainly a loosening of artistic control." The issue of control was the most important for Sutton: the national domestic market had to come first over all other interests.

> The co-production market must always be a small proportion of the whole output, in my opinion. Our concentration must be domestic—we must maintain and improve our national flavours and talents and excellencies, otherwise the output becomes leavened down into a sort of flat, boring international stew, with all the individual taste taken out of it.[53]

This anticipates later criticisms of "Europudding" productions that Hjort along with many other critics have derided. John Stringer sounded a similar cautious note a few months later: "I think one of the points we have to accept is that a co-production is no longer a BBC programme. It is a joint programme with some other party and the other party's interests have also to be given considerable weight."[54] And, despite Sutton's disclaimers, that party looked to be increasingly American. Even co-productions with European partners often took place with the American market in mind; as Robin Scott recalls, "there were some French and German companies keen to invest money in joint productions ... on generous terms in order to gain a foothold in the lucrative American market in association with the BBC"

(Scott 1976, 7). These were the horns of the co-production dilemma as the BBC perceived it in 1970; fortunately, they had arrived at a workable relationship, for the time being at least, with their main American partner, Time-Life Films.

In February 1971, 8 out of 36 pending BBC co-productions deals were with American companies; by October 1971 that proportion had risen to 43 out of 51, most with Time-Life. By 1973, 60% of BBC Television's co-production income, more than 2 million pounds, came from co-finance deals, 90% of which derived from the BBC Two's partnership with Time-Life Films.[55] This was the company formed when the Time-Life Corporation—publisher of an empire of magazines and books, producer of *The March of Time*, owner of television stations, soon to go into the burgeoning field of cable television—bought the assets of the Peter M. Robeck organization in 1969. With it came Robeck himself who became president of the new division. Robeck had begun distributing BBC programs in the US in 1958, working closely with BBC Television Enterprises head Dennis Scuse in selling already-produced programs to American buyers, both commercial and educational. Once Time-Life Films took over the relationship and co-production deals replaced off-the-shelf sales as the major business at hand, Scuse took a back seat and the major players on the BBC side became David Attenborough, Director of Television Programs, and his two lieutenants, Shaun Sutton, Head of Drama, and Aubrey Singer, Head of Features.[56] This triumvirate, in cooperation with Time-Life Films, supervised production of most of the high-profile drama and documentary programs aired on PBS over the next decade, far more than any single equivalent American team or production company. On the other side, the majority of BBC Two's high-profile documentary and period drama series of that decade (and beyond) were in fact British/American co-productions, with all the tensions over control and quality—and over marking and un-marking—that these original memos anticipated.

One of the first projects of the new Time-Life Films division, and for a long time the major jewel in its crown, was investment in Kenneth Clark's *Civilisation* series—perhaps the first global documentary blockbuster, and the progenitor of the BBC's tradition of the "authored documentary" (A. Clark 2010a). In this case, production planning for the series had begun in 1966, when Huw Weldon and David Attenborough reached an agreement with prominent art historian Sir (later Lord) Kenneth Clark to produce a thirteen-part series on what Attenborough conceived as a showcase, in color, of the world's "most beautiful things" and what Clark re-defined as an attempt "to show how two thousand years of the creative urge had moulded western civilization" (A. Clark 2010b). Clark himself wrote and narrated the programs; Michael Gill served as supervising director. It was one of the

BBC's biggest color productions yet, with a budget of £15,000 per episode (not including the cost of salaries and overhead). Only a small fraction of British homes could receive the BBC Two's color television signal when the program debuted in February 1969 and its initial audience was less than 1% of the British population. It was rebroadcast in 1971 on BBC One where it reached a marginally larger audience, almost 8%. These were not block-buster numbers, and critical reception, while respectful, was lukewarm. It was in the United States that the series truly made an impact. Jonathan Conlin quotes Clark from a 1970 London interview, "Kind people stop me in the streets and talk about the programme . . . but they're always Americans" (2009, 98).

By the time the first episode aired in Britain, Peter Robeck had already decided that it was a good investment, and brought the project to Time-Life when he launched its Films division in 1970.[57] His confidence was rewarded when the CPB contributed $350,000 to bring it to PBS, and the Xerox Corporation stepped in with $1 million in underwriting, a portion of which was earmarked to promote the program (the BBC itself received only $300,000 of this) (Conlin 2009, 111). An important aspect of the promotion was the creation of a special hour-length compilation program that aired on NBC with Xerox sponsorship on September 8, 1970, in a pre-primetime slot (6:30 on a Tuesday); Xerox also invested heavily in print ads. By the time the first episode went out on PBS stations around the country on October 7 and on subsequent Sunday nights for thirteen weeks (with repeats on Wednesday evenings), anticipation was higher than for any public television program since *Forsyte*. It did not disappoint; viewers all over the country praised it and some credit (or blame) it with going a long way towards saving PBS from Richard Nixon's attempts to kill off public broadcasting (Conlin 2009; Ouellette 2002). In November, the US National Gallery of Arts (where a special premiere had helped to build anticipation for the series) awarded Clark a medal for distinguished service for his achievement; at the ceremony the NEH announced that, with help from Xerox, it would fund the provision of copies of the series to colleges and universities throughout the US.[58]

Marked clearly and triumphantly as British, largely via the persona of Lord Clark, the success of *Civilisation* launched a period during which, as Conlin puts it, "PBS began to look like a fully-owned and -operated subsidiary of the BBC" (2009, 8); it has been held up by critics of PBS's cultural mission as a prime exemplar of its strategies for cultivating a conservative cultural elite (Ouellette, 91–99). In Britain, though attracting some criticism at the time, it is now remembered as "an international success" that "went on to change the shape of cultural television. Without it, none of the large-scale didactic series that came after (Alistair Cooke's *America*, BBC, 1972–73; Dr Jacob Bronowski's *The Ascent of Man*, BBC, 1973) would have been made" (Vahimagi in "Clark, Lord Kenneth (1903–1983)"). What goes unmarked here is how much the large-scale "authored documentary," as well as the period costume drama, is in fact a transnational form. The BBC produced them; American investment drove their success and shaped their development. And worldwide sales of the series confirmed their commercial viability and influenced program producers around the globe.

The next major project taken on by the BBC in cooperation with Time-Life was the less successful and now rarely mentioned series *The British Empire*. Based on a book by James Morris, *Pax Britannica*, the thirteen-part series that aired on BBC Two beginning in January 1972 was accompanied by a series of pamphlets published by Time-Life, which had invested in the program to the tune of one-third of its production budget. This series, never picked up by an American outlet, became controversial in Britain not only for its subject matter—the episode on India attracted criticism from all sides—but for its outright "plug" for the Time-Life book series at the end of each program, in the profits from which the BBC would have shared. This smacked uncomfortably of sponsorship, in many Britons' eyes, and even though BBC spokesmen denied emphatically that considerations of the US market or of ancillary profits played any role in the production, a long and contradictory list of the program's ills were laid at the door of American influence.[59] When the next major Time-Life financed drama series *Search for the Nile* debuted on BBC Two in the fall of 1971, such protestations were renewed, now out of the Letters page and into the critics' columns in influential newspapers like the *Guardian*. As a stellar line-up of new productions was announced—particularly the two mentioned above, *The Ascent of Man* and *America*—the BBC's public denials of any transatlantic influence clashed with increased pressure from Time-Life behind the scenes to protect their growing, and not yet profitable, investment in British co-production.

Now that Time-Life was no longer confining itself to the purchase of US distribution rights after the fact, but putting up funds in the planning stages of production, it increasingly demanded the right to know what its partner was planning and to have some say in the process. Robeck appointed L. Richard "Dick" Ellison Time-Life's representative in London. Ellison was a freelance writer/director who would go on to produce the controversial PBS series *Vietnam: A Television History* (1983), itself a co-production with French and British partners. This was a new situation; having someone from their largest co-producing organization constantly on hand with an assignment to look after Time-Life's interests caused Aubrey Singer to issue a warning in March 1971:

> Under no circumstances . . . should [Ellison] be allowed to approach producers direct. Of course we must acknowledge our obligation

to consult with our co-producers – but, at the risk of being reiterative, they are minor partners getting major product very cheaply. Their involvement is marginally helpful and useful at this time – Heaven help us if it ever becomes essential.[60]

But Robeck's division was losing money fast, and if the relationship was to survive some degree of consultation seemed necessary—just as, despite Singer's fears, American investment was in fact quickly becoming essential to a certain type of BBC production. After a long series of letters back and forth and a flurry of internal memos, some guidelines were hammered out.

> The BBC will have the final artistic and editorial control of each programme. The BBC will consult with Dick Ellison on behalf of Time Life Films on the form and content of the programmes at all significant stages of the production. This will be interpreted to mean that Dick Ellison will be invited to comment at the script and/or treatment stage, the rough-cut stage (where appropriate), and the recording stage of each production.[61]

It is not clear how much Ellison's and Robeck's comments were taken into account, but Time-Life's concerns must have been met in some way because it is certain that the list of BBC/Time-Life co-productions continued to mount. By the end of 1972, with 90% of the BBC's co-production revenues stemming from Time-Life investment, David Attenborough suggested to his colleagues that Time-Life should now be given first option on everything BBC Television produced.[62]

So perhaps it is not surprising that in December 1972, with *The Search for the Nile* much publicized for its Emmy award in the States, the blockbuster 20-part adaptation of Tolstoy's *War and Peace* just wrapping up its first run on BBC Two after months of US-financed shooting in Yugoslavia, and plans for Alistair Cooke's *America* series announced in the press, the BBC found it necessary to produce for public circulation a statement on their co-production policies, not the last that they would issue over the next decade. Titled "BBC Television Co-Productions: The Why, How and What," it ran through a series of questions, from "Are co-productions something new, or have they been going on for some time?" (answer: not new, but recently more important) and "How do you choose your co-producers?" ("Very carefully indeed") to matters of more public concern:

> But surely nobody puts large amounts of money into a series and simply steps aside? (answer: 'Yes they do,' citing Time-Life and *The British Empire*).

And they had no say in the series at all? In that case, what do co-producers get for their money? (Particularly in the case of other television organizations, the co-producer gains very valuable experience from working with the BBC on a programme or series. We're not just sharing cost. We're sharing experience and know-how too.)

The final segment addressed the question that critics and the BBC's regulators had recently brought up, and that recent negotiations with Robeck and Ellison had thrown into question:

You've done a number of co-productions with Time-Life. Why them? ('Because they are obvious partners for co-productions. They have a very good reputation, they understand television, and, most importantly, they already have strong connections with us as our distributors in the United States. . . . They are enthusiastic about our projects, they are prepared to invest enough money to enable us to produce series on the scale they should be produced, and they are happy to leave us to produce the programmes.')[63]

But on Time-Life's end, this policy had resulted in a growing inventory of programs sitting on the shelf, unsold; between 1970 and 1973, Time-Life Films lost nearly $3 million out of a $5 million investment (Prendergast 1986, 287–88).

Its greatest success under Robeck's aegis was achieved with the debut of the next major BBC/Time-Life venture, the thirteen-part series *America*, written and presented by Alistair Cooke. Once again produced by Michael Gill, this series—actually entitled *America: A Personal History of the United States*—proved a great success on both sides of the Atlantic. Though many commented on the irony of the first major television retrospective on American history coming from the BBC—as Dennis Scuse scoffed in a magazine interview, "Just think of it—America buying a series about its own country from a foreign producer" (J. Lewis 1972)—in the context of the transnational cultural economy it was a predictable development. Though the production team was British, its author and organizing persona was a naturalized American with a considerable expertise in observing his adopted country; he had come to personify the growing space where British and American culture overlapped. And Time-Life Films did more than simply "buy" the project; it was involved it from the beginning, though the original notion seems to have come from Gill, who presented the idea to Cooke as an "American *Civilisation*" (Clarke 1999, 413)—a notion clearly designed to appeal as much to the American market as to the British, if not more. With production funds from Time-Life the project got underway in 1971; Cooke's biographer recounts that the original compensation offered to Cooke was quite modest, since all involved imagined PBS as the most likely US outlet. When Robeck managed to convince the Xerox Corporation to invest to the tune of $4 million, then sold the series to NBC, it activated a clause Cooke's lawyer had presciently written into his contract giving Cooke 10% of gross profits for all US and British sales. And though the BBC had agreed that Time-Life would publish a book based on the series, Cooke was able under the terms of his contract to take the work to his publisher, Alfred Knopf, in the States while the BBC retained publishing rights in the UK. This left Time-Life largely cut out of what proved to be the most profitable part of the venture, since the book became an international best-seller. Cooke made sufficient money that he retired from his long-time position as correspondent for the *Guardian*.

The series ran in thirteen installments on NBC every other Tuesday evening, beginning on November 14, 1972, a few weeks before its debut on BBC Two, which occurred on December 11. Xerox followed a British model of advertising, limiting its announcements to two 90-second spots at the beginning of each episode and two at the end.[64] In June of 1973 Xerox sponsored a further, syndicated run aimed at younger audiences, which ran on various commercial stations in the early evenings. PBS picked up the series in September 1974 and broadcast it, with numerous repeats and a wide variety of corporate and non-profit underwriters, through March 1975. Reviews were largely enthusiastic, though some British commentators felt Cooke had been too soft on America's historical record, especially in the contemporary era, and some American commentators found his account "belittling" and dismissive of America's true accomplishments.[65] Clearly, though, here was the formula for successful US/UK co-production: a focus on events to which Americans could easily relate (unlike *The British Empire*) and the presence of a compelling authorial personality capable of bridging transatlantic divides.

This was confirmed in the next large-scale US/UK co-productions, documentary mathematician and scientist (and former *Brains Trust* panelist) Jacob Bronowski's sweeping *The Ascent of Man,* which "attempted to do for science what *Civilisation* had done for art" (Clark 2010a). Filmed in various locations around the world in 1971 and 72, it aired in Britain from May through July, 1973, and in Canada shortly thereafter; US broadcast was delayed because no major sponsor or network showed immediate interest, and Robeck was holding out for a big sale to recoup Time-Life's considerable investment (Prendergast 1986, 389). As with *Civilisation,* a special preview for press and VIPs of the scientific and literary establishment was arranged in January, 1974 in Washington, DC, this time at the Smithsonian. Their glowing reviews caused the Smithsonian to add two week's worth of additional screenings, and Time-Life took out slightly plaintive ads in major newspapers around the country: "Now that the response to 'The Ascent of Man' is so definitely established, we would welcome inquiries from US corporations interested in presenting this major television event in 1974."[66] This time the Mobil Oil Corporation, *Masterpiece Theatre*'s backer, stepped up to the plate with a matching grant from the Arthur Vining Davis Foundation, and the series aired not on a commercial network but on PBS beginning in January 1975 to great acclaim (but very little profit to Time-Life). Book sales once again enriched both producing organizations.

By this time the way such productions were promoted in Britain and in the United States had begun to diverge remarkably. In Britain, the BBC worked hard to bury any mention of Time-Life's involvement in one of the last paragraphs of any given story, and often a pre-emptively defensive spin preceded it: Bronowski commented in the *Times*, shortly before the series debuted, that he was "convinced that a series like *The Ascent of Man* could only have been produced in England. 'Highly literate science and art can be put in powerful terms to the man in the street here without betraying intellectual heritage.'"[67] In the US, on the other hand, Time-Life began to take out full-page ads in the *New York Times* trumpeting its role in such "co-productions of Time-Life Films and BBC-TV" as "grownup television" and boasting of their many awards. These ads were aimed at attracting sponsors and network/syndication sales as much as viewers.[68] However, they also proved Peter Robeck's swan song. By the end of 1973 he had been removed from his post as president of the division, which had failed to produce any profits for its parent organization, and a new man, Bruce Paisner, took over. At about the same time David Attenborough departed his post as Director of Television Programs to go into independent production, after being offered and briefly considering the post of Director-General of the BBC. He would become one of the best-known natural history documentarists in the world with such large-scale co-productions as *Life on Earth* (BBC/Turner Broadcasting) and *The Living Planet* (BBC/Time-Life). His position was filled by Alasdair Milne, who would succeed to the Director-General post for several tempestuous years in the 80s.

Attenborough's departure removed one of the most co-production-friendly executives at the BBC, and Paisner's arrival ratcheted up Time-Life's demands on the relationship. One of Paisner's first actions was to try to intervene more effectively in the company's co-production arrangements with the BBC, causing a second wave of alarm to ripple through Television Centre. Aubrey Singer fired off an irate memo:

Paisner willfully refuses to understand in any way whatsoever that we, the BBC, cannot embark on the lowering of standards implicit in "Mid Atlantic" production. Time and time again he has been told (and obviously it has not sunk in) that our programmes are designed for British audiences, that the majority of the money in co-productions is British licence holders' money, that the editorial thrust must therefore be aimed at the British audience and not between both audiences. . . . There is a tacit assumption on Time Life's part that their knowledge of the American market is better than the BBC's. I question this.[69]

Singer had a point; by this time bountiful evidence existed that BBC Two's audience resembled PBS's viewership far more closely than either matched the majority audience in their home countries. A highly educated transnational minority propped up "quality" production at both institutions. BBC/PBS partnership on such continuing series as *NOVA*, introduced in 1974 patterned after (and frequently co-produced with) the BBC series *Horizon*, featuring documentaries on topics of science and nature, and the *Mystery!* series introduced in 1977, continues this arrangement into the present day. By contrast, Time-Life's vision of reaching a larger, more diverse audience (and larger profits) on more commercial outlets produced only limited success.

But in 1975 conditions stood on the verge of change. A series of developments, both technological and industry-related, took the stage in the mid 1970s that would set the transatlantic cultural economy into a steep spin towards revolution in global culture. Satellite-distributed cable television and the video cassette market, along with the effects of the fin/syn rules in the US and continued financial problems for both the BBC and independent broadcasters in the UK, ushered in a period of rapidly escalating co-production and program trade, along with increasing anxieties over media imperialization and unbalanced program flows. The period of deregulation and privatization under Reagan and Thatcher in the 1980s, along with the debut of Britain's Channel 4 in 1982, shifted the dynamic again, just as the era of globalization dawned in earnest and a whole new field of scholarship along with it. The concluding chapter will take a brisk sweep through these decades, identifying a few key points that relate to the US/UK transnational dialogue most strongly.

But it is worth noting in closing that it was not only the culture and practice of public television in the US, nor only BBC Two in the UK, that was influenced by the programs that co-production made possible. As *New York Times* TV critic Les Brown wrote in 1977, "millions of viewers who never tune to PBS are nevertheless affected by public television because, in recent years, it has profoundly influenced the programming of the commercial networks." He points to the incursion of new forms of television, such as the mini-series, serialized adaptations of novels (mostly popular, like *Roots* and *Rich Man, Poor Man*), and prime-time soap operas like *Peyton Place* and soon *Dallas*, all first introduced on PBS with "much of it imported from Britain."[70] As cable television opened up new markets, with an economic structure and marketing strategy that differed from commercial broadcasting, this influence would become ever stronger. On the British side, despite widespread disavowal of the notion, American programs continued to inflect British television culture. From soaps and quiz programs to cop and adventure shows, American aesthetics and televisual practices had become absorbed into the British idiom, even as key distinctions were maintained, at least discursively (see Weissman 2009). And though Anthony Smith could later claim "PBS has had no discernible influence on TV within the UK apart from acting as part of the inspiration for Channel 4," it is hard to imagine that the presence of the American market and American cofinancing didn't at the very least support and encourage the kinds of programs increasingly important to the BBC's financing and identity. Even Smith admits that "the export of UK programmes has helped to make British politicians aware of the fact that they might be destroying something useful if they further undermine British public TV."[71] This seems influence enough.

Part 3 Conclusion
Going Global

Between 1946 and 1975, the growth of television around the world created a whole new "world information order," to quote a phrase that would become globally resonant in the next decade. When Nordenstreng and Varis published their influential UNESCO report in 1974, they noted that until 1962, "The United States alone had more television sets than the rest of the world put together" (1974, 3) in absolute numbers; by percentages Britain, France and Germany lagged only slightly behind. By the mid-70s television had been introduced into virtually every country across the globe, and alongside the programs produced and broadcast by each individual nation appeared an increasing assortment of programs purchased from other national suppliers; the economics as well as the basic visuality of television drove this first wave of televisual globalization far beyond what radio had accomplished. Further, if most (though not all) of radio's international expansion had been driven by politics—the politics of nation and of empire—television programs spread via the circuits of commodity exchange, along the lines that the cinema had pursued since its earliest days. A similar movement was happening in radio—these chapters have regrettably had to leave out the fascinating but well documented story of popular radio's transformation in the 1960s and 70s, and its increasing domination by the economics of the global popular music industry (see Barnard 1989; Fornatale and Mills 1980; Wall 2003).

As with radio decades earlier, two of the most well-established and affluent nations to embark on the business of production for the world's markets were the United States and Great Britain, and these chapters have traced the arc of their mutual resistance and cooperation across television's formative decades. By the mid 1970s, a transnational vocabulary of television had evolved, the filmed series had become the backbone of national schedules and of international trade (Bielby and Harrington 2008; Havens 2006; Steemers 2004), and in most nations—even those that maintained public monopolies—commercial forms and practices had emerged to compete with public funding. In the US the opposite trajectory finally permitted a public broadcaster to emerge, deeply entangled both with commercial underwriting and with the transatlantic cultural economy.

Yet the extent and nature of transnational exchange on the global stage had yet to rise to the peak of contestation that emerging technologies and changing politics would motivate in the 1980s. The familiar push-pull remains: for public broadcasters, survival as an institution depends on the existence of audience-building programs acquired from foreign producers, usually American, more cheaply than they can be produced domestically (particularly in the area of drama), allowing scarce public monies to go into more urgently nationally specific program genres such as news and public affairs. And revenues from foreign sales and co-production agreements bring much-needed boosts in overall funding available, even as they encourage a widening-out of the focus of a program beyond the borders of the nation. The concluding chapter traces the development of the interwoven transnational culture that television production evolved in the last decades of the twentieth century, leading up to our digitally linked present era.

CHAPTER 10

Towards "Globalization"

As these chapters have demonstrated, media globalization has a history, one that goes back far beyond the 1980s. First came the state-based reign of radio, delineating the cultural boundaries of the nation-state and spreading its empire-building politics through the ether, creating a new stage on which the nation was performed. Nations defined themselves against an array of global "others," both internal and external, and circulated the preferred national culture more broadly and accessibly than ever before possible, projecting it outwards during wartime conflicts in a way that acted to transnationalize the national address, in return. When broadcasting met the already globalized commodity culture of film in the second half of the decade, television's transnational dispersion began, ushering in a period of increasingly global media exchange.[1] I have argued here for a more nuanced understanding of the relationship between nations in broadcasting, one that peers beneath the sweeping generalizations of the globalization discourse to trace specific currents of flow and circuits of exchange in one particularly productive, and powerful, transnational relationship.

The transnational cultural economy created between Britain and the United States in the twentieth century by no means exists as the only important transnational circuit of ethereal exchange across history. Each sector of the globe shows a similar network of relationships in the construction and circulation of radio and television, depending on larger contexts of cultural proximity—with shared language a dominant factor—as well as political and economic dominance. And, for both Britain and the US, other highly productive transnational relationships deserve an equally detailed study. The records of the BBC demonstrate not only its struggles with internal national identities—Scotland, Ireland, Wales (see Lucas 1981; MacDowell 1992; McLoone 2000; Medhurst 2010; R. Savage 1996)—but also show the important influence of other major European broadcasters, notably Germany before the war and France throughout, along with the offshore broadcasters whose history Sean Street traces. A history of the influence of the BBC throughout the British Empire, both directly and as a model, has only just been written; Simon Potter's recent book traces its impact on such national systems as All India Radio (AIR), the CBC in Canada, ABC in Australia, and across the Dominions and the Commonwealth. The United States has had an extensive exchange with Canada ever since broadcasting began that has been more reviled than explored (though see Collins 1990a; Tinic 2005; Vipond 1992); even less recognized are the circuits of influence and cultural adaptation within Latin America and the Spanish speaking world (though see Rivero 2009; Sinclair 1996, 1999). Some very good studies explore specific periods and areas of US/Latin America transnational flow (Hayes 2000, McCann 2004; Schwoch 1987, 2008) but few have traced the influence the other way, on US broadcasting culture (though see Casillas 2006). Yet Spanish language media have existed in the US radio and television landscape since its earliest years, and important transnational routes of distribution and co-production have operated in a productive cultural exchange that now addresses over 15% of the US population on a regular basis. One of the very first satellite-distributed services to operate in US airspace was not HBO or ESPN, but SIN, the Spanish International Network, originally operated as the US arm of Mexican media giant Televisa, later nationalized as Univision (Rodriguez 1997). It is my hope that this historical study, by concentrating on forms of cultural exchange that go beyond the industrial and political into the more difficult to discern but fundamentally important fields of creative practice, cultural impact, and the social discourses that shape them, will inspire similar studies of other sites of transnational interest.

Though such conduits of exchange, such *histoires croisées*, have existed since the very beginning of radio, so that we cannot understand national broadcasting without taking the shaping pressures of the transnational into account, in the late 1970s and 80s changes began to accumulate worldwide that reshaped the cultural role of media and communications and moved us towards a more broadly globalized world. Some of the roots of this change were technological—the introduction of cable television, communications satellites, and VCRs, leading to the digital revolution of the 90s—and some were political and economic, such as the rise of market-based political ideologies ushered in during the Reagan and Thatcher era, during which public broadcasting systems were privatized and restructured to compete in the marketplace and a philosophy of deregulation reigned. Other roots can be found in the movement of people and of finance in the decades since the 1970s, as Arjun Appadurai sketched out in 1996 in his architecture of the social imaginary as a series of "scapes"—ethnoscapes, mediascapes, technoscapes, financescapes, and ideoscapes—by which globalization works its transformations (Appadurai 1996). Such shape-shifting geographies move us from a system in which nations could at least attempt to legislate and control access to culture, to one where nations certainly still produce and circulate culture but everyday people's ability to take up and participate in cultural flows from all over has escaped the bounds of national policy. This is one of the larger narratives of the twentieth century, taking off at warp speed into the twenty-first.

In this concluding chapter I want to first trace, briefly, a few of the more specific events and developments that moved the transnational cultural economy of Britain and the US from the twentieth century into the twenty-first, as well as the ways in which scholars have responded to various phases in the exchange. I want then to point to the larger issues that this history has, I hope, raised or complicated through sheer accumulation of historical density.

In Britain, the last quarter of the twentieth century was marked by significant structural changes, notably the introduction of independent local radio in the 1970s (national commercial radio would be held off until the 90s), followed by the debut of Channel 4 in 1982, the long-awaited fourth television channel. Both ILR and Channel 4 attempted to split the commercial/public service divide: ILR along the lines of Independent Television, a mixture of private and public ownership under public regulation; Channel Four, on the other hand, owned by the state but supported by commercial advertising and regulated by the Independent Broadcasting Authority.[2] Its mandate to serve minority communities and interests through an emphasis on independently produced programs, along with the growing market for such productions on cable television channels in the US, helped to set off a second major wave of US/British program exchange and co-production.

The BBC expanded its US co-productions and sales significantly in these years. Dropping Time/Life as their intermediary in 1980, BBC Enterprises, now operating as an independent profit-making subsidiary (renamed BBC Worldwide in 1994), moved aggressively into the global marketplace. Philip Schlesinger quotes Roy Gibbs, sales director of BBC Enterprises, in 1984: "We are the BBC's major co-producer. We know what programmes will be made two to three years down the line and can go out and pre-sell them" (Schlesinger1986, 276). Much of this trade at first was done with the US-based Arts and Entertainment cable channel (A&E) which became the BBC's most significant partner over the next two decades, with more than 50% of its schedule originating in Britain (Steemers 2004, 112). In 1985, debut of the Discovery Channel launched a new empire of transatlantic documentary production (Chris 2002), which soon began to outweigh the BBC's volume of exchange with PBS—though PBS's ongoing reliance on co-produced British programming remained.

These developments had been made possible by the introduction of widespread satellite broadcasting in the mid 1980s. In the US satellite transmission became linked to the rapidly growing field of cable television to inaugurate a new multi-channel world of national cable channels, distributed by satellite, able to provide specialized programming through a combination of advertising and direct subscription. In Britain it became a political hot potato, tossed between regulatory and commercial interests, until Rupert Murdoch jumped the queue and launched his Sky service in 1989, which became BSkyB in 1991 (see Collins 1990b). In the 1990s pan-European commercial broadcasting became a reality, with channels like Eurosport, Canal Plus, ARTE, and Euronews attempting to create and sustain a European identity in the air, to counterbalance the growing abundance of American films and television programs available via satellite. However, with the European Community Directive on Television in 1989 (known as "Television Without Frontiers") that any satellite service authorized in one European country must be allowed to transmit into any other, Britain, via Murdoch, became once again a conduit for American programming in Europe—though limits were also applied. To complement the television of abundance, VCRs debuted in the early 80s, commodifying film in a new way that brought it into closer conjunction with the television set, and beginning the user-driven recording of television programs that added a new, individually controlled sector of distribution, outside the usual channels of control.

By the late 1990s, however, a fresh current began to flow, stimulated by the advent of digital satellite communications and the growing online distribution and digital recording sectors. Public service and regulated commercial broadcasters in Europe but also notably in Japan, squeezed by competition and under mandate to broaden and democratize their audience base, moved more aggressively into the global television market. One result was the introduction of a new wave of reality-based formats that soon began to circulate around the world, reversing some of the old patterns of program flow (Moran 1998; Selznick 2008; Steemers 2004). These included not only traditional documentary formats, now seen on such channels as Discovery, National Geographic, Animal Planet, The History Channel and TLC, not only in the US but worldwide—but game shows (*Who Wants to be a Millionaire?*, *The Weakest Link*), cooking programs (*Top Chef, Iron Chef*), makeover shows (*What Not to Wear, Extreme Makeover: Home Edition*), talent competitions (*Pop Idol/American Idol, America's Next Top Model*), and the structured and staged situational reality shows that became particular hits, such as the globally successful *Big Brother* and *Survivor* franchises. These truly transnational programs—relatively inexpensive to produce, easy to "nationalize" by encouraging local participation, and blamelessly focused on "fact"—might pop up anywhere on the new expanded digital cable and satellite universe, or they might have an entire channel devoted to the genre (The Food Channel, Home and Garden Network, etc.); in the US, most came from Britain or via a British translation of a format originated in another country.

Another notable moment in the British/American relationship was the debut of the cable channel BBC America in 1998, owned and operated by BBC Worldwide. Unabashedly commercial, it presents not only BBC but UK commercial programs with a sensibility that stands the old refined PBS Britishness on its head (C. Becker 2007). However, this dedicated channel represents a very small part of the remarkable expansion of BBC Worldwide in the early 2000s. Their own website best expresses the evolution of the Enterprises division launched under Hugh Carleton Greene and Ronald Waldman more than 50 years before:

> BBC Worldwide, the commercial arm of the BBC, is a fast-growing media and entertainment company. Our mission is to maximise profits on behalf of the BBC by creating, acquiring, developing and exploiting media content and media brands around the world. We are self-funded and return profits to the BBC to be reinvested in programmes and services to help keep the UK licence fee as low as possible. Our primary purpose is to bring value to the BBC in the form of profits and programme investment. We acquire the commercial rights to great programmes such as *Planet Earth*, *Doctor Who* and *Top Gear* and find ways of earning money from these across different media and markets. We then channel funds back to the BBC to be invested in new programmes and services.[3]

By 2010, the company reported an income of more than £1 billion, generating nearly £150 million in profits from its "seven core businesses": channels, content and production, digital media, sales and distribution, magazines and children's licensing, home entertainment, and global brands.

Besides BBC America, wholly owned channels include BBC Entertainment, BBC HD, BBC Knowledge, BBC Lifestyle, CBeebies (children's programs), and UKTV in Australia. All have global reach and are delivered via direct broadcast satellite. Other channels are co-partnered ventures, such as Animal Planet and People+Arts, partnerships with the US-based Discovery Communications corporation. Ten UKTV domestic channels are a joint venture with Virgin Media, and three services operate in conjunction with Canada's two largest commercial networks, CanWest and CTV. BBC Worldwide's Content and Production arm invests in independent and co-production ventures with companies around the world, and is responsible for two of the biggest international hits of recent years, *Dancing With the Stars* and *Strictly Come Dancing*. Its Sales and Distribution arm bills itself as "one of the world's most successful exporters of television programmes, second only to the big US studios" and goes on to claim, "The business accounts for around half of the UK's total television exports with around 40,000 hours of programming sold in the last year."[4] Top selling programs in 2008–09 were *Top Gear, Robin Hood, Dr. Who, Primeval,* and *Spooks* (titled *MI5* in the US).

Such programs, though they might be produced for domestic markets, keep a clear eye aimed at international audiences. US program producers have always done this, but in the 2000s a new kind of headline began cropping up in American newspapers, such as "Britons Revamp American TV"[5] and "Brit Invasion of TV Shows Keeps Growing."[6] The first article referred to the game and reality show "invasion" and the second to a broader pattern of adaptations, imports, and formats noticeable a few years later, indicating "a growing reliance on series concepts from abroad."[7] And not only from Britain; most articles noted the influence of Latin American imports and adaptations on the offerings of such channels as Univision. Another hall-mark of US television drama in the 2000s was the high-profile drama series with an international cast, like ABC's successful *Lost* and less successful *Heroes*, often with subtitled dialogue for lengthy scenes conducted in another language (unusual in American TV). In another twist, some US producers began adapting their own programs for international audiences in conjunction with foreign partners. US producer Dick Wolf's incredibly prolific *Law & Order* franchise was one of the first to take on what might be termed "original adaptations"; *Paris Enquêtes Criminelles* debuted in 2007 on TF1 as a version of *Law & Order: Criminal Intent* specifically shaped to fit the French legal system (no reading of Miranda rights) and French cultural sensibilities. Produced by Alma Productions, a French company based in Paris, it was overseen with obsessive care by its creator, Wolf, especially regarding the use of the trademark "ca-ching" sound (which "should never be used more than two times per act, and should be used to signal a shift in the storytelling, not just a change in location").[8] A British version, *Law & Order: UK*, debuted on ITV in 2009, produced by Kudos Film and Television and set in London but again held tightly to the original. Two different iterations of the franchise have also been adapted for Russian television, set in Moscow; their translated titles are *Law & Order: Division of Field Investigation* (patterned on *Special Victims Unit*) and *Law & Order: Criminal Intent*.

Such attempts to nationalize within a scripted and highly controlled aesthetic mark a shift from both the earlier period of unacknowledged borrowing and the stark domestic/import distinction of the 60s and 70s towards a new era in franchised media: *television croissée*. Today's media properties increasingly extend themselves not only across episodes and seasons, in television's traditional pattern, but across media platforms– from television to film, videogames, and online sites, building complex storyworlds in a transmedia universe (Jenkins 2006)—and across national "platforms" as well (see D. Johnson 2009; Rixon 2006). A resurgence in transnationally oriented regional production has sent other programs off on unprecedented adventures. The best example may be the wildly successful comedy *Yo soy Betty, la fea*, originated in Colombia for Latin American distribution but adapted worldwide, in the US as *Ugly Betty*. Its circuits are worth considering for a moment: not only did the original Colombian series air in more than 30 countries, it was adapted into more than 20 national versions, many of which departed considerably from the original while maintaining key elements, however loosely defined. A few of these "original adaptations" themselves were sold to secondary markets: third generation iterations that demonstrate the complex and contradictory flows of media culture in a transnational age.[9]

How we Talk about Transnational Media

The trajectory of these developments in the media universe is mirrored by the waves of understanding it has produced in scholarly discourse. The first "media imperialism" wave in the mid 1970s reflected the slow roll-out and maturation of national over-the-air television systems around the world, most of them heavily dependent on imported programs and technologies as they ramped up domestic operations. The resulting escalation of international sales and co-productions in the late 1960s and 1970s engendered not only the concerns expressed in the Nordenstreng and Varis UNESCO report of 1974 but also such influential works as Herbert Schiller's *Mass Communication and American Empire* in 1969 and his *Communication and Cultural Domination* in 1976. These studies showed an overwhelmingly dominant US media engine driving world cultures towards homogenization and the erasure of national differences. An upsurge of anxieties over "Americanization" can also be seen in Britain during this period, despite the UK's own considerable global impact, due least in part to BBC efforts to justify an increase in the license fee (Weissman 2009). This first wave of globalization scholarship may perhaps have culminated in the critical furor caused by the huge international success in 1980–81 of *Dallas*, the American prime-time soap (itself made thinkable on US schedules through the success of BBC co-produced literary adaptation serials) whose popularity with audiences around the world gave rise to iconic terms of anxiety like "wall-to-wall Dallas" and "Dallasification." However, the force of the critical reaction against *Dallas* can also be read as confirmation of the secure status by this time of national television systems in most countries, and the established dominance of domestic production to which *Dallas* provided either a welcome contrast or an unwelcome intruder (and a model—see Collins 1986).

The second wave of globalization discourse reacted to technological and political developments of the late 1980s and early 1990s, theorized through anxieties over the "erosion of the public sphere" and the shift of emphasis from "citizen to consumer."[10] In the British context, this wave was sparked by the deliberations of the Peacock Committee, convened under Margaret Thatcher, and in the US by the deregulatory activities of the FCC under Reagan appointee Mark Fowler. The 1986 Peacock Report's strongly market-based recommendations set off alarm bells across Europe and among apprehensive US media scholars as well, leading to an impressive spate of articles and books characterizing the globalization and heightened commercialization of national television in highly negative terms.[11] On both sides of the Atlantic, commercial media were contrasted to public service media in inflammatory tones, with much of the criticism of the BBC that came from the left in earlier decades now buried beneath a new "Americanization" scare, fed by fears that the global market spearheaded by Hollywood might decisively win out over publicly financed national culture (see Blumler 1991; Curran 1991; Garnham 1983; among others). At the same time, a particularly contentious period in BBC operations fanned the flames, as John Birt replaced Alisdair Milne in 1992 and proceeded to introduce internal competition and "outsourcing" to BBC production practices. In the US, the expiration of the fin/syn rules brought a new wave of mergers between the film and television industries and the formation of new, vertically integrated over-the-air networks: Rupert Murdoch's FOX, the WB (Warners) and UPN (Paramount). This period is also marked by some of the first scholarly analyses of the actual dimensions of imports, exports, and co-productions (Collins 1986; Schlesinger 1986) and by the beginning of consideration of the ways that audiences understood and used such media (Ang 2001; Morley and Robbins 1995).

By the late 1990s, however, some of these second wave fears had begun to seem almost quaint as the digital revolution swept across the globe, multiplying the number of available channels in each nation exponentially while the internet provided a virtually stateless new cultural domain. A third wave of scholarship continues to develop, less certain of the basic assumptions of the nation-based frameworks that preceded it and crossing media boundaries as well as national ones. The advent of the European Union and its trans-nationalizing cultural initiatives helped to reframe the terms of the debate, as did the increase during the 1990s in migration of populations from the outposts of empire and from the margins of the former Soviet Union, creating new levels of cultural diversity within national boundaries. National identities and national cultures became more contested grounds, less firmly held by elites. A new, permeable form of national culture became the norm, with immigrant populations able to tune into channels from home via satellite even as they switched between domestic and other imported offerings. As new media capitals rose (Bombay, Hong Kong, Lagos) new ways of theorizing global cultural flows began to appear (Appadurai 1990, 1996; Bhabha 2004; García Canclini 2001; Ong 1999) and with them considerations of media culture willing to reconsider the old oppositions and to analyze ever more complex circuits of exchange (Bielby and Harrington 2008; Havens 2006; Kumar 2008). Along with transnational intersections came a growing number of trans-media studies, looking particularly at the ways in which digital media have transformed the forms and formats of film, television, music and added entirely new media venues, such as video games and online worlds, and created a new digital world of intertextuality and expanding global franchises (J. Gray 2010; D. Johnson 2009; Jenkins 2006).

Final Points

The theme of cultural "globalization" of every kind has produced a wide range of scholarship as the third wave continues, including not only studies of the contemporary scene but histories such as this one, that use a globalized sensibility to cast a skeptical eye on some of the givens of previous eras as well as on some of the enthusiasms of the present. Interrogating that sensibility by taking a transnational cultural perspective, in the mode of the *histoire croisée* with nation as the primary variable, enables a few themes to emerge that readers might take away from this volume as a revision of accepted knowledge in the field of broadcasting and cultural history more generally.

First of all, the central aim of this book has been to place broadcasting at the heart of the history of nation-building in the twentieth century rather than at its periphery. This includes not only the institutions of radio and television but the practices they inspire and texts they produce and circulate, and the ways in which such manifestations resonate within the larger political and cultural contexts of their times. Our empires of the air cannot be disregarded as transparent conveyers of more meaningful content, nor as trivial pursuits best left to the pundits of the day, but must be acknowledged as meaningful historical forces in their own right. Now that the digital era has brought audio and video texts out of obscurity and into increasing availability on the web, historians of all types will be able—and should feel obligated—to give sound and screen texts the same kind of attention and evidential weight they have long attached to the press and the printed page, and to count the media themselves as powerful actors in historical processes. The online world, both amateur and professional, has made radio and television texts more widely available than ever before, but efforts must continue to render such materials as accessible to scholars as are historical print media. Audio-visual archives have only existed for roughly fifty years; their fragile holdings present unique challenges for preserving, cataloguing and providing access to the vital historical records they contain. This task runs into barriers rooted in the national remits and complex rights situations that often surround such multiple-authored texts, as well. Thus it is imperative that we as scholars work with archivists and collectors to identify and preserve significant materials, resolve rights issues, and create platforms through which our global radio and television heritage can be opened to all.[12]

Placing broadcasting at the heart of national cultures also mandates reconsideration of the concept of "Americanization" as it has been deployed across the decades, given how central a role the United States has played in the development of modern media. This is a term, as Berghahn points out (2004), that has undergone substantial changes in its more than 100 year history. Its political valence reached a peak in the Cold War era but it continues to resonate in its cultural form today, though as he argues it may now be in decline under the pressures of globalization and the many counterbalances to the influence of the US in the world. Yet "Americanization" has been one of the more powerful words with which to conjure change, and resistance to change, across the twentieth century. This history may serve to elucidate how that vague but weighty concept has been mobilized in one particular, highly influential, context and thus to deconstruct the many essentialisms that it implies. Within the cultural economy of British broadcasting, the invocation of "Americanization" was a powerful strategic tool, used in the early decades to uphold a class-based hierarchy under which elements of popular culture could be decried as "American" and thus rendered illegitimate, de-nationalized. Under that label the tastes and interests of the working class could be justifiably resisted by the reigning Arnoldian philosophy, one that celebrated a top-down dissemination of national elite culture to the masses while suppressing the bottom-up development of a truly popular British culture on the national airwaves (as others have argued; see Camporesi 1994, 200; Scannell with Cardiff 1991). This changed with the war, as a more genuinely democratic broadcasting culture evolved in Britain (Cardiff and Scannell 1986; Nicholas

1996). But the strategy remained to adapt and borrow from American popular forms and to reap the benefits of their popularity while publicly denigrating their quality as well as, in the case of the BBC, the value of the entire system that produced them (Lealand 1984; Weissman 2009). When not only independent television but the BBC itself began to benefit from an embrace of popular, commercial forms and their sale worldwide—and when American co-finance became an important underwriter of elements of "quality" public service fare—the dynamic began to change. However, the "Americanization" card can still be effectively deployed in the British context when deemed necessary. Thus in 2001, with the BBC's public funding once again under attack, Director General Greg Dyke could say, "We are told the world is globalising—that's not true: it is Americanising. It is essential that TV, radio and online should reflect the cultures of particular countries."[13] There is much truth in this, but this history should serve to indicate some of the more complex truths behind it that go unstated.

For instance, too little attention has been paid to the productive function of transnational flows. Sweeping invocations of "Americanization" or globalization tend to obscure the ways that cultural influence works, and always has worked, across lines of many different kinds of which the nation is only one, and a recent arrival at that. Though national literatures and musical traditions, for example, are highlighted and cherished wherever they exist, it is widely recognized that influence is not the same as erasure, and that artists at all levels borrow from a great variety of inspirations both domestic and challengingly exotic. In such cases, the cultural identity of a work is typically guaranteed by the nationality of its author; in the some-what more difficult arena of the cinema, where not only multiple authorship but multi-national productions have become increasingly the norm, the "marking" of national identity has become a process of complex political and economic negotiations (Hjort 2010). As I have argued throughout, for the dedicated national institutions of radio and television too little attention has been paid to the highly productive aspects of global (often but not always American) influence. This applies not only to popular methods of pre-sentation, narrative modes, and genres that might first appear in the US but are quickly adapted to serve a variety of domestic contexts, but also to those programs and modes that develop in specific opposition to perceived transnational influence—such as the British tradition of the "realistic" working-class type of early evening serial, as in *Coronation Street* or *EastEnders*. Also too little taken into account are the specific techniques of domestication that broadcasting's unique distribution and textual systems not only permit, but mandate. With its serial texts, slotted into domestic schedules and stretched out over months or years, promoted and delivered into the midst of the nation's living rooms, broadcasting has embedded the transnational within the authorized national address since its inception (see Rixon 2006). In a sense, it is the very "nationalness" of broadcasting that has *produced* the category of the non-national, but also the many techniques for managing it, from simple "unmarking" and denial to the careful and productive deployment traced in these pages.

This study has also attempted to question the scholarly and popular discourse produced over the years that starkly differentiates commercial and public service media, from the pronouncements of John Reith to the public sphere debates of the 1990s. I wish particularly to encourage a more nuanced understanding of the relationship between the economic, political, and cultural roles of complex media systems. By focusing on the commercial aspects of the BBC and on the role of private broadcasters in Britain, and conversely on the overlooked history of educational and public service broadcasting in the United States, not only are transnational circuits of exchange brought out but "hidden histories" are revealed. Each era produces its own instrumental histories, and in the period of national differentiation and strategic rivalry British broadcasting's substantial role in the marketplace and US broadcasting's considerable investment in public service were suppressed. Though a number of recent accounts have begun to redress these omissions (D. Goodman 2007b; Johnson and Turnock 2005; Russo 2009; Slotten 2009; Sean Street 2006) there are still many important stories to be told. Of course the major argument of this book is that one history most often hidden or suppressed is that of transnational exchange itself, as contrary to the assumed predominant national preoccupation of broadcasting as a medium and as a subject of study. As the pendulum of the globalization discourse swings back a bit in years to come, many more such transnational circuits will be revealed.

Finally, on a note that links me back to my original intellectual roots in the study of comparative literature, it is my hope that this history contributes something towards an improved critical understanding of the aesthetics, forms, and structures of the broadcasting medium: more broadly, of the way that it constructs narratives, makes meanings, and circulates powerful representations that are read and taken in as knowledge around the globe. The tensions between seriality and the stand-alone text, between the transmission of live events and the production of recorded textual commodities, between the expressive modes of sound and vision, between the aesthetics of the specific and the local versus the common and the universal, between the controlled iterations of authorized national culture and the popular (often transnational) constructions that burble up beneath them: these are threads that run through this book. The unique expressive qualities of the televisual text—and the aural forms that preceded and coexist with it—have been given serious consideration for only a few short years and in widely dispersed locations. The study of broadcast forms must link more deeply with the tradition of literary and cinematic study within the humanities, to fulfill the vision that John Marshall of the Rockefeller Foundation enjoined so many decades ago. Not only nationalism but elite disdain for popular culture worked to marginalize media study in the twentieth century; now that academic disciplines of all types are rushing to embrace the promise of the digital there is a danger that an important part of digital media's heritage—the audio/visual tradition of radio and television, in all their national and transnational specificities—will be overlooked, or overleaped, again.

On the other hand, the digital realm has provided a godsend for historians and those interested in media's past. The ephemeral, nearly forgotten domain of radio has been endowed with a new permanence thanks to web-based audio sites that not only preserve both current and historical audio works but effectively make them available to audiences around the world. A far cry from the awkward system of my early years of research—mailing off audio cassettes to the few "old-time radio" organizations that heroically maintained this aspect of our nation's culture, then waiting anxiously, often for weeks, for them to arrive! The same is true for television, increasingly, and for our film heritage too. Just as film study got its start when independent cinemas made retrospectives and non-Hollywood films available, and television study became possible with the advent of the VCR, now the digital world of the web ironically does a better job of re-presenting older media than of preserving its own past. Though this study has stayed primarily in the traditional historians' domain of institutional records and print-based traces of the past, it is a concern and involvement with the forms and aesthetics of radio and television that has driven the project, and most likely that drives readers of this tome as well. I hope my study will be useful to them, and that scholarship on radio and television will factor large in our defense of the humanities in the digital era.

Notes

Introduction: Thinking Transnationally—The Anglo-American Axis

1 Alan Riding, "A Common Culture (From the U.S.A.) Binds Europeans Ever Closer," *New York Times* (April 26, 2004) B1.

2 See also Winston (2004).

3 Film historiography also took on a primarily national focus, as national cinemas evolved in resistance to and in conversation with Hollywood.

4 I invoke Arjun Appadurai's concept of the "global cultural economy" (Appadurai 1990) but with a focus on the particular circulation between two dominant nations rather than the more diffuse global patterns that he traces.

5 One of the fundamental precepts of media studies that is all too often overlooked by historians and critics of other cultural forms is that the structures and practices of the media themselves—whether radio, television, newspapers, magazines, recordings, films, or the internet—have an effect on the works and information communicated through them. I would not echo Marshall McLuhan's "the medium is the message" here, but the media most emphatically do shape and influence the message. Too often historians, for example, treat texts conveyed via media as though the medium itself were transparent and unproblematic, simply "relaying" information without any intervening influence. This is a considerable misperception, the correction of which forms one of the framing assumptions of this work.

6 See also De Bens and de Smaele (2001).

7 This is almost commensurate with the extraordinary effort of will required from historians of twentieth-century culture to ignore the presence and effect of broadcasting in the midst of nearly every national development.

8 Though see Bourdon (2004) and Bignell and Fickers (2008), as well as *Media History* 16.1 (2010) for some recent work that moves in this direction. See also Simon Potter (2011).

9 A few recent media histories have developed this context: Scannel with Cardiff (1991), Hayes (2000), McCann (2004).

10 Philip Schlesinger points this out (1979). Clearly there is a gender distinction working here too—sport is seen as the semi-acceptable popular culture pursuit of men, while cinema and television are too feminized to be worth serious scholarship.

11 Much of this work stems from readings of Habermas, whose own neglect of the national dimension of his theories Nancy Fraser has criticized (2010).

12 A growing literature on this subject exists, though it often overlooks the specific role of radio and television.

13 Norimitsu Onishi, "For China's Youth, Culture Made in South Korea" *New York Times* (Jan 2, 2006) A1.
14 Or, as Appadurai himself notes, "the simplification of these many forces (and fears) of homogenization can also be exploited by nation-states in relation to their own minorities, by posing global commoditization (or capitalism, or some other such external enemy) as more real than the threat of its own hegemonic strategies" (1990) 6.
15 *World Film News* 1937—quoted in Jaikumar (2006) 9.

Part 1 The Nations Imagine Radio, 1922–1938

1 John Reith, undated speech @1926, R44/540/2. WAC.
2 Hard (1933) 113.
3 This project will not cover Germany's development, but the treatment of broadcasting by its emerging National Socialist Party—often referred to as the propaganda model of broad-casting—served as a disturbing reminder of the power of radio in the hands of the state. See Lacey (1996).

1 Chaos and Control

1 For deeper discussion of this period, see Susan Douglas (1987).
2 Briggs refers to the formation of RCA, and its annexation of American Marconi, as a "a product of American nationalism" (1961, 60) but he fails to mention the similar transformation of British Westinghouse into Metropolitan Vickers by the forced buy-out of all non-British stockholders that same year—equally a product of British nationalism.
3 "This Word 'Citizen'" *QST* July 1921, 34. See Hilmes (1997) for further discussion. Earlier, the ARRL had lobbied hard against the Poindexter Bill of 1920 which proposed placing radio under the control of the US Navy, calling it "un-American" and blaming it on the efforts of "Naval officers who were abroad during the war and there acquired the 'imperialistic' views of Europe on matters affecting communication." "Dangerous Legislation Confronts Us," *QST* (December 1920) 6.
4 These are the forefathers of the "ham" radio operators of today.
5 "Businesses Engaged In By Owners of Broadcasting Stations," *Radio Broadcast* (April 1923) 524.
6 "Transatlantic Tests Succeed!" *QST* (January 1922) n.p.
7 See "The Visit of G2NM", *QST* (June 1924) for instance, as well as M. B. Sleeper, "Development of Radio Broadcasting in the United States" *Wireless World*, (September 19, 1922) 763; and "American Amateurs Visit England" *Wireless World* (April 15, 1925) 302.
8 "Music By Wireless—First Transmission for Amateurs" *Times* (Feb 15, 1922) 7.
9 "Progress of Radio in Foreign Lands—England's Broadcasting Problem" *Radio Broadcast* (September 1922) 442–43. American amateurs frequently used such characterizations to their advantage, often invoking European restraints to argue for the "American-ness" of keeping radio in unrestricted, private hands.
10 "Wireless for All – Interest at the G.P.O. – 'Radio' Activity in America" *Times* (April 20, 1922) 14.
11 "Wireless for All – An Organized Service – Mr. Godrey Isaacs's Forecast" *Times* (April 19, 1922) 12.
12 Sir Henry Norman (Chairman of the Wireless Sub-Committee of the Imperial Communications Committee), "Wireless For All – Rapid American Progress – The Difficulties of 'Broadcasting' – Controlling Private Installations." *Times* (May 8, 1922) 17.
13 See Hilmes (2003).
14 F. J. Brown, "The Story of Broadcasting in England" *Radio Broadcast* June 1925, 175–82. This quote is from a letter Brown states that he wrote to a friend back home in February, 1922.
15 Sending representatives to the US to observe radio broadcasting there became a rite of passage for many nations at this time; for instance, in the spring of 1922 the German Reichspost "sent a team of experts to the United States" according to Kaspar Maase (2004) 80.

16   Brown, Ibid.
17   Specifically, Postmaster General Kellaway stated: "I have decided to allow the establishment of a limited number of radio telephone broadcasting stations. Permission for these stations will only be granted to British firms who are bona fide manufacturers of wireless apparatus. What I am doing is to ask all those who apply – the various firms who have applied – to come together at the Post Office and to co-operate so that an efficient service may be rendered and that there may be no danger of monopoly and that each service shall not be interfering with the efficient working of the other." "Summary of statement by Mr. Kellaway, Postmaster General, in House of Commons today in regard to broadcasting stations, (4 May 1922)," CO2 British Broadcasting Company – Broadcasting Committee – General Correspondence 1922, WAC.
18   "Memo to Western Electric Company Ltd from General Post Office, London, 15 May 1922," CO2, WAC.
19   "Memo to Western Electric Company Ltd from General Post Office, London, 15 May 1922" CO2, WAC. C. A. Lewis put a slightly different spin on the plan in 1924: "The system on which broadcasting was launched in England was far from perfect, but it did at least establish the great principle *that the concerts had to be paid for by the public, who received and derived entertainment or instruction from them.*" (C. A. Lewis (1924) 9) Emphasis in the original.
20   Sir Henry Norman, MP, "Wireless for All. II. The British Plans – Possibilities of the System" *Times* (9 May, 1922), 21.
21   "Notes of Meeting at the Institute of Electrical Engineers 2nd June 1922" CO1/1, WAC.
22   Letter from G.E.S. Murray, GPO to F. Gill, chair of committee, 12 July 1922. CO38/1, WAC.
23   "Meeting of Committee Tues 8th Aug 1922," CO1/2, WAC
24   "Statement to press at meeting of 18 Oct 1922," Ibid.
25   "Testimony of Mr. F. J. Brown, C.B., C.B.E., Assistant Secretary, General Post Office," May 1923, pp. 38–39. R4/64/1 2, WAC. Already selective institutional memory is at work: Brown asserts that he does "not quite know where the suggestion first came from" to form a single company (when as the records show it had come directly from the Post Office itself), and that "as far as [he] was aware" no one had proposed a competitive privately run scheme along the lines of the US (when it is clear from the minutes of the meetings that Godfrey Isaacs of Marconi repeatedly proposed exactly that option, before agreeing to a public service compromise).
26   Ibid. pp. 46–47.
27   "Lord Gainsford's Statement," July 31, 1923. R4/67/1, WAC.
28   "Broadcasting Question: Official Statement by BBC" April 14, 1923. CO38/2, WAC.
29   "Testimony of Mr. F. J. Brown, C.B., C.B.E., Assistant Secretary, General Post Office" p. 46–47, R4/64/1, WAC.

2   National Broadcasting in Britain

1   "Exchange Greetings With London on Air" *New York Times* (Jan 2, 1926) A1.
2   Meanwhile, Canada boasted over 50 operating stations in 1926 (Vipond (1992) 48); Mexico had 12 (Barbour 1940).
3   "Europe Achieves Unity in Radio Broadcasting," *New York Times* June 28, 1925, XX16.
4   "Exchange Greetings," op. cit.
5   "British On the Air 65,869 Hours in Year" *New York Times* Feb 20, 1927, 19.
6   See Briggs, as well as Scannell with Cardiff (1991) for a discussion of the impact of this key moment on British broadcasting history.
7   Reith, "Memorandum of Information on the Scope and Conduct of the Broadcasting Service submitted as evidence to The Broadcasting Committee, 1925" R4/27/1, WAC.
8   Reith, "Memorandum of Information on the Scope and Conduct of the Broadcasting Service submitted as evidence to The Broadcasting Committee, 1925" R4/27/1, WAC.
9   Quoted in Scannell and Cardiff (1991) 10.
10   Briggs (1965) 306, quoting Control Board Minutes, Nov10 and 17, 1926.
11   V199 Hansard Commons Deb 5s c1573–1650, Nov 15, 1926.
12   R44/540/2, WAC.
13   Gerald Cock, "Memorandum on American control of the Entertainment Industry" n.d. @1929, R34/928/1, WAC.

14 This point was not lost on American broadcasters; in a letter to Owen D. Young, Chairman of the Board of the General Electric Co., Merlin Aylesworth writes: "I can find no greater argument which can possibly be made to Mr. Ochs [publisher of the New York Times] in support of the National Broadcasting Company program than what the British Government is doing to the newspapers in the form of the new British Broadcasting Company [sic]" (Dec 15, 1926). B2 F67, NBC.
15 P. P. Eckersley, "American Radio Broadcasting," (1927) 1. E15/57, WAC.
16 Radio Times "Financial Broadcasting: 'Realism' and Reality" (June 21, 1929) 610–11.
17 Radio Times, "The Big Broadcast" (Feb 17, 1933) 383.
18 Staff Visits Abroad—JCW Reith (Canada and USA) 1933. E15/178, WAC.
19 Memo from P. T. Salisbury to Mark J. Woods, "Comparison Between Organization and Structures of NBC and BBC" (Feb 2, 1934), quoting Popular Wireless, (Dec 2, 1933). B24 F25, NBC.
20 Countries—America. Sir Noel Ashbridge. File 1, 1934–46. E1/120/1, WAC.
21 "Praise from an Englishman," New York Times (Oct 9, 1932) 10. Eckersley had been named in a divorce suit, and Reith's strict supervision of company morals meant that he had to leave the Corporation.
22 Charles Siepmann, "Report on the Regions" (Jan 1936). R34/734/1, WAC.

3 The "American System"

1 "New Broadcasters Aim at Happiness," New York Times, (Oct 28, 1926) 12.
2 "How American Broadcasts Differ From Foreign Programs" New York Times (Aug 3, 1924) XX15.
3 New York Times (April 19, 1925) XX15.
4 "Public Body May Govern British Ether," New York Times, (Mar 21, 1926) 20.
5 New York Times, (Sep 14, 1926) 27. The full announcement is reproduced in NBC, 1926, 10–12.
6 Goodman and Gring examine the Progressive underpinnings of this legislation (2000).
7 See Mander (1984), Benjamin (2001).
8 NBC reported owning 10 stations in 1939, and managing—providing both network and local programs for—5 more, though these stations were owned by others. See NBC, 1926, 15–16.
9 Brainard to Mr. C. B. Donovan, Acme Apparatus Company, Nov 26, 1926. B2 F3 NBC.
10 Llewellyn White provides an extensive and highly critical analysis of the economics of network operations in his study done for the Commission on Freedom of the Press (1947).
11 Radio Times, "Both Sides—Hail, Columbia!" (Feb 5, 1932) 298.
12 Radio Times, (July 14, 1933) "Both Sides—A l'Americaine"
13 B52 F 25, NBC.
14 Letter Aylesworth to Reith, Dec 18, 1933. B16 F27, NBC.
15 Briggs (1965), 48—quoting Reith's Diary from May 1931.
16 "Radio Differs Across the Sea," New York Times (May 31, 1931) 9.
17 H. L. Mencken, "Radio Programs," The Balitmore Evening Sun, (June 29, 1931).
18 Quoted in Education by Radio (Dec 24, 1931) 156.
19 Memo from Janet Quigley to Mr. Marriott and Miss Reeves, July 8, 1936: "Armstrong Perry is rather a nuisance. His is the rival gang to Levering Tyson's National Advisory Council [in original] on Radio in Education." Memo from Quigley to CPR, January 7, 1936, re Perry's request for rebuttal of Broadcasting article: "The NCER is one of the most fanatical opposers of the present system of broadcasting in America and is inclined to turn everything they can induce us to say into ammunition for their attacks on the commercial broadcasters." E1/197 WAC.
20 These included Gladstone Murray, a native Canadian currently serving as director of public relations for the BBC, Joy Elmer Morgan of NCER, and Lee DeForest, one of US radio's earliest inventors, now a harsh critic of the American system.
21 William Hard, "Europe's Air and Ours," The Atlantic Monthly, (Oct 1932) 499–509.
22 Telegram from Bate to Aylesworth, Jan 10, 1934. B24 F25 NBC.
23 Telegram from Reith to Aylesworth, Jan 12, 1934. B24 F27 NBC.
24 Letter from Aylesworth to Reith, Jan 12, 1934. B24 F27 NBC.
25 See Greene's reports in E1/113/1, WAC.

4 Enormous Changes at the Last Minute

1 Memo Gielgud to DP through ACP, May 12, 1930, "Listeners' Reaction to Programmes". R44/23/1, WAC.
2 Memo from Stobart to Siepmann, May 29, 1930, R44/23/1 WAC.
3 "Report of Programme Revision Committee," 1934, R34/874/2.
4 Another key person in this move, according to Silvey, was A. P. Ryan, later key in the development of the Forces programme, as discussed below (Silvey).
5 "BBC Symphony in Smaller Doses . . ." *Variety* (March 18, 1936) 42.
6 "A memorandum on 'Advertising by Wireless'", March 1932. File 31, NBC/LC. That this unattributed 15 page report was found in NBC's files, though it is obviously written from a British point of view, points to the interest US broadcasters took in the possibilities of British commercial radio. The report lists 14 British firms that had experimented with offshore radio advertising, including Selfridge's Department Store (long known for innovative marketing techniques—see Le Mahieu) and Decca Gramophone Company, making a use of radio at this time forbidden in the US but prescient of later times—to sell popular recorded music.
7 Advertisement from *Advertisers Weekly*, (May 25, 1933) 239. HAT.
8 *Radio Pictorial* (Jan 19, 1934).
9 "Plot to Capture . . .", *Daily Sketch*, (April 9, 1934). B 90 F 61, NBC.
10 Memo Morton to Bate, June 11, 1934. B 91 F 2, NBC.
11 International Broadcasting Company Ltd. "Survey of Radio Advertising Penetration" 1935. The Brian Henry Collection Chronological Notes on UK Television (1949–1987) HAT 31/3/2/3.
12 "£10 a Minute," *Shelf Appeal*, October 1935, p. 24–32. R34/959, WAC.
13 "British Advertisers Clamoring for Commercial Radio Outlets," *Broadcasting* (Dec 1, 1935) 22.
14 *Radio Pictorial* (March 3, 1939) 5. In many ways this is reminiscent of the "border blaster" stations operating in Mexico just over the US border, home to many a broadcasting practice forbidden by FCC regulations. See Fowler and Crawford (1987); Loviglio (2005).
15 The JWT studios were located in Bush House, after 1940 the home of the BBC World Service. Philip M. Taylor (1999) weaves an interesting story in his chapter "Handling the Unavowable: Propaganda and Psychological Warfare, 1935–1940," claiming that the British government itself backed Luxembourg and Wireless Publicity Inc as "a useful part of British 'cultural propaganda', supplementing the more highbrow work of the British Council targeted at elites," (131) even to the extent of possibly paying for the JWT studios in the basement of Bush House. "Did they belong to J. Walter Thompson or to Wireless Publicity Ltd? And who paid for them?" (132) It is certain that after 1940 they were used by the BBC Overseas Service.
16 *Radio Pictorial*, (Feb 10, 1939), back cover, BLN. Two more serials, according to Sean Street, were inspired by US models but created by British producers: *Love in an Attic* and *Marmaduke Brown*, both 1939. Another serial, this time on the adventure model, was *Vic Samson, Special Investigator* (250).
17 He was replaced by Sir Frederick Wolff Ogilvie, who resigned in 1942 to give way to a joint directorship by Sir Cecil Graves and Robert W. Foote.
18 Though transmitted on the Regional network only, against the BBC Symphony on the National.
19 However, it was with Askey's next program, the much-accoladed *It's That Man Again (ITMA)*, that the BBC set out, in Briggs' words, "for the first time deliberately to produce British programmes with American-style quick-fire patter." Their immediate model was the *Burns and Allen Show*. (Briggs (1965) 118)
20 As Cardiff and Scannell state, "The working class had never been integrated into the National Programme before the war. . . . This changed dramatically with the crisis in the summer of 1940" (1986) 98.
21 "A Report on the Variety (Light Entertainment) Listening Barometer October–December 1937—Part II: Light Entertainment 'Foreground' Programmes (Vaudeville, Radio Presentations, Serials, Rough Funny Shows, Sophisticated Shows, Musical Comedy, 'Interest' Programmes, Theatre O.B.'s, and Variety Features)" June 15, 1938. R9/9/1, WAC.
22 Letters to the Editor, *Daily Telegraph* (Mar 8, 10, 1942) BLN.
23 See Taylor, 1999, as well as Briggs (1965).

24 R34/269/1 Policy: Broadcasts for the Fighting Forces—File 1A 1939, WAC.
25 R34/269/1 Policy: Broadcasts for the Fighting Forces—File 1A 1939, WAC.
26 "Report by Controller (Programmes) on the Forces Programme" Jan 1, 1942. R34/269/7, WAC.
27 Quoted in Nicholas (1996) 52.
28 "Report on USA Attitude to European War," Gerald Cock, 1940. E1/103, WAC.
29 Very little historical attention has been paid to this service, which lasted from 1940 to 1961, aside from an article by Peter Spence that focuses on its political origins—though see Potter (2011). Its considerable innovations in broadcasting, as well as its influence on broadcasting practices at the BBC after the war, deserve further research.
30 "BBC Announcement: Afternoon Relays From America," B36 F48, NBC.
31 Letter from John Royal to Richard C. Patterson, 4/12/35. B36 F48, NBC.
32 "Lesson in Timing," *Daily Express*, (Feb 19, 1935) n.p.
33 Letter from Fred Bate to Phillips Carlin, April 2, 1936. B46 F15, NBC.
34 Felix Greene, "Report" 27 December 1935. E1/113/1 File 1, WAC.
35 He would go on to become a documentary filmmaker, whose controversial television documentary *Inside North Vietnam* would have an impact on US public television policy in the 1970s.
36 *Variety* (Feb 9, 1938), 37.
37 Later spoofed, of course, as Alistair Cookie on *The Muppet Show's* parody, "Monsterpiece Theater".
38 Talks—Cooke, Alistair—1931–35. WAC.
39 "The American Half-Hour" No. 2, script. B33 F60, NBC.
40 B33 F60, NBC.
41 Memo from ADPP to DPP Feb 12, 1940. Talks—Cooke, Alistair—1936–40, WAC.
42 Bushnell would return to Canada to take up the post of General Director of Programs of the CBC in 1944, and rise to become Vice President in 1958.
43 "When the first three Controllers of the Light Programme were all taken from the wartime Overseas Services the invasion of domestic broadcasting by Overseas presentation standards was complete." R34/323 "Report by Mr. R. A. Rendall" July 1950, WAC.
44 *Time*, (July 9, 1940).
45 See Gorham (1948) 118.
46 See Camporesi (2000) 140–43.

5 The Politics and Poetics of Neutrality

1 S. J. Woolf, "Corwin Presents – Britain at War" *New York Times* (Aug 2, 1941), SM13.
2 Powell (29) cites an essay by C. M. Jansky, an engineer originally involved with the University of Minnesota's pioneering station and later an advisor to the FRC, in Levering Tyson's collected volume *Radio and Education.* Jansky's essay disputes the notion that commercial interests led in the decline of educational stations; instead, he lays the blame on educators and education departments themselves for failing to take an early and serious interest in the potential of radio in education (Jansky (1932) 216–17).
3 Peters and Simonson (2004). See also Frost (1937).
4 Another key Rockefeller project was the Social Science Research Council, founded in 1923 and controlled by the RF under the direction of Beardsley Ruml. See Fisher (1993).
5 These are most familiar to American readers as college football leagues. The Big 10 includes the significant university radio innovation centers of Wisconsin, Ohio, Indiana, Illinois, Iowa, Minnesota, and Michigan; the Big Seven (now the Big Eight) includes Colorado, Washington, Missouri, Kansas, Oklahoma, and Nebraska. All of these are land-grant institutions, supported by their respective states with a corresponding mission to serve their citizens and state governments. They are the much-overlooked "mini-BBC's" of the US broadcasting experience, though different enough that the comparison is a bit stretched (see Slotten (2006)).
6 Both the Carnegie and Rockefeller organizations have a focus that is international, but it is interesting that both have focused considerable attention to British causes as well as American. Carnegie, an immigrant from Scotland to the US in the 1800s, concentrated on libraries and higher education; he founded the University of Birmingham in 1899.

7 By contrast, state governments found themselves quite comfortable with a system of indirect funding through public universities, supplemented by stations' solicitation of private foundation funds.

8 This is also true in other key areas such as medical research, foreign policy, the foundation of key cultural and arts institutions, and education.

9 The major foundations such as Rockefeller must also be seen as part of the "WASP" Eastern establishment that was pro-British generally and that worked in close relationship in education, politics, arts, and social policy.

10 In 1931 Ruml was instrumental in forming a committee on Pressure Groups and Propaganda, chaired by Harold D. Lasswell and with Robert Lynd as secretary, one of the first of the Chicago-oriented projects that would lead to the institutionalization of communications research in the US. The University of Chicago Round Table grew out of a Rockefeller grant in 1935, as did the Rocky Mountain Radio Council and Cleveland station WBOE. Ruml also provided crucial funding ($7.5 million over ten years) for the Yale Institute of Psychology, founded by Angell at Yale, the precursor of Angell's Institute of Human Relations. One historian has called the IHR a "watershed in the development of the social and behavioral sciences . . . and formation of a technoscientific elite" (Capshew (1999) 143–44).

11 See the Richardson and Fisher volume for an assessment of Ruml's and the Rockefeller Foundation's impact on the field of social science research.

12 *Round Table*'s producer, George Probst, also benefited from training at the BBC and will play a prominent role in the development of US public broadcasting as discussed in the next chapter.

13 See Marshall, "Diary" Aug 36, RAC. Grierson himself had earlier benefited from a Rockefeller Fellowship to study public relations at the University of Chicago in the 1920s.

14 Memo from Graves to Quigley, Aug 28, 1935. E1/303 WAC.

15 P/F E15/198 Staff Visits Abroad—Siepmann, C. A. 1936–37, WAC. Marshall also proposed a plan to fund fellowships to permit American recipients to study radio technique at the BBC's recently-organized staff college. One person to receive such a fellowship was Philip Cohen of the Library of Congress, who will be discussed in the next section. Over the next few years, a goodly number of BBC personnel would take advantage of Rockefeller funding to study American radio as well.

16 Memo from Greene to C(P) Jan 4, 1937, P/F E15/198, WAC.

17 In June of 1937 Felix Greene wrote a letter to John Royal of NBC, proposing Siepmann for a position under the newly-appointed NBC Director of Educational Programming, James Rowland Angell, recently retired from Yale. Apparently Royal had met with Siepmann during his 1937 visit and discussed such a position; Siepmann was most interested. As Greene put it, "He is very strongly attracted to the idea of throwing his lot in with America, though the pulls of security and personal loyalties this side are very powerful." In July, Siepmann in his eagerness wrote directly to Angell, telling him that Royal had suggested bringing him in as Angell's assistant. Angell, unaware of any such arrangement, wrote to Royal to ask how to respond; Royal took offense at Siepmann's presumption and snapped, in a note to Fred Bate (NBC's London representative) "As far as I am concerned, the whole thing is off." (Memo Royal to Bate, Sept 3, 1937, B56 F72, NBC).

18 John Marshall, "Frame for a Picture" 1938, RG 1.1, Series 700, Box 22A F 162C, RAC.

19 Buxton 145, quoting Marshall Oral History, *Interview #9*, note 25, 303, RFA.

20 Indeed, Iris Barry was a former British film critic whose writings for the *Daily Mail* in the 1920s had been influential in championing "quality" Hollywood films while deploring the impact of the "lesser" kind on British culture. See Glancy (2006).

21 Both Brett Gary and William Buxton have provided insightful analyses of these seminars.

22 Letter from Siepmann to Royal, Dec 13, 1939, B72 F47, NBC. Siepmann faced considerable loss of face in Britain for seeming to abandon his country in time of war, but apparently it was a love relationship that prompted it. Siepmann married his American wife that same year.

23 Letter from William Barber, Educational Director, W1XAL to BBC, Jan 2, 1935. E1/303 WAC.

24 "Quicker Fox," *Time*, (July 11, 1938).

25 "Worldwide Broadcasting Station," *Education by Radio* 5:15 (Nov 7, 1935) 1.

26 "W1XAL is, from what he told me, very likely to be able to be of considerable help, including financial help, to us in relaying programmes – feature programmes and conceivably some talks – from America." Memo IDB to CP, 6 Aug 1937. E1/303, WAC.

27 Memo from Miss Reeves to Mr. Macgregor, MOI Jan 10, 1940. E1/303, WAC. Reeves also notes a putative connection between WRUL and the Christian Science Church; interestingly, the British Ambassador to the US during this period, Lord Lothian, who aggressively pushed for propaganda plans in America, was a member of the Christian Science faith as well—a belief that may have contributed to his sudden death in December 1940.
28 Telegram sent from Ogilvie to Cock, 29 April 1941. E1/299, WAC
29 Written at Stephenson's behest by former subordinates Ronald Highet, Tom Hill and Roald Dahl, known now for his children's books. Twenty copies were run off in Canada, though only a few survive. It was published with a foreword by Nigel West in 1998, though much of it appeared verbatim in Hartford Montgomery Hyde's biography of Stephenson, *The Quiet Canadian,* in 1962.
30 Telegram Aug 1 1940 from Gerald Cock to Tallents. E1/246, WAC.
31 It is hard to know why this particular episode has received so little attention over the ten years since the BSC report was published. William Boyd speculates in its most recent outcropping in the *Guardian* that the idea of British secret services propagandizing the American public seems inconsequential since most Americans believe the British were right about the need for the US to enter the war, and WWII still enjoys its historical reputation as the "good war," unlike the state of affairs following WWI.
32 Draft Letter of Instructions, Sir Walter Monckton to Mr. R. E. L. Wellington, BBC April 16, 1941. E1/299, WAC.
33 Letter from Ogilvie to Wellington, May 6, 1941. Ibid. WAC.
34 Letter from Wellington to Ogilvie, June 30, 1941, Ibid.
35 Letter from McCarty to WHA staff, Mar 30, 1943, B57 F "OWI Memos 1943", McCarty.
36 By war's end he was deputy director of the OWI's San Francisco Office "responsible for broadcast propaganda to Japan, to China, and to Japanese occupied territories" (Siepmann resume, April 12, 1965, B95 F5 NAEB).
37 Letter from Siepmann to McCarty, Dec 26, 1945. B 80 F "C. A. Siepmann", McCarty.
38 Damrosch began his radio career with a series of highly successful concert/lectures in 1926 under the sponsorship of the Fansteel Corporation, makers of Balkite radios, on NBC's Red network. The concerts continued under RCA's own sponsorship on Saturday evenings on Red, the more commercial and less public-service oriented of NBC's two networks, but switched to the Blue network in 1929. Damrosch himself became a member of NBC's Advisory Council in 1927, serving also as the network's music advisor.
39 During the networks' first decade, the number of "concert music" programs—ranging from symphonies to band and choir performances—held fairly steady at about 26 weekly half-hour evening programs (with 5 or 6 more during the day) from 1928 to 1938, then declined slightly during the war years. About half were sponsored, and half sustaining (Summers (1993)).
40 Letter from Fred Bate to John Royal, Mar 31, 1939, B 66 F56, NBC.
41 Earlier, in 1937 producer Roger Wilson of the BBC Manchester regional station visited the US, admired *The Chicago Round Table,* and came back with the idea to "'use the idea better' than the Americans had done, in the North Region." Two short series, *Why Do You Believe That?* and *Public Enquiry,* used a live audience to ask questions of two speakers in a way rarely done on British air at the time. According to Briggs, "This programme was so successful . . . that it was due to be included in the National programme in the autumn of 1939. War, of course, intervened." (Briggs (1965) 151) *Freedom Forum* itself was considered "too inflammatory for home consumption" during the war years, according to Peter Spence (1982, 367).
42 This tradition would be taken up in the post-war years by British producers like Charles Parker and Ewan MacColl, though the indisputable influence of the pre-war and wartime broadcasters traced here, in both Britain and the US, has been neglected. See Long (2004); Madsen (2005).
43 Batten, Barton, Durstine, and Osborne.
44 This feature was not only repeated several times on British airwaves, but was used for many years as an exemplar of the height of what radio could achieve by the BBC Staff College in the late 1930s and 40s.
45 It is a shame that later works on the British tradition of television drama do not credit radio producers like Shapely and Bridson with pioneering many of the techniques and genres later carried over onto TV. John Caughie's account, for instance, makes mention of Charles Parker

and Ewan McColl, but both of these important radio docu-dramatists were influenced by Shapely and Bridson, and by American radio innovators like Corwin and Lomax as well.

46 And also to the new technique of actuality recording on film; Street reports that Manchester most likely possessed one of the Philips-Miller sound on film systems (Sean Street (2006) 131). See below under the Library of Congress Radio Project.

47 Reproduced in Barnouw (1968) 63–64; Barnouw also astutely places this new post in the context of the network's desire to win back control over programming from sponsors.

48 However, the prestige and high budget of the show meant that most shows were recorded as they were broadcast, for posterity as well as for wider distribution and for replay; many are available today.

49 "Where the Play's the Thing," *New York Times,* (Aug 15, 1937) 38.

50 See also Val Gielgud, (1957) 69.

51 Wylie is not entirely accurate—documentary programs had featured on US schedules for years and the BBC made only very limited use of non-scripted actuality—but he seems to be referring specifically to its new incarnation in the form of the public service drama/feature production traced here. See also the claims of D. G. Bridson, below.

52 Richard O'Brien, "A Cradle of Drama," *New York Times* (July 30, 1939) X10.

53 However, though the BBC was willing to air programs about unemployment in the US that American networks eschewed, it was not anxious to produce similar programs about unemployment in Britain, as D. G. Bridson complained (Bridson (1971) 93).

54 At the time of this writing Norman Corwin is still alive and living in California. His own website has an excellent chronology of his career, complete with audio clips: http://www.normancorwin.com/Classic.html

55 This was a fairly common format on US radio; one of its earliest and longest-running exemplars was NBC's "Cheerio" (1925–40), though Corwin's version was distinctly more highbrow.

56 In one of history's strange coincidences, Houseman had spent several years of his boyhood in the household of the Siepmann family; he counted Charles Siepmann and his brother Eric as his oldest friends. (Houseman (1972) 18–19).

57 See Hilmes (1997) for a more extensive account of *The Mercury Theater on the Air;* also see Heyer (2005).

58 These quotes are taken from Gevinson (2002, 99) who quotes from the original grant application in the Papers of the Radio Research Project (RRP), Library of Congress.

59 Another precedent for the LOC drama/documentary project was the series of recordings made by John Lomax, called *The Ballad Hunter,* which mixed recordings of folk songs performed by ordinary people in their home environments, along with bits of dialogue as they explain themselves and their music, arranged and narrated by Lomax (Cohen 1941). The LOC marketed them as a transcription series to radio stations in 1941 (*Time Magazine,* "Ballad Hunter," July 7, 1941).

60 Gevinson, p 103, quoting MacLeish, RRP, LC.

61 Quoted in Gevinson (2002) 118.

62 From a document reproduced in Gevinson (2002) 114, from a 1941 report on the project.

63 See http://www.radiomuseum.org/forum/philips_the_philips_miller_audio_recording_system. html. This tape was known as "Philimil" or the "Philips-Miller system" in Europe, where it was distributed through the Phillips Company in Eindhoven, Holland. See Sean Street (2006) 127–33. An article in *Time* magazine ("Miller's Way," March 13, 1939) claims that it was used in 1939 for "cutting the hour-long Ironized Yeast Good Will Hour into half-hour (2,000 foot) recordings for transmission from 46 local stations in the U.S. and Canada." A *Newsweek* article claims that its first use was on station WQXR on August 26, 1938 ("Transmission by Tape: N.Y. Station Uses Innovation for the First Time in America," September 26, 1938, p. 27). See also David Morton (2000), especially Chapter 2, "The End of the 'Canned Music' Debate in American Broadcasting" 48–73.

64 Both these transcriptions and some of the original recordings from which the programs were made have been preserved can still be heard at the Library of Congress; see http://www.loc. gov/folklife/guides/Radio.html as well as the listing for the *This Is History!* recordings in the LOC's SONIC catalogue of recorded sound. Though the LOC first released this series of six programs on disc in 1942 under the title *Americans Talk Back,* it is the OWI re-release of the series under the title *This Is History!* that still exists in the LOC Recorded Sound Collection.

6 In It Together: Wartime Radio

1　Previously he had served as assistant director of the Institute of International Education, a Rockefeller and Carnegie-sponsored organization that encouraged international exchange. He worked specifically with the Emergency Committee to Aid Displaced German Scholars, finding teaching and research positions for European refugee intellectuals—excellent connections for a "Talks" director.

2　Roger Eckersley, "Report on the year's work of the American unit, BBC" 1940. R61/46 WAC.

3　Amongst these were Mary Marvin Breckinridge, Dorothy Thompson, and Janet Flanner.

4　Julian relates the story that Corwin's opening sentences, meant to evoke the atmosphere of shortwave exchange— "Hello? . . . Hello? . . . What's the matter with this line?" (followed by brief silence)—was so successful that NBC engineers assumed the transmission was having real difficulties and dropped it (Julian (1975) 86).

5　*New York Times* (Feb 14, 1943) X9.

6　"People to People, *Time* (Mar 22, 1943) 65.

7　"Radio: An Englishman Looks at the U.S." *Time* (Jan 23, 1944) 32.

8　Letter from Stephen Fry to Warren Macalpine, Jan 31, 1945, E1/110 "Counties-America— Programme Exchange" 1936–50. WAC.

9　Memo from Pelletier to DES (Rendall), Jan 15, 1941. R45/30, WAC.

10　See Paul Long for a perceptive critique of this tradition in the work of Charles Parker, a later radio documentarist known for his "radio ballads."

11　Hilmes (2007a).

12　Quoted in Stursberg (1971) 94.

13　Elise Sprott discusses BBC programs for women in Sprott (1938): confined to one hour a day, devoted to instructional material.

14　Memo from Gilliam to PO(F) May 16, 1941 "Front Line Family", R19/1047/1a, WAC.

15　Mrs. Ronnie Colley, "Background Material for Subsequent Synopsis on "Front Line Family" Oct 23, 1941, R19/1047/1a, WAC.

16　Memo from DFD (Gielgud) to ADF (Gilliam) Dec 11 41, R19/1047/1a, WAC.

17　It should be pointed out as well that with the entry of the US into the war in early December, reaching an American audience was no longer of the highest priority for the series.

18　Memo from AD Features (Laurence Gilliam) to DEP (S. J. de Lotbiniere) "Front Line Family" 4 February 1942, R19/1047/1a, WAC.

19　Ironically, the program was never rebroadcast on an established US network because of its status as a recording—recorded programs had long been regarded as a violation of public service standards in the US and networks prided themselves on their all-live schedules. This, along with the FLF's awkward generic status—a "nighttime" show in a "daytime" format— kept it from reaching more than the tiny fraction of US listeners who sought out BBC programs via shortwave, or lived near the Canadian border.

20　Quoted on the bookflap of Jonquil Antony and Lesley Wilson, *More About the Robinson Family*, a book continuing the story of the serial published "by arrangement with the BBC" in 1948 (London: A & E Publishers).

21　Memo from Davenport to DEP (Lotbiniere), May 11, 1942, R/19/1047/1b, WAC.

22　"Audience Research Unit—Programme Reaction Report—Front Line Family" August 28, 1942. R19/1047/1b, WAC.

23　Memo from DFD (Gielgud) to AC (CS), NASD (Gorham) May 8, 1942, R19/1047/1b. In a handwritten note at the bottom, Gorham has scrawled: "Davenport's memo seems to answer DFD's question so I shall not need to challenge his claim to 'quite normal human experience.'"

24　Memo COS (Clark) to CP 2 May 43, R19/1047/1b, WAC.

25　"Stumpers Across the Sea," *Time* (February 12, 1945) n.p.

26　Memo Royal to Mullen, Mar 31, 1943; letter Trammell to Mullen, Oct 25, 1943; letter Hedges to Kirby, Nov 4, 1943. Box 114 F18, NBC.

27　R34/907/1, WAC. Quoted in P. Morley (2001) 14.

28　See P. Morley (2001) and Kirby and Harris (1948). For an excellent history of the AFRS, see Brylawski (1985).

29　Memo from Laurence Gilliam (Assistant Director Features) to ADT "Programmes for American Troops in England" Aug 10, 1942. R34/913, WAC.

30　*Variety* (May 19, 1943) 31.

31 "British Study Shift to American Plan," *Broadcasting*, (Sept 6, 1943) 1.
32 For a more extended discussion, see Baade (2011).

Part 2 Conclusion: Post-War Visions

1 Memo from DG to C(N), C(H), C(P), C(Eur.S), A/C(O.E), 26 Jan 1945 "Americansation." R34/420, WAC.
2 All in R34/578/1 Policy—post War Planning—General, 1942–44. WAC.
3 *Broadcasting* (Mar 27, 1944) 40.
4 *Broadcasting* (Sept 18, 1944) 28.
5 *Broadcasting* (July 24, 1944) 16.

Part 3 Television, Trade, and Transculturation, 1946–1975

1 Letter from George Barnes to Robert M. Hutchins, Mar 6, 1951. T8/88/2, WAC.
2 Extracts from speeches by Mr. J. Arthur Rank—Note by the secretary—Nov 15, 1946. HO 258/31, Kew.
3 *Business Week*, (Nov 24, 1956).

7 Disentangling and Differentiation, 1946–1955

1 John Chabot Smith, "Britain's Bid to Rule the Air Waves," *The Saturday Evening Post* 219 (Nov 16, 1946) 32+.
2 HO256/426 (BB/90/03/II), Kew.
3 P/F E15/220 "Staff Visits Abroad—Waldman, Ronald, 1949–1953" WAC.
4 The reform and restructuring of broadcasting systems in the defeated Axis nations took place as a high priority, guided variously by the US, Britain, and the Soviet Union. As newly independent nations emerged after the war, an ironic aspect of the process is that broadcasting systems often remained patterned closely after the structures of the former colonial power (see Oren (2004)). In much of Latin America, where state broadcasting had achieved a tenuous foothold in many countries during the war years, renewed commercial interest on the part of American advertisers and networks sustained a dual system (McCann).
5 *Broadcasting* (July 24, 1944) 16.
6 *Broadcasting* (September 3, 1945) 17.
7 Memo William S. Hedges to Management Committee, "Two Year Forecasts" Sept 26,1945. B114 F80, NBC.
8 "Dissenter Durr," *Newsweek* June 24, 1946, 42.
9 See Sterling (2007) for a succinct summary of the FCC network inquiry.
10 Smythe would later achieve considerable recognition as a communications scholar—see Smythe (1981).
11 Interview with Clifford Durr, December 29, 1974. Interview B-0017. Southern Oral History Program Collection (#4007). http://docsouth.unc.edu/sohp/B-0017/B-0017.html.
12 Interview, p. 27.
13 See Pickard (2011) for an analysis of the Blue Book's history and significance.
14 Robert K. Richards, "BBC Expert Probes Procedure for FCC," *Broadcasting* (July 30, 1945) 16.
15 Robert K. Richards, "Seipmann Finds Flaws in US Radio" *Broadcasting* (Aug 6, 1945) 20.
16 "The Great Program Hoax," *Broadcasting* (August 13, 1945) 42.
17 Editorial, "Straws in the Air," *Broadcasting* (Nov 19, 1945) 56.
18 "F(ederal) C(ensorship) C(omission)", *Broadcasting* (Mar 18, 1946) 58.
19 *Variety*, advertisement (March 27, 1946) 33.
20 From an interview with Seipmann conducted in December 1960 by Richard J. Meyer. His two articles on the Blue Book and its reception appeared in the *Journal of Broadcasting* in 1962. See also Berkman (1985) and Dell (1997).
21 "Editorial," *Broadcasting* (June 17, 1946) 52.
22 "Freer BBC Desired," *Broadcasting* (April 15, 1946) 82.

23 James, E. H. "BBC May Consider Going Commercial" *Broadcasting* (April 22, 1946) 46.
24 "Editorial" (June 17, 1946) 52.
25 Edward Brecher, however, published a widely read explanation and defense of the report in *The Atlantic Monthly* in August 1946 (Brecher (1946)).
26 However, there was certainly a strong movement in the US itself against soaps, led by "women's groups", as Kathy Newman (2004) and Jennifer Hyland Wang (2002) have demonstrated.
27 Quoted in "The Revolt Against Radio" *Fortune* 35 (Mar 1947) 100+.
28 Other titles examined the movies, government and mass communications, international communications, and basic principles (see Commission on Freedom of the Press). A reviewer in 1948 noted that Ruth Inglis's volume on the movies never mentioned what might have seemed, to a Commission on the Press, a particularly relevant category of films: the newsreels—at a moment when the *March of Time* series, owned by the Commission's major benefactor, was at its height of influence.
29 Jack Gould, "Matter of Credit," *New York Times* (April 18, 1948) 25.
30 H. L. Mencken, Letter to the editors, *Fortune* 35 (April 1947) 29.
31 Bob Musel, "BBC Faces Prestige Loss," *Variety* (May 19, 1943) 31.
32 "British Advertisers Disclose Desire to Employ Radio on Commercial Basis," *Broadcasting* (Sept 18, 1944) 28.
33 "A Plan for Broadcasting – I" *The Economist* (Oct 28, 1944) 564–65
34 "A Plan for Broadcasting – II" *The Economist* (Nov 4, 1944) 597–98. Coase analyzes this series of articles at length.
35 Sir Frederic Ogilvie, "Future of the BBC" *Times* (June 26, 1946) 5.
36 For a detailed recounting of the Parliamentary and press debates during this period, see H. Wilson (1961).
37 Hudson (1951) 237.
38 Memo from Pelletier to BBC management, Nov 14, 1952. E1/194/2 WAC.
39 "University Radio Stations in the USA," report from NASD (MacAlpine) to C(OS), Sept 18, 1946. E1/150/1, WAC.
40 Letter from Wilbur Schramm to Richard B. Hull, May 18, 1949. B39 F5 NAEB.
41 Quoted in "Export of United Kingdom Television Material to Canada" Draft report by BT Jan 55. HO (BB90/06) Overseas Television Service—Export of TV Material—Solicitors Advice, Kew.
42 "Establishment of Overseas Television Service" Oct 22, 1953. HO256/426 (BB/90/03/II) Overseas Television Service—BBC Proposals, Kew. Though no author is given for this report, it may very well have stemmed from the efforts of Hugh Carleton Green, then Assistant Controller of the Overseas Service, who wrote an essay making a very similar argument in the *BBC Quarterly* in Spring 1953.
43 See Kaye (2007) for an explanation of the negotiations and maneuvering between these parties between 1954 and 1964, when the Central Office of Information (COI) decisively took over.
44 "Third Report—NAEB Advisory Committee to the President of the Educational Television and Radio Center," August 7, 1953. B50 F2 NAEB.
45 Though it has been well-traced by historians; see Saunders (1999) and McCarthy (1987).
46 Other officers of the Ford Foundation who had served the Marshall Plan included Waldemar Nielsen, Milton Katz, Richard Bissell, and Shepard Stone (Schwoch (2008) 62).
47 See Saunders (1999), in particular, for a highly personalized account of these dense networks of interrelationships.
48 Encyclopedia Britannica Films grew out of a joint venture by the University of Chicago and Electrical Research Products, Inc. (ERPI) educational films division, which merged under the direction of Robert Hutchins in 1943; ERPI had been a leader in the development of educational sound films since 1929.
49 "Benton, William," *Current Biography*, 1945.
50 Carlson (1968) 135.
51 Memo from H. Rooney Pelletier, November 14, 1952. E1/194/2.
52 "Ivory Towers Sound," *Broadcasting-Telecasting* (Oct 6, 1952).
53 "NAEB's Bill Harley, Statesman in a Pivotal Period for Pubcasting" *Current* (Nov 23, 1998).
54 Charles Parker, "The Wisconsin State Broadcasting Service," June 28, 1953. E15/3, WAC.

55   Memo from Hugh Carleton Green, Assistant Controller, BBC Overseas Services to Graydon Ausmus, President, NAEB, July 10, 1953. B23 F7, NAEB.

56   Later, Basil Thornton blamed Graydon Ausmus, the Alabama-based director of the NAEB, for this: "It may be remembered that we had all but fixed a grant from the Ford Foundation of $100,000 for Third Program broadcasting material to be made available to the NAEB, but Ausmus sabotaged the operation." Letter Thornton to Donald Stephenson, Aug 24, 1962. 9/7/7, NET.

57   Letter from Val Gielgud to Robert Barr Sept 17, 1952, Letter to Barr from Gielgud Sept 25, 1952. E1/194/2, WAC.

58   Letter H. Newburn to George Barnes, June 24, 1954. 8B/3/3, NET.

59   John Crosby, "No Place Else on Television" (Aug 26, 1952) n.p.

60   Not to mention the "othering" of non-white culture, exhibited both in what one review called "the primitive dance of the voodoo ritual" (Gould, New York Times, Nov 16, 1952) and in Gilbert and Sullivan's Mikado.

61   In the course of his defense, it is Welch who directed the famous plaint at McCarthy: "You've done enough. Have you no sense of decency, sir? At long last, have you left no sense of decency?"

62   Memo William S. Hedges to Frank White, Feb 27, 1953. B582 F47, NBC.

63   Including Willys-Overland, Greyhound, Remington Rand, Scott Paper, Union Carbide, and American Machine & Foundry.

64   Jack Gould, "Weaver, Saudek Making TV Plans." New York Times (Feb 25, 1957) 47.

65   Val Adams, "News and Notes of TV and Radio: 'Omnibus'" New York Times (Nov 20, 1960) 19.

66   Gould, quoted in Macdonald (1956) 91.

8 New Directions and Disputes, 1955–1964

1   Jonah Barrington, "Coronation Kicks for toothpaste TV" Daily Sketch, June 8, 1953, 11, BLN.

2   Josephine Ripley, "Age of Kings," Christian Science Monitor (Dec 12, 1961) 32.

3   "Finescriber—Coronation" B580 F 30, NBC

4   Ibid.

5   See Freedman (1999) and H. Wilson (1961) for a full account of this process.

6   An account of this whole process was later published by the BBC as a book, "The Year That Made the Day," 1954.

7   "Television Plans for Coronation," Times (May 6, 1953) 4.

8   "U.S. Broadcasts of Coronation," Times (June 9, 1953) 6.

9   Letter from Romney Wheeler to Warren MacAlpine (Feb 18, 1953). B279 F44, NBC.

10   Memo Mort Werner to Sydney Eiges, "Today's Coronation Coverage", June 2, 1953. B164 F 10, NBC.

11   Kudner Agency, "TV Commercial Sponsor Identification Lines for Both TV Film Programs" May 14, 1953. B279 F44, NBC.

12   "Finescriber—Coronation" B580 F30 NBC.

13   Larry Wolters, "Television News and Views," Chicago Tribune (June 3, 1953) 22; Val Adams, "The Coronation Ceremonies on TV and Radio," New York Times (May 31, 1953) 9.

14   "Canada's Network First to Get Films," New York Times (June 3, 1953) 16.

15   "Finescriber—Coronation" B580 F30 NBC.

16   Display ad 57, New York Times, (June 3, 1953) 64.

17   Display ad 10, New York Times, (June 3, 1953) 12.

18   Display ad 35, New York Times, (June 3, 1953) 35.

19   Jack Gould, "Coronation Marks Birth of World TV", New York Times (June 3, 1953) 46.

20   Quoted in H. Wilson (1961) 156–57.

21   Jack Gould, "Coronation on Video" New York Times (June 7, 1953) 9.

22   "Queen Insulted by Coronation TV, Say British" Chicago Daily Tribune (June 7, 1953) 6.

23   It was only an audio version of the coronation that NBC's Today show was able to air at this early point in the day. Since the TV footage had not yet arrived, NBC's Today Show, with J. Fred Muggs the chimp as Dave Garroway's comic sidekick, went out as usual, occasionally airing an audio clip or two accompanied by stills.

24 "Informal Protest Reported," *New York Times* (June 8, 1953) 12.
25 "BBC Protests to Americans" *Daily Express* (June 8, 1953) 1, BLN.
26 Jonah Barrington, "Coronation Kicks for toothpaste TV" *Daily Sketch*, (June 8, 1953) 11, BLN.
27 B580 F30 "Fineschriber—Coronation—1953"
28 "That TV Row: BBC Say 'We Have Proof'" *Daily Mail* (June 9, 1953) 1, BLN. ABC, meantime, came out smelling like a rose in its decision to simply run the CBC's non-commercial footage.
29 "The TV Threat," *Daily Herald*, (June 8, 1953) 4, BLN.
30 *Variety* (June 10, 1953) 23.
31 Alan Dick, "This is Plug-TV" *Daily Herald* (June 10, 1953) 4, BLN.
32 "The TV Threat" ibid.
33 "An Ape Intervenes," *Time* (July 13, 1953) 90.
34 "A selection of materials on Britain's Coronation" B137 F8, NBC.
35 "The Great TV Row" *Daily Mail* (June 8, 1953) 1+, BLN.
36 "US Coronation TV in British Politics," *New York Times* (June 14, 1953) 32.
37 Memo William R. McAndrew to William H. Fineschriber, June 12, 1953. B580 F30, NBC.
38 Letter from Romney Wheeler to Davidson Taylor, July 2, 1953. B279 F16, NBC.
39 Letter from George Barnes to Davidson Taylor, July 20, 1953, B278 F59, NBC. However, the Corporation did take the precaution in September of employing Charles Siepmann to prepare a "Collection and Analysis of Prevailing Criticisms of Television Programming" in US newspapers and journals from 1950 to 1953, which bears a notation on the cover "Please keep the fact we have this confidential." T8/88/3, WAC. Clearly the BBC wanted to be able to marshall anti-commercial arguments in the coming months while maintaining a façade of impartiality.
40 "Plugged TV: the crowning insult" *Daily Herald* June 11, 1953, 2, BLN.
41 *Manchester Guardian*, Nov 17, 1953, 6.
42 *Manchester Guardian*, Nov 24, 1953, 8.
43 "Letter from London," *The New Yorker* Dec 21, 1953, 160.
44 "Peers' Ire Vented at Commercial TV" *New York Times*, Nov 26, 1953, 24.
45 Memo Aubrey Singer to CP Tel, "Situation Comedy, Dramatic and Documentary Film Series," March 4, 1955. R125/1, 002/1.
46 For the US case, see Boddy (1990) and Hilmes (1990). In the British case, a BBC document from 1946 tells the story: "With or without advertising, the type of television programmes produced by the film industry would tend to be of a lower standard than that of the public Television Service. The standard of film entertainment is already generally regarded as being lower ethically and socially than that of BBC broadcasts, and the same factors would apply to television programmes produced by the film industry . . . BBC television has no interest whatever in harming the films; the film industry has every incentive of profit and self-interest to kill the public Television Service." ("Television and the Cinema—note by the BBC" Oct 18, 1946. HO 258/31 Kew).
47 Conversely, television's episodic schedule gave filmed narratives the chance to develop over time and across narrative variations in a way rarely possible in theatrical cinema. See Hilmes (2011).
48 Report on "West Coast Television" from Sam J. Slate to Norman Luker, April 26, 1949. T8/88/1, WAC.
49 I am indebted throughout this section to the pioneering research of Steven Neale, whose several publications on Sapphire and other production companies of this period are greatly illuminating of the complex issues involved.
50 Linda Gross, "She Battles for Minorities," *LA Times* (Jul 28, 1977) 14.
51 ATV at first allied itself with an American distributor, the Jack Wrather Organization, to serve as its arm in the US and the rest of North and South America. In 1960 ATV purchased the company (Tankel (1984) 139).
52 Board of Trade, "Production of Television Films in the United Kingdom" Nov 2, 1953. HO256/426 (BB/90/03/II). Kew. They were listed with the number of titles currently in production: "Merton Park Studios (3), Busby and Meyer (3), Rayant Pictures (1 for NBC; series under discussion), Vandyke Picture Corporation (4), Max Bygraves (1 or more), James Mason (ditto), Joel Riordan (ditto), Danziger Brothers (2 series and 2 films), Derick Williams Productions (26 short thrillers), Douglas Fairbanks Ltd. (39 films), Gilbert Church (13),

Anthony Beauchamp (8), Harold Webber Television Varieties Inc., High Definition Films Ltd. (1 series)."

53 See Tankel (1984), who upholds Towers as the original genius behind British television exports.

54 Paper No. 78, ITA Memorandum (Review Paper XII) (October 1960) From Tankel (1984) 212–124.

55 Ibid.

56 William H. Stringer, "State of the Nations: TV In, Big Sponsors Out?" *Christian Science Monitor* (Oct 31, 1959) 1.

57 "Report of the CBS Special Committee" March 3, 1959. Box 1 F 25, Mickelson.

58 Richard Austin Smith, "TV: The Coming Showdown," *Fortune* (Sept 1953) 138+.

59 Alfred J. Jaffe, "Are Agencies Earning Their 15% on Net TV Shows," *Sponsor* (Oct 18, 1954) 29+.

60 L. Marsland Gander, "Quiz Shows in Britain," *New York Times* (Nov 22, 1959) 43.

61 Richard Austin Smith, "Television: The Light That Failed," *Fortune* 60 (Dec 1958) 96+.

62 Memo from Kaemmerle to Stanley, Sept 25, 1956. B339 F2, NBC.

63 Memo on American Scene, nd. B339 F2, NBC.

64 Letter from White to Stanley, Nov 30 1959. B338 F69, NBC. Someone at NBC penciled "wrong" in the margin next to these allegations. Stanley and NBC had already struck off on their own with a grant from the Ford Foundation to produce *Continental Classroom,* a instructional program giving college credit across a number of subjects from 1957 through 1963, broadcast at 6:30 am each morning—a time much less likely to be pre-empted for commercial programming.

65 Walter Lippman, "The TV Problem," *New York Herald Tribune* (Oct 27, 1959).

66 William H. Stringer, "State of the Nations: TV In, Big Sponsors Out?" *Christian Science Monitor* (Oct 31, 1959) 1.

67 "TV Blows a Fuse," *Fortune* (December 1959) 96+.

68 "Is British-type TV right for US?" *Sponsor* (Dec 12, 1959) 41+.

69 "Report of CBS Special Committee," March 3, 1959, 21. Box 1 F 25, Mickelson.

70 "Magazine Concept a Panacea For Program Evils? Hardly" *Variety* (Nov 25, 1959) 34.

71 Memo from Russell to Clark, "NBC and a 'Fourth Network'" Jan 8, 1960, E1/1568/1, WAC.

72 Few noted that the BBC's top-rated show, *Juke Box Jury,* was an adaptation of an American program as well; by 1962, when the BBC began to fight business seriously, it used *Wagon Train* to put it over the top. ITV had also adopted American-style scheduling techniques (Sendall I 325)—placing the same programs in the same time slots each week—in contrast with early BBC TV; eventually the BBC adopted the same practices.

73 BBC press release, "Education in Broadcasting" Mar 7, 1961. 9/7/6, NET.

74 The subject of education within the BBC's remit would lead eventually it its collaboration with the Open University beginning in the late 1960s, a subject Briggs traces in some detail in Volume 5 of his history.

75 Letter Bartley to Thornton, June 28, 1960. 9/7/1, NET.

76 Letter Wedell to Thornton, Nov 24, 1960. 9/6/7, NET.

77 Letter Bessborough to White, Jan 17, 1962, 9/6/6; Letter Thornton to Greene, 21 Feb 1962; letter Greene to Thornton Feb 23, 1962, 9/7/7, NET.

78 "Decommercialisation," *Guardian,* (June 28, 1962) 8.

79 Gunn (1965) 48.

80 Donald Mainwaring, "BBC Courting U. S. Clients," *Christian Science Monitor* (21 May 1963) n.p. 8/3/5, NET.

81 Pamphlet, "BBC Transcriptions in the U.S.A." @ July 1956. B23 F8, NAEB.

82 "Renaissance in Communication: An Outline of the Broadcasting Foundation of America, Its Background and Purposes," January 1956. 9/1/10, NET.

83 Brochure, Broadcasting Foundation of America, n.d. @ 1958. 8B/4/1, NET.

84 John Marshall, Interview with Seymour Siegel, January 5, 1957. RF RG 1.2 Series 200R, Box 299, Folder 2797, RFA

85 Ibid.

86 Brochure, Broadcasting Foundation of America, n.d. @ 1958. 8B/4/1, NET. They were also the only recordings for which non-profit stations had to pay: "a modest charge of $1.75 a 12" LP is made, payable directly to the BBC."

87 Letter from Robert B Hudson, Program Coordinator, to Hugh Carleton Greene, Dec. 16, 1954. 8b/3/3, NET.
88 Letter Hudson to Thornton, June 22, 1955. 8B/3/3, NET.
89 Letter from Miall to Newburn July 20, 1956. 8B/3/4, NET.
90 Letter from Cyril Connor to Robert Hudson, Sept 25, 1957. 9/7/5, NET.
91 Memo Hudson to Program File, ETRC, June 9, 1958. 8B/3/4, NET.
92 Letter from Thornton to Donald Stephenson, Aug 24, 1962. 9/7/7/, NET.
93 Somewhat confusingly, the BFA maintained its radio distribution services to NAEB stations, even as it ventured into television under the NET's new mandate.
94 "World's Biggest TV Program Centre Opens June 29," BBC press release June 22, 1960. 8B/3/5, NET.
95 "The General Overseas Service of the BBC", September 1959, E2/803/2, as quoted in Briggs (1995) 691–92.
96 Scuse to Donley F. Fedderson, NETRC, July 9, 1962. 8B/3/5, NET.
97 Memo Waldman to D. Tel., Oct 12,1962. R125/1/1, WAC.
98 Ibid.
99 Ibid.
100 Ibid.
101 Letter from White to del Strother, March 21, 1961, 9/7/6, NET.
102 Letter from del Strother to White, Feb 1, 1961; letter from White to del Strother, March 21, 1961; Memo from Don Feddersen to Gene Alienikoff and Basil Thornton, Aug 18, 1961; Memo Alienikoff to Feddersen Aug 21, 1961. 9/7/6, NET.
103 Because the BBC had already sold rights to NETRC, they had to request that NETRC relinquish its rights in order to make the sale to the New York and LA stations, markets in which no educational station existed. Standard Oil sponsored the program. NET 8C/6/8.
104 Letter Scuse to White, Jan 3, 1961. 8C/6/8/, NET.
105 Budget, March 14, 1962, 8C/6/8, NET.
106 Thornton to White and Kraetzer, Feb 26, 1963. 8B/3/5, NET.
107 Memo Fedderson to Program Managers, May 27, 1963 9/3/5, NET.
108 Donald Mainwaring, "BBC Courting US Clients" *Christian Science Monitor*, May 21, 1963. n.p. 8B/3/5, NET.
109 Letter Bartley to Thornton, Nov 6, 1960. 8B/2/5, NET.
110 Westinghouse had long been the sponsor of CBS's acclaimed live anthology drama program, *Studio One*. With the decline of live drama, Westinghouse had been squeezed out of that program in 1959. Owner of five powerful stations, Westinghouse needed not only high-profile programming to provide to its stations, but public service credits as well.
111 Richard F. Shepard, "INTERTEL: One Year of Progress." *New York Times* May 27, 1962, 13.
112 *Intertel*, n.d. @ 1963. 8H/1/7, NET.
113 8H/1/7, NET.
114 Letter Gayler to Hudson, June 14, 62. NET 8C/39/1.
115 *New York Times* (May 27, 1962).
116 Letter Leiterman to Hudson, Jan 15, 1961. 8H/1/5, NET. See also Bluem, 234–39.
117 Associated-Rediffusion, "Research Report—INTERTEL Programmes" n.d. 8C/38/3, NET.
118 As in European broadcasting more generally; see Bourdon (2004).

9 Transatlantic Partnerships, 1964–1975

1 The 1974 report estimated total US export sales at between 100,000 and 200,000 hours annually, with the BBC at approximately 60,000 hours, counting all US stations separately. About half of the BBC's export hours went to the US; only about 10–15% of US export hours went to Britain, but Britain had become the single largest national importer of US programs, and furthermore, as the report notes, "London has been one centre for American penetration into Europe, and still holds its position as a centre of American distribution of both programmes and news material to Europe." (23)
2 With the implementation of the fin/syn rules, all three major networks had spun off their distribution arms.

3 I diverge from Hjort's general definition of the transnational by including works that, while produced in one cultural context, are distributed and viewed in another. These might simply be considered "foreign" films or television programs, but within broadcasting's distinctly national discourse, I argue, along with Jeffrey Miller, that imported programs are rendered effectively transnational—relating in some distinct way both to the host culture and the originating culture—by their placement within television's highly national context. Though I suspect Hjort would disagree with me, I would argue that Hollywood-style American films, television, and music often function as effectively transnational in this sense, across many national contexts. Here, again (as in the Introduction) we are talking about transnationalism understood as relating to *reception* practices and contexts as well as production.

4 Along these lines, Lealand's 1984 survey of British audiences revealed that over 12% of viewers of the American show *The A-Team* could not identify its national source, while more than 50% of viewers of a British-produced series on (John F.) *Kennedy* identified it as originating in the US. (74)

5 It is truly amazing how very little mention ITV's four official volumes make to the thriving trade in American imports, just as Briggs barely recognizes the growing dependence of the BBC on American co-production financing in the 1970s. This is echoed in American accounts of the development of educational and public broadcasting, where one of the few volumes to focus on Britain's central contributions to PBS is written from an overtly conservative political agenda, "exposing" PBS's Britishness in scandalized tones (Jarvik (1999)).

6 W. Stephen Gilbert, "Sydney Newman: TV's Feisty Dramatiser," *Guardian* (Nov 3, 1997) 15; see also Cook (2000).

7 See also Blaine Allen, "CBC Television Series, 1952–1982," http://www.film.queensu.ca/CBC/G.html.

8 She also argues that, "this link between production in the US and Canada . . . suggested a sense of skill, professionalism, and a 'slickness' which had not been seen on British television before" (2007, 37). But surely by 1958 quite a bit of "slick," professional American television had been seen in Britain; perhaps it would be more accurate to say that no effort had before been made to apply North American commercial production techniques to live "prestige" British production.

9 "ABC Television" *World's Press News* (Nov 14, 1958). Box 17, Folder 9, James.

10 Leonard Miall, "Obituary: Sydney Newman" *The Independent*, Nov 4, 1997, p. 22.

11 Minutes, Midland Regional Advisory Council, Oct 18, 1963. T16/62/3, WAC.

12 See, in particular, Cook ("Start" and "Between") MacMurraugh-Kavanagh, Lez Cooke (2003), and Jacobs (2000).

13 Memo from Sydney Newman to D. Tel re: Annual Planning July 28, 1964. T16/62/3 WAC.

14 Quoted in J. Miller (2000) 65.

15 It is very difficult to document American series that aired on British television; no one has attempted a definitive listing, and the task is made difficult by the way such shows were scheduled and the ways that ratings were compiled. The analysis below drawn on a variety of popular sources, including *40 Years of British Television* by Jane Harbourd and Jeff Wright and *The Radio Times Guide to TV Comedy* by Mark Lewinsohn. This information is supplemented by the BFI's otherwise excellent Screenonline, which unfortunately does not include information about shows produced in the US, no matter how central to British television culture, nor is it very accurate about giving credit to American models for British programming.

16 "Non-Whites on British Television" VR/72/56 16 Feb 1972, R9/10/8. WAC.

17 Though *Coronation Street* proved a greater success, credit is usually given to the BBC's serial drama *Compact* (1962–65), written by Hazel Adair of *Mrs. Dale's Diary* experience and set in the glamorous world of magazine publishing, and also sometimes to *The Grove Family* (BBC 1954–57) though there is some dispute as to whether this family drama belongs to the genre—see Su Holmes, "The Grove Family", http://www.birth-of-tv.org/birth/assetView.do?asset=1413260435_1147261168.

18 Letter from Betty Cope to David Stewart, Papers of David Stewart, Director, International Activities, CPB. Series 1 Box 1, File "Correspondence re: UK and US public TV 1994–1995," NPBA.

19 Letter from David Leonard to David Stewart, Papers of David Stewart, Director, International Activities, CPB. Series 1 Box 1, File "Correspondence re: UK and US public TV 1994–1995," NPBA.

20 For an excellent history of the political and cultural context of the founding of the NEA, see Bienkiewicz (2004)—though she nowhere mentions the many connections between policy on educational radio and television and the arts.

21 Fletcher had retired in 1961, though he continued to be active as a consultant to the NAEB as they took over educational broadcasting lobbying activities from NET, as required by the terms of the Ford Foundation's 1962 grant.

22 Memo from Edwin R. Bayley to John F. White, "Ford Foundation Conversations", June 15, 1964. James Day papers, Series 5, Box 32 Folder 9, NPBA.

23 All above quotes, ibid. Siepmann himself produced a document in the NPBA files titled "Educational Television: Blueprint for a Network" that is both mind-numbingly broad and arbitrarily specific: after reflecting generally on the nature of man, the essence of education, and "the human situation in America today," he comes up with a schedule of proposed programs complete with cost estimates that seem to have been pulled out of thin air.

24 Up to that point, the Foundation had required that 50% of NET's program budget be dispersed to affiliate stations, who produced their own programs for distribution over the network.

25 Both in NET, Series 3, Box 2, Folder 17, WHS.

26 Letter William Kobin to Cyril Bennett (Rediffusion), July 20, 1966. 8A/3/5, NET.

27 Memo from head of School Broadcasting, Television to CA to DG 7 July 1966 "Visit of Dr. David Henry, President of the University of Illinois", E1/1540/1, WAC.

28 John Crosby, "Television in Britain" May 1966. Box 5 Folder 4, CC.

29 James Ridgeway, "Not So Educational TV," *The New Republic* 153:8–9 (Aug 21, 1965) 26–28.

30 For detailed accounts of this history, see Pepper (1975), Carlson (1968), Mitchell (2005), Day (1995).

31 See Pepper for a full history of the struggles over interconnection of the public radio system.

32 Despite a wonderful but short-lived flourishing in the form of the Public Broadcasting Laboratory (1967–69), a cutting-edge live newsmagazine program funded directly by the Ford Foundation and produced by Fred T. Friendly, Edward R. Murrow's old partner at CBS. Some claim that the venerable CBS newsmagazine *60 Minutes* was inspired by *PBL*—it began the very next year and still airs today.

33 A little information about American public television's somewhat complicated structure may be useful here. Unlike the NEA and the NEH, which are federal agencies, the Corporation for Public Broadcasting was constituted as a private, nonprofit corporation that receives funds from Congress for distribution amongst the various players in the educational/public broadcasting sphere. Some of those funds go to PBS, set up in 1969 to manage the newly-installed system of wired (later satellite) interconnection that at last linked public television stations together into a national system. PBS also acquires programs, packages them into a national schedule, and distributes them; PBS itself does not produce programming. That is done through a system of CPB funding, mainly to network affiliates (all independent, mostly run by community groups and educational institutions), with seven stations designated as the system's primary program producers: WGBH-Boston, WETA-Washington, WNET-New York, WQED-Pittsburgh, WTTW-Chicago, KCET-Los Angeles, and KQED-San Francisco. It partners with other government-funded groups, including the NEA, the NEH, and the American Film Institute (itself created by the NEA) as well as with independent producers from around the world, such as the Children's Television Workshop (producer of *Sesame Street*) and, by the 1970s, BBC Enterprises Ltd. Additionally, PBS seeks out non-governmental funding for the system, from foundations, corporations, and other groups, both public and private; individual stations carry out these activities as well.

34 Fred Ferretti, "Forsyte Saga Will Unfold on Channel 13", *New York Times* (Oct 4, 1969) 70.

35 Christopher Sarson interview, June 1990. Series 1.1, Box 2 Fl4, Laurence A. Jarvik Papers, NPBA.

36 Jack Pitman, "BBC-TV Gandering U.S. Sales Push Under New Setup Giving Program Toppers Authority to Make Deals," *Variety* (Jan 14, 1970) 45. According to this article, the re-organization was a result of a management study commissioned by the BBC in 1969 from the New York-based firm McKinsey & Co.

37 David Stewart, "How Should Public TV Follow up the Forsyte Sage success?" *Current* (April 14, 1997)

38 PBS has preserved this opening sequence on their website: http://www.pbs.org/wgbh/masterpiece/cooke/onmpt.html

39 Thus, the rejection of one of the titles initially proposed for the series: "The BBC Presents."
40 The best example in this case is the WNET original drama series *The Adams Chronicles*, funded by PBS and underwriters to celebrate the Centennial in 1976.
41 *Variety* (Jan 27, 1971) 28; (July 14, 1971) 35; (July 21, 1971) 38.
42 See http://www.pbs.org/wgbh/masterpiece/americancollection/amc.html
43 Memo, John W. Macy, "BBC-June 1971", September 15, 1971. CPB Box 23 F 12, NPBA.
44 Letter Webster to Attenborough, Mar 8, 1972. T62/154/1, WAC.
45 Memo Scuse to Attenborough, March 24, 1972. T62/154/1, WAC.
46 In 1976, controversy would erupt when the CPB proposed to directly fund the BBC's planned "Shakespeare Series," adaptations of the entire canon of Shakespeare plays to be produced entirely in Britain and aired on PBS. Both Joseph Papp of the New York Shakespeare Festival and American talent and craft unions objected strenuously to the idea of using American taxpayer monies to fund foreign production. CPB withdrew from its co-financing plans but did fund distribution to schools and additional educational materials.
47 Memo from John Stringer head of business, co-productions, television to C.Tel.A, Nov 25, 1970. R125/1, 002/1 Co-Productions—Policy, 1955-1981, WAC.
48 R125/1, 002/1 Co-Productions—Policy, 1955–1981, WAC.
49 Time-Life Films also began producing their own original series as the American syndication market heated up in the 1970s, the most successful of which was *The Wild, Wild World of Animals*.
50 Memo from Shaun Sutton, "Co-Production Policies and Methods," Aug 19, 1970. T41/305/1, WAC.
51 Ibid.
52 Note by D. P. Tel. (Attenborough), "Co-Production Arrangements" Nov 19, 1969. T41/306/1 WAC.
53 All from Sutton "Co-Production Policies and Methods", above.
54 Memo from John Stringer to C.Tel.A, 25 Nov, 1970. R125/1, 002/1, WAC.
55 "Synopsis for General Advisory Council paper on Co-Productions" June 4, 1979. R125/1, 002/1, WAC.
56 Another important figure on the administrative side was Robin Scott, head of BBC-2. See Scott (1976).
57 Laurence Jarvik, "Interview with Peter Robeck" Mar 19, 1991. Jarvik Collection, NPBA.
58 "Award for Civilization", *The Times* (Nov 19, 1970), 6.
59 See *The Times*, Letters (Jan 31, 1972) 13; Letters (Feb 4, 1972) 13; "BBC rejects protests about 'bias' on Empire," (Feb 14, 1972) 2; "BBC link with 'Time-Life' for new series," (April 10, 1972) 2. See also Vickers and Gilbert, "BBC defends co-production ventures" *Campaign* (June 2, 1972) 30+.
60 Memo from Singer, March 26, 1971. T42/110/2, WAC.
61 Undated memo, T42/110/2, WAC.
62 Memo Attenborough to DC Tel (Weldon), Nov 29, 1972. T62/154/1, WAC.
63 "BBC Television co-Productions: The Why, How and What" (Dec 1, 1972). T41/306/1, WAC.
64 John J. O'Connor, "TV: NBC Gives a Personal View of 'America'" *New York Times* (Nov 15, 1972) 95.
65 James Thomas Flexner, "How America's Goose Was Cooked," *New York Times* (Jan 14, 1973) 137.
66 *New York Times* (Jan 9, 1974) 72.
67 Geoffrey Wansell, "Bronowski, messiah of culture," *Times* (April 25, 1973) 18.
68 *New York Times* (April 30, 1973) 32.
69 Memo Singer to Attenborough, March 22, 1974. T42/110/2, WAC.
70 Les Brown, "Public Broadcasting Serves as Incubator for Commercial Networks," *New York Times* (Mar 29, 1977) 33.
71 Letter from Anthony Smith, President, Magadalen College, Oxford, Dec 9, 1994. File "Correspondence re: UK and US public TV 1994–1995." Papers of David Stewart, Series 1 Box 1. NPBA.

10 Towards "Globalization"

1 Similarly, radio's intersection with recorded music did the same in the audio band, as various histories have traced.
2 The 1981 Broadcasting Act that created Channel 4 also inaugurated Sianel Pedwar Cumru (S4C, or Channel 4 Wales).
3 http://www.bbcworldwide.com/bbc-worldwide.aspx. Accessed July 22, 2010.
4 http://www.bbcworldwide.com/sales—distribution.aspx. Accessed July 22, 2010.
5 Bill Carter, "Britons Revamp American TV" *New York Times* (July 18, 2000) B1.
6 "Brit Invasion of TV shows keeps growing" AP (London) (Feb 26, 2008).
7 Stuart Elliott, "U.S. Television Taps More Imported Series," *New York Times* (May 19, 2008) C7.
8 Brooks Barnes, "NBC Faces Trials Bringing 'Law & Order' to France" *Wall Street Journal* (Mar 1, 2007) 1.
9 In the UK, for example, no British adaptation was done; instead the US version aired for several seasons on Channel 4. The same is true for most of the English speaking countries: Canada, Ireland, Australia, New Zealand, and South Africa all imported the US version: an imported adaptation of an imported program.
10 These terms show the influence of the ideas of German philosopher Jurgen Habermas, whose *Structural Transformation of the Public Sphere* appeared in its first English translation in 1989, though few of the second wave works gave his complex theories an adequate reading.
11 Though, as essays in Tom O'Malley's volume emphasize, it warded off the introduction of advertising to BBC, one of the Conservative governments primary goals (O'Malley (2009)).
12 For more on recent archival activities, see *Critical Studies in Television* 5:2 (2010).
13 "Outgoing Auntie," *The Economist* (16 Aug, 2001) n.p.

Manuscript Collections

Wisconsin Historical Society (WHS)
  Collections:
  National Broadcasting Company (NBC)
  National Association of Educational Broadcasters (NAEB)
  National Educational Television (NET)
  Carnegie Commission on Educational Television (CC)
  Harold A. McCarty papers (McCarty)
  Sig Mickelson papers (Mickelson)
  E. P. H. James papers (James)
British Broadcasting Corporation Written Archives Center (WAC)
British National Archives (Kew)
British Film Institute (BFI)
British Library Newspapers. Colindale (BLN)
History of Advertising Trust, UK (HAT)
Library of Congress (LC)
  National Broadcasting Company collection (LC/NBC)
  Radio Research Project (RRP)
National Public Broadcasting Archives. University of Maryland (NPBA)
Rockefeller Foundation Archives (RFA)

Bibliography

Alexander, Jeffrey. "The Mass Media in Systemic, Historical, and Comparative Perspective." *Mass Media and Social Change*. Ed. E. Katz and T. Szecsko. London and Beverly Hills: Sage, 1981, 17–52.

Allen, Robert C. *Speaking of Soap Operas*. Chapel Hill: University of North Carolina Press, 1985.

Altman, Wilfred, Denis Thomas, David Sawers. *TV: From Monopoly to Competition—And Back?* London: Institute of Economic Affairs, 1962.

Anderson, Benedict. *Imagined Communities: Reflections on the Origin and Spread of Nationalism*. London: Verso, 1991.

Anderson, Kurt. *Television Fraud: The History and Implications of the Quiz Show Scandals*. Westport, CT: Greenwood Press, 1978.

Ang, Ien. *Desperately Seeking the Audience*. New York: Routledge, 2001.

Appadurai, Arjun. "Disjuncture and Difference in the Global Economy." *Public Culture* 2:2 (1990) 1–24.

——. *Modernity at Large: Cultural Dimensions of Globalization*. Minneapolis: University of Minnesota Press, 1996.

Baade, Christina. *Victory Through Harmony: The BBC and Popular Music in World War II*. New York: Oxford University Press, 2011.

Balio, Tino. *Hollywood in the Age of Television*. Cambridge: Unwin Hyman, 1990.

Bannerman, R. Leroy. *Norman Corwin and Radio: The Golden Years*. Tuscaloosa: University of Alabama Press, 1986.

Barbour, Philip L. "Commercial and Cultural Broadcasting in Mexico" *Annals of the American Academy of Political and Social Science*. 208: Mexico Today (March 1940) 94–102.

Barlow, William. *Voice-Over: The Making of Black Radio*. Philadelphia: Temple University Press, 1999.

Barnard, Stephen. *On the Radio: Music Radio in Britain*. Milton Keynes: Open University Press, 1989.

Barnouw. Erik. *Radio Drama in Action: Twenty-Five Plays of a Changing World*. New York: Farrar & Rinehart, 1945.

——. *The Golden Web: A History of Broadcasting in the United States, Volume II, 1933–1953*. New York: Oxford University Press, 1968.

——. "Mister Ledford and the TVA." *Alan Lomax: Selected Writings 1934–1997*." Ed. Ronald D. Cohen. New York: Routledge, 2003. 77–79.

Beachcroft. T. O. *Calling All Nations*. London: BBC 1943.

Beam, Alex. *A Great Idea at the Time: The Rise, Fall, and Curious Afterlife of the Great Books*. New York: Public Affairs, 2008.

Becker, Christine. "From High Culture to Hip Culture: The Transformation of the BBC Into BBC

America." *Anglo-American Media Interactions, 1850–2000.* Ed. Mark Hampton and Joel Wiener. New York: Palgrave Macmillan, 2007. 275–94.

Benjamin, Louise M. "Birth of a Network's 'Conscience': The NBC Advisory Council. 1927." *Journalism Quarterly* 66 (1988) 587–90.

——. *Freedom of the Air and the Public Interest: First Amendment Rights in Broadcasting to 1935.* Carbondale: Southern Illinois University, 2001.

Bennett, Tony and Janet Woollacott. *Bond and Beyond: The Political Career of a Popular Hero.* London: Macmillan, 1987.

Bensman, Marvin R. "Regulation of Broadcasting by the Department of Commerce, 1921–1927." *American Broadcasting.* Ed. Lawrence W. Lichty and Malachi C. Topping. New York: Hastings House, 1985. 54–55.

Berghahn, Volker R. "Awkward Relations: American Perspectives on Europe, European Perspectives on America." In *Americanization and Anti-American: The German Encounter with American Culture after 1945.* Ed. Alexander Stephan. Oxford: Berghahn Books, 2004.

Bernstein, Walter. *Inside Out: A Memoir of the Blacklist.* New York: Knopf, 1996.

Berkman, Dave. "The 'Blue Book' and Charles Siepmann – as Reported in *Broadcasting* Magazine." *American Journalism* 11:1 (1985) 37–48.

Bhabha, Homi K. *The Location of Culture.* New York: Routledge, 2004

Bielby, Denise and Lee Harrington. *Global TV: Exporting Television and Culture in the World Market.* New York: New York University Press. 2008.

Bignell, Jonathan. "And the Rest is History: Lew Grade. Creation Narratives and Television Historiography." *ITV Cultures: Independent Television Over Fifty Years.* Ed. Catherine Johnson and Rob Turnock. London: Open University Press, 2005. 57–70.

——. "Transatlantic Spaces: Production. Location and Style in 1960s–1970s Action-Adventure TV Series." *Media History* 16:1 (February 2010) 31–52.

—— and Andreas Fickers, eds. *A European Television History.* London: Wiley-Blackwell, 2008.

——, Stephen Lacey, and Madeleine Macmurraugh-Kavanagh, eds. *British Television Drama.* London: Palgrave, 2000.

Billig, Michael. *Banal Nationalism.* London: Sage, 1995.

Binkiewicz, Donna M. *Federalizing the Muse: United States Arts Policy and the National Endowment for the Arts. 1965–1980.* Chapel Hill: University of North Carolina Press, 2004.

Blakeley, Robert J. *To Serve the Public Interest: Educational Broadcasting in the United States.* Syracuse: Syracuse University Press, 1979.

Blue, Howard. *Words at War: World War II Era Radio Drama and the Postwar Broadcasting Industry Blacklist.* Lanham, MD: Scarecrow Press, 2002.

Bluem, A. William. *Documentary in American Television.* New York: Hastings House, 1965.

Blumler, Jay. "The New Television Marketplace: Imperatives. Implications. Issues." *Mass Media and Society.* Ed. James Curran and Michael Gurevich. London: Arnold, 1991. 194–215.

Boddy, William. "Building the World's Largest Advertising Medium: CBS and Television, 1940–1960." *Hollywood in the Age of Television.* Ed. Tino Balio. Cambridge: Unwin Hyman, 1990. 63–89.

——. *Fifties Television.* Urbana: University of Illinois Press, 1990.

——. "Operation frontal lobes versus the living room toy: the battle over programme control in early television." *Media, Culture and Society* 9 (1987) 347–68.

Bordwell, David, Janet Staiger, and Kristin Thompson. *The Classical Hollywood Cinema: Film Style and Mode of Production to 1960.* New York: Columbia University Press, 1985.

Bourdon, Jérome. "Old and New Ghosts: Public Service Television and the Popular—A History". *European Journal of Cultural Studies* 7:3 (2004) 283–304.

Boyd, William. "The Secret Persuaders." *Guardian* (Aug 19, 2006) 6.

Boyle, Andrew. *Only the Wind Will Listen: Reith of the BBC.* London: Hutchinson, 1972

Brecher, Edward. "Whose Radio?" *The Atlantic Monthly* (August 1946) 47–51.

Bridson, D. G. *Prospero and Ariel.* London: Victor Gollancz Ltd., 1971.

Briggs, Asa. *The History of Broadcasting in the United Kingdom. Vol. I: The Birth of Broadcasting.* Oxford: Oxford University Press, 1961.

——. *Vol. II: The Golden Age of Wireless.* Oxford: Oxford University Press, 1965.

——. *Vol. III: The War of Words.* Oxford: Oxford University Press, 1970.

——. *Vol. IV: Sound and Vision.* Oxford: Oxford University Press, 1979.

——. *Vol. V: Competition.* Oxford: Oxford University Press, 1995.

Brinson, Susan L. *Personal and Public Interests: Frieda B. Hennock and the Federal Communications Commission.* Greenwood Publishing Group, 2002.

British Broadcasting Corporation. *BBC Year-Book 1930.* London: BBC, 1930.

——. *BBC Year-Book 1933.* London: BBC, 1933.

——. *BBC Annual 1935.* London: BBC, 1935.

——. *BBC Handbook 1941.* London: BBC, 1941.

——. *BBC Yearbook 1968–69.* London: BBC, 1969.

——. *BBC Yearbook 1970–71.* London: BBC, 1971.

British Security Coordination: The Secret History of British Intelligence in the Americas. 1940–1945. Introduction by Nigel West. New York: Fromm International, 1999.

Brooke. Michael. "An Age of Kings (1960)" BFI: Screenonline 2009. http://www.screenonline.org.uk/tv/id/527213/

Brooks, Carolyn N. "Documentary Programming and the Emergence of the National Educational Television Center as a Network, 1958–1972." Ph.D. dissertation. University of Wisconsin-Madison, 1994.

Brown. F. J. "The Story of Broadcasting in England." *Radio Broadcast* vol. 7 #2 (June 1925) 175–82.

Brylawski, Samuel. "Armed Forces Radio Service: The Invisible Highway Abroad." *Wonderful Inventions: Motion Pictures, Broadcasting, and Recorded Sound at the Library of Congress.* Ed. Iris Newsom. Washington: Library of Congress, 1985. 333–44.

Bryson, Lyman. et al. "Needed Research in Communication" (excerpt) *Mass Communication and American Social Thought.* Ed. John Durham Peters and Peter Simonson. Lanham, MD: Rowman and Littlefield, 2004. 136–38.

Buonanno, Milly, ed. *Continuity and Change: Television Fiction in Europe.* Luton: University of Luton Press, 2000.

Burns, Tom. *The BBC: Public Institution and Private World.* London: Macmillan, 1977.

Burrows, A. R. *The Story of Broadcasting.* London: Cassell, 1924.

Buscombe, Edward, ed. *British Television: A Reader.* Oxford: Oxford University Press. 2000.

——. "Nationhood, Culture, and Media Boundaries: Britain." *Quarterly Review of Film and Video* 14:3 (1993) 25–34.

Buxton, William J. "Reaching Human Minds: Rockefeller Philanthropy and Communications, 1935–1939." *The Development of the Social Sciences in the United States and Canada: The Role of Philanthropy.* Ed. Theresa Richardson and Donald Fisher. Stamford: Ablex, 1999. 177–92.

—— "John Marshall and the Humanities in Europe: Shifting Patterns of Rockefeller Foundation Support." *Minerva* 41:2 (2003) 133–53.

Calhoun, Craig. *Nationalism.* Minneapolis: Univ. of Minnesota Press, 1998.

Camporesi, Valeria. "The BBC and American Broadcasting. 1922–55". *Media, Culture and Society* 16:4 (1994) 625–39.

——. *Mass Culture and National Traditions: The BBC and American Broadcasting 1922–1954.* Fecucchio, Italy: European Press Academic Publishing, 2000.

Capshew, James H. "The Yale Connection in American Psychology: Philanthropy, War, and the Emergence of an Academic Elite." *The Development of the Social Sciences in the United States and Canada: The Role of Philanthropy.* Ed. Theresa Richardson and Donald Fisher. Stamford: Ablex, 1999. 143–54.

Cardiff, David. "Mass Middlebrow Laughter: The Origins of BBC Comedy." *Media, Culture and Society* 10:1 (1988) 41–60.

——. "The Serious and the Popular: Aspects of the Evolution of Style in the Radio Talk 1928–1935". *Media, Culture and Society: A Critical Reader.* Ed. Richard Collins et al. London: Sage, 1986.

—— and Paddy Scannell. "'Good Luck War Workers!' Class, Politics and Entertainment in Wartime Broadcasting." *Popular Culture and Social Relations.* Ed. Tony Bennett, Colin Mercer, and Janet Woollacott. London: Open University Press, 1986.

——. "Broadcasting and National Unity." *Impacts and Influences.* Ed. Richard Curran, Anthony Smith, and Pauline Wingate. London: Methuen, 1987. 157–73.

Carlson, Robert A. "The National Educational Television Network: Case History of an Adult Education Organization." *Adult Education* 17:3 (Spring 1967) 134–151.

——. "The creation and development of educational television as an institution of adult education: a case study in American history." Unpublished PhD dissertation. University of Wisconsin-Madison, 1968.

Carpenter, Humphrey. *The Envy of the World: Fifty Years of the BBC Third Programme and Radio 3, 1946–1996.* London: Weidenfeld and Nicolson, 1996.

Carson. Saul. "The American Radio." *The Yale Law Journal* 57:5 (1948) 910–12.

——. "Notes Towards an Examination of the Radio Documentary." *Hollywood Quarterly* 4:1 (Autumn 1949) 69–74.

Casillas, Dolores Inés. "Sounds of Belonging: A Cultural History of Spanish-language Radio in the United States, 1922–2004." Ph.D. dissertation, University of Michigan, 2006.

Caughie, John. *Television Drama: Realism, Modernism, and British Culture.* London: Oxford, 2000.

Chaney, David. "Audience Research and the BBC in the 1930s: A Mass Medium Comes into Being." *Impacts and Influences.* Ed. Richard Curran, Anthony Smith, and Pauline Wingate. London: Methuen, 1987. 259–77.

Chapman, James. *Saints and Avengers: British Adventure Series of the 1960s.* London: I. B. Tauris, 2004.

Chris, Cynthia. "All Documentary, All the Time? Discovery Communications Inc. and Trends in Cable Television." *Television and New Media* 3:6 (2002) 7–28.

Clark, Anthony. "Authored Documentary." Screenonline, accessed June 12, 2010a. http://www.screenonline.org.uk/tv/id/898488/

——. "Civilisation" Screenonline, accessed June 8, 2010b. http://www.screenonline.org.uk/tv/id/549750/

Clarke, Nick. *Alistair Cooke: A Biography.* New York: Arcade, 1999.

Clements, Robert J. "Foreign Language Broadcasting of 'Radio Boston'". *Modern Language Journal* 27:3 (March 1943) 175–80.

Coase, R. H. *British Broadcasting: A Study in Monopoly.* London: Longmans, Green, 1950.

Cohen, Philip. "Documentary Programs: A Demonstration and Discussion." *Education on the Air 1941.* Institute for Education by Radio. Columbus: Ohio State University Press, 1941. 245–72.

—— and Jerome B. Wiesner. "Showing the American People to Themselves." *Journal of the Association for Education by Radio* (January 1942) 3, 12.

Collins, Richard. *Culture, Communication and National Identity: The Case of Canadian Television.* Toronto: University of Toronto Press, 1990.

——. *Satellite Broadcasting in Western Europe.* London: Libbey, 1990.

——. "Wall-To-Wall 'Dallas'? The US-UK Trade in Television." *Screen* 27:5 (1986) 66–76.

Commission on Freedom of the Press. *The American Radio.* By Llewellyn White. Chicago: University of Chicago Press, 1947.

——. *A Free and Responsible Press.* Chicago: University of Chicago Press, 1947.

——. *Freedom of the Movies.* By Ruth A. Inglis. Chicago: University of Chicago Press, 1947.

——. *Freedom of the Press: A Framework of Principles.* By William E. Hocking. Chicago: University of Chicago Press, 1947.

——. *Government and Mass Communications.* By Zecheriah Chaffee, Jr. Chicago: University of Chicago Press, 1947.

——. *Peoples speaking to peoples; a report on international mass communication.* By Llewllyn White and Robert E. Lee. Chicago: University of Chicago Press, 1947.

Conlin, Jonathan. *Civilisation.* London: BFI, 2009.

Cook, John R. "Start Big and Then Build': Sydney Newman and British Television Drama." *Mediated Drama. Dramatized Media.* Ed. Eckarts Voigts-Virchow. Trier: Wissenschaftlicher Verlag, 2000. 118–34.

——. "Between Grierson and Barnum: Sydney Newman and the Development of the Single Television Play at the BBC, 1963–7." *Journal of British Cinema and Television* 2 (2005) 211–25.

Cooke, Lez. *British Television Drama: A History.* London: BFI, 2003.

Coulter, Douglas, ed. *Columbia Workshop Plays.* New York: McGraw Hill, 1939.

Crosby, John. "Stalled: Radio and Who Makes It." *Atlantic Monthly* 181 (Jan 1948) 23–29.

Culbert, David. *News for Everyman: radio and foreign affairs in thirties America.* Westport, CT: Greenwood Press, 1976.

Cull, Nicholas J. "Radio Propaganda and the Art of Understatement: British Broadcasting and American Neutrality 1939–1941." *Historical Journal of Film, Radio and Television* 13:4 (1993) 413–31.

——. *Selling War: The British Propaganda Campaign against American 'Neutrality' in World War Two.* New York: Oxford University Press, 1995.

Curran, James. "Mass Media and Democracy: A Reappraisal." *Mass Media and Society.* Ed. James Curran and Michael Gurevich. London: Arnold, 1991.

—— and Jean Seaton. *Power Without Responsibility: The Press and Broadcasting in Britain.* London: Routledge, 1991.

Curtin, Michael. *Redeeming the Wasteland: Television Documentary and Cold War Politics.* NJ: Rutgers University Press, 1999.

Czitrom, Daniel J. *Media and the American Mind: From Morse to McLuhan.* Chapel Hill: University of North Carolina Press. 1982.

Day, James. *The Vanishing Vision: The Inside Story of Public Television.* Berkeley: University of California Press, 1995.

Dean, Pamala S. "Good Times." *Encyclopedia of Television.* Ed. Horace Newcomb. http://www. museum.tv/eotvsection.php?entrycode=goodtimes. Accessed 2 December 2010.

De Bens, Els and Hedwig de Smaele. "The Inflow of American Television Fiction on European Broadcasting Channels Revisited." *European Journal of Communication* 16:1 (2001) 51–76.

De Moragas Spa, Miguel, Carmelo Garitaonandia and Bernat Lopez, eds. *Television on Your Doorstep: Decentralisation Experiences in the European Union.* Luton: University of Luton Press. 1999

Dell, Chad. "Red-Baiting. Regulation and the Broadcast Industry: A Revisionist History of the 'Blue Book.'" Unpublished paper.

Deutsch, Karl. *Nationalism and Social Communications.* Cambridge, MA: Cambridge University Press, 1966.

Dickinson, Margaret and Sarah Street. *Cinema and State: The Film Industry and the British Government, 1927–1984.* London: BFI 1985.

Donaldson, Frances. *The Marconi Scandal.* New York: Harcourt Brace, 1962.

Douglas, Susan J. *Inventing American Broadcasting.* Baltimore: Johns Hopkins University Press, 1987.

Doyle, Laura. "Towards a Philosophy of Transnationalism." *Journal of Transnational American Studies* 1:1 (2009) 1–31.

Drakakis, John. ed. *British Radio Drama.* Cambridge: Cambridge University Press. 1981.

Dunlap, Orrin E. Jr. *Marconi: The Man and His Wireless.* New York: Arno. 1971

Dunning, John. *On the Air: The Encyclopedia of Old-Time Radio.* New York: Oxford University Press, 1998.

Durovicova, Natasa and Kathleen Newman, eds. *World Cinemas, Transnational Perspectives.* New York: Routledge, 2009.

The Economist. "The Finance and Future of Broadcasters" (March 13, 1926) 15.

Edwards, Bob. *Edward R. Murrow and the Birth of Broadcast Journalism.* New York: John Wiley and Sons, 2004.

Elliott, Philip. "Intellectuals, the 'Information Society' and the Disappearance of the Public Sphere". *Media, Culture and Society* 4:3 (1982) 243–53.

—— and Geoff Matthews. "Broadcasting Culture: Innovation, Accommodation and Routinization in the early BBC." *Impacts and Influences.* Ed. James Curran, Anthony Smith, and Janet Wingate. London: Methuen, 1987. 235–58.

Federal Communications Commission. *Public Service Responsibility of Broadcast Licensees.* Washington, DC: US Government Printing Office, 1946.

Federal Radio Commission. *Third Annual Report of the Federal Radio Commission to the Congress of the United States Covering the Period from October 1, 1928 to November 1, 1929.* Washington. D.C.: US Government Printing Office, 1929.

Fielding, Raymond. *The March of Time, 1935–1951.* New York: Oxford, 1978.

Finch, John. ed. *Granada Television: The First Generation.* Manchester: Manchester University Press, 2003.

Finney, Robert G. "The Radio Corporation of America." *Encyclopedia of Radio.* Ed. Christopher H. Sterling. Vol. 3. New York: Fitzroy Dearborn, 2004. 1163–65.

Fisher, Donald. *Fundamental Development of the Social Sciences: Rockefeller Philanthropy and the United States Social Science Research Council.* Ann Arbor: University of Michigan Press, 1993.

Ford Foundation, *Report.* New York: Ford Foundation, 1936.

—— *Report, 1953.* New York: Ford Foundation, 1953.

Forman, Sir Denis. "A Kind of Happy Magic." *Granada Television: The First Generation.* Ed. John Finch. Manchester: Manchester University Press, 2003. 32–34.

Fornatale, Peter, and Joshua E. Mills. *Radio in the Television Age.* Woodstock, New York: Overlook Press, 1980.

Fortune, "The Revolt Against Radio." 35:3 (March 1947) 101+.

Fosdick, Raymond B.. *The Story of the Rockefeller Foundation.* New York: Harper, 1952.

Fowler, Gene and Bill Crawford. *Border Radio.* Austin, TX: Texas Monthly Press, 1987.

Fraser, Nancy. "Transnationalizing the Public Sphere", accessed Nov 14, 2010. http://www.republicart.net/disc/publicum/fraser01_en.html.

Freedman, Des. "How Her Majesty's Opposition Grew to Like Commercial Television: The Labour Party and the Origins of ITV." *Media History* 5:1 (1999) 19–32.

Frost, S. E. Jr. "The Licensing of Educational Broadcasting Stations: A Retrospect." *Education on the Air 1937.* Institute for Education by Radio. Columbus: Ohio State University Press, 1937.

García Canclini, Néstor. *Consumers and Citizens: Globalization and Multicultural Conflicts.* Minneapolis: University of Minnesota Press, 2001.

Gardner, Carl and John Wyver. "The Single Play: From Reithian Reverence to Cost-Accounting and Censorship." *Screen* 24:4/5 (1983) 114–29.

Garnham, Nicholas. "Public Service Versus the Market: Nicholas Garnham Considers the Impact of New Information Technologies on the Future of British Broadcasting." *Screen* 24:1 (1983) 6–27.

Gary, Brett. "Communication Research, the Rockefeller Foundation, and Mobilization for the War on Words. 1938–1944." *Journal of Communication* 46:3 (Summer 1996) 124–48.

——. *The Nervous Liberals: Propaganda Anxieties from World War I to the Cold War.* New York: Columbia University Press, 1999.

Gellner, Ernest. *Nations and Nationalism.* Oxford: Blackwell, 1993.

Gevinson, Alan. "'What the Neighbors Say': The Radio Research Project of the Library of Congress." *Performing Arts: Broadcasting.* Ed. Iris Newson. Washington DC: The Library of Congress, 2002.

Gielgud, Val. *British Radio Drama 1922–1956.* London: Harrap, 1957.

Glancy, Mark. "Temporary American Citizens? British Audiences, Hollywood Films, and the Threat of Americanization in the 1920s." *Historical Journal of Film. Radio and Television* 26:4 (Oct 2006) 461–84.

Goetz, William. "The Canadian Wartime Documentary: 'Canada Carries On' and 'The World in Action.'" *Cinema Journal* 16:2 (Spring 1977) 59–80.

Gomery, Douglas. "Talent Raids and Package Deals: NBC Loses Its Leadership in the 1950s." *NBC: America's Network.* Ed. Michele Hilmes. Berkeley: University of California Press, 2007. 153–69.

Goode, Kenneth M. *What About Radio?* New York and London: Harper Bros. 1937.

Goodman, David. "Loving and Hating Britain: Rereading the Isolationist Debate in the USA." *Britishness Abroad: Transnational Movements and Imperial Cultures.* Ed. Kate Darian-Smith, Patricia Grimshaw and Stuart Macintyre. Melbourne: University of Melbourne Press, 2007. 187–204.

——. "Programming in the Public Interest: *America's Town Meeting of the Air*". *NBC: America's Network.* Ed. Michele Hilmes. Berkeley: University of California Press, 2007. 25–43.

Goodman, Mark and Mark Gring. "The Radio Act of 1927: Progressive Ideology, Epistemology, and Praxis." *Rhetoric and Public Affairs* 3:2 (2000) 397–418.

Gorham, Maurice. *Sound and Fury: Twenty-One Years in the BBC.* London: Percival Marshall, 1948.

Gray, Jonathan. *Show Sold Separately: Promos, Spoilers, and other Media Paratexts.* New York: New York University Press, 2010.

Gray, L. C. "London Calling!" *Current History* (April 1941) 20–22.

Great Britain. *Broadcasting: Memorandum on Television Policy.* November 1963. Cmd. 9005. London: H. M. Stationery Office, 1963.

Great Britain, Broadcasting Committee. *Report of the Broadcasting Committee* (Chaired by Lord Crawford). Cmd. 2599. London: H. M. Stationery Office, 1926.

——. *Report of the Broadcasting Committee.* (Chaired by Lord Beveridge). Cmd. 8116 and Cmd. 8117. London: H. M. Stationery Office, 1951.

——. *Report of the Broadcasting Committee.* (Chaired by Lord Pilkington). Cmnd. 1753. London: H. M. Stationery Office, 1961–62.

Greene, Hugh Carleton. "Television Transcription: The Economic Possibilities." *BBC Quarterly* 7 (1953) 216–21.

——. *The Third Floor Front: A View of Broadcasting in the Sixties.* London: the Bodley Head, 1969.

Greenfeld, Liah. 1992. *Nationalism: Five Roads to Modernity.* Cambridge. Mass.: Harvard University Press.

Gregory, E. David. "Lomax In London: Alan Lomax, the BBC and the Folk-Song Revival in England, 1950–1958." *Folk Music Journal* 8:2 (2002) 136–54.

Gripsrud, Jostein. *The Dynasty Years: Hollywood Television and Critical Media Studies.* London: Routledge, 1995

Gunn, Hartford N. Jr. "A Station Manager's View of the Problems of Programming." *Educational Television: The Next Ten Years.* Washington. DC: US Department of Health, Education, and Welfare, 1965.

Habermas, Jurgen. *The Structural Transformation of the Public Sphere.* Cambridge, MA: MIT Press, 1993.

Hajkowski, Thomas. *The BBC and National Identity, 1922–1953.* Manchester: Manchester University Press, 2010.

Hall, John A. ed. *The State of the Nation: Ernest Gellner and the Theory of Nationalism.* Cambridge: Cambridge University Press, 1998.

Hall, Randall. *9XM Talking: WHA Radio and the Wisconsin Idea.* Madison: University of Wisconsin Press, 2006.

Hamilton. Mary Agnes. "Broadcasting—A British View". *Harper's Monthly Magazine* (December 1934) pp. 59–67.

Hanson. O. B. "Broadcasting in Europe." *Broadcast News* (January 1932) 4–5.

Harbourd, Jane and Jeff Wright. *40 Years of British Television.* London: Boxtree, 1995.

Hard, William. "William Hard Has a Few Things to Say." *Broadcasting in the United States.* Ed. National Association of Broadcasters. Washington. D.C.: NAB Press, 1933. 110–15.

Havens, Timothy. *Global Television Marketplace.* London: BFI, 2006.

Havig, Alan. "Frederic Wakeman's *The Hucksters* and the Postwar Debate over Commercial Radio." *Journal of Broadcasting* 28:2 (Spring 1984) 187–99.

Hayes, Joy E. *Radio Nation: Communication, Popular Culture, and Nationalism in Mexico, 1920–1950.* Tucson: University of Arizona Press, 2000.

Head, Martin. "The Beginnings of Radio Luxembourg 1930–1939." PhD Dissertation. Polytechnic of Central London, 1980.

Henry, Brian, ed. *British Television Advertising: The first 30 years.* London: Century Benham/History of Advertising Trust, 1987.

Heyer, Paul. *The Medium and the Magician: Orson Welles, The Radio Years 1934–52.* Lanham, MD: Rowman and Littlefield, 2005.

Higson, Andrew. *Waving the Flag: Constructing a National Cinema in Britain.* Oxford: Clarendon, 1995.

Hilmes, Michele. "British Quality, American Chaos: Historical Dualisms and What They Leave Out." *The Radio Journal.* 1:1 (Spring 2003) 2–16.

——. "Cinema and the Age of Television, 1945–1975," *Blackwell's History of American Film.* Ed. Cynthia A. Lucia et al. London: Blackwell, 2011.

——. "*Front Line Family*: Women's Culture Comes to the BBC." *Media, Culture and Society* 29:1 (January 2007) 5–29.

——. *Hollywood and Broadcasting: From Radio to Cable.* Urbana: University of Illinois Press, 1990.

——, ed. *NBC: America's Network.* Berkeley: University of California Press, 2007.

——. *Radio Voices: American Broadcasting 1922–1952.* Minneapolis: University of Minnesota Press, 1997.

—— and Jason Loviglio, eds. *Radio Reader: Essays in the Cultural History of Radio.* New York: Routledge, 2001.

Hjort, Mette. "On the Plurality of Cinematic Transnationalism." *World Cinemas. Transnational Perspectives.* Ed. Natasa Durovicova and Kathleen Newman. New York: Routledge. 2010. 12–33.

Hobsbawm, Eric J. *Nations and Nationalism since 1780: Programme, Myth, Reality.* Cambridge: Cambridge University Press, 1990.

—— and Terence Ranger, eds. *The Invention of Tradition.* Cambridge: Cambridge University Press, 1992.

Hoerschelmann, Olaf. "Quiz and Game Shows" in *Encyclopedia of Television.* Vol. 3. Ed. Horace Newcomb. New York: Fitzroy Dearborn, 1994, 1871–74.

Holmes, Su. *British TV & Film Culture in the 1950s: Coming to a TV Near You.* Bristol: Intellect, 2005.

Houseman, John. *Run-Through. 1902–1941.* New York: Simon and Schuster, 1972.

———. *Front and Center. 1942–1955*. New York: Simon and Schuster, 1979.

Hudson, Robert B. "Allerton House 1949, 1950." *Hollywood Quarterly* 5:3 (Spring 1951) 237–50.

Hull, Richard B. "A Note on the History Behind ETV." In *Educational Television: The Next Ten Years*. Ed. US Department of Health, Education, and Welfare, Office of Education. Washington. DC: US Government Printing Office,1965. 334–45.

Hutchens, John K. "That Realm, That England" *New York Times* (Aug 16, 1942) X8.

Hyde, H. Montgomery. *The Quiet Canadian: The Secret Service Story of Sir William Stephenson*. London: H. Hamilton, 1962.

Ignatius, David. "How Churchill's Agents Secretly Manipulated the U.S. Before Pearl Harbor." *The Washington Post* (Sept 17, 1989): C1.

Iriye, Akira. *Cultural Internationalism and World Order*. Baltimore: Johns Hopkins Press, 1997.

Jacobs, Jason. *The Intimate Screen: Early British Television Drama*. London: Oxford, 2000.

Jaikumar, Priya. *Cinema at the End of Empire: A Politics of Transition in Britain and India*. Durham: Duke University Press, 2006.

Jansky, C. M. Jr. "The Problem of the Institutionally Owned Station." In *Radio and Education*. Ed. Levering Tyson/National Advisory Council on Radio in Education. Chicago: University of Chicago Press, 1932: 213–23.

Jarvik, Laurence A. *Masterpiece Theatre and the Politics of Quality*. Lanham. MD: Scarecrow Press, 1999.

Jenkins, Henry. *Convergence Culture: Where Old and New Media Collide*. New York: New York University Press, 2006.

Johnson, Catherine and Rob Turnock. "From Start-Up to Consolidation: Institutions. Regions and Regulation over the History of ITV." *ITV Cultures: Independent Television Over Fifty Years*. Ed. Catherine Johnson and Rob Turnock. London: Open University Press, 2005. 15–35.

Johnson, Derek. "Franchising Media Worlds: Content Networks and the Collaborative Production of Culture." Unpublished Ph.D. dissertation, University of Wisconsin-Madison, 2009.

Jolly, W. P. *Marconi*. London: Constable, 1972.

Jones, William M. and Andrew Walworth, "Saudek's *Omnibus:* Ambitious Forerunner of Public TV." *Current* (13 Dec 1999). Accessed 12/5/2009, http://www.current.org/coop/coopomni.html.

Julian, Joseph. *This Was Radio*. New York: Viking Press, 1975.

Kaye, Linda. "Reconciling Policy and Propaganda: The British Overseas Television Service. 1954–1964." *Historical Journal of Film. Radio and Television*. 27:2 (June 2007). 215–36.

Keith, Michael and Christopher Sterling, *Sounds of Change: A History of FM Broadcasting in America*. Chapel Hill: University of North Carolina Press, 2008.

Kelly, Frank K. *Court of Reason: Robert Hutchins and the Fund for the Republic*. New York: The Free Press, 1981.

Kepley, Vance. "From 'Frontal Lobes' to the 'Bob-and-Bob' Show: NBC Management and Programming Strategies, 1949–1965." *Hollywood in the Age of Television*. Ed. Tino Balio. Cambridge: Unwin Hyman, 1990. 41–61.

Kerwin, Jerome G. "The Control of Radio." *Public Policy Pamphlets No. 10*. Chicago: University of Chicago Press, 1934.

King-Hall, Stephen. "Radio—The British Way". *The Rotarian* (May 1934) 12+.

Kirby, Edward M. and Jack W. Harris. *Star-Spangled Radio*. Chicago: Ziff-Davis, 1948.

Kirkpatrick, Bill. "Localism in American Media. 1920–1934." Unpublished Ph.D. dissertation. University of Wisconsin-Madison, 2006.

Kraidy, Marwan. *Hybridity, or the Cultural Logic of Globalization*. Philadelphia: Temple University Press, 2005.

Kumar, Shanti. *Gandhi Meets Primetime: Globalization and Nationalism in Indian Television*. Urbana: University of Illinois Press, 2008.

Lacey, Kate. "From *Plauderei* to Propaganda: On Women's Radio in Germany, 1924–35". *Media, Culture and Society* 16:4 (1994) 589–607.

———. *Feminine Frequencies: Gender, German Radio, and the Public Sphere. 1923–1945*. Ann Arbor: University of Michigan Press, 1996.

Lagemann, Ellen Condliffe. *The Politics of Knowledge: The Carnegie Corporation, Philanthropy, and Public Policy*. Middletown: Wesleyan University Press, 1989.

Lambert, Stephen. *Channel Four: Television with a Difference?* London: BFI, 1982.

Lancashire, Geoff. "Best and Worst." *GranadaTelevision: The First Generation*. Ed. John Finch. Manchester: Manchester University Press, 2003. 42–45.

Landry, Robert. "Edward R. Murrow." *Scribner's Magazine* (December 1938) 32.
Lardner, Ring Jr. *I'd Hate Myself in the Morning: A Memoir.* New York: Nation Books, 2000.
Lash, Joseph. *From the Diaries of Felix Frankfurter.* New York: Norton, 1975.
Lashner, Marilyn A. "The Role of Foundations in Public Broadcasting: Part I: Development and Trends." *Journal of Broadcasting* 20:4 (Fall 1976) 529–47.
Leach, Eugene E. "Tuning Out Education: The Cooperation Doctrine in Radio, 1922-1938." *Current* (Jan 1983), accessed November 3, 2009. http://www.current.org/coop/coop2.shtml.
Lealand, Geoffrey. "American Television Programmes on British Screens." London: Broadcasting Research Unit/BFI, 1984.
LeMahieu, D. L. *A Culture for Democracy: Mass Communication and the Cultivated Mind in Britain Between the Wars.* London: Oxford University Press, 1988.
Lenthall, Bruce. "Critical Reception: Public Intellectuals Decry Depression-Era Radio, Mass Culture, and Modern America." *The Radio Reader.* Ed. Michele Hilmes and Jason Loviglio. New York: Routledge, 2002. 41–62.
——. *Radio's America: The Great Depression and the Rise of Modern Mass Culture.* Chicago: University of Chicago Press, 2007.
Lewis, C. A. *Broadcasting From Within.* London: George Newnes, 1924.
Lewis, James. "The Enterprising 'Beeb'". *The Director* (March 1972) n.p.
Lewis, Peter, ed. *Radio Drama.* London: Longman, 1981.
Lewinsohn, Mark. *The Radio Times Guide to TV Comedy.* 2nd ed. London: BBC Books, 2003.
Long, Paul. "British Radio and the Politics of Culture in Post-War Britain: The Work of Charles Parker." *The Radio Journal* 2:3 (2004) 131–52.
Loviglio, Jason. *Radio's Intimate Public.* Minneapolis: University of Minnesota Press, 2005.
Lucas, Rowland. *The Voice of a Nation? A Concise Account of the BBC in Wales 1923–1973.* Dyfed: Gomer Press, 1981.
Luckett, Moya. "The Avengers." *The Encyclopedia of Television.* Ed. Horace Newcomb. New York: Fitzroy Dearborn, 2004. 197–98.
Maase, Kaspar. "From Nightmare to Model? Why German Broadcasting Became Americanized." *Americanization and Anti-Americanism.* Ed. Alexander Stephan. London: Berghan, 2004.
MacCabe, Colin and Olivia Stewart, eds. *The BBC and Public Service Broadcasting.* Manchester: Manchester University Press, 1986.
Macdonald, Dwight. *The Ford Foundation: The Men and the Millions.* New York: Reynal & Co, 1956.
MacKenzie, John M. "'In Touch With the Infinite' The BBC and the Empire. 1923–1953." *Imperialism and Popular Culture.* Ed. John M. MacKenzie. Manchester: University of Manchester Press, 1986.
MacMurraugh-Kavanagh, Madeleine K. "The BBC and the Birth of *The Wednesday Play*, 1962–66: Institutional Containment versus 'Agitational Contemporaneity'". *Historical Journal of Film, Radio and Television* 17:3 (Aug 1997) 367–82.
Macy, John Jr. *To Irrigate a Wasteland: The Struggle to Shape a Public Television System in the United States.* Berkeley: University of California Press, 1974.
Madsen, Virginia. "Radio and the Documentary Imagination: Thirty Years of Experiment, Innovation, and Revelation." *The Radio Journal* 3:3 (2005) 189–98.
Mander, Mary S. "The Public Debate About Broadcasting in the Twenties: An Interpretive History." *Journal of Broadcasting* 25 (Spring 1984) 167–85.
Mann, Dave. "From Obscurity to Authority? The Changing Status of the Screenwriter During the Transition from 'B' Features to TV/Film Series (1946–64)". *Journal of British Cinema and Television* 5:2 (2008) 280–99.
Mansell. Gerard. *Let Truth Be Told: 50 Years of BBC External Broadcasting.* London: Weidenfeld and Nicolson, 1982.
Matheson. Hilda. "The Record of the BBC: Programmes of Speech and Entertainment". *Political Quarterly* 6:4 (1935) 506–18.
Mattelart. Armand. *Multinational Corporations and the Control of Culture: The Ideological Apparatuses of Imperialism.* Sussex: Harvester Press, 1979.
McCann, Bryan. *Hello, Hello Brazil: Popular Music in the Making of Modern Brazil.* Durham: Duke University Press, 2004.
McCarthy, Kathleen D. "From Cold War to Cultural Development: The International Cultural Activities of the Ford Foundation, 1950–1980." *Daedelus* 116:1 (Winter 1987) 93–117.
McChesney. Robert W. *Telecommunications, Mass Media and Democracy.* New York: Oxford University Press, 1993.

McDowell, W. H. *The History of BBC Broadcasting in Scotland, 1923–1983*. Edinburgh: Edinburgh University Press, 1992.

McLoone, Martin. "Music Hall Dope and British Propaganda: Cultural Identity and Early Broadcasting in Ireland." *Historical Journal of Film, Radio and Television* 20:3 (2000) 301–16.

McNicholas, Anthony. "Wrenching the Machine Around: *EastEnders*, the BBC, and Institutional Change." *Media, Culture and Society* 26:4 (2004) 491–512.

Maltby, Richard and Ruth Vasey. "'Temporary American Citizens': Cultural Anxieties and Industrial Strategies in the Americanisation of European Cinema." *'Film Europe' and 'Film America': Cinema, Commerce and Cultural Exchange 1920–1939.* Ed. Andrew Higson and Richard Maltby. Exeter: University of Exeter Press, 1999. 32–45.

Maxwell, Richard. *The Spectacle of Democracy: Spanish Television, Nationalism, and Political Transition*. Minneapolis: University of Minnesota Press, 1995.

Meadel, Cecile. "Between Corporatism and Representation: The Birth of a Public Radio Service in France". *Media, Culture and Society* 16:4 (1994) 609–23.

Medhurst, Jamie. *A History of Independent Television in Wales*. Aberystwyth: University of Wales Press, 2010.

Meyer, Richard J. "The Blue Book." *Journal of Broadcasting* 6 (Summer 1962) 197–207.

———. "Reaction to the 'Blue Book'" *Journal of Broadcasting* 6 (Fall 1962) 295–312.

Miller, Jeffrey S. *Something Completely Different: British Television and American Culture*. Minneapolis: University of Minnesota Press, 2000.

Miller, Mary Jane. *Turn Up the Contrast: CBC Television Drama Since 1952*. Vancouver: University of British Columbia Press, 1987.

Minihan, Janet. *The Nationalization of Culture: The Development of State Subsidies to the Arts in Great Britain*. London: Hamish Hamilton, 1977.

Minogue, Kenneth R. *Nationalism*. New York: Basic Books, 1967.

Mitchell, Jack W. *Listener Supported: The Culture and History of Public Radio*. Westport. CT: Praeger, 2005.

Moran, Albert. *Copycat Television: Globalisation, Program Formats, and Cultural Identity*. Luton: University of Luton Press, 1998.

Morley, David and Kevin Robins. *Spaces of Identity*. London: Routledge, 1995.

Morley, Patrick. *"This is the American Forces Network:" The Anglo-American Battle of the Air Waves in World War II*. Westport, CT: Praeger, 2001.

Morrison, Toni. *Playing in the Dark: Whiteness and the Literary Imagination*. New York: Vintage Books, 1993.

Morton, David. *Off the Record: The Technology and Culture of Sound Recording in America*. New Brunswick, NJ: Rutgers University Press, 2000.

Murrow, Edward R. "Preparation of the Documentary Broadcast." *Education on the Air 1947.* Institute for Education by Radio. Columbus: Ohio State University Press, 1947. 377–90.

Museum of Broadcasting. *BBC Television: Fifty Years*. New York: Museum of Broadcasting, 1987.

National Association of Broadcasters. *Broadcasting in the United States*. Washington. D.C., 1933.

———. *Broadcasting and the Bill of Rights*. Washington. D.C., 1947.

National Broadcasting Company. *Broadcasting in the Public Interest*. New York: NBC. 1939.

Neale, Steve. "Pseudonyms, Sapphire, and Salt: 'Un-American' Contributions to Television Costume Adventure Series in the 1950s." *Historical Journal of Film, Radio and Television* 23:3 (2003) 245–57.

———. "Transatlantic Ventures and Robin Hood." *ITV Cultures.* Ed. Catherine Johnson and Rob Turnock. London: Open University Press, 2005. 73–87.

Nelson, Robin. *TV Drama in Transition: Forms, Values, and Cultural Change*. London: St. Martin's Press, 1997.

Newman, Kathy M. *Radio Active: Advertising and Consumer Activism, 1935–1947*. Berkeley: University of California Press, 2004.

Newson, Iris. ed. *Performing Arts: Broadcasting*. Washington DC: The Library of Congress, 2002.

Newton, Gregory D. "Localism in Radio: U.S. Regulatory Approach." In *Encyclopedia of Radio.* Ed. Christopher H. Sterling. New York: Fitzroy Dearborn. 2004. 869–72.

Nicholas, Sian. *The Echo of War: Homefront Propaganda and the Wartime BBC, 1939–1945*. Manchester: Manchester University Press, 1996.

——. "'Brushing Up Your Empire': Dominion and Colonial Propaganda on the BBC's Home Services. 1939–1945." *The British World: Diaspora. Culture and Identity.* Ed. Carl Bridge and Kent Fedorowich. London: Frank Cass, 2003. 207–30.

Nichols, Richard. *Radio Luxembourg: The Station of the Stars.* London: Allen, 1983.

Nordenstreng. Kaarle and Tapio Varis. "Television Traffic: A One-Way Street?" *UNESCO Reports and Papers on Mass Communication.* No. 70. Paris: UNESCO, 1974.

O'Malley, Thomas and Janet Jones, eds. *The Peacock Committee and UK Broadcasting Policy.* London: Palgrave Macmillan, 2009.

Ong, Aihwa. *Flexible Citizenship: The Cultural Logics of Transnationality.* Durham: Duke University Press, 1999.

Oren, Tasha. *The Demon in the Box: Jews, Arabs, Politics, and Culture in the Making of Israeli Television.* New Brunswick, NJ: Rutgers University Press, 2004.

O'Regan, Tom. "The International Circulation of British Television." *British Television: A Reader.* Ed. Edward Buscombe. London: Oxford University Press, 2000. 303–21.

Ouellette, Laurie. *Viewers Like You? How Public TV Failed the People.* New York: Columbia University Press, 2002.

Paley, William S. "Radio—American or European System?" *Broadcasting* 25 (15 Nov 1943) 11.

Parker, Derek. *Radio: The Great Years.* London: David and Charles, 1977.

Parker, Lester Ward. *School Broadcasting in Great Britain.* Chicago: University of Chicago Press, 1937.

Paulu, Burton. *British Broadcasting: Radio and Television in the United Kingdom.* Minneapolis: University of Minnesota Press, 1956.

——. *British Broadcasting in Transition.* Minneapolis: University of Minnesota Press, 1961.

Pegg, Mark. *Broadcasting and Society. 1918–1939.* Breckenham: Croom Helm,1993.

Pepper, Robert M. "The Formation of the Public Broadcasting Service." Unpublished PhD dissertation, University of Wisconsin-Madison, 1975.

Persico, Joseph. *Edward R. Murrow: An American Original.* New York: McGraw Hill, 1988.

Peters, John Durham and Peter Simonson, eds. *Mass Communication and American Social Thought: Key Texts. 1919–1968.* Lanham, MD: Rowman and Littlefield, 2004.

Phipps, Stephen. "'Order Out of Chaos': A Reexamination of the Historical Basis for the Scarcity of Channels Concept", *Journal of Broadcasting and Electronic Media*, 45:1 (Winter 2001) 57–74.

Pickard, Victor. "The Battle Over the FCC Blue Book: Determining the Role of Broadcast Media in a Democratic Society, 1945–1948" *Media, Culture and Society* 33:2 (2011) 171–91.

Pickering, Michael "The BBC's Kentucky Minstrels. 1933–1950: Blackface Entertainment on British Radio" *Historical Journal of Film Radio and Television* 16:2 (2002)161–95.

Pilsworth, Michael. "Buddy, Can You Spare A Dime? The Television Co-Production Business in Britain." *Sight and Sound* 49:1 (1979–80) 51+.

Potter, Jeremy. *Independent Television in Britain. Vol. 3: Politics and Control, 1968–1980.* London: Macmillan, 1989

——. *Independent Television in Britain. Vol.4: Companies and Programmes, 1968–1980.* London: Macmillan, 1990

Potter, Simon. "Britishness, the BBC, and the Birth of Canadian Public Broadcasting. 1928–1936." *Communicating in Canada's Past: Approaches to the History of Print and Broadcast Media.* Ed. Gene Allen and Daniel Robinson. Toronto: University of Toronto Press, 2009.

——. *Broadcasting Empire: The BBC and the British World, 1922–1970.* London: Oxford University Press, 2011.

Powell, John W. *Channels of Learning: The Story of Educational Television.* Washington, DC: Public Affairs Press, 1962.

Prendergast, Curtis, with Geoffrey Colvin. *The World of Time Inc. Vol. 3: 1960–1980.* New York: Atheneum, 1986.

Price, Monroe E. *Media and Sovereignty: The Global Information Revolution and its Challenge to State Power.* Cambridge. MA: MIT Press, 2002.

Radio and Television Who's Who 3rd edition. London: George Young Publications, 1954.

Real, Michael. "The Great Quiz Show Scandal: Why America Remains Fascinated." *Television Quarterly* 27 (Winter 1995) 2–27.

Reeves, Earl. "Radio—The American Way." *The Rotarian* (May 1934) 14–15, 60–62.

Reith, John. *Broadcast Over Britain.* London: Hodder and Stoughton, 1924.

——. "Broadcasting in America." *The Nineteenth Century* 110 (August 1931) 204–12.

——. *Into the Wind*. London: Hodder and Stoughton, 1949.

Reynolds. David. "Whitehall. Washington and the Promotion of American Studies in Britain during World War Two." *American Studies* 16:2 (1982) 165–88.

Richards, David A. "America Conquers Britain: Anglo-American Conflict in the Popular Media during the 1920s." *Journal of American Culture* 3:1 (1980) 95–103.

Richardson, Kay and Ulrike H. Meinhof. *Worlds in Common?: Television Discourse in a Changing Europe*. London: Routledge, 1999.

Richardson, Maurice. "Eternity Street." *The Observer Magazine* (12 Sept, 1965) 12–14. Clippings files ITV 1955, BFI.

Richardson, Theresa and Donald Fisher, eds. *The Development of the Social Sciences in the United States and Canada: The Role of Philanthropy*. Stamford, CT: Ablex, 1999.

Richardson, Theresa R. and Erwin V. Johanningmeier. "Educational Radio, Childhood, and Philanthropy: A New Role for the Humanities in Popular Culture." *Journal of Radio Studies* 13:1 (May 2006) 1–18.

Rivero, Yeidy. ""Havana as a 1940s–1950s Latin American Media Capital." *Critical Studies in Media Communication*. 26:3 (August 2009) 275–93.

Rixon, Paul. *American Television on British Screens: A Story of Cultural Interaction*. Basingstoke: Palgrave Macmillan, 2006.

Robertson, Jim. *Televisionaries: In Their Own Words Public Television's Founders Tell How it all Began."* Charlotte Harbor, FL: Tabby House Books, 1993.

Robson, William A. "The BBC as an Institution." *Political Quarterly* 6:4 (1935) 468–88.

Rockefeller Foundation. *Annual Report*. New York: Rockefeller Foundation, 1935, 1936, 1937, 1938, 1939, 1940, 1941.

Rodgers, Daniel T. *Atlantic Crossings: Social Politics in a Progressive Age*. Cambridge, MA: Belknap/Harvard. 1998.

Rodriguez, America. "Creating an Audience and Remapping a Nation: A Brief History of US Spanish Language Broadcasting 1930–1980." *Quarterly Review of Film and Video* 16:3–4 (1997) 357–74.

Roelofs, Joan. *Foundations and Public Policy: The Mask of Pluralism*. Albany, NY: State University of New York Press, 2003.

Rogers, Dave. *The Complete Avengers*. London: Boxtree, 1989.

Rolo, Charles J. *Radio Goes to War: The 'Fourth Front'*. New York: Putnam, 1942.

Rowland, Willard and Michael Tracey, "Worldwide Challenges to Public Service Broadcasting." *Journal of Communication* (Spring 1990) 8–27.

Rubin, Joan Shelley. *The Making of Middlebrow Culture*. Chapel Hill: University of North Carolina Press, 1992.

Russo, Alexander. *Points on the Dial: Golden Age Radio Beyond the Networks*. Durham: Duke University Press, 2009.

Saerchinger, Cesar. *Hello America! Radio Adventures in Europe*. Boston: Houghton Mifflin, 1938.

Saudek, Robert. "Experiment in Video Programming." *New York Times* (9 Nov 1952) 13.

Saunders, Frances Stonor. *The Cultural Cold War: The CIA and the World of Arts and Letters*. New York: New Press, 1999.

Savage, Barbara. *Broadcasting Freedom: Radio, War, and the Politics of Race, 1938–1948*. Chapel Hill: University of North Carolina Press, 1999.

Savage, Robert J. *Irish Television: The Political and Social Origins*. Westport: Praeger, 1996.

Sayre, Jeannette. "An Analysis of the Radiobroadcasting Activities of Federal Agencies." *Studies in the Control of Radio* #3 (June 1941) 23–56.

Scannell, Paddy. "Public Service Broadcasting and Modern Public Life". *Media, Culture and Society* 11:2 (1989) 135–166.

——. "'The Stuff of Radio': Developments in Radio Features and Documentaries Before the War." *Documentary and the Mass Media*. Ed. John Corner. London: Arnold, 1986. 1–26

Scannell, Paddy with David Cardiff. *A Social History of British Broadcasting, Volume One, 1922–1939: Serving the Nation*. London: Blackwell, 1991.

Schiller, Herbert. *Communication and Cultural Domination*. White Plains. New York: International Arts and Sciences Press, 1976.

Schlesinger, Philip. *Putting 'Reality' Together: BBC News*. London: Constable, 1979.

——. "Trading in Fictions: What Do We Know about British Television Imports and Exports?" *European Journal of Communication* 1:3 (1986) 263–87.

Schwoch, James. "The American Radio Industry and International Communications Conferences, 1919–1927" *Historical Journal of Film, Radio and Television* 7:3 (1987) 289–309.

——. *Global TV: New Media and the Cold War, 1946–69.* Urbana: University of Illinois, 2008.

Schudson, Michael. "Good Citizens and Bad History: Today's Political Ideals in Historical Perspective." *Communication Review* 4:1 (Oct 2000) 1–19.

——. *The Good Citizen: A History of American Civic Life.* New York: Free Press, 1998.

Scott, Robin. "Going It Together: An account of BBC Television's experience with co-productions." *EBU Review* 27:1 (Jan 1976) 6–10.

Seaton, Jean and Ben Pimlott, eds. *The Media in British Politics.* London: Avebury, 1987.

Selznick, Barbara J. *Global Television: Co-Producing Culture.* Philadelphia: Temple University Press, 2008.

Sendall, Bernard. *Independent Television in Britain, V. 1: Origin and Foundation, 1946–62.* London: Macmillan, 1982.

——. *Independent Television in Britain, V 2: Expansion and Change, 1958–68.* London: Macmillan, 1983.

Serpico, *Edward R. Murrow: An American Original.* New York: McGraw Hill, 1988.

Shapley, Olive. *Broadcasting a Life.* London: Scarlet Press, 1996.

Short, K. R. M. "A Note on BBC Television News and the Munich Crisis, 1938." *Historical Journal of Film, Radio and Television* 9:2 (1989) 165–79.

Shulman, Holly Cowan. *The Voice of America: Propaganda and Democracy, 1941–45.* Madison: University of Wisconsin Press, 1990.

Shubick, Irene. *Play for Today: The Evolution of Television Drama.* London: Davis-Poyntner, 1975.

Siepmann. Charles A. "American Radio in Wartime." *Radio Research 1942–1943.* Ed. Paul F. Lazarsfeld and Frank N. Stanton. New York: Duell, Sloan and Pearce, 1944. 111–50.

——. "Can Radio Educate?" *Journal of Educational Sociology* 14 (February 1941a) 346–57.

——. "Further Thoughts on Radio Criticism." *Public Opinion Quarterly* 5:2 (June 1941b) 308–12.

——. "Needed Techniques in Educational Broadcast." *Education on the Air.* Ed. Josephine A. MacLatchy. Columbus: Ohio State University Press, 1940.

——. "Radio." *The Communication of Ideas.* Ed. Lyman Bryson. New York: Institute for Religious and Social Studies, 1948. 181–84.

——. "Radio's big chance." *The New Republic* 106 (January 12 1942a) 46–48.

——. *Radio in Wartime.* New York: Oxford University Press, 1942b.

——. "Radio's Operation Crossroads." *The Nation* (7 Dec 1946a) 644–45.

——. *Radio's Second Chance.* Boston: Little Brown, 1946b.

——. "Storm in the Radio World." *The American Mercury* (August 1946c) 24+.

——. "What Is Wrong With TV—And With Us." *New York Times Sunday Magazine* (19 April 1964) 13+.

Silvey, Robert. *Who's Listening? The Story of BBC Audience Research.* London: Allen & Unwin, 1974.

Simon, Ernest Darwin (Lord Simon of Wythenshawe). *The BBC From Within.* London: Gollancz, 1953

Sinclair, John. *Latin American Television: A Global View.* New York: Oxford University Press. 1999.

——, Elizabeth Jacka and Stuart Cunningham, eds. *New Patterns in Global Television: Peripheral Vision.* London: Oxford University Press, 1996.

Slate, Sam J. and Joe Cook. *It Sounds Impossible.* New York: Macmillan, 1963.

Slotten, Hugh R. *Radio's Hidden Voice: The Origins of Public Broadcasting in the United States.* Urbana: University of Illinois Press, 2009.

——. "Universities, Public Service Experimentation, and the Origins of Radio Broadcasting in the United States." *Historical Journal of Film, Radio and Television* 26:4 (October 2006) 485–504.

Smith. Anthony D., ed. *British Broadcasting.* London: David and Charles, 1974.

——. *Nationalism: Theory, Ideology, History.* Cambridge: Polity, 2001

Smith, Judith E. "Radio's 'Cultural Front,' 1938–1948." *The Radio Reader.* Ed. Michele Hilmes and Jason Loviglio. New York: Routledge, 2002. 209–30.

Smith, Sally Bedell. *In All His Glory: The Life of William S. Paley.* New York: Simon and Schuster, 1990.

Smulyan, Susan. *Selling Radio: The Commercialization of American Broadcasting, 1920–1934.* Washington, DC: Smithsonian Institution Press, 1994.

Smythe, Dallas W. *Dependency Road: Communications, Capitalism, Consciousness and Canada.* Norwood. NJ: Ablex, 1981.

Sound Broadcasting Society. *Unsound Broadcasting: The Case Against the BBC's New Policy.* London: Faber & Faber, 1957.

Snagge, John and Michael Barsley. *Those Vintage Years of Radio.* London: Pitman, 1972.

Spence, Peter. "The BBC North American Service 1939–1945." *Media, Culture and Society* 4:3 (October 1982) 361–75.

Spencer, Philip and Howard Wollman, eds. *Nations and Nationalism: A Reader.* Edinburgh: Edinburgh University Press, 2005.

Sperber, A. M. *Murrow: His Life and Times* New York: Freundlich Books, 1986.

Sprott, Elise. "Planning Broadcasts for Women in Great Britain." *Education on the Air 1938.* Institute for Education by Radio. Columbus: Ohio State University Press, 1938.

Spry, Graham. "The Canadian Broadcasting Issue." *Canadian Forum* 11 (1931) 246–49.

Steemers, Jeanette. *Selling Television: British Television in the Global Marketplace.* London: BFI, 2004.

Sterling, Christopher H. "Breaking Chains: NBC and the FCC Inquiry. 1938–43." *NBC: America's Network.* Ed. Michele Hilmes. Berkeley: University of California Press, 2007. 85–97.

—— and Michael Keith. *Sounds of Change: A History of FM Broadcasting in America.* Chapel Hill: University of North Carolina Press, 2009.

—— and John Michael Kittross. *Stay Tuned: A History of American Broadcasting,* 3rd ed. Mahwah: Erlbaum, 2002.

Stevens, Mark. "Already We Serve the World: The Federal Theatre Radio Division's Contributions to Radio's Growth in America. 1936–1939." Unpublished Ph.D. dissertation. Kent State University, 1974.

Stewart, David. *The PBS Companion.* New York: TV Books, 1999.

Stole, Inger. "The *Kate Smith Hour* and the Struggle for Control of Television Programming in the Early 1950s." *Historical Journal of Film, Radio and Television* 20:4 (2000) 549–64.

Straubhaar. Joseph. "Beyond Media Imperialism: Asymetrical Interdependence and Cultural Proximity." *Critical Studies in Mass Communication* 8 (2002) 39–59.

Street, Sarah. *British National Cinema.* 2nd edition. London: Routledge, 2009.

Street, Sean. *Crossing the Ether: British Public Service Radio and Commercial Competition 1922–1945.* London: John Libbey, 2006.

Stursberg, Peter. *Mister Broadcasting: The Ernie Bushnell Story.* Toronto: Martin 1971.

Summerfield, P. "Women, War, and Social Change: Women in Britain in World War II." *Total War and Social Change.* Ed. A. Marwick. London: Macmillan, 1988. 95–118

Summers, Harrison B. *A Thirty-Year History of Programs Carried on National Radio Networks in the United States, 1926–1956.* Salem, NH: Ayer Company, 1993.

Sutton, Shaun. *The Largest Theatre in the World: Thirty Years of Television Drama.* London: BBC, 1982.

Swing, Raymond Gram. *'Good Evening!': A Professional Memoir.* New York: Harcourt, Brace and World, 1964.

Sydney-Smith, Susan. *Beyond Dixon of Dock Green: Early British Police Series.* London: I. B. Tauris, 2002.

Tallents, Stephen. *The Projection of England.* London: Faber and Faber, 1932.

Tankel, Jonathan. "The ITV Thriller: The Interaction of Media Systems and Popular Culture." Unpublished Ph.D. dissertation, University of Wisconsin-Madison, 1984.

Taylor, Don. *Days of Vision: Working with David Mercer: Television Drama Then and Now.* London: Methuen, 1990.

Taylor, Philip M. *British Propaganda in the Twentieth Century: Selling Democracy.* Edinburgh: Edinburgh University Press, 1999.

Thomas, Howard. *The Truth About Television.* London: Weidenfield and Nicolson. 1962.

Thomas, Ivor. "Systems of Broadcasting." *Political Quarterly* 6:4. (1935) 489–505.

Tinic, Serra. *On Location: Canada's Television Industry in a Global Market.* Toronto: University of Toronto Press, 2005.

Torre, Paul. "Block Booking Migrates to Television: the Rise and Fall of the International Output Deal." *Television and New Media* 10:6 (Nov 2009) 501–20.

Tree, Ronald. *When The Moon Was High: Memoirs of Peace and War 1897–1942.* London: MacMillan, 1975.

Tunstall, Jeremy. *The Media Are American.* New York: Columbia University Press. 1977.

—— and David Machin. *The Anglo-American Media Connection.* New York: Oxford University Press, 1999.

Vahimagi, Tisa. "Clark, Lord Kenneth (1903–1983)." *Screenonline*, accessed June 8, 2010. http://www.screenonline.org.uk/people/id/549769/index.html
——. "Greene, Sir Hugh (1910-1987)." *Screenonline*, accessed March 3, 2010. http://www.screen online.org.uk/people/id/1172363/
——. "Newman, Sydney (1917-1997)." *Screenonline*, accessed Nov 12 2010. http://www.screen online.org.uk/people/id/522017/
Van Loon, Hendrik. "WRUL." *Current History* 52:1 (May 1941) 22–23+.
Varis, Tapio. "The International Flow of Television Programmes." *Journal of Communication* (1984) 143–52.
Vasey, Ruth L. and Richard Maltby. "Temporary American Citizens: Cultural Anxieties and Industrial Strategies in the Americanisation of European cinema." *The European Cinema Reader.* Ed. Catherine Fowler. London: Routledge, 2002. 180–93.
Vickers, Doug and Nick Gilbert. "BBC Defends Co-production Ventures". *Campaign* June 2, 1972. p. 30+.
Vipond, Mary. *Listening In: The First Decade of Canadian Broadcasting. 1922–1932.* Montreal: McGill-Queen's University Press, 1992.
Wall, Tim. *Studying Popular Music Culture.* London: Arnold, 2003.
Wang, Jennifer Hyland. "'The Case of the Radioactive Housewife': Relocating Radio in the Age of Television." *Radio Reader.* Ed. Michele Hilmes and Jason Loviglio. New York: Routledge 2002. 343–66.
——. "Convenient Fictions: The Construction of the Daytime Broadcast Audience, 1927–1960." Unpublished Ph.D. dissertation, University of Wisconsin-Madison, 2006.
Waymark, Peter Aseley Grosvenor. *Television and the Cultural Revolution: The BBC Under Hugh Carleton Greene.* Unpublished Ph.D. dissertation. Open University. 2006.
Weaver, Pat (with Thomas M. Coffey). *The Best Seat in the House: The Golden Years of Radio and Television.* New York: Knopf, 1994.
Weinberg, Sydney. "What to Tell America: The Writers' Quarrel in the Office of War Information." *Journal of American History* 55:1 (June 1968) 73–89.
Weissmann, Elke. "Paying for Fewer Imports: The BBC License Fee 1975–1981 and Attitudes Towards American Imports." *Television and New Media* 10:6 (Nov 2009) 482–500.
Werner, Michael and Bénédicte Zimmermann. "Beyond Comparison: *Histoire Croisée* and the Challenge of Reflexivity." *History and Theory* 45 (Feb 2006) 30–50.
Wheatley, Helen. "'And Now for Your Sunday Night Experimental Drama . . .': Experimentation and *Armchair Theatre.*" *Experimental British Television.* Ed. Laura Mulvey and Jamie Sexton. Manchester: University of Manchester Press, 2007. 31–47.
White, Llewellyn. *The American Radio: Repoprt from the Commission on the Freedom of the Press.* Chicago: University of Chicago Press, 1947.
Wildeblood, Peter. "The Hindsight Saga." *Granada Television: The First Generation.* Ed. John Finch. Manchester: Manchester University Press, 2003. 1332–34.
Williams, Raymond. *Communications.* Revised Edition. London: Chatto and Windus, 1966.
Wilson, H. Hubert. *Pressure Group: The Campaign for Commercial Television.* London: Secker & Warburg, 1961.
Wilson, K. M. "Watching 'This New Power of Wireless': Correspondence Between Sir J. Reith of the BBC and H. A. Gwynne of 'The Morning Post', 1936–1937." *Historical Journal of Film. Radio and Television.* 4:2 (1984) 203–11.
Wilson, Pamela. "NBC Television's 'Operation Frontal Lobes': Cultural Hegemony and Fifties' Programming." *Historical Journal of Film and Television* 15:1 (1995) 83–104.
Winick, Stephen D. "Alistair Cooke: A Radio and TV Icon in the Archive of Folk Culture." *Folklife Center News* (Winter/Spring 2005) 6–8.
Winston, Brian. "Is 'British Cinema' a Zebra?" *Journal of British Cinema and Television* 1:1 (May 2004) 14–20.
Wylie, Max. *Best Broadcasts of 1939.* New York: Whittlesey House, 1939.

Index

Seeger, Pete 146
Selwyn Lloyd, John 184–5
serial drama form 273–4. *see also Front Line Family*
Shapley, Olive 123–4
shortwave transmissions 97–9, 141, 237
Shubik, Irene 262
Siegel, Seymour 239
Siepmann, Charles: as author of Blue Book 169, 174–8; and BBC listener research 88; and BBC regional broadcasting 61; on Beveridge Committee and Report (1949–51) 181, 183–4; and broadcast news 135; and "Communication Seminars" 114–15; criticism of popular culture 178; and National Educational Television network (NET) 275–6; and OWI 119; on post-WWII US radio 173; *Radio's Second Chance* 177; and US educational radio 112–13
Silvey, Robert J. 90
Singer, Aubrey 217, 289, 291, 295–6
Sklar, Michael 251–2
Slate, Sam 219
Smythe, Dallas 174
Spanish International Network (SIN) 301
spelling bees 99
Spry, Graham 74
spy adventure genre 269–71
Stanley, Edward 230
Stempel, Herbert 227
Stephenson, William 116
Steptoe and Son (television program) 271–2
Stevens, David H. 110
Stewart, James 143
Stobart, J. C. 88–9
Stocks, Mary 184–5
Stringer, John 285, 288
Stringer, William H. 225, 232
Studebaker, John W. 124
Sutton, Shaun 264, 286–8
Swing, Raymond Gram 99
Sykes Committee (1923) 42–4

Taishoff, Sol 175, 177
Tallents, Stephen 89, 102
Taylor, Davidson 214, 230
technology: advancements in radio after World War I 31–2, 237–8; cable 167, 257, 260, 285, 289, 296, 302–4; digital 303, 307–9, 312; Millertape system 130–1; satellites 4, 15, 21, 24, 170, 237, 296, 301–4, 308, 330n3; television 238, 296
Televisa 301
This Is War! (radio program) 143
Thomas, Norman 216
Thornton, Basil 235–6, 240, 249
Till Death Us Do Part (television program)

271–2
Time-Life Films 288–96
Today (television program) 212–13
Toscanini, Arturo 120–1
Trammell, Niles 155
Transatlantic Call: People to People (radio program) 145
Transatlantic Quiz (radio program) 153–4
transatlantic radio programs 141–7, 153–5
transnationalism: anxieties over 167–8, 186, 207, 251, 257; as concept 2–5; and cultural internationalism 9–10; and educational radio 193, 239–42; and film 2–3, 11, 167, 219; and globalization 14-15, 300; and high culture 14, 296; marked vs. unmarked 257–9, 265–7; "marking" of *Masterpiece Theatre* 281–2; in media historiography 3, 5–11; and popular culture 14, 16; productive work of 20–1, 28, 259–65, 267–79, 290, 300–1; and Rockefeller Foundation 108–10
transnational cultural economy 4, 20, 22, 257; *see also histoire croisée*
transnational figures: *see* Cooke, Alistair; Murrow, Edward R.; Newman, Sydney; Siepmann, Charles; Weinstein, Hannah
transcriptions 61, 142; *see also* BBC, Transcription Service; recording
Travis, Joseph 77
Trout, Robert 145
Tyler, Tracy 73–4
Tyson, Levering 73–4, 107

Ugly Betty (television program) 306
Ullswater Committee (1935–6) 92
UNESCO 256
United States Department of Commerce 34–5
University of Chicago 107–8
University of Chicago Round Table (radio program) 111, 193
Univision 301

Van Doren, Charles 227
vinyl records 237–8
Voice of America 118

W1XAL *see* WRUL
Wakeman, Frederic 179–80
Waldman, Ronald 160, 171–2, 246–7, 304
Walker, Paul 194
Waller, Judith 121
Warren, Tony 273
Wasserman, Lew 219
Waters, Ethel 146
Watt, John 135
Wayne, Jenifer 145
Weaver, Sylvester "Pat" 200–1, 225–6, 230